St Andrews Studies in Reformation History

Editorial Board:

Bruce Gordon, Andrew Pettegree and John Guy,
St Andrews Reformation Studies Institute,
Amy Nelson Burnett, University of Nebraska at Lincoln,
Euan Cameron, University of Newcastle upon Tyne and
Kaspar von Greyerz, University of Basel

'Practical Divinity'

Frontispiece   Greenham's communion cup. This silver cup, made in the 1570s or 1580s, bears the initials 'R.G.'. It is on display in the Fitzwilliam Museum, Cambridge, but is still owned by the parish church in Dry Drayton. Photographed by permission of the priest-in-charge and the wardens of the parish church of St Peter and St Paul, Dry Drayton.

'Practical Divinity'

The Works and Life of
Revd Richard Greenham

KENNETH L. PARKER and
ERIC J. CARLSON

Ashgate

Aldershot • Brookfield USA • Singapore • Sydney

Published by
Ashgate Publishing Limited
Gower House
Croft Road
Aldershot
Hants GU11 3HR
England

Ashgate Publishing Company
Old Post Road
Brookfield
Vermont 05036-9704
USA

British Library Cataloguing in Publication Data

Parker, Kenneth L.
    'Practical Divinity': The Works and Life of Revd Richard Greenham.
    (St Andrews Studies in Reformation History)
    1. Greenham, Richard. 2. Anglicans — England — Biography.
    I Title. II. Carlson, Eric Josef.
    283.4'2'092

Library of Congress Cataloging-in-Publication Data

Parker, Kenneth L.
    'Practical divinity': the works and life of Revd Richard Greenham/
    Kenneth L. Parker and Eric J. Carlson.
        p.   cm. - (St Andrews Studies in Reformation History)
    Includes bibliographical references and index.
    ISBN 1-84014-200-6 (hardbound)
    1. Greenham, Richard. 2. Puritans—England—Clergy—Biography.
    3. Pastoral theology—Church of England—Early works to 1800.
    4. Pastoral theology—England—History of doctrines—16th century.
    I. Carlson, Eric Josef. II. Title. III. Series.
    BX9339.G74P37   1998
    283'.42—dc21
                                                            97–38530
                                                            CIP

ISBN 1 84014 200 6

This book is printed on acid-free paper

Typeset in Sabon by Express Typesetters Ltd

Printed in Great Britain by Galliard (Printers) Ltd, Great Yarmouth

Contents

List of figures

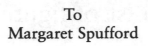

To
Margaret Spufford

Acknowledgements

Scholarship requires collaboration. We believe this to be true and exhort our students to act on this maxim. While we have benefited from the synergy of working together, this project, with its demanding attention to detail and exploration of diverse topics, has required the resources of a community of scholars and friends to whom we owe a great debt.

Richard Greenham believed that the formation of ministers should take place in his rectory, where not only his words but also his example could guide, instruct and form young ordinands from Cambridge University. Professor Margaret Spufford has provided a similar model for aspiring scholars of early modern England, for she has opened her home and life to her students. In Haddenham, on Bateman Street, and now in Whittlesford, she has not only guided students towards lives of effective scholarship, but has also provided a model of mentoring that respects and addresses the humanity of those who seek her guidance. We have been among the greatest beneficiaries of her time, attention and hospitality. She is the person responsible for the genesis of this project and our friendship. Declaring that editing manuscripts did not suit her temperament, she nevertheless recognized that the Greenham sayings in Rylands English Manuscript 524 should be made available in a critical edition. She introduced us to one another, and we soon found that our interests in Elizabethan parochial life, ministry and theology made us natural partners in this work. Having benefited from her tutelage, friendship and advice on this and other projects, we dedicate this book to her, as a token of our thanks, affection and admiration. She not only 'framed' our lives of scholarship, but taught us how to be human in the midst of it.

Our debt to other mentors and scholars is no less significant. Dr Eamon Duffy and Professor Wallace MacCaffrey continue to exercise a profound influence on our research and provide inspiration, guidance and support. Dr Dorothy Owen deserves our special thanks, not only for her generosity in guiding and assisting our understanding of sixteenth-century palaeography and documents from this period, but also for proofing an early transcription of the Greenham sayings and offering advice on its preparation for publication. Professor Patrick Collinson encouraged us in this project in its various stages and has offered valuable insights and helpful corrections as the work has proceeded. Professor Peter Lake has also provided suggestions and encouragement that have helped shape the project. Professor Walter Ong gave time and enthusiastic attention to discussions about the commonplace tradition. Professor David Cressy generously permitted advance use of unpublished material, which helped guide our reflections in the introduction and annotations.

We wish to thank the Director and the University Librarian at the John Rylands University Library of Manchester for permission to publish this critical edition of Rylands English Manuscript 524, folios 1–72. Our special gratitude goes to Dr M.A. Pegg, former Director and University Librarian, for his initial willingness to allow the project to proceed, and to Miss Glenise Matheson, whose hospitality and cooperation made the work possible. We also wish to thank Mr John Tuck, Dr Peter McNiven and Dr Dorothy Clayton for their role in making the final arrangements for this edition to come to print.

Research would have been greatly impeded had it not been for the kind and generous assistance of the Cambridge University Library staffs of the Rare Books Reading Room and the Manuscripts Reading Room. We both owe special thanks to Mr Godfrey Waller in this regard. The library staffs at Gustavus Adolphus College and Saint Louis University deserve our gratitude for their patient and tireless efforts. Ellen Ausenthie of Saint Louis University managed more than one miracle in tracing and obtaining inter-library loans needed for this book.

Our research and writing has also profited from the critical response, suggestions and encouragement of many colleagues and students. In particular, we must thank Professor David Cressy and Dr Lori Anne Ferrell, directors of an NEH-funded Summer Institute (1996) on 'Religion and Society in Early Modern England', and all the participants for their encouragement and advice as we discussed Greenham in sessions, evening colloquia, and over meals. Mr Peter Vlahutin, Revd Douglas Grandon and Mr John Bequette served as research assistants on this project and provided invaluable service that we deeply appreciated. Officers and council members of the Church of England Record Society have given much-needed guidance as this project has proceeded. Members of the Interdisciplinary Faculty Research Colloquium at Saint Louis University, Charles Parker, Georgia Johnston, Matthew Mirow, Richard Valantasis, Carol Needham, Brian Goldstein and Joya Uraizee, have offered a welcome forum for various versions of our introduction. Graduate students in historical theology and history at Saint Louis University have been among the first to respond to our edition of the Greenham sayings and have provided a critical audience that has enhanced the final version of the introduction.

Mr Michael Sekulla, Dr Richard Gould, Dr Matthew Mirow, Dr Mary Crane, Dr Ann Moss, Revd Dr Judith Maltby, Dr Gerald Bray and Dr David George deserve special thanks for their help with particular challenges that this project presented. The Revd Geoffrey Lay, the Priest-in-Charge of the Parish of St Peter and St Paul in Dry Drayton, and Mrs Lay have our gratitude for their hospitality, and for arranging permission to photograph Richard Greenham's communion cup.

This book would not have been possible without the financial support of grants and institutions. A research grant awarded from the Archbishop Cranmer Fund, administered by the Faculty of History, University of Cambridge, provided the initial funding for the transcription of Rylands English Manuscript 524. Grants received from the National Endowment for the Humanities enabled us to work together for five weeks at Claremont in 1996. Research support received from Saint Louis University and Gustavus Adolphus College provided the means to bring this project to completion. Special thanks go to Professor William Shea, chair of the Department of Theological Studies, and Dean Shirley Dowdy, of the College of Arts and Sciences at Saint Louis University, for providing release time from administrative duties for Kenneth Parker in the final stages of the writing.

We know that Ms Janine Genelin of Gustavus Adolphus College, and Ms Mary Boles and Ms Lori Hunt of Saint Louis University have made much of this project manageable, not just with their secretarial support – which was considerable – but also with their generous spirit and supportive attitude. They keep our lives, with the many demands we face, from sinking into chaos. They deserve our thanks for all the miracles, large and small, that must be credited to them.

We wish to express our deep appreciation for the impact that Dr Peter Spufford has had on our lives. While he is a renowned scholar in the field of medieval economic history, we know him as a friend and the ever-generous host who welcomed us on our many visits to consult with Margaret Spufford. His graciousness in the face of our numerous impositions has taught us much about hospitality and what it means to live in a loving, supportive relationship.

Finally, we must thank our friends and loved ones who tolerated our all-consuming obsession with Richard Greenham in the final stages of this project. Eric thanks Caroline Litzenberger and Larissa Taylor for their encouragement. Most of all, Eric thanks Doug Rorapaugh who began his own parish ministry while patiently enduring too much talk about a minister long dead. Kenneth is deeply grateful to Matthew Mirow and Patrick McCarthy for their attentive and watchful concern. Most especially, Kenneth owes a great debt of thanks to his spouse, Tanya, for her support and encouragement, even as she faced the challenges of childbirth and the early months of motherhood. Geoffrey Michael Parker, born on 31 January 1997, taught his father during the last months of writing and revision about what really matters in life.

To these and the many that could not be named in this short space, we express our thanks and gratitude. Our lives are richer because of the kindnesses we have received. We hope that this book repays the investment made in our lives and scholarship by so many.

Abbreviations

Manuscripts

BL	British Library, London
CRO	Cambridgeshire Record Office, Cambridge
EDR	Ely Diocesan Records, Cambridge University Library, Cambridge
GLRO	Greater London Record Office
GL	Guildhall Library, London
PCC	Prerogative Court of Canterbury
PRO	Public Record Office, London
REM 524	Rylands English Manuscript 524, John Rylands Library, University of Manchester, Manchester
St Bart's Hosp.	St Bartholomew's Hospital, Archives Department

Books

DNB	*Dictionary of National Biography*
VCH, Cambs.	*A History of the County of Cambridge and the Isle of Ely*, ed C.R. Elrington, et al., 9 vols to date (London and Oxford: various publishers, 1938–　)
First Edition	Richard Greenham, *The Works of the Reverend and Faithfull Servant of Jesus Christ M. Richard Greenham, Minister and Preacher of the word of God: Examined, Corrected, and published, for the further building of all such as love the trueth, and desire to know the power of godlines*. Edited by Henry Holland. London, 1599.
Second Edition	Richard Greenham, *The Workes of the Reverend and Faithfull servant of Jesus Christ M. Richard Greenham, Minister and Preacher of the Word of God: The Second Edition, Revised, Corrected, and published, for the further building of all such as love the trueth, and desire to know the power of godlines*. Edited by Henry Holland. 2nd edn. London, 1599.
Third Edition	Richard Greenham, *The Workes of the Reverend and Faithfull Servant of Jesus Christ M. Richard*

Greenham, Minister and Preacher of the Word of God, collected into one volume: Revised, Corrected, and Published, for the Further Building of all Such as love the trueth, and desire to know the power of godlinesse. Edited by Henry Holland. 3rd edn. London, 1601.

Fourth Edition   Richard Greenham, *The Workes of the Reverend and Faithfull Servant of Jesus Christ M. Richard Greenham, Minister and Preacher of the Word of God, collected into one volume: Revised, Corrected, and Published, for the further building of all such as love the trueth, and desire to know the power of godlinesse.* Edited by Henry Holland. 4th edn. London, 1605.

Fifth Edition   Richard Greenham, *The Workes of the Reverend and Faithfull Servant of Jesus Christ M. Richard Greenham, Minister and Preacher of the Word of God, collected into one volume: Revised, Corrected, and Published, for the further building of all such as love the trueth, and desire to know the power of godlinesse.* Edited by [Stephen Egerton]. 5th edn. London, 1612.

Propositions   Richard Greenham, *Propositions Containing Answers to Certaine demaunds in divers spirituall matters, specially concerning the conscience oppressed with the griefe of sinne. With an Epistle Against hardnes of heart, made by that woorthie Preacher of the Gospell of Christ, M.R. Greenham Pastor of Drayton.* Edinburgh, 1597.

Two Treatises   *ΠΑΡΑΜΥΘΙΟΝ. Two Treatises of the comforting of an afflicted conscience, written by M. Richard Greenham, with certaine Epistles of the same argument. Hereunto are added two Sermons, with certaine grave and wise counsells and answeres of the same Author and argument.* London, 1598.

PART ONE

Greenham's life and legacy

CHAPTER ONE

Introduction[1]

In 1624, preaching the sermon *ad clerum* in St Paul's Cathedral for the opening of Convocation, Joseph Hall listed Richard Greenham among 21 great lights of the church (*magna illa Ecclesiae lumina*) who had recently (*nuper*) died. Although Greenham had been buried inside the London parish church of Christ Church, Newgate some three decades earlier, Hall exhumed him for verbal reinterment in a pantheon which included John Foxe, John Whitgift, William Perkins and Richard Hooker.[2] It was not Hall's first public praise of Greenham. He penned two laudatory epigrams printed at the beginning of every edition of Greenham's posthumous *Works* and, in 1606, described Greenham in print as 'that saint of ours'.[3]

Neither was Hall's 1624 sermon the first or last occasion that Greenham would be found posthumously in such distinguished company. In 1608, the divine Thomas Cooper, writing of 'the manie excellent treatises & larger discourses concerning the power of godlines, which it hath pleased the Lord of glorie to furnish his Church withall in these last daies', noted in the margin that he referred to the works of 'Greenham. Perkins. [Richard] Rogers. [John] Downam. and Arthur Dent, &c'.[4] Greenham was second to none – not even to Perkins, the most important English Reformed theologian of his day. This was far from uncommon. Charles Richardson, a London minister and author, in describing the duties of a godly minister, recommended reading four

---

[1] Portions of what follows will appear as ' "Practical Divinity": Richard Greenham's Ministry in Elizabethan England' in Eric Josef Carlson (ed.), *Religion and the English People 1500-1640: New Voices/New Perspectives*, Sixteenth Century Essays and Studies (Kirksville, MO: Thomas Jefferson University Press, 1998).

[2] *The Works of the Right Reverend Joseph Hall, D.D.*, ed. Philip Wynter (10 vols, Oxford, 1863), 10: 29.

[3] First Edition, A8v, reprinted in *The Collected Poems of Joseph Hall, Bishop of Exeter and Norwich*, ed. A. Davenport (Liverpool: Liverpool University Press, 1949), 102-3; Joseph Hall, *Heaven vpon earth, Or Of true Peace, and Tranquillitie of Minde* (London, 1606), §9.

[4] Thomas Cooper, *The Christians Daily Sacrifice: Containing a daily direction for a settled course of Sanctification* (1608), A5r. Thomas Cooper, not to be confused with the Bishop of Winchester who bore the same name, was a preacher who enjoyed the patronage of the Lord Chief Justice, later Earl of Manchester and dedicated anti-Laudian, Henry Montagu.

authors: Greenham, Perkins, John Dod and Andrew Willett.[5] Enemies of puritanism also twinned Greenham and Perkins as its most significant patriarchs. The poet-bishop Richard Corbett, in his satirical poem 'The Distracted Puritane', places the names of only two writers in the mouth of his speaker: Greenham and Perkins. In Perkins's writing, according to Corbett's caricature, the puritan 'observ'd the black Lines of Damnation' and feared for the fate of his soul; although 'in dispaire Five times a yeare', he was 'cur'd by reading Greenham'.[6]

Reading Greenham was indeed a godly practice. On the last Sunday of December in 1599, for example, Lady Margaret Hoby recorded in her diary that she and her husband, Sir Thomas Posthumous Hoby, returned home following the afternoon sermon and 'reed of Grenhame'. In what seems like an eternity and a world away from the Hobys' peaceful, godly household, Edward, Lord Montagu, turned to Greenham's writings for solace. In 1642, as the political crisis deepened and his own personal anxiety intensified, Montagu copied out several pieces of advice, including that men must first 'seeke the councell of God in his word, then to give ourselves to fervent prayer and after to use the meanes which God hath appointed'.[7]

Montagu may have become familiar with Greenham through the books of the puritan preacher Robert Bolton,[8] who dedicated *Some Generall Directions for a Comfortable Walking with God* to Montagu. The book contains many excerpts from Greenham's works.[9] Perhaps he

---

[5] Charles Richardson, *A Workeman, That Needeth Not to be Ashamed: Or The faithfull Steward of Gods house. A sermon describing the duety of a godly minister, both in his Doctrine and in his Life* (London, 1616), 29-30. We are grateful to Neal Enssle for this reference.

[6] *The Poems of Richard Corbett*, ed. J.A.W. Bennett and H.R. Trevor-Roper (Oxford: Clarendon Press, 1955), 58.

[7] *Diary of Lady Margaret Hoby 1599-1605*, ed. Dorothy M. Meads (London: George Routledge & Sons, 1930), 93; Esther S. Cope, *The Life of a Public Man: Edward, First Baron Montagu of Boughton, 1562-1644* (Philadelphia, PA, The American Philosophical Society, 1981), 190-91. We are grateful to Professor Cope for bringing Montagu to our attention.

[8] On Bolton, see Peter Lake, '"A Charitable Christian Hatred": The Godly and their Enemies in the 1630s', in Christopher Durston and Jacqueline Eales (eds), *The Culture of English Puritanism, 1560-1700* (Basingstoke: Macmillan, 1996), 145-83. We are grateful to Peter Lake for pointing out Bolton's use of Greenham to us.

[9] Robert Bolton, *Some Generall Directions for a Comfortable Walking with God: Delivered in the Lecture at Kettering in Northamptonshire, with enlargement* (2nd edn, 1626), e.g. 286-7. Quoting Greenham was common practice for Bolton: see his *Instructions For a Right comforting Afflicted Conciences: With speciall Antidotes against some grievous Temptations. Delivered for the most part in the Lecture at Kettering in Northamptonshire* (3rd edn, 1640), dedicatory letter.

owned his own copy of Greenham's *Works*. Many did, and prized them highly. For example, Philip Bisse, parson of Batcombe (Somerset), had four books which he deemed worthy of mention in his will in 1612: a herbal, a Hebrew Bible, and the *Works* of Perkins and Greenham. Philip Kettle, Fellow of Cambridge's St John's College, who died in 1606, owned Greenham's *Works*, which was considered significant enough to be the second – after Perkins's *Works* – of thirteen books listed by name in his post-mortem inventory.[10] Corporate libraries also considered Greenham's *Works* to be worthy acquisitions. Editions could be found, for example, in the More parish library (Salop) and in the Ipswich town library, established in 1599 to serve the town preachers.[11] Small wonder that one post-Restoration owner of the first edition of his *Works* wrote in his copy: 'Greenham altho he is Dead/His works on Earth shall always spread'.[12]

These volumes of his sermons and sayings were not, however, the real foundation of Greenham's extraordinary contemporary reputation. Greenham's death in 1594 was (in the words of his disciple Henry Holland) 'no small wrack to the Church and people of God'[13] not because his pen would no longer pour forth godly guidance – it had singularly failed to do so before his death, as will be seen below[14] – but because of his exceptional work as a parish minister, teacher and comforter of afflicted consciences. Contemporaries believed that 'for practicall divinity ... he was inferiour to few or none in his time'.[15]

---

[10] Margaret Steig, *Laud's Laboratory: The Diocese of Bath and Wells in the Early Seventeenth Century* (Lewisburg, PA: Bucknell University Press, 1983), 353; E.S. Leedham-Green, *Books in Cambridge Inventories. Book-Lists from Vice-Chancellor's Court Probate Inventories in the Tudor and Stuart Periods* (2 vols, Cambridge: Cambridge University Press, 1986), 554–5. Kettle's inventory also included a dozen unnamed books and a final entry for 'all the rest of his books'. This was not unusual. Only the largest and most obviously valuable books were likely to be inventoried by name. Testators like Bisse might own many more books but named in their wills only those books for which they wanted to make special provision, especially if they would not be able to give the book to the chosen beneficiary personally before death.

[11] Conal Condren, 'More Parish Library, Salop', *Library History*, 7 (1987), 114; John Blatchly, *The Town Library of Ipswich, Provided for the use of the Town Preachers in 1599: A History and Catalogue* (Wolfeboro, NH: Boydell & Brewer, 1989), 114–15, 178. We are grateful to Paul Griffiths for the first reference.

[12] Folger Library copy of First Edition, A6r. The owner of this copy, in 1713, was Shadrash Alderson.

[13] Ibid., A2v.

[14] See below, Appendix 1.

[15] The words are those of the eminent London nonconformist Stephen Egerton in the dedicatory letter which precedes the fourth part of the fourth edition of Greenham's posthumous collected works: Fourth Edition, 724.

Joseph Hall wrote to William Bedell, a Fellow of Emmanuel College, that Greenham 'excelled in experimental divinity; and knew well how to stay a weak conscience, how to raise a fallen, how to strike a remorseless ...'.[16]

In the century following Greenham's death, it was those pastoral efforts for which he was remembered – and in the most extravagant terms of late seventeenth-century hagiography. Thomas Fuller devoted less than two pages of his monumental study of British church history to Greenham, but his was the first explicitly biographical approach to the subject. Greenham was the selfless and sedulous pastor who 'often watered [the parish] with [his] tears, and oftner with his prayers and preaching, moistened the rich with his counsel, [and] the poor with his charity'. Though noted for his preaching, 'his master-piece was in comforting wounded consciences' and in that way he was 'an instrument of good to many, who came to him with weeping eyes, and went from him with cheerful souls'.[17]

The great puritan biographer/hagiographer Samuel Clarke published a substantial study of Greenham in 1677. As did Fuller, Clarke emphasized Greenham's 'excellent Faculty to relieve and comfort distressed Consciences'. For Clarke, Greenham was clearly a heroic figure and every aspect of his life and work – his learning and study, his preaching and catechizing, his charity to bodies and souls, his love of the queen and abhorrence of schism – was set out in the most heroic terms. When this paragon 'resigned up his Spirit unto God', the cause was his exhaustion in the service of the Lord.[18]

---

[16] Works of ... Joseph Hall, 6: 150.

[17] Thomas Fuller, The Church History of Britain from the Birth of Jesus Christ until the Year M.DC.XLVIII (London, 1655), 219-20. Much of Fuller's material apparently came from his father, who knew Richard Warfield, Greenham's successor as rector of Dry Drayton: untitled note by C.F.S. Warren, Notes and Queries, 6th ser., 7 (12 May 1883), 366.

[18] Samuel Clarke, 'Life of Master Richard Greenham', The Lives of Thirty-Two English Divines (3d edn, London, 1677), 12-15. An annotated edition may be found in Carlson, 'Practical Divinity', forthcoming. On Samuel Clarke, see: Patrick Collinson, '"A Magazine of Religious Patterns": An Erasmian Topic Transposed in English Protestantism' in his Godly People: Essays on English Protestantism and Puritanism (London: The Hambledon Press, 1983), 499-525; Jacqueline Eales, 'Samuel Clarke and the "Lives" of Godly Women in Seventeenth-Century England' in Women in the Church, ed. W.J. Sheils and Diana Webb, Studies in Church History, 27 (Oxford: Blackwell, 1990), 365-76; and Jessica Martin, Recollected Dust: Izaak Walton and the Beginning of Literary Biography (Woodbridge, Suffolk: Boydell, forthcoming), a revision of her superb 1993 Cambridge Ph.D. dissertation, 'Izaak Walton and his Precursors: A Literary Study of the Emergence of the Ecclesiastical Life'.

This traditional emphasis on Greenham's pastoral work, on 'experimental divinity', can be seen in Marshall Knappen's 1927 doctoral dissertation entitled 'Richard Greenham and the Practical Puritans under Elizabeth'.[19] For details of Greenham's life, Knappen depended on Clarke. Where Knappen's work goes beyond Clarke is in his identification of a group of clerics who were part of the tradition which emerged from Hugh Latimer (via Thomas Bilney) which subordinated structural and theological issues to 'praxis'. Like Latimer, these men were not theologians in the systematic tradition of scholasticism, but 'practical religious leader[s] of the people' whose sermons were about 'practical righteousness' such as the necessity of living in justice and peace with one's neighbours. 'The general object of this school of Reformers', according to Knappen, 'was to concentrate on supplying the religious needs of the average man'.[20] Although Knappen's thesis addressed more than Greenham, Greenham's spirit hovers over virtually every page of the text. Through his title, Knappen clearly identified Greenham as the unofficial leader and most important of all the 'practical' divines – a judgement entirely congruent with that of Elizabethans themselves.

Since Knappen, however, Greenham has not appeared in historical accounts of the Elizabethan Church with anything approaching the prominence that contemporaries ascribed to him.[21] Names of sixteenth-century divines are not expected to come dancing off the tongues of modern undergraduates, but even experts give the impression by their infrequent and modest references that Greenham ranks as a decidedly secondary figure, especially in comparison with such men as Edward Dering or Laurence Chaderton. R.T. Kendall, for example, describes Greenham as 'a patriarchal figure', but then assigns him the role of one of William Perkins's precursors.[22] But, as we have seen, rather than regarding Greenham as John the Baptist to Perkins's Messiah, contemporaries saw them as equals.

One notable exception to this pattern is the 1958 monograph on the Reformation in Cambridge by H.C. Porter. Porter both fully appreciated Greenham's relative importance and emphasized his standing as the epitome of the godly pastor. In a work about Cambridge University, Dr

---

[19] Unpublished Ph.D. dissertation, Cornell University, 1927.

[20] Ibid., 13, 20-28.

[21] For a detailed discussion and references to modern historical works, see Carlson, 'Practical Divinity', forthcoming.

[22] R.T. Kendall, *Calvin and English Calvinism to 1649* (Oxford: Oxford University Press, 1979), 45-7.

Porter understandably stressed, however, not Greenham's pastoral work in his parish but his training there of future ministers in a 'Puritan Academe, with a touch of Little Gidding'.[23] Margaret Spufford went down the muddy road to which Porter had pointed, to the parish of Dry Drayton, and undertook the first archival research on Greenham since that of Samuel Clarke. Working with the wills and ecclesiastical court records in the Ely diocesan archives, Professor Spufford began to piece together a picture of Greenham with his parishioners, establishing 'the first model Puritan parish in the country'.[24] Spufford's Greenham is recognizably closer to the man whose death was such a blow to the godly. Even in Spufford's sympathetic account, however, we see only partially the life and career of the man who was one of the wonders of the Elizabethan Church and whose death extinguished one of its great lights.

In this volume, we continue the work begun by Professor Spufford, seeking to restore Greenham to his proper place in accounts of the Elizabethan Church. Through introductory essays, a critical edition of an early collection of Greenham's sayings, and a representative sample of posthumously published works, the reader will not only discover Greenham's influence on early modern parochial ministry and his skill in curing afflicted consciences, but also how his legacy was claimed and used in the seventeenth century by conformists and nonconformists alike. This paradoxical fact has confounded accounts of Greenham in twentieth-century scholarship. The man encountered here was a pastor, intensely loyal to the Church of England, and obsessed with the realization of a visible godly community in every English parish. Greenham's practical divinity defies our categories of 'Anglican'/'conformist' and 'puritan'/'nonconformist', and points to a broader category of clergy too concerned with establishing 'true religion' and fighting popery in the parish to tolerate an overscrupulosity that detracted from the work of Protestant evangelization. His life and works are a testimony to the complex character of an Elizabethan religion that will not bow to the idols of traditional historiographical models, and call for progress beyond the current impasse, with its endless debates over the nature and character of 'Anglicans' and 'puritans'. Greenham points us to a way forward.

---

[23] H.C. Porter, *Reformation and Reaction in Tudor Cambridge* (Cambridge: Cambridge University Press, 1958), 216-17, 243, 267.

[24] Margaret Spufford, *Contrasting Communities: English Villagers in the Sixteenth and Seventeenth Centuries* (Cambridge: Cambridge University Press, 1974), 327-8.

CHAPTER TWO

A biographical sketch of Greenham's life

In his 1677 biography of Greenham, Samuel Clarke admitted that he had been unable to learn details of his subject's 'Contrey, Parentage, orfirst [sic] Education'.[1] Most of those details remain mysteries to this day. We have Greenham's own statement that he was a 'child' during the reign of Mary Tudor[2] which, together with his May 1559 matriculation from Pembroke Hall,[3] suggests that he was probably born between 1540 and 1545. From 1559, Greenham was in Cambridge, and he became a Fellow of Pembroke in 1567. The college proved a powerful influence on his later life.

Its Edwardian Master, Nicholas Ridley, described Pembroke Hall as 'a great setter-forth of Christ's gospel, and of God's true word'.[4] By the time Ridley became Master, it had for over two decades been the home and training-ground of prominent evangelicals, including Thomas Becon, John Rogers, and William Turner. Many of its alumni and fellowship, including Ridley, would die for their views. For a small house, Pembroke fledged more than its share of Marian exiles and martyrs.[5]

Although it was religiously divided when Greenham arrived in 1559, Pembroke Hall's dominant influence was Edmund Grindal, *de facto* Master for most of Edward VI's reign due to Ridley's absences and, from 1559 to 1562, Master in his own right.[6] The spirit brooding over the waters of Master Grindal's ecclesiology was Martin Bucer and, if Greenham's later words and actions are any evidence, the young scholar not only drank deeply from but also washed often and thoroughly in those waters. Because of their importance for Greenham's career it is worth briefly examining Bucer's and Grindal's vision of ministry.

For Bucer, according to Patrick Collinson, 'pastoral ministry was ... a

---

[1] Clarke, 'Life of Master Richard Greenham', 12.

[2] REM 524, fol. 16v.

[3] J. Venn and J.A. Venn (eds), *Alumni Cantabrigienses, Part I: From the earliest times to 1751* (4 vols, Cambridge: Cambridge University Press, 1922-27), sub 'Greenham, Richard'.

[4] Patrick Collinson, *Archbishop Grindal 1519-1583: The Struggle for a Reformed Church* (Berkeley and Los Angeles, CA: University of California Press, 1979), 38.

[5] See Porter, *Reformation and Reaction*, chap. 4.

[6] Collinson, *Archbishop Grindal*, 37-40.

1 Pembroke College, Cambridge. One of two significant sections which were standing during Greenham's time at what was then known as Pembroke Hall.

matter of extreme importance, a theme to which his preaching and writings constantly returned ...'. Notoriously hostile to 'extreme scrupulosity' over externals such as ceremonies and institutions, Bucer subjected all matters which were *adiaphora* to the test of their impact on ministry. In 1550, when John Hooper refused to be consecrated as Bishop of Gloucester wearing the (in Hooper's view) 'popish' vestments required by the Ordinal, Bucer would not support him. For Bucer, 'a pastor whose principles had landed him in the Fleet prison rather than in the neglected diocese where his talents were so much needed' deserved censure rather than support. Grindal also would indulge nonconformity if shown 'valid pastoral reasons', but, as Professor Collinson shows, 'where a rigid puritan scrupulosity seemed to threaten both the progress of the Gospel and the unity of the Church the puritans had no more resolute opponent'.[7]

In 1562, Matthew Hutton replaced Grindal, but his priorities remained in place during Hutton's tenure. In November 1565, for example, he demonstrated his support for moderation in the service of the church's peace and unity when he signed a letter to William Cecil asking him, as chancellor, to moderate enforcement of regulations concerning vestments.[8] John Whitgift, holder in succession of the two most prestigious chairs in divinity and very briefly Hutton's successor as Master, also signed this letter. In the mid-1560s, Whitgift was widely regarded as entirely in the tradition of Ridley and Grindal, and suspected by some of favouring 'precisians'.[9] Although Whitgift would part company with the kindred spirits of his Pembroke Hall days, he, Grindal and Hutton were direct influences as teachers on Richard Greenham in the 1560s, and it was the air of Pembroke Hall, redolent with its rich history of evangelical godliness and the aroma of Bucer's ideal of ministry, which he breathed every day for over a decade.

Greenham made a choice in 1570 that would profoundly alter his own life and change him from one of scores of forgettable godly academics to the acknowledged pioneer in godly parish ministry when he accepted John Hutton's offer to become rector of Dry Drayton. There are few direct clues to explain either his decision or his sense of calling. He did not make the decision hastily or privately; he believed that it was sinful to enter the ministry without a process of discerning 'affection and gifts'

---

[7] Ibid., 49–56.

[8] Ibid., 37; Peter Lake, 'Matthew Hutton - A Puritan Bishop?' *History*, 64 (1979), 183-4.

[9] Patrick Collinson, 'The "Nott Conformytye" of the Young John Whitgift' in *Godly People*, 325-33.

2 The parish church of St Peter and St Paul, Dry Drayton. The exterior of the church is essentially as it was during Greenham's two decades as rector.

and decided 'with the consent of the most godly and learned brethren'.[10] His long delay in moving from university to parish might be understood in light of his later criticism of 'the preposterous zeal and hasty runing of yong men into the ministry'. Mere book-learning was insufficient, argued Greenham, because 'stayednes, and moderation, use, experience, gravity in ordering affections, and having some mastery over his corruptions was needful in him that should govern the church'.[11] But if education itself did not justify undertaking parish ministry, it was none the less the case that Greenham believed that it was sinful to store up knowledge of God's word without sharing it. What he would later say of ministers provides some clues to what might have been in his mind as a Fellow of Pembroke: the minister must not always stay in his study 'filling himselfe with knowledge, till he becomes as a tunne that will not sound when one knocketh upon it: but hee must come out of his closet and preach the word of God and deliver forth holsome doctrine ...'. Learning which did not advance another's salvation, he argued, was without purpose; indeed, it was even sinful.

> The Minister therefore of Gods word must not onely bee learned but must teach also: for how can hee bee a minister of doctrine, but in this respect that he teacheth executing the office of his ministry? ... Whosoever therfore shall not thus labour is not the minister of the Lord, but a robber and spoiler of the people of God which thrust themselves into the ministerie to fill their belly onely with the sweate of other mens browes.[12]

So, intending to fulfil God's will by sharing God's word with others, Greenham resigned his fellowship and moved the five muddy miles from Cambridge to Dry Drayton.

Dry Drayton was an average-sized Cambridgeshire village.[13] Its boundaries included a large area of heavy and wet boulder clay better suited for grazing than cereal crops, as well as an area of river valley which was part chalk and part alluvium. Barley was the main crop. For a village of its size, it was relatively underpopulated for much of the sixteenth century. In 1524, as English population was recovering from its post-plague lows, Dry Drayton had fewer than 35 households and in 1563 only 31 households. The surplus of baptisms over burials in the 1570s and 1580s implies a staggering population increase in those

[10] REM 524, fols 1v, 67v.

[11] Ibid., fols 54r-v.

[12] Fourth Edition, 781-2.

[13] For Dry Drayton, see especially *A History of the County of Cambridge and the Isle of Ely*, ed. C.R. Elrington et al., (9 vols to date, London and Oxford: various publishers, 1938-), 9: 71, 77-81; and Carlson, 'Practical Divinity', in which the sources are described and analysed in detail.

decades, though outmigration might have kept the population from overwhelming the village's limited resources.

For much of its history, lordship in Dry Drayton had been monastic.[14] In 1543, Henry VIII granted the dissolved Crowland Abbey's manor and advowson of Dry Drayton to Thomas Hutton.[15] The incumbent rector, John Clever, was a non-resident pluralist, known to have been living with a woman (apparently not his wife) in Leicestershire in the 1560s.[16] His successor, William Fairclough, who became rector in 1567, also misbehaved sexually. In December 1568 he was charged, in the Bishop of Ely's court, with adultery with Agnes Lakers. He admitted the charge, but refused to perform his penance and was excommunicated for several months until he submitted.[17] The charges against Fairclough had been brought by the churchwardens, which argues that his adultery had become an intractable public scandal since churchwardens worked hard to resolve matters internally, and only handed cases over to the ecclesiastical courts as a last resort.[18] Fairclough died in July 1570,[19] creating the opening for Greenham.

John Hutton[20] (Thomas's heir), whose duty it was to replace Fairclough, was a gentleman of zealous inclinations. He was apparently related to Greenham's Master at Pembroke Hall, Matthew Hutton. Matthew, sensing perhaps that Greenham was being drawn to parish ministry, probably advised his kinsman John to offer the living to Greenham. The offer was attractive since Dry Drayton was close enough to Cambridge for Greenham to maintain his contacts there and to continue preaching at Great St Mary's and – as was to be important later – for people to come to him with little inconvenience. Although it lacked glebe lands, Dry Drayton was still one of the more lucrative livings in the diocese.[21] For Greenham, unmarried at the time, there were no financial reasons to hesitate.

---

[14] D. and S. Lysons, *Magna Britannia* (Cambridge, 1808), 2[1], 179; *VCH, Cambs.*, IX, 74-7; Frances M. Page, *The Estates of Crowland Abbey: A Study in Manorial Organization* (Cambridge: Cambridge University Press, 1934), 19-28.

[15] *Letters and Papers, Foreign and Domestic of the Reign of Henry VIII*, ed. J.S. Brewer, et al. (21 vols, London, 1862-1920), 18[2]: no. 107(9).

[16] EDR, B/2/3, fols 93, 130.

[17] EDR, B/2/6, 32, 74; D/2/8, fols 9v, 11v, 20r, 27r.

[18] Eric Josef Carlson, *Marriage and the English Reformation* (Oxford: Blackwell, 1994), chap. 7, esp. 142-56.

[19] He was buried on 6 July: CRO, Dry Drayton original parish register.

[20] On John Hutton, see P.W. Hasler, *The House of Commons 1558-1603* (3 vols, London: HMSO, 1981), II, 359-60.

[21] The value in 1535 was £21 0s 14d.: *Valor Ecclesiasticus* (6 vols, London, 1817), III, 502. It would be reasonable to estimate a doubling in the monetary value of the living by 1570: see R.B. Outhwaite, *Inflation in Tudor and Early Stuart England* (2nd edn, London and Basingstoke: Macmillan, 1982). Glebe terrier: EDR, H/1/3.

He remained unmarried for another three years, but in August 1573 he married Katherine Bownd, a physician's widow. Katherine's sister Sibill was married to John Hutton's brother James, and Katherine probably moved to Dry Drayton after her husband's death in order to be with her family, to whom she remained close until her own death in 1612.[22] Given Greenham's antipathy towards the married state,[23] one can scarcely imagine what the courtship must have been like, and the cynical can be excused for believing that he married for domestic convenience if not also for the political connection. The marriage might technically have been illegal, because Greenham does not appear to have complied with the requirement that a minister, before marrying, obtain the advice and consent of his bishop and two justices of the peace. The requirement, put into place in 1559, was designed to combat the 'offense and ... slander' which had been caused 'by lack of discreet and sober behaviour in many ministers ... in choosing of their wives ...'.[24] For failing to comply, Greenham could have been removed from his ministry. However, given that he was marrying an undeniably respectable woman, related by marriage to the most powerful man in the vicinity, there can have been no question of subjecting her to an investigation into her character nor any real danger that she would prove to be an embarrassment to the ministry.

There was, in fact, a much greater threat to Greenham's continued ministry in 1573, and it sprang from another (more serious) bit of nonconformity. In 1571, all ministers in the diocese had been ordered to sign a statement to the effect that the Prayer Book was 'such as conteynethe nothing in yt repugnynge or contrarie to the word of God', that the required apparel (especially the surplice and square cap) was 'not wicked but tollerable and to be used obediently for order and comeliness only', and that the Articles of Religion contained 'most godlye and holsome doctryne agreeable unto Gods holye worde'. Greenham could not and did not subscribe.[25] For some time, he was not

---

[22] CRO, Dry Drayton original parish register. Katherine's will is PRO, PROB 11/119; Prerogative Court of Canterbury, 41 Fenne. We are very grateful to Michael Sekulla for providing us with a copy of this important source.

[23] See below, 77-9.

[24] Injunction 29, Royal Visitation of 1559: *Documents of the English Reformation*, ed. Gerald Bray (Minneapolis, MN: Fortress Press, 1994), 342. For a discussion of this text, see Eric Josef Carlson, 'Clerical Marriage and the English Reformation', *Journal of British Studies*, 31 (1992), 13-21.

[25] EDR, B/2/6, 198. For these issues in general, and especially for resistance to such subscription campaigns, see Patrick Collinson, *The Elizabethan Puritan Movement* (London: Jonathan Cape, 1967).

troubled by the authorities, but in 1573 his non-subscription caught up with him and he faced suspension.

It was on that occasion that he wrote one of the pieces upon which his reputation was built: 'The Apologie or aunswere of Maister Grenham, Minister of Dreaton, unto the Bishop of Ely, being commaunded to subscribe, and to use the Romish habite, with allowance of the com[munion] booke'.[26] While making clear that he would not wear the apparel 'nor subscribe unto it, or the communion booke', Greenham refused to say why 'unlesse [he] be forced thereto'. He begged Bishop Cox to leave him alone, assuring the bishop that he dissented out of conscience and not perversity, but would voluntarily say no more. He claimed – disingenuously – to be a simple country lad unable to match wits with Cox or the 'godly learned' who debated these issues; rather, he 'occupied [him]selfe daylie ... in preaching Christ crucified unto [him]selfe and Country people' and did not stir them up with debates over ceremonies or surplices. Instead, at all times and in all places, he would 'by all meanes seeke peace and pursue it ...'. Greenham saw the Devil's hand in these divisions over externals: 'I doe not doubt but that the common adversarie hath shrouded in on both parties, wolves in sheepes cloathing, to cause the children of God, more egarlie to fight togither, so that the common worke of the Lorde beinge hindered, he might the more prevayle.' To carry out this common work had to be deemed more important than differences over externals; to remove from his parish a man who was loyal to the queen and the church, who was no schismatic or papist, served no interests except those of Satan, the common adversary.[27]

While his impatience with 'preciseness' had been growing with every passing day, Cox chose to take no action against Greenham. Cox was known to be pragmatic not dogmatic, and had previously shown willingness to make allowances for individual consciences.[28] Moreover, he could not afford to lose Greenham. Cox's first priority was to place in every parish a minister who was well educated in the Bible and would reside in his parish to teach his flock. In 1560, he had found the diocese in a miserable state. Many parishes lacked incumbents and the shortage

---

[26] This was printed shortly before his death in *A parte of a register, contayninge sundrie memorable matters written by divers godly and learned in our time, which stande for and desire the reformation of our Church, in discipline and ceremonies, according to the pure worde of God, and the lawe of our lande* (Middleburg, 1593), 86-93.

[27] See also Margo Todd, '"An act of discretion": Evangelical Conformity and the Puritan Dons', *Albion*, 18 (1986), 581-99.

[28] Felicity Margaret Heal, 'The Bishops of Ely and Their Diocese during the Reformation Period: ca. 1515-1600' (unpublished Ph.D. dissertation, Cambridge University, 1972), 120-21.

of suitable candidates was acute. Too many of those parishes which had incumbents (including Dry Drayton) had them in name only, since they were permanently non-resident. At first, Cox was so eager to fill vacancies that the screening process was scarcely more than a formality and, although a few were rejected, he ordained almost anyone with testicles and a pulse. As the 1560s progressed, he raised his standards and rejected unfit prospective ordinands – more than one-third of the candidates in 1568, for example – and began depriving non-residents.[29] Greenham was exactly the sort of well-educated cleric whose services Cox craved and sorely needed. He could ill afford to lose him, especially with the qualified replacements barely able to fill the vacancies which would occur from other causes.

Cox was also obsessively afraid of Catholicism. In letters to William Cecil, he regularly perched between paranoia and hysteria on the subject.[30] His zeal over parochial staffing was very much related to this fear, for an educated catechizing and preaching ministry was essential to wipe out superstition and defeat the menace of popery. Because of this, Cox did not resist lay patronage of nonconformists in the diocese, and he personally placed them in livings in the Isle of Ely, 'remote and ignorant' as it was. The urgent need for teaching the word of God, in Cox's view, overrode any differences over *adiaphora*, at least if those with whom he differed proved willing to preach Christ crucified and restrict their sentiments about 'abuses' in the church to their consciences and keep them out of pulpits.[31] Greenham's description of his single-minded efforts to preach Christ crucified and battle against the 'common adversarie' would help Cox to see him as an ally in the anti-Catholic struggle.

Finally, Greenham was allowed to continue because the effects of his nonconformity were moderated by the high value he placed on preserving peace in the church. Shortly before he left Cambridge in late 1570, Greenham joined other Cantabrigians in signing two letters to William Cecil in support of Thomas Cartwright, who had given a controversial series of lectures on the Acts of the Apostles for which he was ultimately removed from his position as Lady Margaret professor of divinity.[32] Greenham did not long remain among Cartwright's

---

[29] BL, Add. MS 5813, fols 63ff.; EDR, A/5/1; Heal, 'Bishops of Ely', 106-31; Dorothy Owen, 'The Enforcement of the Reformation in the Diocese of Ely' in *Miscellanea Historiae Ecclesiasticae. III, Colloque de Cambridge, 24-28 Septembre 1968*, ed. Derek Baker (Louvain: Publications Universitaires de Louvain, 1970), 172-4.

[30] Heal, 'Bishops of Ely', 134.

[31] Ibid., 129.

[32] A.F. Scott Pearson, *Thomas Cartwright and Elizabethan Puritanism, 1535-1603* (Cambridge: Cambridge University Press, 1925), 422-4, 426-7; Collinson, *Elizabethan Puritan Movement*, 112-13.

supporters, however. When the controversy spilled outside of the
university and threatened the stability of the church, Greenham lent his
talents to a different cause. George Downame later recalled that during
his university days Greenham had rebuked students from the pulpit of
Great St Mary's for being drawn into bootless, unedifying debates rather
than attending to the studies which would prepare them for the real
work of preaching and teaching.[33]

One of his followers would later record him saying that in 'a meer
outward thing' he 'would not break the peace of the church', and in 'the
lesser adjuncts of religion ... hee would not withstand or condemn any
but leav them to ther own reason, seing very good men do soe dissagree
in them, or change ther opinion in them'; only when 'it came to the
essence of gods worship ... must wee bee strickt'.[34] A good example of
what this meant in practice can be seen in the stinging rebuke he
delivered to a 'godly minister' who outraged his parishioners by pulling
down 'certain painted glasse windowes' in the church. Greenham
scoldingly told him that the minister's first duty was not to destroy but
to teach, and that he should first have taught his parishioners and
obtained their consent to replace the windows with plain glass.[35] He
advised another 'to preach faith and repentance from sin: and when god
shal have given you some power, and credit in ther consciences', then to
take up denouncing abuses.[36]

Rather than removing Greenham in 1573, as he clearly would have
been justified in doing, Cox soon employed him in sensitive conferences
with recusants and members of the heretical sect, the Family of Love. In
1580, for example, Mary Johnson, a Cambridgeshire recusant, was
ordered by Cox to confer with Greenham.[37] Greenham played a central
role in the diocesan campaign against the Family of Love in the same
year, devising the articles to which suspects would subscribe and,
through personal conversation, returning some of the tractable to
'orthodoxy'. He met with Mrs Margaret Colevyll, a widowed
gentlewoman, and he 'gently and lovingly confuted her errors by the
scriptures, and ... she by degrees yielded and in the end freely gave up her

---

[33] George Downame, *Two sermons, the one commending the ministrie in general: the
other defending the office of bishops in particular* (London, 1608), dedicatory epistle. See
also Charles Henry Cooper and Thompson Cooper, *Athenae Cantabrigiensis* (2 vols,
Cambridge, 1858-61), 2: 143-4.

[34] REM 524, fols 54v-55r. In another place, he said 'wee may yeeld just obedience, so
it bee in things meerly outward ... Let us do as much as wee can with the peace of the
Church lest wee make the remedy of the evil wors then the evil it self': ibid., fol. 10v.

[35] Ibid., fols 36v-37r.

[36] Ibid., fols 39v-40r.

[37] EDR, D/2/10, fols 195v-196r.

book [of Familist writings], acknowledg[ing] her errors with many tears before sufficient witnesses'.[38]

The Family of Love, which was quite active in Cambridgeshire, roused Greenham to extreme language as few other things could. He described the sect as 'pestilent' and 'that phreneticall fansie'.[39] Their hypocrisy was a recurring theme.[40] The juxtaposition of Catholics and Familists in Cox's assignments to Greenham is not surprising. Catholics and Familists both threatened the unity of the church; they were cut from the same cloth, and its weaver was Satan. Followers recorded many different occasions when he linked the two.[41] Typically, his comments on these two enemies of the church expressed a sense of urgency:

> Look but to the Papists and Familie of love, how painfull and cunning they are to goe, to runne, to ride, to make one like of their heresies; see, how they will looke for you at markets, how they will entertaine you, what meekness, what mildnes they will use to salute you. This ought to shame us, this ought to make us labour more for knowledge, that when temptations invade us, when Satan accuseth us, when heresie shall assault us, we may stand stedfast and unremoveable, we may edifie one another, and in persecution not be dismaied, but resist constantly unto blood.[42]

The church, Greenham believed, was itself to blame for these heresies. Common people were drawn to them because their parish churches failed to offer the sort of teaching and preaching necessary to meet their spiritual needs. This was also the key to crushing both Papists and Familists, for what linked the two most notably was their confidence in the works and words of men rather than of God: 'If we take away ... the Fathers traditions from the Papist, or the eight man his revelations from the Familist, and urge them with the word, they are gone: so that it is onely word of God, maugre the head of the divell, that unblindfoldeth all their errors, and is able to move them, and convert so many to truth as God will have saved'.[43] This was, for example, his experience with Margaret Colevyll.

Although Greenham sincerely advocated peace, he could apparently wield a fierce verbal sword against separatists. As noted above, he gave

---

[38] *Tudor Royal Proclamations*, ed. Paul L. Hughes and James F. Larkin (3 vols, New Haven: Yale University Press, 1964-69), no. 652; Gonville and Caius College, Cambridge, MS 53/30, fols 126v-129r; Christopher W. Marsh, *The Family of Love in English Society, 1550-1630* (Cambridge: Cambridge University Press, 1993).

[39] Fourth Edition, 803, 853.

[40] For example, Third Edition, 273, 472, 490; Fourth Edition, 803.

[41] For example, REM 524, fols 56v-57r.

[42] Fourth Edition, 854-5.

[43] Ibid., 843. The reference to 'the eight man his revelations' is to the writings of H.N.: see Marsh, *The Family of Love.*

Cambridge students a memorable shaking-up over their attention to Thomas Cartwright. A telling indication of Greenham's stature as an anti-separatist preacher can be found in Job Throckmorton's published attack on Greenham's Cambridge contemporary, Robert Some.[44] Some had signed the pro-Cartwright letters to Cecil and, as Peter Lake describes his positions, he had much else in common with Greenham. By 1588, Some had become a writer of fairly unimpressive anti-separatist polemic. In response to his attack on John Penry, Throckmorton suggested that Some's recent interest in ingratiating himself with Archbishop Whitgift had led Some to be too much around Lambeth, where the damp air had addled his previous good sense. For the sake of his health, Throckmorton urged Some to 'get him into the country in th'open aire, & to make his onely residence & ordinary aboade upon Girton benefice ... [and] to take paines with his poore parishners, aswel by publike teaching & catechising of them, as by private admonishment & familiar conferences ...'. After this dig at Some for his non-residence, Throckmorton concluded: 'And let him ask M. Grenham whether this be not an excellent medicine for the shortnes of breath, I warrant you he hath tried it, and hath found good of it, for he hath winde at wil ye see, & as shril pipes as most men'. Greenham was apparently never short of words and energy for a sermon against separatists. Since none of those sermons survive, their tone and effect can only be gauged by observations like these. Had Greenham been a publishing polemicist, there would no doubt be published rebuttals from the separatists, but that was not the case. Still, the separatists saw him as an important and effective enough foe to single him out for bitter asides such as this one.

It is worth noting the common thread woven through his activities outside the parish during the 1570s and 1580s: conferring with Mary Johnson and with the Familists, and preaching in Cambridge against Thomas Cartwright and Martin Marprelate. In each instance, Greenham acted to preserve the peace and unity of the church. A sometime nonconformist Greenham might be, but could Cox hope to do any better? By the mid-1570s, John Hutton was part of Lord North's political circle, and engaged in a full-blown power struggle with Cox.[45] Cox had no reason to be sanguine about the prospects for a more

---

[44] [Job Throckmorton], M. *Some laid open in his coulers: Wherein the Indifferent Reader may easily see, howe wretchedly and loosely he hath handeled the cause against M. Penri* (La Rochelle, 1589), 121-2. We are indebted to Peter Lake for this important reference. See P. Lake, 'Robert Some and the Ambiguities of Moderation', *Archiv für Reformationsgeschichte*, 71 (1980), 254-79.

[45] E.J. Bourgeois II, 'The Queen, a Bishop, and a Peer: A Clash for Power in Mid-Elizabethan Cambridgeshire', *Sixteenth Century Journal*, 26 (1995), 3-15.

conformable incumbent for Dry Drayton if he forced Greenham out and created a vacancy; nor could he expect anyone who would lend his efforts so effectively to the causes which agitated the ageing bishop.

Through the surviving visitation records it is clear, *inter alia*, that Greenham continued to eschew wearing the surplice.[46] Yet after 1573 neither Cox nor any other Ely diocesan official troubled Greenham over his nonconformity. He was not among the eleven Cambridgeshire ministers threatened with suspension by Archbishop Whitgift in 1584.[47] Instead, he laboured away at the business of parish ministry for almost two decades.[48]

That we know so much of his parish ministry is due almost entirely to the household seminary which sprouted in Dry Drayton. It was the first of its kind and a truly significant innovation in clerical education, filling a crucial gap: the absence of any *practical* training for ministry.[49] Whether its germination was intentional or not remains unknown; however, some of Greenham's reported sayings suggest that this work developed after serious reflection. Many recognized a need for some intermediate stage between the university and the parish, since the university provided no real practical preparation in ministerial duties.[50] As shown above, Greenham decried 'the preposterous zeal and hasty runing of yong men into the ministry'.[51] Instead of allowing unseasoned men to take up ministry on the basis of book-learning alone, Greenham stated that 'it were an happy nourcery for this church if every grounded pastor' would take on 'some toward schollar' as his assistant for a time; after some experience, 'hee may commend him to the church goverment,

---

[46] There was no surplice in Dry Drayton, according to reports shortly after his departure: EDR, B/2/11, fol. 89v.

[47] *The Seconde Parte of a Register; being a calendar of manuscripts under that title intended for publication by the Puritans about 1593, and now in Dr William's library, London*, ed. A. Peel (2 vols, Cambridge: Cambridge University Press, 1915), I, 227-8. John Hutton was one of the seven local gentlemen who wrote to Whitgift on their behalf, making it likely that Greenham would have been mentioned if he were under threat.

[48] See below, 59-86.

[49] From the comment of Samuel Ward, it appears that William Perkins gave advice to men who were already working ministers, rather than training men before they took up parish work: *Two Elizabethan Puritan Diaries*, ed. M.M. Knappen (Chicago: American Society of Church History, 1933), 130. The need for 'how to' training was later also filled by handbooks on ministry: see Patrick Collinson, 'Shepherds, Sheepdogs, and Hirelings: The Pastoral Ministry in Post-Reformation England', *The Ministry: Clerical and Lay*, ed. W.J. Sheils and Diana Wood, *Studies in Church History*, 26 (Oxford: Blackwell, 1989), 194-8; Neal R. Ennsle, 'Patterns of Godly Life: The Ideal Parish Minister in Sixteenth and Seventeenth Century English Thought', *Sixteenth Century Journal*, 28 (1997), 3-28.

[50] John Morgan, *Godly Learning: Puritan Attitudes towards Reason, Learning, and Education, 1560-1640* (Cambridge: Cambridge University Press, 1986), 293.

[51] REM 524, fols 54r-v; see above, 11.

and being happily discharged of one', take on another apprentice from the university 'to bee framed in like manner fit for the work of the lord'.[52]

Greenham intended at least this much, but found himself with more than one assistant at a time. His location so close to Cambridge certainly fostered that, and he would have been well known to godly students since he preached occasionally at Great St Mary's. Thus, he trained more than his share of 'toward schollars' who became major figures in the English Church, such as Arthur Hildersham and Henry Smith. He established a precedent followed by many in the next century[53] but, more importantly, as his protégés dispersed into the rectories, vicarages and pulpits of England, Greenham's example in Dry Drayton went with them and, presumably, helped to define the shape of their own ministries. Literally thousands of English lay people were, by the 1620s, in some sense the flock of Richard Greenham.

During his two decades at Dry Drayton, his friends and admirers reportedly had 'often laboured' him to leave it. Although unwilling, when pressed 'hee seemed to offer these conditions. First if they would remoove him his stipend should not bee one penny more then in his present place 2ly hee requested to have the choice of the pastor 3ly hee required such a place as might not bee far from his charge present, beecause hee would stil use his fatherly care to his people as to his natural childeren in the preaching of the gospel.'[54] In 1591, Greenham did leave Dry Drayton for London, where he remained until his death. When he moved, he met one, possibly two, of his conditions. He was influential in the choice of Richard Warfield as his successor. His stipend in London will never be known, but it seems unlikely that he would have used the move to improve himself financially.[55] He clearly did not meet the third condition, however; London was too far from Dry Drayton for regular visits.

What were his motives for leaving his parish after twenty years? Thomas Fuller's father told the historian of a conversation in 1616 which

---

[52] Ibid., fol. 57v. He cited biblical precedents for the duty of 'every godly learned minister' to 'trayn up some yong schollar': fol. 58r.

[53] An excellent discussion of early seventeenth-century seminaries is in Kenneth Shipp, 'Lay Patronage of East Anglian Puritan Clerics in Pre-Revolutionary England' (unpublished Ph.D. dissertation, Yale University, 1971), App. II. See also Morgan, *Godly Learning*, 295-9.

[54] REM 524, fol. 2r. Fuller (*Church History*, 220) reported that Greenham's friends described Dry Drayton as 'but a bushel' and urged him to leave it.

[55] Patrick Collinson describes Greenham's move as to 'a more lucrative and comfortable post', but he gives no evidence that it was more lucrative – which seems unlikely – and it was certainly not more comfortable: 'Shepherds, Sheepdogs, and Hirelings', 200.

he had with Richard Warfield, in which he reported receiving these parting words from Greenham: 'Mr. Warfield (saith hee) God blesse you, and send you more fruit of yor labours then I have had: ffor I perceive now good wrought by ministerie on any but one familie.' Samuel Clarke reported that Greenham left because of 'the untractableness and unteachableness of that people among whom he had taken such exceeding great pains'.[56] Is this credible? Ministers often asked Greenham to comment on how to respond to troubles in one's calling and place of residence. One man who asked 'whither for some trobles hee might not depart from his calling' was told by Greenham that 'if for every troble or for many trobles a man might forsake his calling hee should bee out of any calling, for-as-much as every calling hath his lets and impediments'.[57] Moving provided no relief from troubles, for wherever one 'did purpose to live for a good christian, the crosse of christ would follow him'.[58]

Greenham's recorded sayings convey mixed messages about whether perceived failures in ministry could justify giving up a calling. On the one hand, he had a finely developed sense of delayed gratification: like 'a good fieldsman, hee would long after hee had sowen looke for the increas, not measuring the fruit of his labor by the time present but by the tyme to come ...'.[59] On the other hand, he professed that continuing in a calling depended on God's blessing. When he first entered the ministry, his intention was that 'if the lord denying his grace and blessing would seme to refuse him, hee would publickly in the congregation to the glory of god and shaming of himself confes his unhability and unwoorthines of the place and so depart'.[60]

However, there is good reason to believe that Greenham was not a failure in Dry Drayton. While he might have been frustrated at delays in transforming it into a shining village on the clay, that did not demonstrate 'his unhability and unwoorthines of the place'.[61] Greenham left because the Remembrancer of the Exchequer, Thomas Fanshawe, and others persuaded him that, whatever the need for his ministry in Dry

---

[56] Warren, *Notes and Queries*, 366; Clarke, 'Life of Master Richard Greenham', 15.
[57] REM 524, fols 3r–v.
[58] Ibid., fol. 17r.
[59] Ibid , fol. 7v. See also fol. 2r: 'When hee could not see one profit by his doctrine presently hee wold not bee discouraged, for that hee often observed that they presently would rather murmure then profit by his speeches: after examining his speaches when ther cholar was over did much more profit by his doctrine then they that seemed at the first to receiv it very mildly, who after notwithstanding went away without al fruit or would thinck of it again.'
[60] Ibid., fol. 67v.
[61] For our argument that this was not the case, see Carlson, 'Practical Divinity'.

Drayton, there was even greater need in London. By 1591, the church was well supplied with educated ordinands, and a suitable replacement for Greenham could easily be found. But the needs in London were such, so he would have been told, that only he could meet them. His removal to London could not have been presented to him as, nor could he have believed it to be, a comfortable option.

London lectureships had, in the early 1580s, been a safe haven for nonconformists. By 1590, however, Archbishop Whitgift and Bishop Aylmer had brought them under strict episcopal supervision and the number of nonconformists in lectureships had decreased sharply. Those who remained were keenly aware of hot episcopal breath on their unsurpliced backs. Paul Seaver has pointed out that what saved the London nonconformists 'from impotent silence during [the 1590s] was the steady influx of mature nonconformists from the provinces'.[62] Greenham was part of that influx and because of his towering stature among non-separating nonconformists he was recruited to help save their cause in London.

In February 1591/92, Greenham was granted a licence to preach in the diocese of London. This occurred in spite of Greenham's non-subscription. The official registration of his licence stated that 'Mr Thomas Fanshawe armiger de verbo suo promisit ut domini Greenham nullas innovaciones aut contentiones de rebus suscitet vel spargat'.[63] While other preachers were simply licensed 'as long as (*dummodo*)' they did not stir up trouble, Greenham's reputation as a nonconformist patriarch required something more; Bishop Aylmer licensed him only with the personal assurances of his good conduct from a powerful third party.

Whether Aylmer granted the preaching licence only under pressure from the politically powerful Fanshawe, who was one of the most prominent supporters of London nonconformists,[64] is not clear. Aylmer, who became Bishop of London in 1576, was no friend to nonconformists. He had enthusiastically supported Whitgift's subscription campaigns in 1584. But he was similar in important ways to Bishop Cox of Ely. Like Cox, Aylmer had been an exile in Mary's reign and regarded Rome as the great enemy; like Cox, he desired to staff his parishes with educated clergy who could teach and preach.[65] He seemed

---

[62] Paul Seaver, *The Puritan Lectureships: The Politics of Religious Dissent, 1560-1662* (Stanford, CA: Stanford University Press, 1970), 211-20.

[63] GLRO, DL/C/335 (Liber Vicarii Generalis, 1590-95), fol. 60v.

[64] On Fanshawe, see Hasler, *House of Commons*, II, 105-6.

[65] John Strype, *Historical Collections of the Life and Acts of the Right Reverend Father in God, John Aylmer, Lord Bp. of London in the Reign of Queen Elizabeth* (new edn, Oxford, 1821), 16-17, 21-3.

willing, for a good cause, to make compromises with quite radical men. He constructed a naïve scheme to send William Charke, Edmund Chapman, John Field and Thomas Wilcox to Lancashire, Staffordshire 'and such other like barbarous countries, to draw people from Papism and gross ignorance'.[66] George Gifford, suspended in 1584, was restored without subscribing; Gifford was respected for his work in bringing his Essex parish 'to more sobriety and knowledge of true religion' and he emerged as a ferocious opponent of the separatist Henry Barrow.[67] In other words, Aylmer seemed willing to bend a bit, as Cox had been, in order to serve the larger needs of the church, as long as the object of his concessions proved committed to the unity of the church and the defeat of its enemies.

There are even hints of the form which Aylmer's licence for Greenham would take in the 1582 compromise over Robert Wright. Wright, whose patron was Lord Rich, preached without a licence and was known to conduct private services not conforming to the Prayer Book. He was imprisoned but eventually released after he agreed to limited subscription and his 'friends' put up a 'good round sum' as insurance that his future preaching would not be disruptive of church unity.[68] Like Wright, Greenham had a powerful patron who could be called upon to stand surety for him. Perhaps Aylmer remembered the 1582 precedent when faced with a request to license a known nonconformist whose past history in Cambridgeshire showed he would serve the bishop well in defeating common enemies.

Although he had manors in Essex and Hertfordshire, Thomas Fanshawe's London residence – necessary when he attended to Exchequer business and served in Parliament – was in Warwick Lane, and he was active and influential in the affairs of his parish.[69] Although the licence does not specify in which parish Greenham would preach, Fanshawe's activities as recruiter and sponsor make clear that it would be Christ Church, Newgate Street, one of the six largest parishes within London's walls and, in Greenham's day, one of the newest. The parish was founded in December 1546 as part of a scheme to reconstruct the dissolved foundation of St Bartholomew's Hospital. The Hospital itself was re-established by the City authorities as a hospital for the sick, the dissolved Grey Friars (Franciscan) house by Newgate was converted into

---

[66] Ibid., 36. On these men, see Collinson, *Elizabethan Puritan Movement*.

[67] Strype, *Aylmer*, 71-3.

[68] Ibid., 54-7. On Wright, see Seaver, *Puritan Lectureships*, 94-5, 111-12.

[69] He has been identified as a spokesman for the parish in its dealings, for example, with the board of governors of St Bartholomew's Hospital, which had authority over the parish: H. Gareth Owen, 'Tradition and Reform: Ecclesiastical Controversy in an Elizabethan London Parish', *Guildhall Miscellany*, 2 (1961), 63-70.

3 Christ Church Newgate, London. The church in which Greenham preached and was buried was destroyed in the Great Fire. It was rebuilt, but destroyed again during World War II. The remains of the Wren church are now part of a small public park and rose garden on High Holborn. Greenham was buried in a place which must now be under either the pavement or the street.

an orphanage (later known as Christ's Hospital), and the Grey Friars' church became the new parish church of Christ Church. This entire area was under the authority of the governors of St Bartholomew's Hospital.[70]

From its earliest days, the parish was known for its connections with advanced reformers and prominent London religious radicals. Thomas Becon was its first vicar; later vicars included Thomas Gataker. By 1560 the parish had already established a lectureship, held then by Richard Allen, one of the most extreme of London's radical preachers. By 1590 the number of lecturers had risen to four. When the parish was established, part of the pre-Dissolution resources had been used to endow five assistant clerks or 'singing priests'. These conservative fixtures, whose role harked back to the more 'popish' church services of Henry VIII's reign, were peas under the mattresses of the religiously progressive lay folk who dominated the parish. They ultimately succeeded in getting the Hospital governors to remove them. The 'singing priests' gave way to a curate and four lecturers, all paid out of the endowment, which allowed the parish to stop paying for its lecturer from parochial funds. Greenham's status and reputation seemed to demand a position of more prestige and a higher stipend. Fanshawe pressed the Hospital governors to combine the positions and salaries of the four lecturers into one for Greenham. Although seriously considered, the proposal was never adopted[71] and Greenham must have been paid from parish funds or from the contributions of patrons like Fanshawe, who could well afford it.

Very few details are known about Greenham's ministry in London. His pattern of conferring with the disaffected in order to win them back continued, as Aylmer must have hoped and expected. In April 1593, he joined two other divines in visiting John Penry. Since Penry reported to his wife that the ministers had 'authority on their sides', this may have been a commission much like those Greenham carried out for Cox. They found Penry unwilling to accept 'private intermeddling in so public an action' and instead he went to trial for 'having ... feloniously devised and written certain words with intent to excite rebellion and insurrection' and was executed on 29 May 1593.[72]

[70] Owen, 'Tradition and Reform'; Rosemary Weinstein, *Tudor London* (London: HMSO, 1994), 13. The parish was created by pulling down the churches of St Nicholas Shambles and St Ewen, Warwick Lane, and uniting those parishes with some of St Sepulchre within Newgate. We are grateful to Dr Ian Archer for discussions about this parish and for many suggestions of archival resources for this chapter.
[71] St Bart's Hosp., Ha 1/3, fols 86r, 109v.
[72] John Waddington, *John Penry, the Pilgrim Martyr, 1559–1593* (London, 1852), 123; *DNB*, sub Penry, John.

Penry's trial and execution took place while London passed through the final stages of the third deadliest Elizabethan visitation of the plague.[73] By 2 September 1592, the plague had broken out in the area around the parish and the Hospital governors ordered their clerk to obtain the Lord Mayor's decrees and ordinances 'for the avoiding of the same sickness'.[74] The church had its own response: prayer, penance and listening to sermons. As Bishop of London, Grindal had written a service to be used in all churches on Wednesdays and Fridays during time of plague. It was a lengthy service consisting of seven sermons from the Book of Homilies plus one on 'the justice of God in punishing impenitent sinners' composed specially by Alexander Nowell. Bishop Aylmer revised it in 1593, severely reducing its length by cutting all but Nowell's and one other homily. The service would then be not more than an hour long, to discourage both prolonged exposure to infected people and religious 'faction'. Both concerns were raised by Grindal's lengthy programme.[75] Greenham, as a licensed preacher, would not read from the Book of Homilies. Instead, he preached a series of well-attended fast sermons.[76]

Although he exposed himself to danger by remaining in London and carrying out his ministerial functions,[77] it was not the plague that claimed Greenham's life. He had been troubled by a number of health problems for at least a decade; his enormously energetic spirit was clearly confined in a fragile body.[78] He died late in April 1594 of unknown causes and was buried on 25 April in Christ Church; there are no details of his funeral.[79] He left no will, which was not uncommon for

---

[73] Paul Slack, *The Impact of Plague in Tudor and Stuart England* (London: Routledge & Kegan Paul, 1985), 151. The mortality rate in London was 14.5 per cent.

[74] St Bart's Hosp, Ha 1/3, fol. 107r.

[75] Slack, *Impact of Plague*, 229.

[76] GL, MS 9163, fols 305r-305v. According to Ian Archer, the numbers recorded are extremely high. We are grateful to Dr Archer for his evaluation.

[77] Greenham often commented on the need for special pastoral arrangements during epidemics: for example, 'Hee thought that it were meet in the time of plagues that ther should not bee one minister both of the sick and whol, but that the people should provide either one to minister to the sick or els, such an one as should minister to the whole whilest ther own pastor attended on the sick': REM 524, fol. 19r.

[78] For example, ibid., fols 21r ('hee was troubled with most greevous toothaches, and with a most lamentable Fistula'); fol 37r (stomach problems).

[79] GL, MS 9163, fol. 320v, is a list of receipts for burials. It includes a note of eight shillings received 'for the buriall of Mr Richarde Grenhame oure lat preacher a man of worthie memorie who was buried the 25 Apriell 1594'. Roughly two-thirds of all burials in mid-seventeenth-century London took place within two days of death: Stephen Porter, 'From Death to Burial in Seventeenth-Century England', *The Local Historian*, 23 (1993), 199-204. For London funerals, see esp. David Cressy, 'Death and the Social Order: The Funerary Preferences of Elizabethan Gentlemen', *Continuity and Change*, 5 (1989), 99-119; and Clare Gittings, 'Urban Funerals in Late Medieval and Reformation England'

men without children. His widow, who was granted the administration of his goods on 30 April,[80] ultimately returned to Dry Drayton, outlived another husband, and was buried in April 1612.[81]

in Steven Bassett (ed.), *Death in Towns. Urban Responses to the Dying and the Dead, 100-1600* (Leicester: Leicester University Press, 1992), 170-83. Because of the inaccurate information in both Fuller and Clarke (see *DNB*), the year of Greenham's death had been much debated. While our discovery of the burial receipt is conclusive, it should be noted that over a century ago Edward Solly (*Notes and Queries*, 6th ser., 8 [21 July 1883], 55) argued for April 1594 because of Greenham's attendance on Penry and his comments on the Lopez case as recorded in Holland's preface to the First Edition.

[80] GLRO, DL/C/335, fol. 174.

[81] CRO, original parish register of Dry Drayton; PRO, PROB 11/119; Prerogative Court of Canterbury, 41 Fenne.

CHAPTER THREE

Greenham's legacy

Greenham's memory, like his body, might have rested in peace had it not
been for the devotion and enthusiasm of his followers. In the century
following his death, Greenham was claimed by conformists and
nonconformists alike as a 'saint' to be emulated. The edifice of his
seventeenth-century reputation was erected on two sturdy pillars: his raft
of disciples and posthumously published works. His disciples comprised
an eclectic assortment of divines, including Joseph Hall, Henry Smith
and Arthur Hildersham. A Cambridge man with impeccable Reformed
credentials, Hall was a spirited opponent of presbyterians and
separatists, and recruited by Laud as a defender of episcopacy.[1] While his
devotional works reflected a Reformed spirit that seventeenth-century
puritans admired, his polemical works vigorously attacked puritans on
some of their most principled stands.[2] Hall was full of praise for
Greenham. As a defender of episcopacy and the Church of England
generally, Hall not only admired Greenham's abilities as a pastor and
healer of afflicted consciences, but also as a churchman committed to the
unity of the church. Smith was perhaps the most famous preacher of his
day, and his sermons are still easily accessible and frequently cited by
historians.[3] Hildersham, recognized by his peers as one of the political
leaders of the radical nonconformist clergy, actively promoted the
Millenary Petition. Thanks to influential supporters, his long preaching
career extended into the reign of Charles I in spite of his refusal to

---

[1] Hall was born in 1574 in Ashby-de-la-Zouch. He entered Emmanuel College, a
'moderate Puritan' college, according to Peter Lake, in 1589 and was elected Fellow in
1595. Ordained in 1600, he became rector of Hawstead in Suffolk in 1601. He rose
quickly to become chaplain of Prince Henry and chaplain to an embassy to France (1616),
and then Dean of Worcester. In 1618, he was a delegate to the Synod of Dort, though he
left early due to illness. He later became Bishop of Exeter and then (1641) of Norwich.
Dan Steere, '"For the Peace of Both, For the Honour of Neither": Bishop Joseph Hall
Defends the *Via Media* in an Age of Extremes, 1601-1656', *Sixteenth Century Journal*, 27
(1996), 749-65; Peter Lake, 'The Moderate and Irenic Case for Religious War: Joseph
Hall's *Via Media* in Context' in S.D. Amussen and M.A. Kishlansky (eds), *Political Culture
and Cultural Politics in Early Modern Europe. Essays Presented to David Underdown*
(Manchester: Manchester University Press, 1995), 55-83, especially 56.

[2] Steere, 'For the Peace of Both', 749.

[3] See R.B. Jenkins, *Henry Smith: England's Silver-Tongued Preacher* (Macon, GA:
Mercer University Press, 1983).

subscribe.[4] These were but three of many young men whose ministries were strongly influenced by Greenham. Some of these devotees took notes of Greenham's sermons and pastoral advice, and preserved them as a more concrete remembrance of their teacher.

These manuscript notes proved especially important because almost nothing penned by Greenham was published during his lifetime.[5] Thomas Crook, a leading London nonconformist, undertook the task of putting together an omnibus posthumous volume of Greenham's works. When Crook died in 1598, Henry Holland completed his labours and produced a volume in 1599.[6] Ever-thicker editions followed in subsequent years. Holland died in 1603 before completing the fourth edition. Although his widow Elizabeth wrote the dedicatory letter to King James I, fulfilling her husband's dying wish, it was the prominent London preacher and nonconformist Stephen Egerton who took over editorial duties. In 1612, Egerton produced a fifth and final edition of Greenham's works in which the contents were 'digested after a more methodicall manner then heretofore'. There was little new material but the whole composition, which had grown rather haphazardly as Holland received new manuscripts, was thoroughly reorganized and given a comprehensive (and remarkably good) index.[7]

---

[4] In 1583, Archbishop Whitgift required all clergy to sign a statement accepting royal supremacy in temporal and spiritual matters, and affirming that the Prayer Book, the political structure of the church, and the Articles of Religion were in conformity with scripture. Those who refused were to be suspended from performing any clerical functions. Whitgift's Three Articles were essentially incorporated into the Canons of 1604 as Canon XXXVI. For the text, see E. Cardwell, *Synodalia* (2 vols, Oxford, 1842), I, 267-9. On the controversy over subscription and its effect on Hildersham, see Kenneth Fincham, *Prelate as Pastor: The Episcopate of James I* (Oxford: Clarendon Press, 1990), esp. chap. 7. For some other aspects of Hildersham's role as a puritan leader, see Collinson, *Elizabethan Puritan Movement*. Although he was arguably more important in his own time than Henry Smith, Hildersham has not attracted a modern biographer.

[5] See Appendix 1; on Greenham's 'Apologie', see above, 16. We have used the passive voice deliberately in discussing this matter. Whether Greenham consented to or was involved in the publication of either is unknown and, in our view, unlikely.

[6] On Crook's role, see First Edition, A6r. The 1599 edition was not actually the first time since his death that Greenham's works had appeared in print. A handful of brief treatises and collections of miscellaneous sayings appeared in 1595, 1597 and 1598. Holland noted grumpily in the 1599 preface that 'some respecting gaine, and not regarding godlinesse, attempted [after Greenham's death] to publish some fragments of his workes, to the griefe ... of many loving friends, which have long desired and expected this impression of all his workes together' (A6r). A complete listing of all Greenham's published works can be found in Appendix 1.

[7] Elizabeth Holland's letter: Fourth Edition, *3r-*3v. The title of the fifth edition retains the same wording as that of the fourth, including the attribution of editorship to Holland, but concludes with the following new phrasing: *The Fifth and Last Edition:*

Greenham had written very little which could have been intended for publication. Even his major treatise on the Sabbath, which Holland noted had many personal corrections in the original text, had not been completed to Greenham's satisfaction when he died. Meditations on some passages from scripture and a catechism were among his papers, but it remains unclear whether he intended these for the public. The imperfect state of these works confirms what one would expect from a man who, as we shall see, tirelessly devoted himself to pastoral ministry and had little time for the (in his mind) indulgence of writing for the marketplace. As the editor of his posthumously published works noted, 'such were his travels in his life time in preaching and comforting the afflicted, that hee could not possibly leave these works as he desired'.[8]

The hefty volumes of his collected works could not have been produced without the manuscript material that followers sent to Crook and Holland from all over England. A number of people, especially women, sent the editors copies of personal letters of spiritual advice which they had received from Greenham and had obviously preserved and treasured for many years. Letters from Richard Greenham were not ephemera. Devout Elizabethans made a habit, while attending church, of taking careful notes of sermons for later study and discussion. Greenham's editors benefited from this custom and published reconstructed versions of his sermons on the basis of such notes.

The first and subsequent editions of Greenham's works also contained extensive (and ever-growing) sections of aphorisms, apophthegmata, and sometimes lengthy accounts of godly advice, organized in the form of a commonplace collection, a 'literary' genre that will be explored in the next chapter. Holland explained in a marginal note that he received the set of sayings in the first edition from someone identified only as 'Hopkins'.[9] For a second volume, which appeared in 1600, Holland described more fully his editorial efforts. When the first edition met with a positive reception 'of many, both learned and truely religious', Holland

---

In Which Matters Dispersed Before Through the whole booke are methodically drawne to their severall places, and the hundred and nineteenth Psalme perfected: with a more exact Table annexed (London, 1612).

[8] First Edition, A6v.

[9] John Hopkins must be Holland's source. *ΠΑΡΑΜΥΘΙΟΝ. Two Treatises of the comforting of an afflicted conscience, written by M. Richard Greenham, with certaine Epistles of the same argument. Hereunto are added two Sermons, with certaine grave and wise counsells and answeres of the same Author and argument* (London, 1598), contains 'A great number of grave and wise counsels and answers, gathered by Master John Hopkins and others that attended him for that purpose' (A4r). Although there are some minor textual differences, and the order is rather different, this collection contains many of the same sayings as the 'Grave Counsels' printed in the First Edition.

was 'incouraged to seeke out the rest [of Greenham's sayings] carried about in written copies from hand to hand, and dispersed into divers parts of this land'. This he did, collecting 'all the copies I could heare of, and come by; I have set these Meditations in this forme of common places, reducing all to speciall chapters and arguments, whereunto they might seeme to have most relation'. Holland also left out what he 'thought less pertinent, or not so suitable to the rest' of the *Works*. He compared this to the way Peter Martyr's *Commonplaces* – one of the set books for study by the English clergy – were collected 'to the great good of the Church'.[10]

In 1601, Holland published an additional 113 'grave counsels' which had recently been sent to him 'from a godly preacher' identified marginally as John Brodley, the vicar of Sowerby in the West Riding of Yorkshire. Brodley had been a student at St John's College, Cambridge; he matriculated in 1578, and graduated BA in 1582 and MA in 1585. This would place him in Cambridge during the precise years in which Greenham's seminary functioned five miles away at Dry Drayton and makes it highly likely that Brodley took notes at the feet of the master.[11] Such student notebooks circulated, as Holland described it, 'hand to hand', and were copied by others.

One of these copies survived and found a home in the John Rylands Library, Manchester, in 1930.[12] Apart from the name of its early twentieth-century owner, nothing else is known of the manuscript's sojourn of almost four centuries.[13] The collection of sayings make up the first 72 folios of Rylands English Manuscript 524. The other 146 folios include works attributed to Arthur Hildersham and Thomas Cartwright. The first 68 are fair-copy notes of Greenham's sayings, kept in chronological order. The first entry was dated 28 July 1581; the last

---

[10] First Edition, A6v; quotations from the 1600 additions taken from the Third Edition, 251, 254.

[11] Ibid., 463. Brodley was vicar of Sowerby from 1591-1625. This makes almost irresistible our desire to associate the Cambridge University Library copy of the Fifth Edition with Brodley. On the last page of the index of that copy is written: 'This I give to my kinsman Beniamen Crabtre'. Although we have not been able to identify a Benjamin Crabtree, there were Crabtrees in Sowerby and nearby with the right sorts of interests to make them likely recipients of this book: Elias Crabtree, the rector of Dickelburgh (Norfolk) from 1643 until his ejection in 1660, was from Halifax, and Henry Crabtree, curate of Todmorden sometime after the Restoration, was born in Sowerby *c*.1642; both were students at Christ's College, Cambridge. See Venn and Venn, *Alumni Cantabrigienses*.

[12] We are grateful to Miss Glenise Matheson, Keeper of Manuscripts, John Rylands Library, for this information.

[13] Moses Tyson, 'Hand-list of Additions to the Collection of English Manuscripts in the John Rylands Library, 1928-35', *Bulletin of the John Rylands Library*, 19 (1935), 232.

probably dates from 1584. The final four folios include a copy of one of Greenham's well-known epistles, 'A letter against hardnes of hart'. The manuscript is far too neat and carefully written to be notes taken down while Greenham spoke. The scribe of this collection probably prepared this fair copy from someone else's notebook. Professor Collinson was the first modern scholar to call public attention to this valuable source, identifying it with Arthur Hildersham, presumably because of other works of Hildersham bound with the sayings.[14] This attribution has problems, not least of which is the fact that almost 70 per cent of the sayings in the manuscript also appear in the published collection of 'Grave Counsels', suggesting some connection with John Hopkins.[15] While the editors doubt that a positive identification of the original recorder of the sayings is possible, the close connection between the manuscript and published sayings, often verbatim or very close paraphrases, suggests that the Rylands sayings represent an early, well-established and widely circulated collection of sayings.

As editorial remarks in the printed editions make clear, even before his death there was widespread interest in Greenham's counsel and guidance, and he enjoyed, thanks in no small part to his dispersed former students, what can fairly be described as a national reputation. Yet the unauthorized publications of 1597 and 1598,[16] the five editions of his *Works* from 1599 to 1612, as well as the occasional broadsheets and inclusion of individual sermons or other pieces in collections with works of Richard Rogers, William Perkins, John Dod and Robert Cleaver, testify to the substantial market for something more complete and durable than notebooks and letters carefully copied and handed about.[17] Greenham's editors deserve much of the credit for transforming the sedulous pastor and non-publishing divine into one of the most read and respected theologians of early seventeenth-century England.

While Henry Holland likened Greenham to Elijah in 1599, Joseph Hall was the first (in 1606) to canonize Greenham in print as 'that saint of ours'.[18] This hagiographic filter, promoted by Greenham's conformist and nonconformist disciples, gave his literary remains an authority that perpetuated his memory and influence throughout the seventeenth

---

[14] REM 524; Collinson, *Elizabethan Puritan Movement*, 494-5 n.10; Collinson, "'A Magazine of Religious Patterns'", 508 n.36. We are grateful for Professor Collinson's observations on this subject. For the list of works attributed to Hildersham and Cartwright, see: Tyson, 232.

[15] See Appendix 2.

[16] First Edition, A6r.

[17] See Appendix 1.

[18] First Edition, A5v; Hall, *Heaven upon earth*, §9.

century. This was particularly true of the collected sayings. They resonated with a truth and force that gave Greenham a place among English divines which was second to none. Yet the history of circulated manuscript sayings and the compilation of posthumously published commonplaces raises questions which deserve attention: How can one be sure that the sayings and other works attributed to Greenham reflect his own words or even his ideas and beliefs? Why did collections of sayings figure so prominently in the circulated manuscripts and published collections? What purposes did they serve for the original compilers and those who used them in their printed forms? The key to all these questions lies in the commonplace tradition of the sixteenth century. This 'literary' tradition, inherited from antiquity and utilized in modified form during the medieval period, provided a foundation for the humanist pedagogical reform of the sixteenth century that transformed the ways in which knowledge was organized and applied.

CHAPTER FOUR

The Greenham sayings in their literary and historical context

'The lippes of the righteous feede many'. With this saying from the Book of Proverbs, Henry Holland began his 'Preface to the Reader' in the first edition of Richard Greenham's *Works*.[1] This carefully chosen fragment of Old Testament wisdom literature summarized a conception of religious knowledge and its acquisition that Holland's early modern readers understood. His readers in the post-modern era may also find it deceptively simple and straightforward. Yet this proverb is opaque – all but impenetrable. It yields few clues about the sixteenth-century understanding of the nature and use of religious knowledge, the nurturing quality of the righteous man's authoritative voice, or even who qualifies as 'righteous'. This is the challenge of sententious wisdom. Its brevity and lack of sustained argumentation mask a complex set of assumptions that can only be deciphered when examined in the larger social, cultural and religious context.

Therefore, when looking at the Greenham sayings found in Rylands English Manuscript 524 and the printed editions, one must first recognize that the meaning discovered in them by sixteenth-century readers did not derive simply from Greenham as an individual, but from Greenham as a sage who articulated values cherished by his religious community. This dimension of Elizabethan intellectual life poses special problems of interpretation that scholars must understand before the sayings can gain their proper place in the study of early modern English religion. Facing this challenge results in a more critical use of the sayings, a better appreciation of the basis for Greenham's stature among the godly, and a clearer understanding of how his legacy was used in the late Elizabethan and Stuart period.

The special problems posed by commonplaces as a literary form, more than any other factor, explains why Greenham has received only cursory attention in recent generations of scholarship. Apart from the work of Peter Lake, Margo Todd and a few others, theologians and historians have found little use for commonplaces beyond the anecdotal.[2] While

---

[1] Proverbs 10:21; First Edition, A4r.

[2] Peter Lake, *Moderate Puritans and the Elizabethan Church* (Cambridge: Cambridge University Press, 1982), chap. 7; Margo Todd, *Christian Humanism and the Puritan Social Order* (Cambridge: Cambridge University Press, 1987), chap. 3.

acknowledging the praise and high regard given to Greenham by his contemporaries and seventeenth-century divines, scholars rarely do more than dip into his sayings for a choice quote to illustrate a point or highlight an idea. His sayings lack the coherence and sustained argumentation of works by William Perkins and other Elizabethan divines. These other publications took a form which reflected the early modern transition toward a textually oriented intellectual discourse, characterized by systematic organization, reasoned argumentation and narrative structure that endure. They are readily appropriated by the orientation of current historical and theological scholarship.[3] Instead, Greenham's sayings must be read in the context of an orally-oriented tradition. Within the orally-oriented tradition examined here, authority was constructed from collecting copious testimony which was then deployed in rhetorical performances, oral or written, designed to persuade and convince.[4] Such collected testimony emphasized the importance of human experience as a source of truth, yet deferred to earlier voices of authority in the process of collecting. Thus, the method of the commonplace tradition reflected earlier orally-oriented approaches to sententious wisdom and reinforced community beliefs and practices. This approach to intellectual discourse, vigorously promoted by the humanist pedagogical reform of the sixteenth century, found expression in the student notebook transcribed and edited here. A closer examination of this commonplace tradition clarifies why Greenham's

---

[3] Since the 1950s, a lively debate over the importance of orality and textuality in this and other periods has been both intense and productive. It is not possible in this chapter to recapitulate the various aspects of this scholarly dialogue, and the nuances of recent discussions. What is referred to here by textuality was a movement from the humanist privileging of the spoken word toward the spacialization of ideas on the printed page by those who followed Peter Ramus. The Greenham sayings represent the orally-oriented humanist tradition of the sixteenth century. The works of William Perkins, who championed Ramism in the 1580s as the only true approach to the organization of knowledge, represent the textually-oriented tradition that came to dominate print culture. For more details see: Robert Weimann, *Authority and Representation in Early Modern Discourse*, ed. David Hillman (Baltimore, MD: The Johns Hopkins University Press, 1996), 105–12, especially 108–9; Mary Crane, *Framing Authority: Sayings, Self, and Society in Sixteenth-Century England* (Princeton, NJ: Princeton University Press, 1993); Martin Elsky, *Authorizing Words: Speech, Writing, and Print in the English Renaissance* (Ithaca, NY: Cornell University Press, 1989), 4; Walter J. Ong, *Ramus: Method, and the Decay of Dialogue* (Cambridge, MA: Harvard University Press, 1958); Joan Marie Lechner, *Renaissance Concepts of the Commonplaces* (New York: Pageant Press, 1962); John Rechtien, 'The Visual Memory of William Perkins and the End of Theological Dialogue', *Journal of the American Academy of Religion: Supplement*, 45.1 (March 1977), 69–99.

[4] Weimann, *Authority and Representation*, 108.

works have moved from their place of prominence in the early modern period to the margins of recent scholarly discourse.

Study of the Greenham sayings in the context of the commonplace tradition also highlights the impact of his editors on the form and content of the theological ideas transmitted and the image of Greenham projected. The Rylands English Manuscript 524 offers a valuable 'control' heretofore unavailable to scholars, permitting one to judge the extent to which Greenham's 'words' and accounts of his 'actions' were modified or omitted to suit the editors' image of him. This exercise offers an opportunity to re-evaluate Greenham's contemporary reputation and the use made of him in current scholarship.

The commonplace tradition and twentieth-century scholarship

Walter Ong, the noted scholar of orality and textuality in the early modern period, has pointedly asked 'why was the commonplace tradition once so important, since it now seems so affected and boring and aesthetically counterproductive?'[5] Recognized works of scholarship have characterized commonplace books as 'unendurable', with an 'air of triviality that is often very boring to the modern critical reader ...'.[6] One scholar even observed, 'It is pathetic to see the Humanist in all walks of life supposing that the mere writing up on the wall of a wise saying will make a difference to those who read the writing on the wall'.[7]

Uncertain how to appropriate the commonplace tradition, most scholars offer no response to Ong's question, choosing either silently to omit or to marginalize these works in their studies. Some relegate the impact of commonplace collections to the role of technical aids for memory, study and composition.[8] Patrick Collinson has described collections of sayings as the 'raw material' from which more influential

---

[5] Walter J. Ong, *Interfaces of the Word: Studies in the Evolution of Consciousness and Culture* (Ithaca, NY: Cornell University Press, 1977), 148.

[6] C.S. Lewis, *English Literature in the Sixteenth Century* (Oxford: Clarendon Press, 1954), 450; Paul O. Kristeller, 'Humanism and Moral Philosophy' in Albert Rabil, Jr (ed.), *Renaissance Humanism: Foundations, Forms, and Legacy* (3 vols, Philadelphia, PA: University of Pennsylvania Press, 1988), 281.

[7] H.A. Mason, *Humanism and Poetry in the Early Tudor Period* (London: Routledge and Kegan Paul, 1959), 111.

[8] Robert Bolgar, *The Classical Heritage and its Beneficiaries* (Cambridge: Cambridge University Press, 1954), 269. While acknowledging the importance of commonplace books in the humanist tradition, Bolgar limits their impact to that of 'mnemotechnical aids'. Arthur Kinney, *Humanist Poetics: Thought, Rhetoric, and Fiction in Sixteenth-Century*

works were created, and the 'by-product of the pastoral art of resolving cases of conscience'.[9]

This study presents a different approach. The commonplace tradition was not an embarrassment to an otherwise creative era, or merely a technical aid for memory, or unprocessed data for other forms of literature.[10] The genre played a vital role in moulding the intellectual and religious life of sixteenth-century England. It developed from a pedagogical practice with ancient roots, was modified in the course of a long tradition, and held a special place in the humanist agenda of the English Renaissance and Reformation. This line of argument builds on an emerging body of scholarship. Inspired by the work of Walter Ong, the last 40 years have witnessed a resurgent interest in the commonplace tradition, led initially by Ong and his students from the 1950s through the 1970s, and more recently by scholars at various American and British universities. The work thus far has led to a greater understanding of noetic history, the formation of human subjectivity, and the transmission of cultural values in the early modern period.[11] Much work remains to be done on the impact of the commonplace tradition on English religious life, especially regarding its use and adaptation by English divines of the Elizabethan and Stuart periods.

One scholar of sayings has observed, 'the meaning of a proverb is made clear only when side by side ... is given a full account of the accompanying social situation – the reason for its use, its effect, and its

---

England (Amherst, MA: University of Massachusetts Press, 1986), 11, presents the commonplace book tradition as a tool of imitation. William Crane, Wit and Rhetoric in the Renaissance, The Formal Basis of Elizabethan Prose Style (New York: Columbia University Press, 1937), chap. 3, stresses the role of commonplace books as a resource for ornamentation and illustration for compositions.

[9] Collinson, '"A Magazine of Religious Patterns"', 508-9.

[10] M.A. Screech warns that 'The greatest risk of error that we run where commonplaces are concerned is when a combination of insensitivity, carelessness or prejudice reinforces our ignorance'. M.A. Screech, 'Commonplaces of Law, Proverbial Wisdom and Philosophy: Their Importance in Renaissance Scholarship (Rabelais, Joachim du Bellay, Montaigne)' in R.R. Bolgar (ed.), Classical Influences on European Culture A.D. 1500-1700 (Cambridge: Cambridge University Press, 1976), 128.

[11] A sample of this scholarship includes: Ann Moss, Printed Commonplace-Books and the Structuring of Renaissance Thought (Oxford: Clarendon Press, 1996); Mary Crane, Framing Authority; Walter Ong, Ramus, Method, and the Decay of Dialogue; Ong, The Presence of the Word: Some Prolegomena for Cultural and Religious History (New Haven, CT: Yale University Press, 1967), 79-87; Ong, Rhetoric, Romance and Technology: Studies in the Interaction of Expression and Culture (Ithaca, NY: Cornell University Press, 1971), esp. chap. 2; Ong, Interfaces of the Word, esp. chap. 6; Lechner, Renaissance Concepts of the Commonplaces; John Rechtien, 'John Foxe's Comprehensive Collection of Commonplaces: A Renaissance Memory System for Students and Theologians', Sixteenth Century Journal, 9.1 (1978), 83-9; Rechtien, 'The Visual Memory of William Perkins'.

significance in speech'.[12] To understand the signficance of Greenham and his collected sayings in early modern England, we must examine carefully the circumstances in which Greenham's sententious wisdom was gathered in the 1570s and 1580s. We must consider who collected and recorded the sayings, as well as why they collected them in this genre. Equally important, we must assess how they were edited after his death and the significance of editorial decisions made. Greater understanding of these factors will provide a basis for more fruitful study of the Greenham sayings and their impact on seventeenth-century English religious life.

Authorship

Richard Greenham remained reluctant to publish throughout his life. Almost all that we have in print passed through the editorial filters of Thomas Crook, Henry Holland and Stephen Egerton in the various stages of preparing the posthumously published *Works*.[13] This failure to publish reflected his pastoral priorities, not a social or cultural disdain of print common among aristocrats of this period. Miles Mosse complained that 'manie that have the roome of Christ [i.e. ministers] at this daie, are given to write much, though they preach little'.[14] This charge could not be levelled at Greenham, who reportedly preached six times a week, catechized his parishioners every Thursday, prayed with his family twice a day, examined his servants on the preaching they heard, and gave much time and energy to counselling the many who came to him with troubled consciences.[15] Little time or energy remained for the preparation of his works for publication. Despite disclaimers from Holland and Egerton that Greenham did not record or edit his sayings,[16] scholars commonly quote the sayings without acknowledging that they passed through the filter of others. This issue must not be neglected, for on it hinges much of the significance of these sayings. Greenham's sententious wisdom reflected values of the godly community. It was not the work of an individual. Having made this point, we must stress that this notebook reflects values of the godly in the early 1580s - not those of the late

---

[12] Raymond Firth, 'Proverbs in Native Life, with Particular Reference to Those of the Maori', *Folk-Lore*, 37 (1926), 134.

[13] See above, 32.

[14] Thomas Rogers, *Miles Christianus* (London, 1590), 13. We wish to thank John Craig for this reference.

[15] Clarke, 'Life of Master Richard Greenham', 12-15. Also see Holland's remarks: First Edition, A6v.

[16] First Edition, A6v; Fourth Edition, 723.

Elizabethan and early Jacobean periods. Our first task is to understand better the nature of the community in the 1580s that translated Greenham's actions and words into a genre designed to influence and guide readers in their understanding of religious experience and the exercise of their calling as believers and ministers.

There are three things known about the sayings that passed into print. First, Greenham accepted as part of his calling the need to 'traine up some younger men' in the skills of practical divinity, relying on his experience and study of 'cases of conscience'.[17] Second, starting in the 1570s and continuing through the 1580s, a succession of young university men spent time at Dry Drayton, observing his ministry and preparing to model his pastoral practice.[18] Third, these university men, and others who came for direction and counsel, recorded his words and acts in notebooks; a good number of which found their way to Crook, Holland and Egerton, and these provided the basis for the collected sayings and other materials published in the five editions.[19] Only one notebook is known to have survived, and it is edited here. Over 70 per cent of the sayings found in the manuscript also appear verbatim or closely paraphrased in the printed editions.

This information highlights important issues that require investigation and clarification. First, the recorders of Greenham's sayings received their intellectual formation through English schools and universities in the early Elizabethan period. An examination of their education would provide vital clues to their habits of collecting and framing religious knowledge. Second, these young university men, eager to bring a Protestant preaching ministry and 'true religion' to rural parishes, recorded acts and speeches that focused on matters of praxis and addressed difficult and delicate problems associated with 'cases of conscience'. Reflection on the use of Greenham as an authoritative voice, providing what Holland described as the 'best rules for this unknown facultie',[20] may offer important insights into how Elizabethan Protestants justified their religious practices and formed others in the doxa, or common values of the godly.[21] Finally, Crook, Holland and Egerton are names commonly associated with late Elizabethan and

---

[17] First Edition, A5r. Also see REM 524, fol. 57v.

[18] See above, 19-20.

[19] First Edition, A6r-v.

[20] First Edition, A5r.

[21] See: Margo Todd, *Christian Humanism*, 80-85; Margo Todd, 'Puritan Self-fashioning' in Francis Bremer (ed.), *Puritanism: Transatlantic Perspectives on a Seventeenth-Century Anglo-American Faith* (Boston, MA: Massachusetts Historical Society, 1993), 57-87; Stephen Greenblatt, *Renaissance Self-fashioning: From More to Shakespeare* (Chicago, IL: University of Chicago Press, 1980), 1-9, 82-3.

Jacobean puritanism. An examination of their editorial control over Greenham's 'words' may aid our understanding of Greenham's place in the Elizabethan Church and increase our understanding of his canonization as a 'saint' in the seventeenth century.

Greenham's rectory 'seminarians' and their educational formation

The importance of humanism in English intellectual life is a standard feature of scholarship on early modern England. 'Humanism' in this context refers to a pedagogical reform that firmly established itself in English schools and universities during the sixteenth century.[22] Humanists rejected the scholastic project which stressed the articulation of formal, necessary and universal propositions about God and creation using syllogistic logic; they judged that this approach lacked value because abstract speculations could not guide human affairs. In its place they gave priority to classical studies and rhetoric, meaning the persuasive and communicative aspect of language, which they deemed central to directing human society.[23] For the Renaissance and

---

[22] For a review of the scholarship on English humanism, see: Alistair Fox, 'Facts and Fallacies: Interpreting English Humanism' in Alistair Fox and John Guy (eds), *Reassessing the Henrician Age: Humanism, Politics and Reform 1500-1550* (Oxford: Basil Blackwell, 1986), 9-33. For studies of English humanism as a pedagogical reform see: Weimann, *Authority and Representation*, 103-12; Crane, *Framing Authority*, 5-6; Rebecca Bushnell, *The Culture of Teaching: Early Modern Humanism in Theory and Practice* (Ithaca, NY: Cornell University Press, 1996); Hanna Grey, 'Renaissance Humanism: The Pursuit of Eloquence', *Journal of the History of Ideas*, 24 (1963), 497-514. For an examination of humanist pedagogical priorities and their implementation in English schools and universities see: Crane, *Framing Authority*, 53-92; Lisa Jardine, 'The Place of Dialectic Teaching in Sixteenth-Century Cambridge', *Studies in the Renaissance*, 21 (1974), 31-62; Anthony Grafton and Lisa Jardine, *From Humanism to the Humanities: Education and the Liberal Arts in Fifteenth- and Sixteenth-Century Europe* (Cambridge, MA: Harvard University Press, 1986), esp. xii-xvi; Margo Todd, *Christian Humanism*. These works effectively counter the arguments of M.H. Curtis, H. Kearney and W.T. Costello, which characterize the curriculum of the period as conservative and relatively unaffected by the intellectual changes then taking place. See: M.H. Curtis, *Oxford and Cambridge in Transition: 1558-1642* (Oxford: Clarendon Press, 1959); H. Kearney, *Scholars and Gentlemen: Universities and Society in Pre-Industrial Britain 1500-1700* (Ithaca, NY: Cornell University Press, 1970); William T. Costello, *The Scholastic Curriculum at Early Seventeenth-Century Cambridge* (Cambridge, MA: Harvard University Press, 1958), esp. 7-8.

[23] Weimann has observed that 'the humanists, in rejecting ontological positions in logic, substituted "place-logic", which was particularly suited to the needs of rhetoric and literary studies' (*Authority and Representation*, 108). Also see: Victoria Kahn, 'Humanism and the Resistance to Theory' in Patricia Parker and David Quint (eds), *Literary Theory/Renaissance Texts* (Baltimore, MD: The Johns Hopkins University Press, 1986), 375-6; Fox, 'Facts and Fallacies', 18, 21, 31-3.

Reformation humanist, rhetoric cultivated a seamless union of wisdom and style, intended to guide the student toward virtue and right action.[24] This became a generally acknowledged goal of education, especially of theological education. Whether one traces this concept back to Cicero, or demonstrates its impact through the writings of Martin Bucer, Peter Ramus or other sixteenth-century writers, the focus was on praxis, the virtues – wisdom needed for right living.[25] Holland commended Greenham's sayings in this context, acknowledging the importance of pagan wisdom, prized by the humanist tradition, yet associating Greenham's words with a superior form of wisdom. In language characteristic of the commonplace tradition he stated, 'The holy bookes and monuments of the righteous are as strong chests and storehouses, wherin God hath ever reserved most precious foode for posteritie.'[26] These 'strong chests' and 'storehouses' of wisdom can only be understood in the context of the pedagogical reform of sixteenth-century humanists.[27]

While encouraging students to read the works of antiquity, humanists guided them in a practice of gathering quotes that summarized and validated truths they recognized, and organizing them in 'places', from which these fragments could be redeployed as needed. Promoted by Rudolphus Agricola's widely used *De inventione dialectica libri tres*, and the influential works of Erasmus and Melanchthon, the humanist pedagogical reform proved a significant force in sixteenth-century European education.[28] Their ideas and approaches, and those of other noted humanists, were liberally borrowed and adapted by English textbook writers like Roger Ascham, Abraham Fraunce, Richard

---

[24] Grey, 'Renaissance Humanism', 498.

[25] '*Bene beateque vivere*' found in Cicero and Bucer, '*doctrina bene vivendi ... Finis doctrinae non est notitia rerum ipsi subjectarum, sed usus et exercitatio*' in Ramus. Todd, *Christian Humanism*, 68-9; Martin Bucer, *De regno Christi*, trans. Wilhelm Pauck and Paul Larkin, *Library of Christian Classics*, vol. 19, *Melanchthon and Bucer* (Philadelphia, PA: The Westminster Press, 1969), 166 n.18.

[26] First Edition, A4r.

[27] See Crane, *Framing Authority*, 6-7.

[28] Desiderius Erasmus, *Adages*, trans. R.A.B. Mynors and Margaret Mann Phillips, *Collected Works of Erasmus*, vols 31-4 (Toronto: University of Toronto Press, 1982-92); Desiderius Erasmus, *Literary and Educational Writings 2: De Copia/De Ratione Studii*, ed. Craig Thompson, *Collected Works of Erasmus*, vol. 24 (Toronto: University of Toronto Press, 1978); Philip Melanchthon, *Loci Communes Theologici*, trans. Wilhelm Pauck and Paul Larkin, in *Library of Christian Classics*, vol. 19, *Melanchthon and Bucer* (Philadelphia, PA: The Westminster Press, 1969); Grafton and Jardine, *From Humanism to the Humanities*, 125-6; Jardine, 'The Place of Dialectic Teaching', esp. 52; Ong, *Ramus*, chap. 5; Todd, *Christian Humanism*, chap. 3.

Rainolde and Thomas Wilson,[29] whose works provided the model for intellectual development practised in English schools and universities.

From his early days of studies, the schoolboy learned the importance of collecting *exempla* for effective argumentation and improving his style in oral and written discourse. The purpose of these studies was not simply the mastery of Latin and a body of ancient literature, but the cultivation of skills of discourse which drew from and contributed to doxa, or consensus on what was good and true. Boys received established categories into which appropriate quotes should be collected and stored for redeployment when needed.[30] This pedagogical practice was reinforced at university, with an established place in Cambridge colleges by the 1560s.[31]

Walter Ong observed that humanists fashioned a pedagogy adapted to the *Zeitgeist* of the period, 'to what they felt was real "life" and to the real pedagogical situation'.[32] Confronted with many changes in society and culture, humanists sought solutions to these challenges while striving to honour the intellectual traditions they had received. Having marginalized syllogistic logic and the apodictic certainty of scholasticism, the humanists of English Protestantism had to resolve the problem of an impoverished metaphysical stance.[33] The process of gathering *exempla* and framing these sayings in 'places' or *loci* enabled them to engage in a creative process, using the authoritative voices of the past to establish the authenticity of a position, while freeing the framer to recast a saying to suit the needs of the present. Placing recognized authorities of the past at the service of the current consensus defined the humanist project, providing an authenticated language for discourse, while editing out dangerous or undesirable ideas found in the context from which sententious wisdom came.[34] Defining places for these sayings

---

[29] Roger Ascham, *The Scholemaster*, ed. R.J. Schoeck (Don Mills, Ontario: J.M. Dent and Sons, 1966); Abraham Fraunce, *The Arcadian Rhetoric* (London [1588]); Richard Rainolde, *The Foundacion of Rhetorike*, intro. Francis R. Johnson (New York: Scholars' Facsimiles and Reprints, 1945), esp. iii-xxii; Thomas Wilson, *Arte of Rhetorique: 1560*, ed. G.H. Mair (Oxford: Clarendon Press, 1909). For discussions of the impact of these and similar works see: Weimann, *Authority and Representation*, 108-9; Todd, *Christian Humanism*, 60; Crane, *Framing Authority*, 7, 12, 210 n.29; Ong, *Ramus*, 119-20.

[30] Crane, *Framing Authority*, chap. 1; Ong, *Ramus*, chap. 5; Ong, *Rhetoric, Romance, and Technology*, chap. 2; Mary Jane Cherry, 'A Classification and Analysis of Selected "Sayings" in Shakespeare's Plays' (unpublished Ph.D. dissertation, 1981, The Catholic University of America), 27-66.

[31] Jardine, 'The Place of Dialectic Teaching', *passim*.

[32] Ong, *Ramus*, 97.

[33] Weimann, *Authority and Representation*, 108-9; Kahn, 'Humanism and the Resistance to Theory', 377.

[34] Crane, *Framing Authority*, 13, 17.

gave the framer liberty to reorient and creatively alter the meaning of a fragment taken from its original context.[35] In 1583, when the youthful Arthur Hildersham may have been observing and recording Greenham's pastoral practice, Thomas Cartwright sent him a reflection entitled, 'For Direction in the Study of Divinity'. Concerning 'old' and 'new' writers, Cartwright recommended the following:

> As touching the order of reading them, I think the new Writers are to be read before the old, for that we understanding by them what suits there are depending between us and our Adversaries of all sorts, we may both the better know what evidence is layed up in the Monuments of the Old Writers either for us or them, and make our note accordingly.[36]

He named 'new writers' Calvin, Beza, Bucer and Luther as guides to be followed.[37] In this way one grew into an understanding of the nature of truth, as defined and articulated by the Protestant community, and could then be encouraged to explore the works of old writers from which the wheat could be winnowed from the chaff. Printing made possible the production of collections of sayings that had been gathered and framed by Protestant luminaries of the period, modelling for students of theology acceptable patterns of gathering and framing commonplaces.[38]

This method of guiding and forming students in approved patterns of thought and practice gave a central pedagogical role to the notebook and the organization of 'places' for collected fragments of wisdom. While it enabled the student to grow in understanding and accumulate examples of doxa and praxis, it also established limits and controlled the boundaries of accepted ideas and actions.[39] The students and lay people who came to Dry Drayton, and Greenham himself, would have found this means of acquiring knowledge a normal and expected activity for one seeking wisdom and insight into Christian truth and right action. It

---

[35] Crane, *Framing Authority*, chap. 1, esp. 16-18; Ong, *Rhetoric, Romance, and Technology*, 35; Bolgar, *Classical Heritage*, 271-5, 295-301. Alistair Fox's critique of Arthur Ferguson's *The Articulate Citizen and the English Renaissance* (Durham, NC: Duke University Press, 1965), is useful to note here. Fox criticizes Ferguson's attempt to broaden the definition of a 'humanist' to include anyone influenced by what he describes as humanism's reinterpretation of antiquity and its application to current problems. He asks, 'if scholars were employing new criteria, were those criteria necessarily derived from their classical studies at all?' (Fox, 'Facts and Fallacies', 23-4). The argument here takes Fox's point further, giving priority to the method of study, rather than the matter studied.

[36] Thomas Cartwright, *Cartwrightiana*, eds Albert Peel and Leland H. Carlson, Elizabethan Nonconformist Texts, vol. 1 (London: George Allen and Unwin, 1951), 112.

[37] Ibid., 113-15. See Todd, *Christian Humanism*, 66-7 for other examples.

[38] Holland cites four in his Preface: Luther, Beza, Urbanus Rhegius and Jean Taffin (First Edition, A4v).

[39] Crane, *Framing Authority*, 55.

would have been considered an essential practice for one preparing for the ministry, which required effective oral and written communication.

Richard Greenham's authoritative voice

The method of learning outlined in the previous section functioned well for established subjects of theological and spiritual concern. Yet Elizabethan Protestants found that their work took them beyond the standard subjects addressed by ancient authorities, and the new writers offered little supplementary guidance. English ministers wrestled with the challenges of pastoral care as they applied 'true religion' at the parochial level. The need for guidance in these unexplored areas required an authoritative voice that could establish confidence and certainty in unfamiliar territory. Greenham's disciples and editors offered him as just such an authority. This appeal to Greenham as a paradigm of godly thought and action – an authoritative voice of doxa and praxis – could not simply be asserted. It required justification. Three models of authority operative in Elizabethan society served this purpose. First, Greenham's appeal as a theologian in the Christian humanist mould attracted the attention and respect of young university men and other Protestants trained in humanistic studies. Second, the association of his name and actions with biblical, ancient and reformed authorities gave his example and teaching an aura of authenticity normally accorded past or distant figures. Third, the transmission of his ideas in the form of proverbs and sententious wisdom employed a rhetorical form associated with the values and common assumptions of the community – using Greenham as the sage who articulated the corporate values of the godly. These different understandings of authority, and the diverse assumptions which grounded them, functioned together to establish the authoritative voice of this rural Cambridgeshire rector.

Despite the existence of practical divinity written by continental Protestants, Holland characterized this subject as 'an unknowne facultie' and stressed the need for works which addressed ministering to afflicted minds and guided in the 'art and skill to proceede in the practise of this cure'.[40] The Christian humanist focus on experience proved a useful frame of reference in this search for right practice. Holland claimed the Greenham sayings corrected the tendency to 'gesse uncertainly to apply good remedies, and speeches unto the sicke, then know how to proceede by any certaine rule of art, and well grounded practice'.[41]

---

[40] First Edition, A5r.
[41] First Edition, A4v.

Patrick Collinson has observed that Erasmus's *Paraclesis* provides a distillation of the Christian humanist agenda.[42] Erasmus's definition of a theologian focused on experience and *metanoia*:

> To me he is truly a theologian who teaches not by skill with intricate syllogisms but by a disposition of mind, by the very expression and the eyes, by his very life that riches should be disdained, that the Christian should not put his trust in the supports of this world but must rely entirely on heaven ... if anyone under the inspiration of the spirit of Christ preaches this kind of doctrine, inculcates it, exhorts, incites, and encourages men to it, he indeed is truly a theologian .... [L]ife means more than debate, inspiration is preferable to erudition, transformation is a more important matter than intellectual comprehension.[43]

These words lay out the priorities of a movement for which Erasmus proved the most eloquent spokesman and Richard Greenham became a living paradigm.

Samuel Clarke described Greenham's life in terms remarkably similar to Erasmus's theologian. After a detailed account of Greenham's charitable work among the poor, he observed:

> We have before heard of his great charity to men's Bodies: his Charity to Souls was no less exemplary. For having great Experience, and an excellent Faculty to relieve and comfort distressed Consciences, he was sought to, far and near, by such as groaned under spiritual Afflictions and Temptations: all whom he entertained friendly and familiarly, without respecting the person of the rich more than the poor. Yea the fame of this spiritual Physician so spread abroad, that he was sent for to very many, and the Lord was pleased so farre to blesse his labours, that by his knowledge and experience many were restored to joy and comfort, out of unspeakable and insupportable terrours and torments of conscience.[44]

Holland cites Greenham's 'Apologie' to confirm his intent to learn and practise a divinity that grew out of experience, 'to studie the cases of conscience, to succour the perplexed in them: he hath been so filled with compassion to the afflicted, (which God wrought in his heart) as if he had bin distressed with them: He hath seene the manifold blessings of God upon his travell'.[45]

---

[42] Collinson, '"A Magazine of Religious Patterns"', 499.

[43] Desiderius Erasmus, *Christian Humanism and the Reformation: Selected Writings*, ed. John C. Olin (New York: Harper Torchbooks, 1965), 98, 100. This vision of the theologian was adopted by the Protestants of England, but could also be used to describe the impact of Christian humanist ideas in Catholic Europe.

[44] Clarke, 'Life of Master Richard Greenham', 13-14.

[45] First Edition, A5r.

Collinson has argued that English Protestantism, even English puritanism, found Christian truth most convincingly displayed in human experience rather than dogmatic definitions.[46] This humanist conviction had evolved among the Elizabethan godly to incorporate epistemological presuppositions about election, the truth found in scripture, the ability of the elect to live out that truth, and the possibility of recognizing the fruit of election in others and oneself.[47] In this context, knowledge of exemplary lives provided guides to the truth valued by the godly community.[48]

This focus on experience as a guide to truth reveals an important dimension of the sayings found in Rylands English Manuscript 524. The commonplace tradition described thus far focused on the collection of texts, primarily printed and often already selected and situated in a 'place'. The notebook of Greenham's sayings examined here is evidence of an important adaptation of the commonplace tradition by Elizabethan Protestants – especially those who identified with the godly. Holland's preface appealed to Greenham's life, speeches and actions as a guide to the 'best rules for this unknowne facultie'. Greenham's example was promoted as the best means of forming and nurturing young ministers and the godly laity. The appeal to experience among Christian humanists gave Greenham's life, words and actions a self-authenticating quality. He confirmed the ideals and goals of the godly, reinforcing and validating the doxa and praxis of his community. His authority rested, in part, on these grounds. Yet the intellectual and religious life of sixteenth-century England required more than right action.

Protestant adaptations of the humanist pedagogical agenda established an implicit expectation that words and virtuous action be confirmed and ratified by acknowledged authorities of antiquity and the continental Reformation. In his preface, Holland employed marginal notes, direct associations and literary allusions to establish Greenham's place among the authorities acknowledged and respected by the godly. The Old and New Testaments, pagan philosophers and poets, church fathers, Reformation leaders and humanist pedagogues were all used in this effort. Greenham was identified with the 'righteous' man referred to in Proverbs 10. The description of his maturity of faith was a paraphrase of Ephesians 4:13. Greenham was implicitly and explicitly identified with Elijah, with references to 'when God had translated this Elias from us' before he could publish his 'good knowledge'. Greenham's stature as

---

[46] Collinson, '"A Magazine of Religious Patterns"', 499–501.

[47] For a more detailed examination of these presuppositions see below, 98–102.

[48] Margo Todd, 'Puritan Self-fashioning', 57–87; Greenblatt, *Renaissance Self-fashioning*, 1–9, 82–3.

a teacher was associated with that of Tertullian. His wisdom in dealing with afflicted minds and cases of conscience was associated with the practical divinity of Luther, Beza, Urbanus Rhegius and Jean Taffin.[49]

This effort identified Greenham's published works with the authenticated language of recognized authorities, and in so doing established him as a source of truth for the godly. While this effort appears to contradict the emphasis on experience described above, Elizabethans treated these as necessary counterbalances to one another. With the religious changes of the period and the new challenges faced as ministers applied Reformed theology at the parochial level, experiences like those of Greenham modelled how to resolve difficult and delicate pastoral problems. The appeal to scripture and other commonly acknowledged authorities, and the association of Greenham with them, provided an assurance of continuity with an authentic past – so necessary to the sixteenth-century mind.

The third model of authority confirming Greenham's 'voice' derived from the genre of sententious wisdom. This genre enjoyed a prestige comparable to that of scripture,[50] and commanded the respect of both the learned and common folk. The commonplace genre depended on the influence of this form; and its power was explicitly invoked by Tudor texts on rhetoric and logic.[51] Thomas Wilson, in his explanation of 'the storehouse of places' where the arguments and reasons for the proof of 'every matter' were collected, described these rhetorical forms as 'sentences of the sage, whiche are brought to confirme any thyng, either taken out of olde aucthors, or els soche as have been used in this common life'. Within the parameters of his definition he included 'sentences of noble men, the Lawes of any realme, quicke saiyinges, proverbes ... Histories of wise Philosophers, the judgementes of learned men, the common opinion of the multitude ...'.[52] Two sources of sententious wisdom are highlighted here: the 'common opinion of the people' and the 'sage'.[53] The Greenham sayings fall into the latter category. However, the voice of the sage in this form must not be mistaken for the opinion of an individual. The power of his wise sayings rested on the communal nature of the doxa and praxis they endorsed.

[49] First Edition, A4r–A6v.

[50] Friedrich Seiler, *Das Deutsche Sprichwort* (Strassburg: K.J. Trubner, 1918), 10.

[51] Crane, *Framing Authority*, 48–52; Thomas K. Mauch, 'The Role of the Proverb in Early Tudor Literature' (unpublished Ph.D. dissertation, University of California, Los Angeles, 1963), 106–7.

[52] Thomas Wilson, *The Rule of Reason, Conteinyng the Arte of Logike* (London, 1563), fols 36v, 49r–v.

[53] For a discussion of this distinction see: Mauch, 'Role of the Proverb', 108; Archer Taylor, *The Proverb* (Cambridge, MA: Harvard University Press, 1931), 43–4.

Sayings commanded a respect that derived from a corporate interpretation of experience; and that consensus was equated with divine or eternal truths that transcended time and culture.[54] This aspect of sententious wisdom reinforced and enhanced Greenham's authoritative voice.

Given the compact nature of sayings, their impact must be understood in the context of the corporate assumptions about human experience that invested them with meaning.[55] Greenham became for the godly a sage who spoke of how things are, how they should be, and pronounced judgements based on a standard of human behaviour the godly recognized. He made prophetic statements that mirrored the fears of the community and set down rules to follow. When a Greenham saying asserted, 'by nature al men bee papists, heretiques, adulterers, and in al kinds sinners, until god renued them', the community's understanding of the utter corruption of human nature and God's redemptive role was articulated and confirmed.[56] The recommendation that 'civil Holidaies, ... bee the fittest and most convenient times for fasting daies', expressed a corporate sense of how that time should be redeemed.[57] When distinctions between 'true religion' and 'superstition' were made, the saying articulated community standards of belief and practice.[58] In these and many other ways, the Greenham sayings reflected the value of sententious wisdom for a community, using the words and example of Greenham as sage to articulate perceptions of life, fears about the future, and the rules needed to regulate conduct properly. The recording of his sayings in the 1580s, and the gathering and framing that occurred in the late 1590s and early 1600s, demonstrate the communal production of the sententious wisdom attributed to him. While Greenham's name and reputation enhanced the value placed on them, the sayings gained popularity and wide circulation because they mirrored values cherished by the godly community.

In this interplay of models of authority, words and actions attributed

---

[54] In a discussion of the grammatical forms used in sententious wisdom, Greimas explained that in sententious wisdom, 'le présent employé ici devient le temps anhistorique par excellence qui aide à énoncer, sous forme de simples constatations, des *vérités éternelles*. L'impératif à son tour, en instituant une réglementation hors du temps, assure la permanence *d'un ordre moral* sans variations'. Algirdas J. Greimas, *Du Sens: Essais Sémiotiques* (Paris: Editions du Seuil, 1970), 313.

[55] Crane explained that 'these fragments ... reflected common ideas about extratextual things, places in the text where the cultural codes of antiquity, Scripture, and sixteenth-century England intersected'. Crane, *Framing Authority*, 39.

[56] REM 524, fol. 21r.

[57] Ibid., fol. 13v.

[58] Ibid., fols 24v, 25r, 34r, 35v-36r, 54r.

to Greenham achieved recognition among the godly as a source of the consensus and practice for the community. The appeal to experience in the humanist tradition, the association of Greenham with ancient authorities and continental Reformers, and the respect accorded sententious wisdom, all worked together to give Greenham's language an authenticity that made him one of the most revered and respected theologians of his time.

Having said that, we must recall how authoritative voices were used in the commonplace tradition. The gathering and framing process highlighted the points at which the words and reported actions of an authority intersected with the values of a community in a particular period.[59] The commonplace tradition served well the *Zeitgeist* of the times, for it allowed the gatherer of sayings to use the authenticated language of recognized authorities, while lifting it from contexts that no longer reflected the consensus of the community. The gathering of Greenham's sayings and framing into 'places' was a necessary process in the late sixteenth and early seventeenth century; for the notebook edited here, with sayings collected from 1581 to 1584, reflected values and priorities of that period. This consensus had shifted by the turn of the century.

The gathering and framing of Crook, Holland and Egerton

The commonplace tradition, with its practice of gathering and framing the sententious wisdom of authoritative voices, provides important insights into how religious discourse was controlled in late Elizabethan and Jacobean England.[60] The pedagogical reform that gave priority to the commonplace book also gave the gatherer and framer great power over the material. Editors commonly used their control over texts to mould and recast them in ways that suited their purpose. Greenham's late Elizabethan and early Jacobean editors used that power to select, alter and frame the sayings in a manner that modified priorities and principles accepted by the godly in the 1580s. Evidence of the control exercised by Greenham's editors reveals valuable insights into the shifting priorities within the godly community, calls for caution in using the printed sayings as a reflection of Greenham's positions in the 1580s,

---

[59] Crane, *Framing Authority*, 15, 39.

[60] For an examination of the use of the words 'gather' and 'frame' in sixteenth-century England, see: Crane, *Framing Authority*, 3–4, 202 n.6. For other examples of this practice see: Thomas Elyot, *The Banket of Sapience* (1564); Desiderius Erasmus, *Apophthegmata* (1542). We thank Dr Crane for her advice and suggestions in this matter.

and illustrates the value of commonplace books as a resource for the study of English religious life.

Henry Holland stated explicitly the control he exercised in editing the sayings. In the Preface he explained, 'the Treatise of Counsels I found most distracted and corrupted. Of the many hundreds I selected these few, and have reduced them into alphabeticall order, desiring so to dispose them, as that every counsell might be set under one speciall head or argument.'[61] Careful examination of this practice, which can be followed in the annotations of this edition, illustrates the creative process that gathering and framing offered. While it cannot be asserted that Holland worked from the notebook edited here, comparison of the manuscript and printed sayings demonstrates that many sayings derive from a common origin, often matching word for word, or appearing as close paraphrases. *Exempla* from the notebook and the editions of the *Works* illustrate how priorities for gathering and framing shifted and changed – even in the successive editions of the *Works*.

The most obvious examples of control over gathering appear in the alteration of manuscript versions of sayings in successive editions. One of the most dramatic of these concerns advice on the churching of women. In 1583 Greenham is reported to have recommended the following:

> Hee observed many things to bee corrupted by superstition which were good in ther first original, as, when woemen drawing near the tyme of ther deliverance, do require the prayers of the church, as in a farewel commit themselves to the intercessions of the saints, partly for that they are to enter into a dangerous travel, partly for that they shalbee long without the publique means of the assembly, and therfore stand in need of the grace of god watching over them. Again hee thought it civil and seemly in al sicknesses, that the bed should bee comely, adorned with whites, but especialy that this was comely in the sicknes, and after the travel of woemen, so superstition bee avoided. As for the *Chrysmes* which superstitiously are used, hee said they came of this, that men when god blessed the seed of ther body, would testify ther thankfulnes to god by giving something, to the minister, or Pastor, and the pore. Besides, howsoever foolishly, and to strictly women abuse ther liberty, yet hee thought it some equity, that after ther deliverance, they should not prophainly, bee ready to go to other places, before they had given thanks, And as they tasted of the benefit of the praiers of the saincts, both in ther gracious deliverance, and holy preservation of ther soules from evil: soe they should pray the congregation, to bee earnest in thanksgiving for them. This hee did not only require of woemen, but of men also. And yet hee observed that wemen might daily bee brought from ther superstitious *Churchings*, but as hardly are they brought to religious thanksgivings.[62]

---

[61] First Edition, A6r.
[62] REM 524, fols 35v–36r.

The manuscript version explained how this ritual, corrupted by previous practice, might be reformed to bring women from 'superstitious *Churchings*' to 'religious thanksgivings'. The First Edition reproduced verbatim the first sentence of this advice, with its exhortation to seek the 'intercessions of the Saints' before the delivery, but excluded advice on how to prepare the bed and the admonition for mothers *and* fathers to seek a blessing and prayers of thanksgiving from the congregation after the birth. This 'gathering' out of the saying recorded in 1583 is a significant departure from the original sense of the advice recorded – omitting any ritual act after childbirth that might resemble or recall the practice of churching. In 1605 the Fourth Edition excluded the saying altogether, and it did not reappear in the Fifth Edition.[63] This example raises questions about the evolution of godly attitudes toward the reform of the 'superstitious' practices of the old religion and religious exercises which honoured the experience of women. The manuscript saying stressed reform of the practice, asserted the inclusion of men in the blessing, and encouraged clergy to exercise prescriptive control over a re-formed ritual. The first three editions of the sayings excluded 'superstitious *Churchings*' altogether, and simply admonished women to seek prayers before the experience of childbirth with no provisions for thanksgiving after a safe deliverance. The last two editions (1605 and 1612) made no reference to women's experience of childbirth or the need for prayers from the congregation before or after that experience. This example demonstrates how a careful study of the gathering practised by Greenham's editors can yield clues about changing priorities and attitudes of the godly. It also illustrates the dangers of drawing conclusions from the printed editions about Greenham's approach to pastoral care in the 1580s.

The practice of framing can also yield useful information. In 1582, Greenham is reported to have made the following observation: 'One asking him what hee thought of, fayries hee answered hee thought they were spirits: but hee distinguished between these and other spirits, as commonly men distinguish between good witches and bad witches.' Though the saying is brief, the recorder leaves no doubt that Greenham acknowledged the existence of fairies and used the analogy of good and bad witches to illustrate that fairies could be distinguished as good spirits. In the manuscript, which has an incomplete set of 'places' provided in the margins, this passage was framed as a saying on 'fairies'. The import of this saying was dramatically altered by the practice of framing in the printed editions. While the recorder in the 1580s understood the saying to be primarily focused on the existence of fairies

---

[63] Women in Travell 1, First Edition, 75; Second Edition, 74; Third Edition, 42.

and their quality as good spirits, the First Edition shifted the emphasis to the last clause of the sentence, and framed the saying under 'Witchcraft'. The Second Edition (1599) excluded the saying altogether. The Third, Fourth and Fifth Editions (1601, 1605, and 1612) included it again under 'Witchcraft', adding a gloss that left no room for doubt about the problem the editors had with Greenham's reference to 'good witches and bad witches'. In the gloss the reader was told, 'Not for that they are good or lawfull, but of blind people so called and reputed'.[64] While the recorder of Greenham's saying in 1582 exhibited no unease with the good witch/bad witch analogy in the discussion of fairies, either in gathering or framing, by 1599 the mention of witches in the saying was enough to shift the framing of the saying to 'Witchcraft'. By 1601 it was necessary to clarify the language to exonerate Greenham of any suggestion that there might be good witches. This example highlights the creative process of framing a saying, giving emphasis and attention to an issue that in an earlier period was so commonly assumed to be true that it was used by analogy to explain another issue. A closer examination of the practice of framing yields important evidence of how the godly recast the authenticated language of respected authorities, like Greenham, to suit changing attitudes and priorities.

The large number of verbatim or closely paraphrased sayings found both in the manuscript and printed editions suggests that other manuscript sayings, not found in print, may have been among the sayings Holland and others excluded as 'distracted and corrupted'. Consideration of sayings absent from the printed collections provides intriguing circumstantial evidence of how the consensus of the godly community changed from the 1580s to the early seventeenth century. The range of subjects covered by sayings not found in the printed editions raises questions about shifting emphases in the discipline of the godly community and rejection of more moderate approaches to furthering the reformation of the English Church.

A remarkable observation concerning correction from others was expressed in the following saying: 'Hee said two kinds of men should have liberty to admonish him, to wit his enemies and his inferiours, these hee wold alwaies hear, beecaus hee would practise that in himself which hee taught to others.'[65] Why did this apparent expression of humility and consistency in a spiritual mentor not appear in print? Did his editors perceive that it undermined the authority of godly ministers and raised doubts about the purity and clarity of the causes they championed? Its

---

[64] REM 524, fol. 13r; Witchcraft 2, First Edition, 74; Third Edition, 42; Fourth Edition, 42; Fifth Edition, 42.

[65] REM 524, fol. 37v.

absence from the printed collection suggests that it expressed an attitude toward inferiors and enemies of the godly that did not conform to the ideals of the godly community in the early seventeenth century.

One of the most striking examples of moderation is found in a manuscript saying concerning stained glass windows. It was reported that:

> A godly minister complayning to him, that hee was troubled for pulling down certain painted glasse windowes, in his church, hee answered in my Judgement, the minister is *docere non destruere*,[66] hee is to threaten al the plagues of god against them, that should destroy such things, to lay the burden of the wrath of god upon them, but how the minister should do it alone, hee saw not, but as with consent, when by the power of the gospel hee had convinced ther consciences and by his liberality was ready to reare up new white glasse in stead of the old. For stil hee laboured that in a minister ther should bee wisdome; and love mixed with zeal, that when hee shal suffer of the world, hee might have wherwith wisely, hee might defend himself, with a sufficient warrant one of the word, and with a testimony that in a sound caus, hee even used, sound discreet, and loving means.[67]

This plea for moderation and the use of persuasion to bring about right action did not appear in the printed collections of sayings. Was it politically inexpedient to publish on the question of stained glass and advocate for white glass at the end of Elizabeth's reign? Or did Greenham's admonition seem too harsh a judgement on the minister's actions to suit his editors 20 years later? These and many other examples illustrate interesting directions for research that can be pursued when studying sayings that did not appear in print.

Enough evidence has been presented to illustrate the impact of gathering and framing on the meaning and import of the Greenham sayings in the printed editions. Principles and priorities of the 1580s were modified, omitted, or explained away as the editors sought to provide Greenham as an authoritative voice for the godly community while controlling and limiting the meaning of the sayings. This process ensured the viability of the Greenham sayings as authenticated language for the godly community in the seventeenth century and aided his canonization as a 'saint'.

Conclusion

Situating Rylands English Manuscript 524 in the context of the

---

[66] 'to instruct, not to destroy'.
[67] REM 524, fols 36v–37r.

commonplace tradition and the humanist pedagogical reform has highlighted important aspects of Elizabethan religious history that deserve further exploration. When Holland opened his preface with a passage from Proverbs, he redeployed a fragment of wisdom literature that summarized godly assumptions about religious knowledge, sources of authority and the nature of righteousness. The power and influence of the commonplace genre, long neglected by historians and theologians, is evident in the contemporary popularity of the Greenham sayings. The role of commonplace books as a pedagogical tool and 'literary' genre has revealed a complex relationship between acts of gathering and framing, and the power of this exercise to fashion and control the discourse of a community. The authority of Greenham rested on a triad of models that emphasized experience, association with recognized authorities of antiquity and the Reformation, and the power of the sayings as expressions of community values.

The critical edition of Rylands English Manuscript 524 presented in this volume provides scholars and students with an opportunity to observe how the process of gathering and framing enabled those skilled in the practice to select and change the words and reported actions of a respected authority to conform to the consensus of a particular community in another historical context. Greenham's editors used creatively the sayings found in this notebook and elsewhere to fashion a 'saint' who advocated priorities and principles they valued. Anomalies and contradictions to the truth as they understood it were either edited out, explained away, or excluded altogether. While this provides a valuable new resource for the study of English religion in the early seventeenth century, it complicates the use of Greenham's published works in studies of the godly in the 1580s. We are not able to encounter the 'historical Greenham' in this notebook, for the recorder of these sayings also functioned as a gatherer and framer. However, the notebook does provide insights into ideals valued by the godly of that period. What once was considered the 'raw material' for more important literary works has proven to be a significant resource in the continued quest for understanding of Elizabethan religious life and thought.

Having clarified the nature and usefulness of the evidence available to us, we now turn to a closer examination of the context in which the sayings were compiled: Greenham's pastoral ministry. His students documented and his seventeenth-century biographers apotheosized his efforts to erect a shining godly community on Dry Drayton's clay. Greenham, for them, was the paradigmatic godly pastor. It is crucial, therefore, that we gain a clearer understanding of the components of his work and how they contributed to the creation of a Protestant parish ethos.

CHAPTER FIVE

Greenham's pastoral ministry

With admirable brevity but deceptive simplicity, Greenham reportedly summed up pastoral ministry as 'none other thing, but to preach the word of God sincerely, and purely with a care of the glory of God, and a desire of the salvation of our breathern: & secondly a reverent administration of the sacraments, according to the order and institution of our Saviour Jesus Christ'.[1] The lived reality of his ministry was much more complex, since 'preaching' subsumed a variety of teaching functions, including catechizing and conferring, and 'reverent administration of the sacraments' had also to be understood to include a number of rituals which were not (though some had once been) sacraments. Almost a decade ago, Professor Collinson pointed out how little studied was the actual routine of parish ministry.[2] The available sources make it possible to learn a great deal about Greenham's ministry, and such a study is essential since it was on the foundation of that ministry that his contemporary reputation was built.

'To preach the word of God sincerely'

In the course of the Reformation, the whole meaning and nature of ministry had to be redefined. It was no longer a sacrificial ministry created by a sacramental anointing which effected an ontological change in the anointed. It was, nevertheless, still an office of great dignity, and ordination still took place liturgically. The average lay person could easily fail to see most of the differences between the pre- and post-Reformation clergy. This was especially the case with the re-emergence of teaching that emphasized the clergy as mediators between God and the laity, without whom there was no salvation. This is a troubling paradox: that a church founded on each person's unmediated relationship with God should find itself defining its ordained ministry in a way which seemed *mutatis mutandis* startlingly Roman.

The mediatory role of pre-Reformation clergy is, of course, well understood. The priest, through his monopoly over the sacraments, was a crucial channel of the grace necessary for salvation. It was he alone, *in loco Dei*, who spoke the words of absolution and it was he who offered

---

[1] Fourth Edition, 781-82.
[2] Collinson, 'Shepherds, Sheepdogs, and Hirelings', esp. 189-94.

access to the grace which God made available in the other sacraments and the Mass. The Reformation, crudely put, freed people from this clerical power over them and offered them an alternative theology by which unmediated communication with God was not only possible but preferable, and an individual's salvation was a matter between God and that individual alone.

Elizabethan ministers, however, often wrote and preached on the dignity of their calling and began to make heady claims about their importance, their necessity and their mediatory function which, in the most extravagant versions, sound paradoxically like the claims of the detested Roman priesthood. In 1597, Edward Dering wrote:

> The true Minister is the eye of the body, the workman of the harvest, the messenger that calleth unto the Marriage, the Prophet that telleth the will of the Lord, the wise-man that teacheth to discerne betweene good and evill, the Scribe that doeth expound the Law, the servant that occupieth his Maister's Talents unto gaine, the witnesse that beareth testimony of Christ to all people, the dispensers of the misteries of God, the Steward that giveth meate in due time, unto the residue of the housholde, ... the Labourers of God to till his husbandry, and make up his building: the sheepheard to feede the church of God, which he hath purchased with his blood.

In sum, for Dering it was 'the Minister by whom the people doe beleeve'.[3]

Dering is one of many of Greenham's contemporaries with such views. For example, Bishop Jewel wrote that through ministers 'God lighteneth our darkness, he declareth his mind to us, he gathereth together his scattered sheep, and publisheth unto the world the glad tidings of salvation ...'. Ministers, according to Jewel, 'are the eyes of Christ, the pillars of the church, the interpreters of God's will, the watchmen of the Lord's tower, the leaders of Christ's sheep, the salt of the earth, the light of the world'.[4] For Richard Bernard, they were 'Light, Salt, Saviours, Seers, Chariots of Israel, & Horsemen thereof, Pastours, Planters, Waterers, Builders, and Stewards, Watchmen, Soldiers, Nurses ...'. These images were significant for Bernard because ministers were thus compared 'to such things, and callings, as are most common, and also needfull to necessarie uses: that the *necessity* of them heereby may be considered of, both for the Church and Commonwealth'.[5]

---

[3] Edward Dering, *A Briefe and necessarie Catechisme or Instruction, very needfull to be known to all Housholders* (1597), A3v.

[4] *The Works of John Jewel*, ed. John Ayre (4 vols, Cambridge: Cambridge University Press, 1847), II, 1129-30.

[5] Richard Bernard, *The Faithfull Shepheard: Or The Shepheards Faithfulnesse: Wherein is for the matter largely, but for the maner, in few words, set forth the excellencie and necessitie of the Ministerie ...* (1607), 2. (Emphasis added.)

Claims such as Bernard's sit uneasily beside appeals to the unmediated Protestant relationship between God and the individual. Nevertheless, such claims, all carefully supported with marginal references to scriptural passages, were by no means unusual in the clerical writings of the time. As before the Reformation, assertions of ministerial necessity were explained by reference to a clerical monopoly. Elizabethans, however, located the relevant power of the keys in preaching. Bishop Jewel wrote that the principal duty of ministers 'is to preach repentance ... so we may amend our lives, and be converted unto God'.[6] According to Greenham, the Word was 'the very gate of heaven, and the keies thereof are given to the true Ministers of Gods word ...'.[7] This was an extraordinary appropriation of medieval priestly imagery. The medieval priest in his primary work as speaker of the words of absolution succeeded the apostles in controlling – through the power to forgive sins – the keys to the Kingdom. The post-Reformation minister had no less importance and no less power over the eternal life of his neighbours.

For Greenham, preaching provided 'the most principal means to increase and beget faith and repentance in Gods people ... and where this ordinary means of salvation faileth, the people for the most part perish'.[8] In a sermon preached to other clergy, he reportedly compared a congregation without a preaching minister to a flock of sheep scattered and threatened by wolves, for preaching was 'the instrument which God hath appointed to pull his people into the sheepfold of Jesus Christ, where they are without daunger of destruction: when as all they that are without a Pastor are wandering abroad to their owne destruction: such horrible disorder is there, where Gods word is not truly preached'.[9] Some version of this view was not uncommon. Arthur Dent, in that most popular of devotional works *The Plaine Mans Pathway to Heaven*, wrote that:

> Faith commeth by hearing the word preached, then I reason thus:
> No preaching, no faith; no faith, no Christ; no Christ, no eternall life
> ... If we will have heaven, we must have Christ. If we will have
> Christ, we must have faith. If we will have faith, we must have the
> word preached. Then I conclude that preaching ... is of absolute
> necessity into eternall life.[10]

George Downame, who had heard Greenham preach during his student days at Cambridge, called preaching 'the chiefe worke of the Ministerie'

---

[6] *Works of Jewel*, II, 1131.

[7] Fourth Edition, 779.

[8] 'A Profitable Treatise, Containing a Direction for the reading and understanding of the holy Scriptures', in First Edition, reprinted below, pp. 339–46, esp. 339.

[9] Fourth Edition, 778.

[10] Arthur Dent, *The Plaine Mans Pathway to Heaven* (1625), 336–7.

and the duty from which the ministry derived its dignity because 'by the preaching of the worde, men are brought to salvation, and ... without it ordinarily men cannot attaine to salvation'.[11] And the Word would not, Greenham would argue, preach itself any more than sheep would herd themselves.

Since the stakes were so high, Greenham invested a great deal of time and effort in preparing for his sermons. Rising every morning at four to study,[12] he considered this regimen essential since the other demands on his time left him little privacy during the day. He preached twice on Sunday and once every weekday (except Thursday). His weekday sermons began soon after dawn so his parishioners could 'attend upon his Ministry' before beginning their work. Greenham preached in plain style, but that referred 'to content not delivery'.[13] He preached with such energy 'that his shirt would usually be as wet with sweating, as if it had been drenched in water ...'.[14] Some tried to persuade Greenham to preach with more restraint but he predictably refused. He had every reason to believe his technique appropriate, citing the malevolent energy expended by Satan to stop his mouth. This manifested itself as 'very sharp and trembling fears in the flesh' which he experienced before preaching.[15]

And his method appeared to be effective. Once while he was preaching, 'a woman burst out into desperate crying, that shee was a damned soule'. Greenham left the pulpit to console her, saying 'woman didst thou not come into this place to hear of thy sins and of the forgivenes of them in christ: bee of good comfort, and as thou seest thy sins so shalt thou hear pardon of thy sins'.[16] He urged his students not to expect such events, however, and encouraged them to be patient and to persist in their preaching, comparing the preacher to a farmer who 'would long after hee had sowen looke for the increas, not measuring the fruit of his labor by the time present but by the tyme to come ...'.[17]

His reputation for effective preaching was such that he regularly

---

[11] Downame, *Two Sermons*, 26-7.

[12] Greenham noted that sometimes this backfired. When 'hee studied painfully, and laboured exquisitely for a sermon' he would often become thoroughly confused, and he could preach better without any study but with some time to pray for assistance: REM 524, fol. 24v; Clarke, 'Life of Master Richard Greenham', 12.

[13] Francis Bremer and Ellen Rydell, 'Puritans in the Pulpit', *History Today* (September, 1995), 50-54.

[14] Clarke, 'Life of Master Richard Greenham', 12.

[15] REM 524, fols 5v-6r, 43v. See Peter Iver Kaufman, *Prayer, Despair and Drama: Elizabethan Introspection* (Champaign, IL: University of Illinois Press, 1996), 56-7.

[16] REM 524, fols 67v-68r.

[17] Ibid., fol. 7v.

preached outside Dry Drayton as well. We have seen that he continued to preach at Great St Mary's in Cambridge; he was a guest preacher in other churches as well.[18] He also participated in at least one combination lecture, though its location is unknown.[19]

Greenham's preaching was not just within church buildings; he said that it was 'not sufficient that hee preach the word of God [only] in the pulpet'.[20] After his morning sermon, he would change into dry clothes and 'walk out into the Fields, and ... confer with his Neighbours as they were at Plough'.[21] One can only imagine the bewilderment of the village's preoccupied barley farmers as they ploughed around their energetic rector. For Greenham, drenching another shirt with perspiration in the service of truth, his feet immobilized in Dry Drayton's damp clay, was a duty to God, to his flock and to those who learned of ministry from him.

Even more than this, though, true preaching meant that 'hee must goe to every mans house, and there diligently instruct both him and his house in the feare of God'.[22] This ambitious plan was Greenham's response to a pastoral crisis caused by the abolition of mandatory auricular confession.[23] The Elizabethan homily on repentance printed in the official *Certain Sermons or Homilies* (1562) stated that auricular confession had no warrant in God's word and it was against 'true Christian liberty' to require 'the numbering of [one's] sins, as it hath been used heretofore in the time of blindness and ignorance'. Instead, Christians should make 'unfeigned confession and acknowledging of [their] sins unto God'.[24] Greenham also taught that confession ought to be made directly to God. For Christians, relief from 'spiritual greefs' would only come, according to Greenham, 'if wee power forth our greefs into the bosome of the lord who is most faithful to conceal, most loving to take pity and most able to help us in al our greefes whatsoever'.[25]

However, it was also accepted that, after confessing to God, some people would remain 'troubled in conscience', and auricular confession might be expedient. To avoid despair and experience God's mercy, Bishop Jewel advised people to confess sins 'either in the secret thought

---

[18] For example, ibid., fols 67v–68r.

[19] Ibid., fol. 6r.

[20] Fourth Edition, 782.

[21] Clarke, 'Life of Master Richard Greenham', 15.

[22] Fourth Edition, 782.

[23] For this issue, see Eric Josef Carlson, 'Auricular Confession and the English Reformation', unpublished paper, Sixteenth Century Studies Conference, October 1996. This paper is being revised and expanded for publication.

[24] *Certain Sermons or Homilies Appointed to be Read in Churches, In the time of Queen Elizabeth of Famous Memory* (1683), 343–5.

[25] REM 524, fol. 35v.

of thy heart before God, or else *in the hearing and presence of men*'. The latter could 'do much good, if it be well used', though Jewel emphasized 'that every man should be *bound* to their auricular confession, it is no commandment or ordinance of God'.[26] When administering the Lord's Supper, the curate could (at his discretion) formally encourage those who 'requireth further comfort or counsel ... [to] come to me, or some other discreet and learned minister of God's word, and open his grief that he may receive such ghostly counsel, advice, and comfort, as his conscience may be relieved; and that by ministry of God's word he may receive comfort and the benefit of absolution, to the quieting of his conscience'.[27]

Greenham considered this 'the right use of confession' but noted that it was usually 'passed over untaught'.[28] Many ministers felt that confession of any sort, in fact, was commonly ignored. For example, in June 1602, John Buckeridge preached at the Temple Church: 'In tymes past men were ashamed to committ synn, but ready to make confession; nowe the world is changed, for nowe every one dares comitt anie synne, but is ashamed to make confession.'[29] Buried not very far under the surface of Buckeridge's homiletic hyperbole was a feeling shared by Greenham. Although 'Eare confession' had been the object of 'grosse abuses' in the past and 'men were too far gone with Auricular confession', Greenham came to feel that in abolishing it 'our losses have been greater than our winnings' – not only because people failed to confess their sins altogether, but because they 'come too short of christian conferring' with their ministers.[30]

For Greenham, 'christian conferring' was essential for anyone seeking to live a Christian life: 'We must for a time like babes hang at the mouthes of the Ministers, because wee cannot runne before wee goe'.[31] He once observed that 'hee thought it good if men would confer more with ther Pastors saying, Even in earthly things when men cannot try gold themselves, they know to go to the goldsmith'.[32] Thomas Bell also

---

[26] *Works of Jewel*, 2: 1132-3. (Emphasis added.)

[27] *The Two Liturgies ... set forth by authority in the Reign of King Edward VI*, ed. Joseph Ketley (Cambridge, 1844), 273-4, 314. In the homily on repentance, people were encouraged to speak to their curate or 'some other godly learned man ... that they may receive at their hand the comfortable salve of God's word': *Certain Sermons*, 345.

[28] In 'Of the Confession of Sins' in Fourth Edition, 797.

[29] *The Diary of John Manningham of the Middle Temple 1602-1603*, ed. Robert Parker Sorlien (Hanover, NH: University Press of New England, 1976), 73.

[30] Fourth Edition, 797; REM 524, fol. 40r.

[31] 'A Profitable Treatise ...', below, p. 343.

[32] REM 524, fol. 40r. In 'A Profitable Treatise ...', he said: 'In naturall things man standeth in neede of helpe, then much more in spirituall things he standeth in need of others'. (See below, 342.)

encouraged conferring with ministers, and treated it as one of the 'ordinary means' of salvation: a Christian should read the Bible, 'frequent godly sermons' and 'often confer with zealous preachers, for thy better instruction and sound confirmation'.[33] But Bell's model of conferring emphasized its voluntary nature; it depended upon lay initiative. The primary purpose of conferring for Greenham was bringing people to an awareness of their sinfulness, and the urgency of that goal fostered his ambition to 'goe to every mans house', and provided the link between conferring and preaching.

The preacher's duty, according to Bishop Jewel, was 'to preach repentance ... so we may amend our lives, and be converted unto God'. In preaching, 'our filth is laid open before our eyes' and 'we [are] taught ... to see ourselves, to know our weakness, to repent our sins, to believe the forgiveness of our sins, and to turn to God'.[34] Calling sinners to repentance did take place in the pulpit. The episode described above, of the woman moved to tears, indicates that Greenham preached in this way and consciously framed sermons intended to evoke sorrow for sin and a desire for forgiveness.

In every sermon the preacher should present to his auditors a number of appropriate doctrines from the scriptural text. For each doctrine, arguably the most important task at hand was to present its 'applications': the ways in which the doctrine applied to the individual. Richard Bernard, who called this 'home-speaking', described it as 'the sharpe edge of the sword'; it made 'faithfull Ministers teaching, unsavorie to carnall and evill men'. The minister needed blunt and harsh speech to penetrate his hearers' defences, but sinners confronted with such preaching might feel that the minister wagged a finger at them as individuals. Preachers, wrote Bernard, 'are said to name men in the Pulpit, & gall some personally: when no man is named'.[35]

When people became angry over 'particularizing', the consequences for the minister could be devastating. While some of Edward Shepherd's parishioners in Essex 'delighted not to heare him, because he made no application of his doctrine, & did not reprove sin',[36] what even the

---

[33] Thomas Bell, *Motives concerning the Romish Faith and Religion* (1593), ¶3, quoted in C. Haigh, 'Puritan Evangelism in the Reign of Elizabeth I', *English Historical Review*, 92 (1977), 30.

[34] *Works of Jewel*, II, 1132-3.

[35] Bernard, *Faithfull Shepheard*, 71. Bernard's concern proved all too real. In 1634, he was taken to court by James Ashe, the most prominent member of his parish, who denounced Bernard's preaching, accusing him of speaking in particular against an individual: Steig, *Laud's Laboratory*, 202-3.

[36] Jim Sharpe, 'Scandalous and Malignant Priests in Essex: the Impact of Grassroots Puritanism' in Colin Jones, Malyn Newitt, et al. (eds), *Politics and People in Revolutionary England* (Oxford: Basil Blackwell, 1986), 267.

godly might demand in the abstract they might rail against in the particular. As Sir Francis Hastings wrote to his cousin Sir Richard Grenville in 1583:

> I knowe some that shewe great zeale and wilbe accounted earnest professors, and will not sticke to expresse the same by diligent frequentinge the worde preached, and by giveinge good countenance to the minister therof, and this have I sene well perfourmed and continued whilest the precher hath held him in a generall course of doctrine, but if by any occacon (as duetie byndeth him) he be drawen into particuler reprehensions, and the same are felt to touche the quicke, then kicke they, and cannot be quiet till they have hindered them selves of so gret a blessinge ... for no sooner is the precher misliked for his playnes, but then is there such huntinge into his doctrine, and such siftinge of his lif, and so many baites layde for him, that zeale is forgotten, the worde hath lost his due regarde, and the minister for doing his duetie is despised.[37]

Since such preaching could not be avoided without jeopardizing souls (including the preacher's own if he failed to carry out his task), it needed to be handled with great delicacy if it were not to be counterproductive.[38] Naming names and wagging fingers at individuals was emphatically not what godly ministers such as Bernard and Greenham advocated. The preacher should condemn *sin* in the pulpit and confront *individual sinners* privately.

According to Greenham, God held every minister accountable for every soul entrusted to him. There was no more pressing burden on the minister, therefore, than 'to watch over the souls of his people, to be so careful over them, as that he will not suffer one through his negligence to perish'.[39] To save the souls of his flock, 'It is necessarie that the Minister of God, doe very sharply rebuke the people for their sinnes, and that he lay before them Gods grievous judgements against sinners'.[40] For Greenham, the minister's duty could not be confined to the pulpit.

Rebuking sinners was a duty fraught with danger and the quality of the parson's relations with his parish, and thus the success of his ministry, depended on the way he carried it out. Richard Kilby, a curate in Derby, recommended that correction be done 'secretly, and very kindly' because he had been insensitive in rebuking erring parishioners; he advised those reading his book that following his unfortunate example 'will hinder your ministry, and ... put you into more trouble

---

[37] Huntington Library, H.A. 5087, quoted in Claire Cross, 'An Example of Lay Intervention in the Elizabethan Church', *Studies in Church History*, 2 (1965), 278.

[38] Bernard had many suggestions for successfully carrying out this function: *Faithfull Shepheard*, 72-7.

[39] Fifth Edition, 342, 358.

[40] Fifth Edition, 392.

than you can imagine'.[41] The minister of Weston Colville, a village not far from Dry Drayton, was a case in point. Simon Hacksuppe, the godly rector from 1583–1605, buried his ministry in a tidal wave of litigation when he tore his parish apart with finger-wagging denunciations of sinners from the pulpit. Apparently he named names and he named sins. A flood of court cases and bitter divisions in the village resulted.[42]

Greenham, on the other hand, 'observed as a general law that soemuch as with a good conscience might bee, hee would use private warnings before, publique dealings, and gentle and curteous speaches before vehement and sharp speaches and threatnings'. He also recommended seeing if someone other than the minister might be better fitted to the task. Whoever approached the sinner should 'put on the person of the offendor, that as you spare not his sin beecaus of zeale of gods glory, so you pres it not too far beecaus of compassion of a brother'.[43] But if such 'gentle and curteous speaches' failed, then 'vehement and sharp speaches and threatnings'[44] were necessary. The minister, he said, 'must not be ashamed to rebuke and reprove such as will not bee obedient to the Gospell, but remaine still wallowing in their sinne: and if that holesome admonitions will not serve, he must not spare to thunder out the just judgements of God against them, untill he hath beaten them down to hell with the terror thereof ...'.[45]

The frequency with which Greenham's disciples asked him to comment on reprehension and the care with which they recorded his many comments indicates both the importance and the sensitivity of this duty, rendered far more difficult in the absence of a formal sacramental structure. Greenham's experience likewise makes clear a related problem: that successful reprehension could and did lead to despair and spiritual crisis. The sacrament of confession had been, in theory at least, meant to offer consolation to the sinner through the words of absolution. But without the sacramental encounter, how did the minister convey that comfort to the afflicted?

The elect, according to William Perkins, 'feele continually the smart and bitternes of their owne sinnes'. If Christians did not experience a 'lively feeling of misery' from the enormity of their sins piercing their hearts, they could not 'ascertain their election and learn of their salvation'. Misery and consolation were, therefore, somewhat paradoxically intertwined. No pastoral function was more necessary

[41] Richard Kilby, *The burthen of a loaden conscience* (1608), 95.
[42] Carlson, *Marriage and the English Reformation*, 173–4.
[43] REM 524, fols 10v–11r.
[44] Ibid., 12v.
[45] Fourth Edition, 782.

than to encourage 'godly sorrow' in order to be aware of God's grace and mercy.[46] But what if that awareness did not follow?

This was certainly Richard Greenham's experience. He had a national reputation for comforting afflicted consciences and spent much of his time offering consolation to those who came to him 'extreamly througn down' by the burden of their sins.[47] Most of Greenham's counselling seems to have been face to face. Evidence from the Rylands manuscript shows that this work consumed an enormous amount of Greenham's time.[48]

He spent some time writing letters as well.[49] Some of this is evident in the manuscript, such as when a 'Godly learned man' wrote to ask him if it was permissible to use the services of a popish physician.[50] Printed texts of several of his pastoral letters have been preserved in the editions of his *Works*. These include 'A Letter Against hardnesse of heart' (which was also copied into the Rylands manuscript), 'An other comfortable Letter by Master R.G. to Master M.', 'A Letter Consolatorie, written to a friend afflicted in conscience for sinne', and 'A Letter Consolatorie to Mistris Mary Whitehead'.[51] Clearly, the recipients treasured letters of advice received from Greenham and circulated copies for the edification of others. The letter at the end of the Rylands manuscript may well have been appended to the notebook as an example of how to compose a letter of consolation to one troubled with 'hardnes of hart'.

The content of Greenham's godly conferring will be discussed below;[52] at this juncture one should simply note that Greenham considered comforting afflicted consciences one of the principal activities of his ministry. He treated it as an essential part of his vocation to preach the

---

[46] Peter Iver Kaufman, '"Much in Prayer": The Inward Researches of Elizabethan Protestants', *Journal of Religion*, 73 (1993), 166-7.

[47] REM 524, fol. 14r.

[48] Greenham was sometimes asked to counsel someone outside his parish. He was reluctant to do so without some indication of the consent of the person's minister, in order to avoid giving offence and appearing presumptuous in exercising spiritual authority outside his parish: ibid., fol. 46r.

[49] On written spiritual direction, see Patrick Collinson, 'A Mirror of Elizabethan Puritanism: The Life and Letters of "Godly Master Dering"' in his *Godly People*, 316; A. Daniel Frankforter, 'Elizabeth Bowes and John Knox: A Woman and Reformation Theology', *Church History*, 56 (1987), 333-47.

[50] REM 524, fol. 1r.

[51] First Edition, 443-76; Fourth Edition, 874. Greenham was by no means the only minister of his day actively engaged in comforting afflicted consciences. *The Short Title Catalogue* is full of works such as Robert Linaker's, *A Comfortable Treatise for the Relief of such as are Afflicted in Conscience* (1595).

[52] See Chapter 6.

word of God sincerely. As Greenham once said, 'it is a greater thing in a Pastor to deal wisely and comfortably with an afflicted conscience ... then to preach publickly and learnedly'.[53] This did not mean that he saw pastoral counselling as superior to preaching; rather, it was the highest form of preaching – a private preaching to and from the heart, rather than public preaching from books and the mind.

Greenham, along with many other ministers, came increasingly to realize that even the best public preaching fell on deaf ears without preparation, especially in the form of catechizing. William Crashaw, for example, described the catechism as 'such a means of knowledge as without it all preaching is to little purpose'.[54] Greenham's bishop, Richard Cox, was obsessed with catechizing; it dominated his injunctions to the diocesan clergy in 1573.[55] In Elizabeth's reign it became more and more important as a function of pastoral ministry, for if preaching was necessary for saving faith, and preaching could not be understood without preparation, catechizing was necessary for salvation.[56]

Ministers were expected to catechize once a week, usually on Sunday before the second service. As of 1571, two hours of catechizing was the official requirement. That may not have been widely observed,though, as Ian Green argues, 'evidence for moderately frequent, moderately conscientious catechizing in early modern England turns out to be rather better than we had been led to believe ...'.[57] Greenham introduced mid-week catechism sessions (on Thursdays, in place of his sermon), which were rare at that time,[58] in addition to his regular Sunday efforts. He did not limit catechizing to the youth: once when a man 'being negligent to bee taught' brought his infant to Greenham to be baptized, he agreed to do so only after the man confessed his error, and promised to reform his life and present himself for instruction.[59] We know only the most general

---

[53] REM 524, fol. 61r.

[54] Ian Green, '"For Children in Yeeres and Children in Understanding": The Emergence of the English Catechism under Elizabeth and the Early Stuarts', *Journal of Ecclesiastical History*, 37 (1986), 417.

[55] *Visitation Articles and Injunctions of the Period of the Reformation*, eds W.H. Frere and W.P. Kennedy, 3 vols, Alcuin Club Collections xiv-xvi (London: Alcuin Club, 1910), III, 296-7.

[56] Ian Green, *The Christian's ABC: Catechisms and Catechizing in England c.1530-1740* (Oxford: Clarendon Press, 1996), 26-9. For the development of catechizing as ministerial function, ibid., chap. 3.

[57] Green, *The Christian's ABC*, 2. Green is referring especially to Christopher Haigh's claim that catechizing was the most neglected clerical task: 'Puritan Evangelism', 35.

[58] Clarke, 'Life of Master Richard Greenham', 12; Green, 'For Children in Yeeres', 419.

[59] REM 524, fol. 65v.

things about his pedagogy: 'The office of the Catechist is to make his doctrine easie to enter by giving it an edge in perspicuitie, methode, &c. and of the catechized often to goe over the same thing, as a knife doth the whetstone, & to repeate and iterate it, till he have made it his owne.'[60]

Since many ministers, like Greenham, catechized people of many different ages and levels of knowledge, they needed a variety of catechetical materials.[61] The 1549 Prayer Book included a short catechism still in use under Elizabeth, and with the approval of Convocation, Alexander Nowell composed a more advanced catechism. Greenham was one of many other divines who followed with his own volume, developed in response to his own needs.[62]

Greenham's catechism is difficult to evaluate because the surviving text is incomplete. Typically, English catechisms covered four elements: the Decalogue, the Apostles' Creed, the Lord's Prayer, and the sacraments.[63] Greenham's contains the first two, but breaks off early in the treatment of the Lord's Prayer. In the 1602 edition of Greenham's *Works*, Henry Holland added this note to the catechism: 'I cannot as yet finde any more of this Catechisme; If any man have the rest in his private use, he shall doe well to communicate the same unto the Church for the good of many.'[64] Since no more sections were forthcoming, it is unclear whether they ever existed. It is certainly possible that Greenham's catechism was a work in progress, never completed because of the hectic pace of his ministry.[65]

The existing elements of Greenham's catechism are arranged in the same order as those of Luther's *Short Catechism*. Luther, unlike Calvin, placed the Decalogue first because he held that it was the first duty to make sinners aware of their sinfulness and thus their need for Christ. This is consistent with what we have seen of Greenham's views above, and it is unsurprising that his catechism would reflect it. However, more English catechisms began – like John Calvin's – with the Creed. Other

---

[60] Third Edition, 289.

[61] On this topic, see Green, *The Christian's ABC*, chap. 2.

[62] *A Short Forme of Catechising* in First Edition, reprinted below, 265–98. It was also published separately in 1602, with the misleading authorial attribution of 'R.C.': see Appendix 1 below, 362.

[63] On the contents and structures of catechisms, see Green, *The Christian's ABC*, chaps 5–6.

[64] Third Edition, 231.

[65] A further difficulty is that we do not know when Greenham composed his catechism. This is of some importance because, as Green shows, the 1570s and 1580s were decades of major change in the structure of catechism (*The Christian's ABC*, 280–87) and it is difficult to contextualize Greenham's catechism without being able to date it.

than the order of elements, however, Greenham did not imitate Luther; the contents are quite different.

William Perkins, according to Ian Green, designed his 1590 catechism for older parishioners who 'evidently knew the basic formulae but showed little or no comprehension of what they represented for the conscientious Christian'.[66] The same could be said of Greenham. His catechism plainly aims to develop understanding of basic doctrines such as election and justification in ways that could not be intended for the parish youth. With many mid-Elizabethan divines, Greenham preferred many questions with short answers to few questions with long answers.[67] The section which survives contains over 300 questions; few responses are more than one pithy sentence. If the language is not the 'country-like speech' adopted by William Wood in his catechism,[68] neither was it inaccessibly academic. Greenham's efforts to construct a catechism demonstrate that he took very seriously the need to prepare and teach all age levels in his parish – not just the youth. Without such preparation, the seed of his preaching fell on unfurrowed soil. More importantly, souls would be lost without the essential Word preached from his pulpit.

'A reverent administration of the sacraments'

While actually administering the sacraments and other services of the church occupied relatively little of his time,[69] Greenham treated them with no less seriousness than preaching: 'The neglect of Gods Sacraments', he reportedly said, 'doth provoke him against us, as it did against Moses, for the neglect of the Circumcision of his sonne. The Lord met Moses with some such affliction; as that hee was readie to die according to the threatening.'[70] Since the form of almost every ritual of the church was controversial in the 1570s and 1580s, Greenham's responses to questions and challenges have left us with the materials to construct an unusually complete sense of his sacramental and ritual ministry. The focus here will be on the two sacraments of the church,

---

[66] Green, *The Christian's ABC*, 286-7.

[67] Ibid., 243-7.

[68] Ibid., 249.

[69] The parish register, which is complete for Greenham's tenure, records 203 baptisms, 25 marriages, and 63 burials. Greenham performed an average of ten baptisms a year; actual baptisms ranged from a low of three in one year to four years in which there were 17 or 18. Since the exact date of Greenham's arrival in the parish is not known, it is not certain that he was present for all the burials during the 1570 mortality crisis. The figures given are maxima. CRO, Dry Drayton original parish register.

[70] Second Edition, 358.

baptism and the Lord's Supper, and the primary non-sacramental rituals, solemnization of marriage and burial.

The English Church taught that baptism was a sign of regeneration (but did not guarantee it) and a means 'whereby Christian men are ... grafted into the church'.[71] In Greenham's time, there was general agreement on these points.[72] Greenham was part of the broad consensus that held that an unbaptized child, if he or she died in that state, would not be punished. While God had told Abraham that an uncircumcised man would be 'cut off',[73] Greenham reportedly argued that this resulted from man's contempt for God's covenant. The father of an unbaptized child was guilty of contempt for withholding his child from the sacrament; the child, incapable of such contempt, would incur guilt only if he or she chose in adulthood to remain 'in the [same] state of rebellion and contempt against God'.[74]

When baptism had been considered essential for salvation, emergency baptisms by women - especially midwives - had been accepted. The Elizabethan church reluctantly allowed this practice to continue, largely as a concession to custom. Greenham, however, spoke against it: 'The example of Zipporah cannot be followed amongst us, that women should baptize ...; for the ministration of the Sacrament is ioyned to the ministerie of the word, which office none can take, except he be called as Aaron was.'[75]

When Greenham baptized children, the ceremony apparently deviated modestly from the requirements of the Prayer Book, and in fairly predictable ways: Greenham refused to use the sign of the cross when he baptized, which was one of the most common manifestations of Elizabethan nonconformity.[76] He argued that it was redundant - that the sacrament of baptism was itself a sign of the cross:

> When a good man was complained on for that hee used not the cros in Baptism, hee answered thus for himself, I did minister baptism and that is a sign of the cros: now to add another cros is to make the thing signifying, and the thing signified al one, and mee thincks it is against gods ordinance to make a double seal to one thing.[77]

---

[71] *Religion and Society in Early Modern England: A Sourcebook*, eds David Cressy and Lori Anne Ferrell (London: Routledge, 1996), Article 27 of the Thirty-Nine Articles, 66–7.

[72] For an overview, see David Cressy, *Birth, Marriage and Death: Ritual, Religion and the Life Cycle in Sixteenth and Seventeenth Century England* (Oxford: Oxford University Press, 1997), chap. 5.

[73] Genesis 17:14.

[74] Third Edition, 267–8.

[75] Ibid., 267.

[76] See Cressy, *Birth, Marriage and Death*, chap. 6.

[77] REM 524, fol. 29v. See also fols 55v–56r.

He also expressed concern that witnessing the sign of the cross used in rituals might encourage its superstitious use in private and provide a defence for those who used it, which he had himself witnessed. The dangers of renewing past abuses of the sign of the cross outweighed any possible edification in its baptismal use: '[W]hatsoever hath no good use by Gods institution but hath been abused, it is better to have the thing clean taken away then otherwise'.[78]

On the other hand, Greenham used the interrogatories at baptism. These were questions about faith asked of the godparents, who answered on behalf of the child. Some nonconformists more extreme than Greenham objected to these on the grounds that godparents lacked the power to make statements of faith for the child. John Field complained that 'they ask questions of an infant, which cannot answer, and speak unto them, as was wont to be spoken unto men, and unto such as being converted, answered for themselves and were baptized. Which is but a mockery of God, and therefore against the Holy Scriptures.'[79] Apparently, one of Greenham's parishioners was disturbed by this as well: 'Unto one that asked him how hee might keep a good conscience in answering the corrupt interrogationes in Baptism, hee saied as soon I have done, you may say nothing, for as others you may make answer according to a good conscience or els you may keep your self from the action.'[80] As the answer makes clear, Greenham conformed in asking the questions, but would not object to the silence of a conscientious objector. This episode also suggests that Dry Drayton was one of the many parishes in England in which lay people, finding the official service to be intolerably corrupted, took the initiative in trying to shape their children's baptisms.[81] Sacramental nonconformity was not a clerical monopoly, nor was it even something in which clergy were necessarily a step or more ahead of their parishioners.

The godparents, who answered the maligned interrogatories, were themselves a subject of some controversy in the Elizabethan Church. Those who objected most strenuously saw the office as another popish invention lacking any scriptural warrant.[82] Greenham artfully dodged the debate. 'Being demanded what his judgement was of having promisers in Baptism', he replied that it was 'good to have witnesses to testify to the church that wee are christianly baptised' and although he detested 'al frivolous ceremonies and pernitious reliques so for the

---

[78] Ibid., fols 25r, 55v–56r.
[79] John Field, 'A View of Popish Abuses Yet Remaining in the English Church' (1572), in *Religion and Society*, eds Cressy and Ferrell, 85.
[80] REM 524, fol. 10r.
[81] See Cressy, *Birth, Marriage and Death*, chap. 6.
[82] Ibid., chap. 7.

keeping of the peace of the church I would not have refused such holy orders as tend both aedification, to love and to comelines in the church'.[83] Perhaps to defuse some of the tension associated with the term, Greenham seems to have referred to these individuals as witnesses or, most commonly, assistants. This semantic shift reflects the functions which he emphasized that, in his mind, made what the church called godparents 'tend ... to aedification'. For Greenham, a father should delight to have the aid of some other adults 'to teach instruct and reform his child according to christian duties ... for the bringing up of that child, to the means of his salvation'.[84]

Possible popish pollution of the office of godparent was a peripheral issue for Greenham, whose real concern was the practical pastoral matter of assuring children a godly upbringing. This is clear in his repeated attention to the father's role and intentions, as can be seen in a vivid episode recorded by one of his disciples. One Sunday, while 'going ... to his congregation to preach', a man approached him and said, 'Sir, A frind of mine meaneth to send his child to bee baptised of you, but hee himself wil not come and as hee saith hee is sick'. Greenham found that this prospect 'troubled his mind', and he worried about it throughout the service until 'in the very end of this sermon, god taught him how to doe'. When he came to the font and did not see the father present, he asked the people to sing a psalm and sent two men off with these instructions:

> I desire you in the name of the church that ye go to this man and ask him if hee wil refuse to come, if hee were wel, and ask if hee wil come herafter, if god restore him to health. If hee graunt to thes things, aske him further if hee bee willing and desirous to have his child baptised; and if hee bee soe whither being absent in body, hee wil bee present in spirit if hee consent, further request, if for that hee cannot come himself and yet would have his child baptised, hee would make you his delegates, for this tyme to answer in his behalf, and afterward come himself and signify so much to the church of christ.

The absent father agreed to this, and Greenham baptized the child with the two men 'supplying the place of the father'.[85]

A further indication of Greenham's acceptance of godparents in some guise is that his wife is known to have had at least five godchildren in the parish. In her will, Katherine identified as her godchildren the son of Greenham's successor Richard Warfield and children from four important village families.[86]

---

[83] REM 524, fol. 12r.
[84] Ibid., fol. 41r.
[85] Ibid., fol. 11r-v.
[86] PRO, PROB 11/119; PCC, 41 Fenne.

There is only one distinctive feature of Greenham's baptismal practice and it emerges not from his 'sayings' but from the parish register. Shortly after Greenham's arrival, Dry Drayton's children began increasingly to receive biblical baptismal names. Of the ten children baptized in 1575, for example, only one received a traditional parish name (Thomas). Instead, there were Peter, Appia, Daniel, Ursula, Nathaniel, Samuel, Josiah and two Sarahs. They were soon joined by several Deborahs and Rebeccas, along with Jehosabeths and Hananiahs, Gemimah, Solomon, Manasses, Moses, Joshua, Eunice, and even – improbably enough – Lot and Bathsheba. When Greenham left, the traditional names (William, Henry, John, Elizabeth, Alice and Margaret were the most common in Dry Drayton) returned and biblical names were soon no longer chosen.[87]

Biblical names were clustered primarily in seven families. Since some families retained traditional naming patterns, Greenham was not simply changing outward demonstrations of piety through some sort of vulgar blackmail over the font; some individual choice must have been involved.[88] However, parents virtually ceased biblical naming as soon as Greenham was no longer present when they named their babies. Even if the change in practice had been voluntary, it was not deep-rooted enough to withstand the pressure of custom without Greenham present. His successor, Richard Warfield, was not the sort to be antipathetic to the practice, but perhaps he did not care enough to encourage it, and so people returned to customary ways.

The Elizabethan Church acknowledged only one other sacrament in addition to baptism: the Lord's Supper. Greenham's view of the Lord's Supper was conventional. For him, the body and blood of Christ were *represented* by the bread and wine, and they had the effect on the soul that bread and wine had on the body: bread gave strength and wine gave comfort. The sacrament was foremost a remembrance of Christ's death, but it was also a spiritual union with Christ and communion with other members of the body of Christ.[89]

Greenham was only required to administer the sacrament three times a year[90] and he may not have exceeded that. Nevertheless, preparing his

---

[87] CRO, Dry Drayton original parish register. The fashion for naming children with pious ejaculations, used by Dudley Fenner in Cranbrook, did not penetrate much beyond East Sussex and the Kentish weald, but the Hebraicization demonstrated in Dry Drayton's register was found elsewhere beginning in the 1560s. See Nicholas Tyacke, 'Popular Puritan Mentality in Late Elizabethan England' in Peter Clark (ed.), *The English Commonwealth* (Leicester: Leicester University Press, 1974), 77–92.

[88] We are grateful to Michael Sekulla for information and assistance on this subject.

[89] 'Of Examination Before and After the Lords Supper', Fourth Edition, 502–3.

[90] See Jeremy P. Boulton, 'The Limits of Formal Religion: The Administration of Holy Communion in late Elizabethan and early Stuart London', *London Journal*, 10 (1984), 135–54.

congregation to receive the sacrament was one of his most demanding pastoral activities. He reportedly said that when new to a parish a minister should 'stay a good while, after his coming to his people from administering the sacrament, until after a continual publique teaching by some convenient tyme and some requisite trials of the people hee may minister both some comforts, lest doing it before, hee administer to most unworthy receivers'.[91] Before coming 'to eate the flesh and drinke the bloud of Christ', the people 'must eate it by faith out of the word of God'; only then 'the Minister shall administer to [them] the outward seales of bread and wine, to confirm and strengthen [their] faith'.[92] It is no exaggeration to say that every time Greenham preached, catechized, or read publicly from the Bible, he was engaged in preparing people to receive the Lord's Supper.

However, preparation for the Lord's Supper was not solely the work of the minister. Greenham taught that the strength and comfort derived from the sacramental elements came after an intensive self-examination by each potential recipient, whom Greenham instructed literally to indict and try himself or herself. All who undertook this truthfully found themselves guilty of sin, but as Christians they would not need to remain in the state of condemnation. Having been made aware of their unworthiness, sinners turned to Jesus, found pardon, and received the sacrament for strength, nourishment and comfort.[93]

While encouraging this intensely personal and introspective preparation, Greenham exerted himself to further their preparation. When preaching, for two or three days before the appointed Sabbath, he 'alter[ed] his text of purpose to prepare, or els hee diverted his ordinary text' to the subject. He also devoted at least a week 'in calling his people to private conference'.[94] All who wished to receive the sacrament were examined, especially those for whom it was the first time, and required to make a series of promises:

> Hee would take these promises of them, whom first hee admitted to the sacrament, and that in the sight of god and presence of some faithful witnesses, if it might bee first that beecaus the principles of religion and doctrine of beginnings were the word of god, or at least most consonant with the word and not the word of man, they would grow up in the further confirming of them, by further knowledg of the word. Secondly they promised to depart from ther former corrupt conversation, and to labour more for holines of life. Thirdly

[91] REM 524, fol. 2r.

[92] Fourth Edition, 784.

[93] Ibid., 501–2. See also John E. Booty, 'Preparation for the Lord's Supper in Elizabethan England', *Anglican Theological Review*, 49 (1967), 131–48.

[94] REM 524, fol. 38v.

that they would make conscience to keep the sabbath wholy, and throughout in godly exercises to the lord, and as far as ther callings did permit that they would come to bee enstructed, both by publick preaching and by private conference, in the week daies fourthly that if they did fal hereafter into any sin, of disobedience, mallice, filthines, pilfery or slander, or any such like, they would suffer themselves either publickly, or privately to bee admonished of it, according to the censure and quality of the fault. fiftly they promised that if they profited not in knowledg, they would willingly bee suspended from the sacrament hereafter, until they had gotten more forwardnes in knowledg again.[95]

Greenham actively discouraged the unprepared from coming forward to receive the bread and wine, but he was reluctant to exclude the 'indifferently instructed' from the sacrament if they 'lay in noe sin'.[96] By that he meant notorious sinners: 'If a man in his congregation had done evil the church not knowing of it, hee ... would not debar him of the sacrament ... without some orderly or further proceeding in discipline' in order to avoid making the sin known publicly.[97] The value which Greenham placed on the church's peace and unity precluded him from turning away any but those who, in receiving the sacrament, would scandalize the congregation.

The manner in which Greenham's administration of the Lord's Supper differed from the Prayer Book concerned the latitude he permitted in receiving the elements kneeling (as required) or sitting. Greenham identified the posture in which one received the sacrament as one of 'the lesser adjuncts of religion'. On such matters, 'hee would not withstand or condemn any but leav them to ther own reason, seing very good men do soe dissagree in them, or change ther opinion in them'. His comments echo his stinging rebuke of the Cambridge students who had become obsessed with the Cartwright matter: 'Hee said hee found want of judgement in men who would do and not do things without sound reason.'[98] Again, he could find no value in breaking the unity of the church over something which was not essential: 'Let us do as much as wee can with the peace of the church lest wee make the remedy of the evil wors then the evil it self.'[99]

Marriage, although one of the seven medieval sacraments, was not a sacrament in the reformed English Church.[100] However, marriages were still to be advertised in the parish church in the banns and then to be

---

[95] Ibid., fol. 39v.

[96] Ibid., fols 32v–33r.

[97] Ibid., fol. 30r.

[98] Ibid., fol. 54v.

[99] Ibid., fol. 10v.

[100] On this topic, see Carlson, *Marriage and the English Reformation*, chaps 3–4.

solemnized and blessed by the minister in the parish church, using the words of the Prayer Book. They would then be entered in the parish register. Legal disputes over the existence and dissolution of marriage continued to be judged by the church courts using the medieval church's canon law. Marriage remained so profoundly ecclesiastical in its construction, therefore, that the laity could hardly have noticed any practical change as a result of its loss of sacramental status. Greenham's pastoral work, like that of all other parish clergy, had a significant matrimonial element.

In several years, there were no marriages in Dry Drayton. This is not entirely surprising, since there may have been pressure on young people to move out of the parish in order to control population growth.[101] Greenham's attitude towards marriage can have done little to encourage more parochial nuptiality. Indeed, he encouraged people to think of it only as a last resort to avoid fornication:

> One asking his advice how hee might best avoid concupiscence, hee said that a continual examination of your selves by the law, a reverent and daily meditating of the word, a painful walking in our honest calling, an holy shaming of ourselves, and fearing of ourselves before our frinds, a continual temperance in diet, sleep and apparrel, a careful watching over our eies and other parts of our bodies, a zealous geolousy to avoid al occasions, of persons, tymes and places, which might nourish concupiscence, a godly frequenting of times, persons, and places, which breed in us mortification, togither with an humbling of ourselves, with the shame of sins past, with the greefe of sins present, and with the fear of sins to come. lastly a careful using of fasting, praier and watching ... are means to come to mortification herin ...

If all of these - along with moderate exercise - failed, Greenham conceded that 'it is like the lord doth call a man to the holy use of marriage'.[102]

Greenham reportedly warned those already inclined to marry that 'many run hastily into that calling, not using the means of trying ther estate, thorowly before, as namely, whither they by praier, fasting, and avoiding al provocations of concupiscence, have the gift of chastity or no'.[103] Greenham once told an inquirer 'of a certain man, whom hee

---

[101] Legally, unless licensed to do otherwise, couples had to marry in the parish in which one of them resided. Given the likelihood of exogamy at the time, most couples had at least two parishes in which they could marry without a licence. It is possible that the burden of Greenham's marriage preparation programme (described below) simply drove couples to marry elsewhere. We are grateful to Michael Sekulla for suggesting the importance of this factor in curtailing the number of marriages in Dry Drayton.

[102] REM 524, fol. 21v.

[103] Ibid., fol. 16v.

knew wonderfully to bee moved to marriage, and yet attending some longer time on the lord by fervent and continual praier, hee was delivered even from every inward motion, and titillacion therunto'; the man later married but found himself so enfeebled 'that hee cold not use the act of generation'.[104]

According to canon law, valid and indissoluble marriages were contracted when a man and a woman who were free to do so exchanged words in the present tense which indicated their intent to be married: 'I, Thomas, take you Anne to be my wife', for example. These binding contracts did not require the presence of the minister (or, indeed, of any witnesses), and the exchange did not take place in the church.[105] It was the custom for couples to be handfasted (that is, betrothed) in a private setting, usually (but not always) with family and friends in attendance, and then to notify the minister so that he could publish the banns. A few weeks later, the contract would be formally recognized and blessed in what was called the solemnization of the marriage.[106]

Greenham would not publish the banns without questioning the couple on several topics. First he ensured that they were not related to one another in a degree which would make the union illegal. Then he asked whether they were then or had ever been contracted to anyone else (which would bar any valid marriage), whether they had their parents' consent and 'whether they did purpose to continue this action publickly and with the prayers of the church to solemnize ther meeting according to the word'. Next,

> Al these things graunted in the presence of ther Parents or vicegerents, hee would use some exhortation for the general duties both of men and wemen, and after would contract or handfast them (as it is in the common Liturgy) in the sight of god with praier. His exhortation was first a defence of this thing to bee used, of the minister and then a breef discours of the doctrine of the law, and faith applyed to ther estate of marriage and particular callings and to ther most need. Thus of consanguinity and contract and consent the questions asked and answered with prayer and exhortation, hee left them until the further sanctimony of ther meeting.[107]

Paternal consent was so important to Greenham that it moved him to attempt some odd innovations. Once, when the bride's father was not

---

[104] Ibid., fol. 25r.

[105] Carlson, *Marriage and the English Reformation*, chap. 2.

[106] Greenham did not challenge the basic premises of the laws and customs: REM 524, fol. 30v.

[107] Ibid., fol. 43r-v. What is described is clearly a version of what appears in First Edition, 288-99, as 'A Treatise of a Contract before Mariage'. This is reprinted below, 329-38.

present at the solemnization because he had recently died, Greenham noted that it was 'a laudable custome in the church and a tollerable ceremony, that the father should give his daughter, both to shew his authority over her and to witnes his consent in bestowing her'.[108] If the father were dead and thus could not give his daughter, 'hee said then hee would not have the mother to do it, in the congregation, but thought it good for the father in his testament wisely to appoint some vicegerent to do his duty'.[109]

While he lacked legal grounds for refusing to marry anyone for failing to obtain consent of their parents or governors, he could none the less use his considerable authority as minister to impose the requirement in his own church. He could, for example, compel a couple to perform a humiliating public confession of fault during their solemnization before he would play his part. The couple in question 'overslipt in love' and 'intended to marry, without consent of governors'. Greenham eventually blessed the union, after the couple privately confessed their fault to those whose consent they should have sought. Then, at their solemnization,

> they confessed ther fault to the church, they pronounced themselves sorrowful for offending against god and the church, they craved forgivenes they desired al to beware of the like, and praied them, to pray for them that this fault might so humble them, that they might the more warilie walk, without offence the residue of their life.[110]

Such practices amounted to modest *de facto* alterations in marriage law in his parish.

Greenham did the same with the marriage service in the Prayer Book. When the Prayer Book came under attack by Field, Wilcox and Cartwright, the continued use of the ring was the feature most criticized about the marriage service.[111] Greenham had no qualms about the ring itself. John Field raised a further objection that the Prayer Book had the husband 'make an idol of his wife' when he gave her the ring with the words 'with my body I thee worship'.[112] Rather than disturb the parish with a futile attack on a popular custom, Greenham chose to change the words with which it was accompanied:

> Hee refused not the Ring in marriage if it were offered, but took it using thes words, to teach the man to say to his spouse I promis to bee thy faith ful husband and to keep my body proper unto thee and

---

[108] REM 524, fol. 45r.

[109] Ibid., fol. 49v. There is no trace in any of the Dry Drayton wills, including those which Greenham witnessed, of such a scheme being employed.

[110] Ibid., fols 51v–52r.

[111] Carlson, *Marriage and the English Reformation*, 47.

[112] Field, 'View of Popish Abuses' in *Religion and Society*, 86.

to make thee partaker of al my worldly substance. In token wherof
I give thee this ring and with a pure and sincere hart I marry thee.[113]

Again, the pragmatic pastor is seen, guarding the peace of the church
from being broken over externals while undertaking, through words and
teaching, to reshape the meaning of the object or action.

The burial service in the Prayer Book was extremely brief. It required
the minister to meet the funeral procession and corpse at the church stile
and accompany it into church or to the grave site. The body would then
be lowered into the ground while the minister prayed. For Greenham, no
controversy attended this simple service.[114] He used it without objection,
and justified its use in language that reflected his principle of
moderation:

> hee said that whatsoever was not either flatly commanded, or
> plainly forbidden in the word, might sometimes bee used for the
> maintaining of love and some times bee left undone for the avoiding
> of superstition. And for the burial of the dead, beecaus wee read no
> prescript order of it. I thinck wee must follow the general rule, that
> is that al things bee done decently, so that ther bee neither on the one
> side a prophain casting of the body, nor on the other side any
> superstition used in the same ...[115]

Greenham seems to have had little else to say about burying the parish
dead. While he did his duty in the churchyard, he probably spent scarcely
an hour or two each year doing it, since there was an average of only two
burials each year after the 1570 mortality crisis ended. On funeral
sermons, which Field and Cartwright viewed with suspicion, Greenham's
students recorded no views, and there is no indication that he preached
any. By the time a parishioner died, Greenham might have felt that his
work was done; his time and energy were for the living.

To act 'as a man indifferent'

If Greenham himself defined his ministry as one of preaching and
administering the sacraments, he had also to accept that his parishioners
had their own expectations of his public ministry which he could ignore

---

[113] REM 524, fol. 45r.

[114] John Field and others like him objected rather limply that the service seemed to
maintain prayers for the dead. They reserved their primary objections, however, for
customs which were not part of the Prayer Book service: Cressy, *Birth, Marriage and
Death*, chap. 18.

[115] REM 524, fol. 66v. He 'could wish the place to bury the dead in some other place,
then in the church yard', but that too he accepted so long as 'it should bee kept decently
and reverently': fol. 19v.

only at his peril. The most important of these functions was to act as an arbitrator in disputes. Some clergymen based their ministry on the text that Christ came not to bring peace but a sword, and made careers out of disrupting communities at peace with their preaching and efforts to discipline the reprobate. The author and minister George Gifford, for example, believed that one indication of true godly preaching was contention, because if the word of God were truly set out, wicked men 'would storm and fret against' godly preachers.[116]

The more typical godly ministers, however, were noted for the disputes which they tried to end, not those which they provoked. Bernard Gilpin, the most famous sixteenth-century parish minister in northern England, is a good example. In the town of Rothbury, there were two factions engaged in a bitter feud. When Gilpin came to Rothbury to preach, both sides appeared and stood – armed to the teeth – in different parts of the church. Gilpin 'was somewhat moved with this unaccustomed spectacle' but went on with his sermon. The uneasy peace was soon broken, and while Gilpin was still preaching, the sides began to inch towards each other with bloody intentions. Gilpin came out of the pulpit and prevented the imminent clash, but his labours to negotiate a lasting peace failed. The two sides would only agree to remain quiet for the duration of Gilpin's time in the church. He made what use he could of that time, 'disgracing that barbarous and bloody custome of theirs'.[117] Gilpin's biographer considered this incident, in spite of the failure, to be a significant example of the character of his subject's ministry.

The minister's role as peacemaker grew naturally out of his public image, ideally at least, as 'a man indifferent'. For example, in 1602, the parishioners of Market Rasen in Lincolnshire were embroiled in a dispute between the major landowners and freeholders over common rights. One Sunday, after evening prayer, someone raised the matter in the church itself and 'divers hot intemperate speaches' followed. The minister, William Storr, 'disliking so indiscreete a course', told them to regard the place and end their bickering. He suggested that each side choose 'two or three of the fittest, and most substantiall men' to negotiate for the rest. They agreed, but 'intreated him, that he would, as a man indifferent, speake first what he thought concerning the cause'. He

[116] George Gifford, *A briefe discourse of certaine points of the religion, which is among the common sort of Christians, which may bee termed the Countrie Divinitie. With a manifest confutation of the same, after the order of a Dialogue* (London, 1582), fols 47v–48r. Gifford, coincidentally, was born and raised in Dry Drayton but had left before Greenham's arrival. (We are grateful to Michael Sekulla for information on Gifford's lineage.)

[117] George Carleton, *The Life of Bernard Gilpin, a Man Most Holy and renowned among the Northerne English* (1629), 27–8.

refused several times but was finally persuaded 'to intermeddle'. His intervention was disastrous, because it so displeased Francis Cartwright that, a few days later, the young man brutally murdered Storr.[118] The spectacular and scandalous murder is beside the point. It was the work of a deeply disturbed young man and not a typical result of ministerial peacemaking. But because it so scandalized the public, its memory was preserved in pamphlet form and we can see Storr at work as peacemaker, at first at his own initiative and then responding to the demands of his congregation. The minister's role as peacemaker was, above all, one in which he cooperated with the wishes of the laity in order to contain disputes and prevent them spilling outside the boundaries and becoming matters of litigation.

Greenham was remembered as 'a great Friend to, and promoter of Peace and Concord amongst his Neighbours and Acquaintance, insomuch that if any had come to him who were at Variance, he would either have made them friends himself, or if he could not prevail, he would have made use of other Friends to reconcile them together, thereby to prevent their going to Law'.[119] Evidence from the church courts supports this. A well-governed village solved its own problems, and use of church courts was not only as a last recourse but was also a visible sign of the villagers' failure to maintain order in their own affairs.[120] In the decades before and after Greenham's tenure, Dry Drayton was responsible for remarkably little litigation in the church courts. During his tenure that did not change. For example, the two instance cases (that is, cases in which one party sued another) were both suits brought against people from other parishes, cases in which Greenham could have little impact as a settler of conflict. Defamation cases, which were elsewhere common among neighbours, did not occur at all. Since it is unlikely that Greenham succeeded in miraculously curbing the tongues of his parishioners, this suggests that tempers were cooled and disputes settled without going to court. Notably absent is tithe litigation, the most common type of suit in the church courts. This is striking because Dry Drayton apparently had no glebe land, which made Greenham unusually dependent on tithes, and his heroic charity left the household perpetually short of money.[121] *Ex officio* cases tell a

---

[118] Anon., *The Manner of the Cruell Outragious Murther of William Storre Mast. of Art, Minister, and Preacher at Market Raisin in the County of Lincolne Committed By Francis Cartwright. one of his parishioners, the 30. day of August Anno. 1602* (Oxford, 1603), A2r.

[119] Clarke, 'Life of Master Richard Greenham', 13.

[120] Carlson, *Marriage and the English Reformation*, chap. 7.

[121] Clarke, 'Life of Master Richard Greenham', 12-13. Clarke tells of Mrs Greenham being forced to borrow money 'to get in [the] harvest', but that could refer to rented lands.

similar tale: for those same 20 years, presentments against villagers were almost unknown. The only presentments from within the parish were against one incorrigible who had put himself outside the community by refusing to respect its order and two people who had fled the parish and removed themselves from the possibility of peaceful resolution. The others resulted from problems which occurred outside Dry Drayton before the parties became denizens.[122] If Dry Drayton was not the New Jerusalem, it was none the less a well-governed and peaceable place, aided in no small measure by Greenham's passionate commitment to peace in church and state.

Conclusion

The pattern of ministry established by Greenham at Dry Drayton reflected the Bucerian commitment to foster a parish life centred around the word of God, read, preached and taught. This was the great theme of his pastoral practice and his driving passion. The obsession sent him to his study before daybreak, ensured that he was in his pulpit at dawn, and compelled him to chase after farmers in their muddy fields during the day. While the sacraments nurtured and comforted the community, Greenham treated them as teaching moments, and not experiences that conferred grace in and of themselves. Former sacramental acts, such as marriage, continued to have an important place in maintaining and sustaining order in the parish, but Greenham sought to purify and remove elements in them that might encourage or justify 'superstitious' practices. Indeed this became the other theme in Greenham's ministry, for he cautiously excised, altered and adapted practices and ceremonies to wean his parishioners from the 'false' religion of popery. Yet he did not bludgeon his people with harsh or uncompromising discipline and standards. Instead he sought to use his office in a way that fostered love, and nurtured spiritual growth and maturity in members of the community. He even avoided humiliating secret sinners through private admonitions. He mediated and maintained peace between neighbours, and conducted his ministry in a way that respected, within limits, the scruples and religious opinions of those in his charge. These attributes illustrate why his pastoral practice became a model for conformists and

---

Greenham also refused to accept fees for performing services such as marriages, baptisms and burials; instead, he had the fees paid to the parish to be used for the poor: REM 524, fol. 35v.

[122] For a discussion of these cases, See Carlson, *Marriage and the English Reformation*, 160–61.

nonconformists alike. Greenham engaged in the reinvention of parish life to suit the priorities and principles of England's new (Protestant) religion. That he achieved this goal with so little rancour and tension within Dry Drayton reflects his skill and talent as a man of peace and discretion.

Yet he accomplished so much more. His ability to heal afflicted consciences made Dry Drayton a veritable pilgrimage site for those thrown down by spiritual doubts and fears. His students recorded numerous cases of troubled souls who sought his counsel and departed at peace with God and themselves. His disciples regarded this aspect of his work as the greatest achievement of his life. While William Perkins has been credited as the founder of English Reformed casuistry, based on 'cases of conscience', contemporary testimony and the cases recorded by Greenham's students leave little doubt that Greenham was widely acknowledged to be the founder and original practitioner of what became in the seventeenth century a widely practised art.

CHAPTER SIX

The cure of afflicted consciences

From 1581 to 1584 Richard Greenham's student recorded many instances of troubled people – distressed in mind, body or spirit – who sought out the pastor of Dry Drayton for words of comfort, assurance and admonition. These encounters illustrate a religious vision filled with uncertainty and anguish, tempered by the hope and promise of profound spiritual consolation. The spiritual conflict in and around them seemed tangible and touched them personally. Greenham's achievements in 'spiritual physick'[1] rested on his ability to use the fundamental principles of a shared world-view to help his 'patients' understand their anxiety and pain. His 'experimental divinity' proved a convincing response to troubled consciences all too willing to find sin in their lives, and reluctant to claim the presence of the Holy Spirit and the working of God's grace in the midst of their troubles. While Greenham expressed frustration and sadness that few responded to the message of salvation preached,[2] his success as a spiritual physician rested on a self-selected clientele – the godly. This fact is crucial, for his ability to effect cures depended on shared assumptions about human nature, God, satanic temptation, the *loci* of authoritative teaching, and the reasons why some believe and others do not. Working out these assumptions, which will be explored in the next chapter, Greenham assessed the situation of each afflicted conscience. These took the form of physical illness, doubts about the state of one's soul, fears of things to come, and tragedies like the death of a child or a natural disaster. Considering each case in context, Greenham comforted, guided and admonished as each circumstance required.

Because of the testimony of scripture and observation of human experience, Greenham grounded his counsel on the premise that the godly do not escape affliction and trials. Indeed, these were defining moments, when the godly could be distinguished from the rest of humanity. In 1584 Greenham reportedly said:

> As when two Gentlemen ryde together in hunting, it is hard to discern each others hounds beecause they bee mingled together, which afterward is more easily done when the hunters are severed

---

[1] REM 524, fol. 8v.

[2] When discussing the value of preaching, Greenham observed, 'The lord offereth the myne of his mercy to bee devided to them, that wil but hear, and beleev it, and no man almost regardeth it'. Ibid., fol. 38r.

> even so, so long as god and the world walk as it were together, it is
> hard to distinguish between the heires of the one and of the other,
> but when they are severed by persecution, it wil surely bee seen the
> children of god and who bee the heyres of the world.[3]

Whether this involved taking a principled stand in matters of religion, enduring physical suffering, or struggling through periods of spiritual dryness, Greenham's spirituality precluded a Christian life devoid of challenges and pain. His careful observation of human experience, coupled with the principles he shared with the godly and imparted to others, resulted in a counselling style that brought many through periods of spiritual affliction to a greater assurance of their election.[4] For Greenham, the cosmic battle between God and Satan found clear expression in the afflictions of the godly. The trials they endured were diagnosed as either demonic temptation or divine purgation. In either case, the person afflicted required the assistance and guidance of godly counsel, for in the midst of these torments reason was clouded and affections proved untrustworthy.

When Satan tempted a person, the victim often forgot what he knew and this cast 'a mist before his eies that hee cannot discern and corrupteth his tast that hee cannot judg'.[5] The tempter used many different ploys to achieve this goal, but always tailored these to the weaknesses and affections of the person tempted.[6] He might cause one to mourn for spiritual benefits that were absent, or conceal blessings already received that might prove a source of thanksgiving.[7] The adversary might cause discontent with a godly calling or suggest the need to seek something new.[8] One case, recounted in the manuscript sayings, graphically illustrated the destructive power of these temptations. Greenham reportedly described how:

> A certain man afflicted in mind began through the temptation of
> Sathan to mislike his calling and chaunged it, afterward hee thought
> this calling and that calling to bee unlawful and so was almost
> brought to mislike al. Hee felt on a tyme a great pain in his leg, and
> being desirous to go from his bed to his table for booke, hee could
> not his leg remaining sore, then remembring that it was said in the
> scriptures, If thy foot offend thee cut it of,[9] hee streight way laying
> his foot on a block, and taking a hatchet in his hand stroke of his

---

[3] Ibid., fol. 58r.
[4] Ibid., fol. 23r–v.
[5] Ibid., fol. 60r. also see: fols 18v–19r.
[6] Ibid., fol. 67r–v.
[7] Ibid., fol. 57v.
[8] Ibid., fols 48v–49r.
[9] Matthew 5:29–30.

legg not feeling pain: the veynes being so torn hee could not but bleed to death. Howbeit hee died very repentantly. So dangerous a pollicy and so pleasant a temptation is it to an afflicted mind to leav our callings as things unlawful.[10]

Those who yielded to Satan's temptations, even the godly, could suffer destructive delusions. Spiritual joy made one vulnerable to 'carnal joye' and spiritual sorrows might result in 'carnal sorrowes'.[11] In 1583, Greenham reportedly reprimanded one who claimed his affliction was extraordinary. Greenham regarded this as a dangerous satanic temptation for:

You shal reason thus in yourself, that an extraordinary curs must have an extraordinary comfort, and therfore that you must look for some strange and woonderful consolation, wherby Sathan wil almost move you to contemn, or at least not so much to regard, ordinary consolations, which have helped, others, and may help you, and by this means breed in you such unthankfulnes that ere you are aware, one extraordinary affliction shalbee sent indeed.[12]

Greenham assured those who came to him that Satan's power to tempt was limited and that God did not permit the godly to be pressed beyond their ability to withstand and resist the adversary. God used Satan to show the afflicted their sins rather than to condemn them, and would always 'increas our strength and [st]retch it out according to the proportion of our temptation'.[13]

Greenham explained to those who came to him that these adversities, though painful, should be treated as an opportunity, for through them 'God scoureth away the infirmities of his sainicts'. Like the experience of the man who passed through his spiritual afflictions and enjoyed consolation and joy despite great physical pain, these trials could be redeemed and resulted in a deeper sense of God's presence.[14] These experiences were not a breach of God's covenant[15] with the godly, but crosses he allowed them to carry because of their own failings and sins.[16] Indeed, Greenham urged his hearers not to desire to depart from the furnace of affliction, 'until the lord hath purified us as pure gold for his own use'.[17] In all these cases, Greenham encouraged those troubled to use these as occasions to examine their souls, and guided them in

[10] REM 524, fol. 64r-v.
[11] Ibid., fols 2v-3r.
[12] Ibid., fols 38v-39r.
[13] Ibid., fol. 8r.
[14] Ibid., fols 64r-v.
[15] See below, 111.
[16] REM, fol. 59r.
[17] Ibid., fol. 57v.

reflections on their inward corruptions and the possible benefits God sought to make available to them through such experiences.

Greenham found in the pain of affliction and spiritual anxiety the first elements of a cure. In case after case his student reported that Greenham began with a reminder that the very fact that they sought spiritual counsel was a sign of the Holy Spirit working in their life and evidence of grace. The troubled must battle against their affliction in the name of Jesus Christ. They were not to focus on particular sins in their lives, but their disposition toward those transgressions.[18] Explaining that the elect often sin, Greenham emphasized that their transgressions were not like those of the worldly. While the wicked rested in their sins and did not repent, the godly sought 'to please god, though sometime they have a violent fit of syn'.[19] Those who came deeply troubled over particular sins received assurance that 'noe syn is so great, but in christ it is pardonable'.[20] Even the woman who was distressed by her fear that 'shee was with child with the devil', found her sin compared to those of the Apostle Paul and encouraged not to fear Satan or her sin too much and, above all, 'not [to] dout of pardon by repentance'.[21] Greenham's analysis of sin in a 'child of god' proved a complex and nuanced task, always taking into account the person's level of maturity in the Christian life, the nature of the sin, and the circumstance in which it was committed.[22] His method of counselling never allowed a penitent to depart without assurance that particular sins proved no obstacle to God's love and grace.

The tender consciences Greenham healed also came with other types of fear. Some condemned themselves for unbelief or 'dulnes of spirit'. In these cases, Greenham explained that their fears should be a source of comfort, for 'faith being the gift of god, is the most obtained or encreased of god, when you thirsting after the increas of faith, thinck that smale measure obtained to bee no faith'. While great feeling might be one means of increasing faith, another came by 'humbling ourselves before the mercy seat of god for want of our faith'.[23] Greenham reportedly likened this experience to a serious illness, explaining that just as in physical illness, 'life may bee within one, yet it cannot bee felt of the sick body', so with want of feeling, the spirit of God was present even though the graces of God seemed dead.[24] He even went so far as to assert

---

18 Ibid., fols 3v–4r.
19 Ibid., fol. 24r–v.
20 Ibid., fol. 14r.
21 Ibid., fol. 31r.
22 Ibid., fol. 27v.
23 Ibid., fol. 18r.
24 Ibid., fol. 31r.

that the greatest faith could often be found where there was least feeling.[25] Here again, Greenham used concern over spiritual affliction as a sign of God's grace and means of assurance.

In 1582 Greenham reportedly explained that sudden fears that resulted in 'troublesome thoughts' also were signs of God's favour, for they enabled the afflicted to observe the workings of the heart, and to make an 'anatomy' of God's graces at work, or the corruptions towards which the heart was prone. He found this to be his own experience and that of others. In this way God humbled the heart, and encouraged the godly to 'fear and forethinck of evils to come'.[26]

To those suffering from physical illness or personal tragedy, Greenham warned against judging their situations too harshly or too quickly. Such experiences should be welcomed as a mercy, for they kept the believer mindful of God and preserved one from the torments of hell.[27] To a 'godly man' who anguished over the sin that had caused his only son to die by drowning, Greenham explained that while God corrected sin in this tragedy, the father must not assume that he was the one being punished. Instead, Greenham offered a range of possibilities, from the correction of 'others of gods children' to the prevention of a great sin in his son's life. In any case, Greenham urged him to keep in mind that 'such outward things evils do happen, ofter to the most godly, and benefits do abound to the ungodly'. In this affliction, as in all others, Greenham encouraged the grieving father to 'stay himself on the love of god'.[28]

The first step in Greenham's remedy for afflicted consciences emphasized God's forgiveness, power to assist, and use of life's trials to guide and strengthen those who believed. While this approach reflected the practice of spiritual direction in the medieval West and was not in itself unique or innovative, in the context of Reformed English pastoral practice it took on special significance. The stress on humanity's utter corruption and inability to turn to God left the spiritually afflicted to question the state of their election when faced with sin, spiritual dryness, troubling thoughts and personal tragedies. Greenham's counsel used these crises as evidence, not of reprobation, but of God's spirit working in their lives. These afflictions provided opportunities to die to the world and draw nearer to God.[29] Sorrow and sadness for those things that separated one from God provided undeniable proof of grace working in a person's life. Peter Kaufman has effectively demonstrated that

[25] Ibid., fol. 15r.
[26] Ibid., fols 22r–23r.
[27] Ibid., fol. 63r.
[28] Ibid., fol. 41r–v.
[29] Ibid., fol. 64r.

Greenham was among the most skilled counsellors in the godly community that not only used, but also induced through the preaching and counsel, a state of despair intended to draw hearers into a greater awareness of their sins and dependence on God.[30] Yet after despair had been induced by private anxieties, preaching or counsel, troubled souls required more than comfort and reassurances. They also needed to use the 'means' that would restore 'inward joy and peace'.[31]

Greenham divided the 'means' into two categories, identifying 'reading, hearing, and confering' as the best means for increasing judgement and understanding, and 'praying, singing, and meditating' as the ideal means to 'whet up affection'.[32] While these means should be used in times of peace and prosperity, they were most needed in times of affliction, for they offered the best means of comfort and healing. Greenham reportedly explained that these were provided 'for mans help ... though our consciences told us wee used the means but in weaknes, for that the lord pardoneth our infirmities, and crowneth our sincerity in them'.[33] Perseverance in these activities drew the believer nearer to God and provided the best remedy for those afflicted.

Reading scripture, hearing sermons, and conferring with godly counsellors provided the afflicted with greater knowledge of the faith and insight into their particular afflictions and challenges. Greenham sent the afflicted to scripture because it could be used to impart the promises of God. He explained that the word of God was like seed, and though it might take time to grow after planting, it would eventually provide a harvest of consolation and healing.[34] Scripture was the standard by which all inward motions and inclinations should be judged.[35] Preaching provided great riches of knowledge and insight through the words of godly preachers.[36] The preacher could speak to the conscience of a person prepared to hear the word of God.[37] Conferring with a godly pastor or lay person opened the opportunity to have God's admonitions and promises applied to particular problems faced. During periods of affliction and despair godly counsel prevented the afflicted conscience, disoriented by temptation or sin, from misleading the person into acts of spiritual and bodily destruction.[38]

Prayer, singing and meditating prepared the affections to receive

---

[30] Kaufman, *Prayer, Despair, and Drama*, chap. 2.
[31] REM 524, fol. 8v.
[32] Ibid., fol. 3v.
[33] Ibid., fol. 36r-v.
[34] Ibid., fols 6v, 7r. Also see 35r, 36r-v, 38r.
[35] Ibid., fol. 18r-v.
[36] Ibid., fols 37v-38r.
[37] Ibid., fol. 3r.
[38] See above, 87-9.

spiritual consolation. Prayer was the essential beginning for every action of the believer. Whether one was reading or hearing the word of God, or beginning a conference with one of the godly, prayer opened the heart, not only to receive God's truth, but also to feel the Holy Spirit at work.[39] When one was tempted to unbelief, prayer made the affections ready to receive spiritual consolations.[40] In the midst of spiritual dryness the elect should persevere, offering themselves 'into the hand of Jesus Christ' and 'continue in a praier of faith though not of feeling'.[41] Greenham encouraged the singing of the psalms according to need and occasion. This proved particularly important in cases of affliction, for 'those that are most thrown down, might reap fruit in singing the Psalms of greatest comfort'.[42] Meditations, or what Greenham's student identified as 'good thoughts', framed the disposition of the mind and heart, and disposed one to respond to the Holy Spirit. These meditations, based on the word of God and life experience, drew the believer into a deeper understanding of God's work in one's life.[43]

These means were not to be used in isolation, but complemented and aided one another. The means that improved knowledge and judgement required the use of those that cultivated godly affections. In 1584 Greenham reportedly said that 'to read and not to meditate is unfruitful, to meditate and not to read is dangerous for errours, to meditate or to read without praier is hurtful'.[44] All the means worked together to improve the faith of the believer and provide instruction, correction and encouragement, especially during time of affliction.

Another element of Greenham's spiritual physic involved regular association with 'the saincts of god and holy companyes'.[45] Rejecting the company of the ungodly, remaining in a parish with a preaching ministry, reverently keeping the Sabbath day, and participating in godly exercises, fortified the believer in times of affliction and preserved the believer from despair. Greenham warned that frequenting the assemblies of the wicked risked temptation and punishment at God's hand.[46] Participation in a godly community that had recourse to a preaching ministry was essential not only to sanctification, but to one's salvation.[47] God had provided the Sabbath for the nurturing of his children. The assembly for worship and

[39] REM 524, fols 3r, 44r–v.
[40] Ibid., fol. 6v.
[41] Ibid., fol. 15v.
[42] Ibid., fols 33v–34r.
[43] Ibid., fols 4v, 6r–v, 9v–10r, 13r, 21v, 22r, 25r, 37r.
[44] Ibid., fol. 63r.
[45] Ibid., fol. 8v.
[46] Ibid., fol. 2v.
[47] See below, 106–7, and above, 59–60. Also see: fol. 48v–49r.

preaching, as well as the time to reflect with others on the truth imparted within one's family or around the preacher's table, proved an essential means for preserving the godly and healing them in times of affliction.[48] Greenham also encouraged the use of godly exercises during the weekdays, so long as they did not unduly interfere with a person's ordinary calling.[49]

The last feature of Greenham's prescription, though apparently mundane, reflected his appreciation that spiritual healing could not be separated from care of the body. He emphasized that the cure of afflicted consciences required that the troubled avail themselves of 'kitching [kitchen] Physick and a thankful using of the creatures of god'.[50] Denouncing preachers who inveighed against the body as the enemy of the soul, Greenham reportedly stressed that 'wee had need rather to nourish the body, as the frind to the soule for the exercise of repentance, of mortification and sanctification'.[51] For this reason, Greenham's student recorded sayings that dealt with diet, the prudent use of strong drink for medicinal purposes, and ways of restoring the body during periods of bodily and spiritual suffering.[52] Moderation in the use of the 'creatures of god' proved a consistent theme in Greenham's advice. The rules he set for his wife's diet tied this principle to the health of her soul: 'Bee moderate in things most which the appetite liketh of most, and check the too much greedines of an earthly thing, and you shal find this to bee a good physick to the body and an wholesome preservation for the soule'.[53] When confronted with an angry or irritable person, Greenham reportedly prescribed – not a spiritual cure – but food instead. His student noted that 'hee would often provoke one inflamed with cholar to eat, beecaus hee observed by experience, that abstinence nourisheth cholar, and a moderate receiving of gods gifts, alayed it'.[54] This emphasis on moderation and sensible use of food, drink and medicaments that would refresh the body and aid in the healing of the soul illustrates how practical Greenham's 'experimental divinity' could be. Never one to isolate the body from the spirit, Greenham looked at the whole situation of those who came to him and provided means of healing as person, place and circumstance required.

---

[48] See below: *A large Treatise of the Sabbath*, 299–327. Also see: fol. 39v. For an overview of issues related to Sabbath observance see: Kenneth L. Parker, *The English Sabbath: A Study of Doctrine and Discipline from the Reformation to the Civil War* (Cambridge: Cambridge University Press, 1988).

[49] REM 524, fol. 23v.

[50] Ibid., fol. 8v.

[51] Ibid., fol. 20v.

[52] Ibid., fols 9v, 21v, 28r-v, 37v.

[53] Ibid., fol. 38r.

[54] Ibid., fol. 28r.

When Henry Holland commended Greenham's skill in the 'unknowne facultie' of curing afflicted consciences,[55] he offered Greenham's works as an answer to a deeply felt need of the period. The world-view that resulted from Reformed Elizabethan religion had unexpected consequences and produced extreme and troubling cases of personal anxiety which sometimes resulted in a deeper sense of religious insight, and at other times resulted in physical or emotional destruction. Greenham's ability to use the metaphysical and theological assumptions of the godly, mixed with a talent for assessing persons in distress, made his work with afflicted consciences paradigmatic as Reformed casuistry in the late Elizabethan period developed. While a prolific publisher like Perkins is normally credited with the origins of this casuistic tradition,[56] it should not escape notice that the most renowned practitioners of this skill in the next generation, Arthur Hildersham, Richard Rogers, Henry Smith and others, received their first formation in this 'facultie' at Dry Drayton.[57]

A growing body of scholarship explores the phenomenon of anxiety and despair in Elizabethan culture.[58] While this preoccupation is often identified as a defining feature of the godly, there is a growing awareness that it transcended the ecclesiological and theological divides of early modern European Christianity.[59] That Greenham proved a skilful physician to the afflicted within the godly community of the English Church testified to his appreciation that faith was more than theological formulations or academic debates concerning orthodox belief. Ever conscious of the spiritual battles being waged all around him, Greenham's efforts to bring 'true religion' to all those God had chosen for his own proved his chief calling in life. Assisting them through the temptations and tribulations of this life provided the principal focus of his ministry. Greenham, like Perkins and others, found in these periods

---

55 First Edition, A5r.

56 James Keenan, 'William Perkins (1558-1602) and the Birth of British Casuistry', in James Keenan and Thomas Shannon (eds), *The Context of Casuistry* (Washington, DC: Georgetown University Press, 1995), 103-30; Ian Breward, 'William Perkins and the Origins of Reformed Casuistry', *Evangelical Quarterly*, 40.1 (January-March 1968), 3-20.

57 See above, 19-20.

58 Recent examples include: Kaufman, *Prayer, Depair, and Drama*; John Stachniewski, *The Persecutory Imagination: English Puritanism and the Literature of Religious Despair* (Oxford: Clarendon Press, 1991); Charles Cohen, *God's Caress: The Psychology of Puritan Religious Experience* (New York: Oxford University Press, 1986); Martha Tuck Rozett, *The Doctrine of Election and the Emergence of Elizabethan Tragedy* (Princeton, NJ: Princeton University Press, 1984).

59 Kaufman, *Prayer, Depair, and Drama*, 9-11.

of affliction the great moments of the Christian's life.[60] As he reportedly explained in 1582,

> Being with one afflicted in body and mind, unto whom the lord had shewed many tokens of salvation, fruitfully to sanctify the present afflictions, hee said, I fear not the tyme of the visitation of them, that therby do grow in the gifts and graces of god but rather, I fear, the tyme of ther deliverance, should bee overtaken with unthankfulnes, and so woefully they should loose the fruit of that good, which they so dearly purchased of the lord.[61]

Greenham's experimental divinity did not seek to minimize or remove the problem of afflicted conscience; rather he used it as the chief tool to drive those who came to him toward a deeper commitment to God. Final victory over the adversary could not be achieved in this life. Right responses to trials and afflictions marked out the godly and gave them assurance of their election and God's love. This approach, which began with the lived experience of spiritual anxiety, followed by the appropriation of the promises of God and the application of the means of salvation, illustrates Greenham's profound understanding of human experience in his time and place, and his skill in applying the Reformed vision of reality to particular situations.

---

[60] Ibid., especially 17–26, and chap. 2; Cohen, *God's Caress*, 183–4.
[61] REM fol. 15r.

CHAPTER SEVEN

The theological foundations of Greenham's cure of afflicted consciences

Commending Richard Greenham to readers of the *Works*, Henry Holland presented him as the master of a previously 'unknowne facultie' – the cure of afflicted consciences. Greenham achieved his cures by observation of 'cases of conscience' and personal identification with the spiritual affliction of those who suffered. Explaining the difficulty of this practice Holland observed,

> The godly learned know it is a matter far more difficult to judge what secret causes breede the hidden distemper of the soule: and here it is farre more dangerous to proceed only by experience, without art and skill. And here we must as carefully respect all occasions and circumstances of time, place, and persons: *For a word spoken in due time, is like an apple of golde with pictures of silver*: so the contrary, unseasonable and impertinent speeches be most dangerous.[1]

The 'facultie' described here does not reflect the labours commonly associated with 'dogmatic' or 'systematic' theology, with its prescriptive-normative orientation. Greenham's theological reflection employed a descriptive–critical approach that his contemporaries identified as 'practical' or 'experimental' divinity.[2] Taking each case as he found it, Greenham sought to understand the circumstance or person he encountered, and applied his understanding of human experience and the Christian faith in assessing the problem and achieving a solution or cure.[3] Bishop Corbett, no friend of the godly, noted that while Perkins's approach often induced despair, Greenham's

---

[1] First Edition, A4v–A5r. The proverb used is found in Proverbs 25:11.

[2] Much of what follows is influenced by current debates concerning spirituality as a subject of academic research and study. Greenham's sayings and his other published works reflect the concerns and priorities commonly associated with works of spirituality. For examples of the exploration of spirituality as an academic discipline see: Sandra M. Schneiders, 'Spirituality in the Academy', *Theological Studies*, 50 (1989), 676–97; Walter Principe, 'Toward Defining Spirituality', *Studies in Religion/Science Religieuses*, 12.2 (Spring, 1983), 127–41; Philip Sheldrake, *Spirituality and History: Questions of Interpretation and Method* (New York: Crossroads, 1992).

[3] REM 524, fol. 33v.

works proved a comfort and cure for afflicted consciences.[4]

Greenham and those to whom he ministered functioned within a commonly held vision of reality that not only gave definition to the spiritual maladies experienced, but also proved the essential starting-point in effecting a cure. Understanding Greenham's ministry to afflicted consciences requires that a larger set of metaphysical[5] assumptions be explored. We must recognize how Greenham perceived human nature, God and Satan. His distinctions between true religion and false religious practices must also be examined, as well as his beliefs concerning the *locus* of authority and authoritative teaching in religious matters. Finally, the vital question of who is saved – and why – must be carefully considered. Only then can we gain a clearer understanding of how Greenham ministered so effectively to those afflicted in mind about the state of their soul.[6]

Prolegomena

Responding to these questions raises complex problems of historical context, the nature of the evidence available, and the critical–analytical stance of the scholar with regard to the person and religious tradition being examined. Having already explored the historical context of Greenham's ministry and considered the literary nature of the sayings, we must reflect on the presuppositions scholars bring to the task of analysing the practical divinity of a historical figure like Richard Greenham. Margo Todd has warned that these assumptions can lead to 'unconscionably distorting the past', and reflect 'the inadequate

---

[4] *Poems of Richard Corbett*, 58.

[5] This term is not being used here in its classic theological sense. Rather, it refers to any set of assumptions that provide a framework for ordering and interpreting human experience.

[6] Carlos Eire has stressed that the study of theological reflection that starts with human experience requires a close examination of 'the concept of reality that informs any given experience'. In order to analyse the cognitive structures of these experiences (either personal or communal), scholars must identify the epistemological (and metaphysical) assumptions that form the foundation of a truth system. How does that system define God and creation, or the interaction between the divine and humanity? What types of experiences receive attention? What characterizes occasions of self-transcendence? What is the relationship between these experiences and the development of the doxa of the community? In what ways does an accepted belief 'determine' a given experience, and how does experience influence and alter the doxa of a community? Carlos M.N. Eire, 'Major Problems in the Definition of Spirituality as an Academic Discipline', in Bradley C. Hanson (ed.), *Modern Christian Spirituality: Methodological and Historical Essays* (Atlanta, GA: Scholars Press, 1990), 53-61; esp. 58.

perspective of historians on subjects to whom they unabashedly condescend, and whom they are more willing to caricature than to try fully to understand'.[7] If Richard Greenham's 'experimental' divinity is to be understood, the 'otherness' of his world-view must first be acknowledged.

This task is further complicated by the layers of conflicting historiographical and theological models scholars bring to the subject. Assumptions about early modern English religion, politics, economics and society shape the questions asked and guide the selection of evidence. Greenham has been cited by scholars as the minister who established the first 'model Puritan parish',[8] a parish made famous in 'Puritan circles' for two decades by his presence.[9] His ministry has been characterized as subversive, as an attempt to accomplish through the pulpit and by life example what could not be imposed 'by direct control over the establishment'.[10] At least one scholar has used him as the pre-eminent example of the failure of 'Protestant' ministry, despite the most conscientious of efforts.[11] Greenham's theology has been labelled a mixture of Calvinist and Bezean ideas by one scholar,[12] and a system of theological reflection imbued with Lutheran principles by another.[13] While these models provide important scholarly shorthands, they may also distort Greenham's priorities and principles in precisely the ways that Professor Todd warns against.

The limits and difficulties of the sources available for this task must also be appreciated. Greenham's reflections are known primarily through sayings collected by young university men who received training in pastoral ministry at Dry Drayton during the 1570s and 1580s, and sermons and meditations reconstructed from the notes of lay and clerical hearers. These works come to us through the filter of others who recorded and edited his thoughts. This fact makes the ideas found in the sayings a fascinating reflection of a community of faith, but require discretion on the part of scholars who wish to analyse and isolate the 'theology' of Richard Greenham.

---

7 Todd, 'Puritan Self-Fashioning', 58.

8 Spufford, *Contrasting Communities*, 51–2.

9 M.M. Knappen, *Tudor Puritanism: A Chapter in the History of Idealism* (Chicago, IL: University of Chicago Press, 1939), 382.

10 William Haller, *The Rise of Puritanism* (1938; reprint, Philadelphia, PA: University of Pennsylvania Press, 1972), 47–8.

11 Christopher Haigh, 'The Continuity of Catholicism in the English Reformation', in Christopher Haigh (ed.), *The English Reformation Revised* (Cambridge: Cambridge University Press, 1987), 178 n.8.

12 Kendall, *Calvin and English Calvinism*, 46.

13 John H. Primus, 'Lutheran Law and Gospel in the Early Puritan Theology of Richard Greenham', *Lutheran Quarterly*, new series 8 (1994): 287–98.

Only when we encounter these texts with an awareness of our own cultural and 'metaphysical' stance, the scholarly models we have inherited, and the 'voice' that we 'hear' in these works can we begin to appreciate the rich significance of Greenham's sayings and other 'writings'. These texts do not reflect a world marked by 'Puritan' and 'Anglican' theology and church practice. Instead they mark out a world-view that was anti-papist, and concerned with 'true religion' and 'right practice'. They reflect the experience of a pastor focused on parochial religion. The issues and questions addressed in these works illustrate the concerns of young university men preparing to construct a new religious ethos in rural parishes befuddled by three decades of uncertainty about religious practice and norms. Considered in this light Greenham's example becomes more interesting and engaging, but more difficult to squeeze within the established parameters of conventional historical and theological discourse. Indeed, we may find that his example opens up new vistas for scholarly investigation, toward the study of how new patterns of ministry and altered forms of parochial life were cultivated in the first decades of Elizabeth's reign.

In attempting to construct a description of his praxis-oriented theology, we must be specific about the parameters of the study and the goals to be achieved. First, the description found in this chapter will be limited to the sayings recorded between 1581 and 1584. While they are not received directly from Greenham and reflect what was 'heard' rather than what was 'said', they are time-limited and illustrate an ethos that his student recorder recognized as the authentic doxa and praxis of the godly in the early 1580s. Second, this chapter will attempt to reconstruct basic elements of Greenham's religious world-view, and locate these in the context of the theological ideas of the period. The sayings are particularly useful for this purpose, because they reflect a lived application of religious principles, and not a 'learned' treatise influenced by established formulae and summaries of doctrines. Third, by limiting our focus to afflicted consciences, this chapter will illustrate how the basic elements of the religious world-view of the godly shaped the experience of Greenham and the afflicted who came to him with their fears and anxieties, and how Greenham applied this understanding of human experience to provide comfort and assurance, as well as strategies for achieving deliverance from spiritual despair.

Human nature, God and Satan

In his rural parish near Cambridge, Richard Greenham observed the cosmic spiritual battle between God and Satan. These two adversaries and their armies of angels and devils struggled for the souls of those under his care and for the fate of the English people. The tangible nature of this conflict, as described earlier in cases of afflicted conscience, formed the essential foundation on which Greenham's reflections rested. Greenham lived in a theocentric universe, yet the questions he addressed reflected a decidedly anthropocentric world-view.[14] His understanding of human nature, God and Satan not only shaped his explanation of why things are the way they are but also his view of how things should be. The spiritual system within which he functioned grew out of assumptions concerning the corruption of human nature, God's omnipotence and Satan's efforts to mislead and destroy.

Human corruption and weakness marked the essential starting-point of Greenham's spiritual counsel. Men and women could do nothing good or meritorious of their own effort, nor was the evil that they did of their own initiative, for human nature was utterly corrupt and predisposed to evil.[15] Caught in the conflict between God and Satan, humanity lived on the front lines of their battle. Human actions demonstrated allegiance to God or the adversary.

Salvation and all good human actions had their source in God.[16] This was possible because of Jesus Christ's work on the cross, so that those who believed lived under grace that saved.[17] Believers 'serveth christ as a conqueror to pul us out from under the burden of sin, and to rescue us from the clawes of sathan, when our sins and infirmities beat us down'.[18] God proved merciful in his corrections, pardoned infirmities and rewarded sincerity.[19] He warned those who displeased him and comforted those who grieved and sorrowed.[20]

God punished and corrected sin, but he did not treat sins equally. A sinner's disposition and reaction to transgressions proved more important than particular sins. Greenham reportedly explained in 1581 that 'the lord doth not so verily punish particular deserts but general fallings into sin, not smal infirmities, but grosser presumptions: for the particular sin bringeth not wrath, but the lying in that sin, and not repenting of it bringeth wrath which drawing in other sins withal

---

[14] James Keenan and Ian Breward have also noted this anthropocentrism in the theological works of William Perkins. James Keenan, 'William Perkins (1558-1602) and the Birth of British Casuistry', 113; Ian Breward, 'William Perkins and the Origins of Reformed Casuistry', 14.

[15] REM 524, fols 6v–7v, 20r, 21r, 29r–v.

[16] Ibid., fols 6v–7v, 8r–v, 12v, 19r, 24v, 35r.

[17] Ibid., fols 29r–v, 31r–v.

[18] Ibid., fol. 29r–v.

[19] Ibid., fols 36r–v, 52v–53r.

[20] Ibid., fols 35v, 60r, 64v.

draweth in also gods displeasure'.[21] God judged the public and private sins of persons, communities and nations and warned, tried and punished those who disobeyed.[22]

Satan was God's adversary and their battleground was the plane of human existence.[23] Satan was not a horned and clawed caricature to be mocked or ignored, but a 'secret adversary and spiritual tempter' who enticed men and women to reject God's will and pursue ways that led to destruction.[24] As God had his hosts of good angels, Satan had his host of evil angels who sought to influence people's lives.[25] These evil spirits could possess people and even tempt women to conceive with them.[26] Satan's chief weapon was to conceal from men and women the benefits of Christ and entice them to reject God.[27]

Satan's role as tempter was the central theme in all discussions about him.[28] Through scripture and experience his policies and devices could be known.[29] His methods varied according to each individual, attacking people in their weakness; for as Greenham reportedly concluded, 'Sathan so abuseth a mans weaknes that it is easy for a man to deceiv himself in it.'[30] Some he encouraged to make excuses for not doing good or to do small evils without fear. Greenham noted this problem in himself, observing 'that when hee would not do a thing that was good then his own reason and the devil would easily teach him an excuse'.[31] Others he misled through the affections, taking advantage of sorrow, encouraging immoderate feelings, and tempting to despair.[32] Satan not only enticed through ignorance, but also used good desires and the pursuit of truth to deceive and mislead.[33] As in the case of the man who chopped off his leg, the adversary often used discontent or complacency, and through these and other means clouded human judgement.[34]

Those who actively sought God and desired to do God's will did not escape Satan's attempts to snare and entrap. If he could not tempt the

---

[21] Ibid., fols 3v–4r. Also see: fol. 33v.
[22] Ibid., fols 28v–29r, 37r, 41r–v, 44r–v, 47r, 57v–58r, 58v–59r, 60v, 60v–61r, 63r, 64r, 67r.
[23] Ibid., fols 6v–7v.
[24] Ibid., fol. 54r.
[25] Ibid., fol. 49v.
[26] Ibid., fols 10v, 31r–v.
[27] Ibid., fol. 29r–v.
[28] Ibid., fols 21r, 38v–39r, 44v–45r, 64r–v.
[29] Ibid., fols 8r, 24r, 31r–v, 35r–v, 50r.
[30] Ibid., fol. 25r. Also see fol. 67r–v.
[31] Ibid., fol. 65v. Also see fol. 62r.
[32] Ibid., fols 24r–v, 50r, 63v.
[33] Ibid., fols 18v–19r, 45v.
[34] Ibid., fols 64r–v, 58v–59r, 60r.

believer to resist or leave the calling God had given,[35] Satan might attempt to misdirect the conscience and entice the believer to mix spiritual affections with carnal feelings.[36] Greenham reportedly observed that 'Sathan is most ready to make us most unwilling unto that wherin the lord wil most use us to the good of his church'.[37] Satan might thus encourage the godly to focus on smaller sins to distract them from much greater and more serious evils in their lives.[38] He could mislead with a lack of feeling or a fear to speak the truth when it was needed.[39] When all else failed, he might encourage the godly to a lack of moderation in spiritual matters, and through this discredit the godly with the charge of excessive zeal.[40] Greenham found this intemperance expressed in the way some argued for strict Sabbath practice. In 1583 he reportedly observed that,

> When Sathan would not discredit the word by some ordinary shifts, hee would cause men to use reaching, and excessive speaches to discredit the same, which do somuch the more harm, beecaus they commonly passe in zeal and are afforded for a principal mean to credit the truth. As for example, when a man shal say it is as great a sin to boute ['boat'] on the sabbath, as to murther ones father ...[41]

Satan's ceaseless efforts to deceive did not mean that he had an absolute power to tempt human beings. God gave strength to believers, enabling them to resist whatever trials Satan set for the children of God.[42] As the experience of Job demonstrated, Satan was nothing more than a vassal of God; and so the believer might appeal directly to God for preservation and protection from the worst that Satan could inflict.[43] Satan's efforts could ultimately be confounded by the prayers of the faithful.[44]

Many aspects of the metaphysical assumptions described above concerning God and Satan were shared with the dominant Western theological traditions of the ancient and medieval periods. In these matters Greenham reflected the consensus found among Christian humanists, Protestant and Catholic, of the sixteenth century. Yet Greenham's understanding of human nature was decidedly more pessimistic than that of medieval theologians and Catholic thought of the

---

[35] Ibid., fols 48v–49r, 60v, 61r.
[36] Ibid., fols 2v–3r.
[37] Ibid., fol. 61r.
[38] Ibid., fol. 17v.
[39] Ibid., fols 18v–19r, 43v.
[40] Ibid., fols 24r–v, 48r–v.
[41] Ibid., fols 48r–v.
[42] Ibid., fols 8r–v.
[43] Ibid., fols 31r–v.
[44] Ibid., fol. 47r.

sixteenth century. While scholastic theologians taught that the conscience[45] had not been utterly corrupted by the fall, the Greenham sayings leave no doubt that he taught, with other Reformed theologians, that the conscience only had sufficient knowledge of God to render human beings inexcusable.[46]

Greenham's understanding of humanity as utterly corrupt, with no inherent ability to turn to God apart from grace, brought the dichotomous conflict of his spiritual universe into the realm of human experience. His experience in ministry reinforced this radical division between those who served God and those seduced by the adversary. For this reason Greenham's sayings contain the recurring themes of true and false religion, and the distinction between the godly and those who reject God's will. A clearer appreciation of these distinctions will enhance our understanding of his skill in healing afflicted consciences.

True and false religion

This brief saying, recorded in 1582, is the only contemporary evidence concerning Greenham's early life:

> Hee said that being a child in Q Maries daies, hee conceived on a tyme a liking of that religion, which was true, and taught of god, why that should bee the purest religion, in so much that it wrought, in that means, upon him, as hee never had any delight in outward things.[47]

It offers more than a fleeting glimpse at Greenham's youth; it provides a key to understanding his vision of the Christian faith. Greenham knew Mary Tudor's reign first hand. He did not require John Foxe's *Acts and Monuments* to shape his memory of the choices English Protestants made and the consequences experienced by some. As Margo Todd has described with reference to Samuel Ward, this was Greenham's period of 'self-fashioning'.[48] Unlike the early 1580s, with the complexities and

---

[45] Understood here as *synteresis*, or inborn knowledge of the primary principles of moral action.

[46] Breward, 'William Perkins and the Origins of Reformed Casuistry', 13–14; Thomas Aquinas, *Summa Theologica* (London, 1920–25), I.q 79. a 13. ad 1–3; William Perkins, *Workes* (3 vols, London, 1626–31), III, 173. For further discussion of this matter, see below, 112–15.

[47] Ibid., fol. 16v.

[48] During the 1540s and 1550s, the dramatic changes in religious practice required that a self-reflective person 'define himself' and design a religious identity. Greenblatt and others assert that this was a distinctive feature of the Renaissance. Todd, 'Puritan Self-Fashioning', 60; Greenblatt, *Renaissance Self-Fashioning*, 1–2. The work of self-fashioning involved the assimilation of a subjectivity with which one chose to identify.

ambiguities of Elizabethan Protestant experience, 'Q Maries daies' marked the period of his youthful choice between true and false religion. He understood the decision in starkly dualistic terms, and knew himself to be blessed, having been drawn to the religion that was 'true', 'taught of god', 'the purest religion', that fostered in the believer no 'delight in outward things'.[49]

Implicit in this saying are themes explored throughout Greenham's theological reflections. He did not boast of his own insights or youthful wisdom, but acknowledged providential guidance in a period when a choice for 'false religion' might have been expected. He located authoritative teaching not in any earthly intermediary, but in the word of God. Identifying his understanding of Christianity as the 'purest religion', he gave priority to a Christian practice that focused on interior transformation, not external forms and practices.

While this saying referred to the Catholic practice of Mary Tudor's period, and indirectly associated it with the 'false religion' of Elizabethan recusants, the themes outlined also suggest an implicit critique of any practice that diverted attention to outward things. In 1582, to speak of 'true religion', 'taught by god', that was purified of 'outward things' would have conjured more recent memories in the minds of his students. His rejection of 'outward things' would have been associated not only with the popish ceremonies and adornments of Queen Mary's era, but also with Greenham's refusal to use the surplice, his concerns over certain liturgical forms prescribed by the Prayer Book, and other issues that marked his efforts to introduce 'true religion' at Dry Drayton.[50] This distinction between 'true' and 'false' religion, and how he defined each, is essential to understanding Greenham's experimental divinity.

Greenham defined false religion as external observances and superstitious beliefs that did not lead to interior transformation. Acknowledging the original value of many rites and rituals, such as the churching of women and the use of chrisms, these nevertheless had been corrupted and abused as mere external practices, not as a means of drawing the faithful together for prayer and thanksgiving.[51] Use of the sign of the cross at baptism proved a particular concern; for ignorant people were encouraged by the adversary to apply a corrupt logic,

---

This point is intriguing when considered along with the concept of 'framing' found in humanist pedagogy and the sixteenth-century commonplace tradition. Greenham reportedly observed that the task in his rectory seminary consisted of drawing students 'out of the university, to bee framed in like manner fit for the work of the lord' (REM 524, fol. 57v).

[49] Ibid., fol. 16v.
[50] See above, 15–16.
[51] REM 524, fols 35v–36r.

reasoning that since it was permitted at baptism one might use it when preparing to pray.[52] Representative of false religion were people who 'would hear a man willingly in the church and gainsay his doctrine at home wherin they be[t]raied rather that they h[e]ard for solemnity of the place then of any devotion'.[53] Reverencing things, such as churches, and rejecting true teaching provided in sermons, proved distinctive signs of 'false religion' for Greenham.

Yet the danger of false religion did not end with rejection of popish practices. Greenham reportedly expressed concern that many, having been freed from 'the gulf of superstition', were 'too far plagued and swallowed up of prophaines, thincking either that ther is no god or els that hee is not so fearful and merciful as his threatnings and promise commend him to bee'.[54] Having rejected belief in a devil with horns, claws and a hollow voice, Greenham observed that many had no regard for Satan and the threat he posed as a spiritual tempter.[55] This disregard of God and Satan led to great calamity, resulting in spiritual and temporal destruction.

In 1584 Greenham's student recorded the story of one whose life spun out of control after rejecting papistical teaching. Not satisfied with the religion of Protestants, he became familiar with the doctrine of the Family of Love, and through their teaching became an atheist. Doubtful that heaven or hell existed, he decided to grab pleasure where he could, stole a horse, was captured, and condemned to die. Despite valiant attempts by godly ministers to bring him to conversion, he persisted in atheism until his execution day. As he ascended the ladder to die, he turned to the crowd and cried, 'wel let the world say, what they wil: doubtles ther is a god, and the same god is just for ever to his enemies, and everlastingly keeping his mercies with his children ...'. This affirmation of true religion from the mouth of an enemy of God illustrated the consequences of resting in false religion or rejecting the claims of truth.[56] For Greenham there was no middle ground.

Greenham's anti-papist attitudes reflected a general Elizabethan

---

52 Ibid., fol. 25r. Also see: fols 55v–56r.
53 Ibid., fol. 4r.
54 Ibid., fol. 9r.
55 Ibid., fol. 54r.
56 Ibid., fols 56v–57r. For further discussions of last speeches at executions see: Lake, '"A Charitable Christian Hatred": The Godly and their Enemies in the 1630s', especially 145–50; J. Sharpe '"Last Dying Speeches": Religion, Ideology and Public Execution in Seventeenth Century England', *Past and Present*, 107 (1985), 144–67; Peter Lake, 'Deeds Against Nature: Cheap Print, Protestantism and Murder in Early Seventeenth-Century England' in Kevin Sharpe and Peter Lake (eds), *Culture and Politics in Early Stuart England* (Stanford, CA: Stanford University Press, 1993), 257–83.

Protestant conviction that Catholicism represented the essence of false religion. This sentiment proved so strong that it became a defining feature of English nationhood.[57] As has been noted earlier, Greenham proved a valued ally to Bishop Cox in the church's assault on papists and heretics.[58] His concern over lingering 'superstitious' attitudes and practices also proved a distinguishing Protestant characteristic, although the definition of these problems varied widely. Carlos Eire has observed that 'one person's spirituality could be another's superstition'.[59] While Greenham's denunciation of popish superstitions as false religion corresponded with the prevailing Protestant ethos, his modification or rejection of ceremonies and practices permitted by the Prayer Book[60] reflected concerns associated with the godly, who strove for a more thorough reformation of the English Church.[61] His impression that the laity used the Prayer Book to defend lingering papist practices and attitudes was shared by others.[62] His fear that confusion in religion would lead to atheism reflected an anxiety so common among the hotter sort of Protestant that George Gifford gave the name 'Atheos' to the protagonist of his *Country Divinity*.[63]

Greenham's construction of false religion corresponded in a broad sense with the views of any conforming Elizabethan Protestant- false religion was that practised by those who were loyal to the anti-Christian Bishop of Rome. His more particular concerns over popish residue in the life of the English Church marked him as one of the godly. Yet if the religion of Rome was false, and the Prayer Book could not be trusted in all its rites and rubrics, two questions arose: Where was 'true religion' to be found? How was it to be appropriated and practised?

God communicated truth through the written and spoken word.

---

[57] The diverse range of theologians, bishops and nonconformists who expressed anti-papist sentiments illustrates the broad base for this defining feature of English Protestantism. See: Patrick Collinson, *The Birthpangs of Protestant England* (London: Macmillan Press, 1988), 10; Lake, *Moderate Puritans*, 6, 55-76, 93-115; Dewey D. Wallace, Jr, *Puritans and Predestination: Grace in English Protestant Theology* (Chapel Hill, NC: The University of North Carolina Press, 1982), 61-5.

[58] See above, 17-21.

[59] Eire, 'Major Problems in the Definition of Spirituality', 59.

[60] See above, 21, 24-5, 72-4.

[61] Yet even Greenham encountered in his ministry some more scrupulous than himself. Following the lead of Bishop Cox, he permitted silence and avoided confrontation when it touched matters that he did not regard as vital to salvation and the well-being of souls. See above, 73; Eamon Duffy, *The Stripping of the Altars* (New Haven, CT: Yale University Press, 1992), 588-91.

[62] Duffy, *Stripping of the Altars*, 590-91; Gifford, *Countrie Divinitie*, 2-3.

[63] Ibid., *passim*.

Greenham's 'true religion' rested on the premise that sacred scripture, preaching and the counsel of godly ministers and lay people were the normal means of authoritative teaching provided by God. The dramatic shift from ritual and symbol, which characterized medieval Christian practice,[64] to text and word was Greenham's essential starting-point for locating the *ecclesia docens* – the teaching church. Within Greenham's circle of influence, a parish that did not enjoy the benefits of scripture reading, preaching, and the guidance of a godly pastor was no church at all. In October 1581, Greenham reportedly observed that he had often been sought out to 'plant a church' elsewhere. This did not refer to the creation of a separatist congregation in England or abroad, but the establishment of a ministry that provided the word of God read, preached, and mediated through godly counsel in another English parish.[65] These constituted 'the word of god' for Greenham, and it is sometimes difficult to determine, except by context, which one was being described.

God provided sacred scripture to help men and women in their need, to instruct, warn, comfort and encourage.[66] The Bible was distinguished from the esteemed works of Calvin, Beza and others because scripture constituted 'the writings of the holy ghost'.[67] Important truths about human experience and God's promises found clear expression in the Bible.[68] It could be a source of comfort to the faithful in distress, a guide in decisionmaking, and a means of testing 'inward motions'.[69]

Since the time Christ appointed simple fishermen to preach the gospel, God had used preaching to increase love of the truth.[70] Preaching was nothing less than the ordinary means of conveying God's truth, and the most effective means of leading hearers to Christ. Exploring biblical texts that called hearers to consider their salvation was the essential task of preaching.[71] In 1582 Greenham reportedly stated that through preaching 'I drive men out of themselves and send them to christ if they wil, but if they refuse they go worthily to hel: and so to whom hee could not bee the messenger of salvation for ther unbeleef, unto them hee was an

---

[64] Duffy, *Stripping of the Altars, passim.*

[65] REM 524, fol. 2r. We are grateful to Professor Collinson for his insights on this subject.

[66] Ibid., fol. 36r-v.

[67] Greenham did not include the Apochrypha in the canon, asserting that 'the jewes did esteem them as the Papists did the old schoolemen, or as wee do Calvin or Beza, and therfore by continuance of tyme they were corruptly and unadvisedly joyned to the Canonical scriptures'. Ibid., fol. 66r.

[68] Ibid., fols 35r, 6v.

[69] Ibid., fols 69r, 9r, 18r-v.

[70] Ibid., fol. 1r.

[71] For example, ibid., fol. 45v. See above, 61-2.

instrument of condemnation prepared for them'.[72] As a preacher, he experienced the movement of the spirit of God so intensely that he reported at times hearing 'as it were sensibly a voice' that spoke words of guidance, warning or reproof.[73] The preacher became a vessel from which God's truth flowed. While Greenham freely acknowledged the variable quality of preaching,[74] he consistently impressed on his hearers that those who preached were bearers of 'gods word'.[75] While some focused on the humanity of the messenger, Greenham insisted on the divine source of the message. In 1583 he reportedly stated,

> The sitting of one houre receiveth a fruit unto immortality. for howsoever men thinck the ministers of god to speak even whatsoever commeth into ther mouths, it is not so, they speak that, which many years they have studied for, which earnestly they have prayed for, which by woful experience they have bought, and by a painful life dearily paied for. If a prince should give out by portion a myne of money for the fetching, who would spare to go. The lord offereth the myne of his mercy to bee devided to them, that wil but hear, and beleev it, and no man almost regardeth it.[76]

He discouraged lay people from leaving a parish with preaching for a community without a preaching ministry, warning that to do so would endanger their salvation.[77] For Greenham, preaching followed very closely behind the canonical scriptures as the best means of receiving the truth God entrusted to humanity.

The godly counsel of clergy and lay people constituted a third source of truth for Greenham. For the minister, as shown above, godly counsel was in no way inferior to preaching.[78] Though counsel was variable and dependent on the abilities and spiritual maturity given to each person, every godly member of the parish could serve as an instrument of divine wisdom. He considered it 'an unchristian courtesy' (probably meaning a remnant of popish reverence for the person of the priest) that lay people should always defer to the preacher in spiritual matters, 'seing they were annointed with the same spirit, though not with the like measure of like graces'. In 1582 he reportedly urged everyone at table,

> By praier to offer ther speaches to god, and to use them advisedly reverently, and not passing the bounds of ther knowledge, and if they would not speak of any thing, yet they should aske somthing:

---

[72] Ibid., fol. 7v. Also see fol. 35r.
[73] Ibid., fol. 11r.
[74] Ibid., fol. 6r-v.
[75] Ibid., fol. 35r.
[76] Ibid., fols 37v–38r.
[77] Ibid., fol. 51.
[78] See above, 67–9.

> if they could not ask, yet they should speake of the Communion of
> saincts: if they cold say nothing yet at least they should complain of
> ther dul minds, which is a punished mind and even of ther dulnes
> and deadnes should rayse quicknes and life of speach again.[79]

Every member of the godly community had a role to play in
communicating God's will, from the learned and articulate preacher to
the most confused of the laity. For Greenham, 'every man had a special
gift or word or oath and that therfore yee would wish men to search
them selves to that god that hath called them and to use it in prayer'.[80]
Indeed in certain cases he considered it a great sin, risking the judgement
of God not to act when called to be his instrument of instruction,
warning or reproof.[81]

Greenham stressed that the counsel offered by ministers and divinely
empowered lay people should not be treated lightly or dismissed as the
unwanted meddling of another human being. For this reason he would
not tolerate the confutation of his warnings, 'not that hee respected so
much his private person, as that it was a thing against gods glory and
truth and would have men swift to hear admonitions, slowe to crosse'.[82]
To those who refused godly counsel, he offered this fearful caution:

> The next time you awake in the night, when ther shal none bee by
> you, but god and his holy angels. and when you go to pray to the
> lord, consider of my speach in fear and trembling, if you can find
> comfort in your conscience, examine your self without hipocrisy in
> your bed, and do see if the lord graunt your praiers, until you
> acknowledg this to bee a sin, to withstand boldly and openly the
> preacher of gods word, let mee bear the want of credit with you
> hereafter, And when you see god denieth you comfort, or refuseth
> your praiers, yeeld to the truth.[83]

While Greenham defined the limits and offered cautions about the use of
godly counsel, he firmly declared that God used his faithful as oracles of
truth, ministers of comfort and harbingers of judgement. Their words
should be received with the respect and deference due to the master they
served. To reject or dismiss the admonitions of the godly minister or
layman risked offending God and incurring his wrath.

Through these three means of authoritative teaching - scripture,

---

[79] Ibid., fol. 6r.

[80] Ibid., fols 1v, 42v-43r. See Diane Willen, '"Communion of the Saints": Spiritual
Reciprocity and the Godly Community in Early Modern England', *Albion*, 27 (1995), 19-
41; Barbara Donagan, 'Godly Choice: Puritan Decision-Making in Seventeenth-Century
England', *Harvard Theological Review*, 76.3 (1983), 307-34.

[81] REM 524, fols 1v, 4v-5r.

[82] Ibid:, fol. 21v.

[83] Ibid., fol. 35r. See also fol. 23v.

preaching and godly counsel – the Christian community received from God the guidance required to order corporate and private life. These sources of truth existed to transform men and women into godly people who conformed to the will and purpose of God. The canonical scriptures, acknowledged to be the very word of God, provided the standard by which all teaching, doctrine and church practice should be judged. It was the essential starting point for all preaching, godly counsel and private decisions or reflections. Preaching articulated the will of God to the assembled community, and should be received, not with respect for the preacher, but out of reverence for the truth God communicated by that means. Godly counsel, rightly used, offered believers divine assistance in their immediate situation, mediated by a minister or lay person.

While the sacraments of baptism and the Eucharist were described as 'like acquittances to absolv' believers of sin[84] and built up the community of the faithful, and the liturgy and rites of the church (properly cleansed of superstitious practices) aided in the worship of God and the edification of believers, they were not the focus of Greenham's reflections on the means to salvation.[85] In repeated references to the sacraments, Greenham tied their use to proper instruction and personal affirmation of the doxa and praxis of the community.[86] The efficacy of sacraments received was directly tied to the faith of the recipient.[87] Regeneration and interior transformation came through divinely enabled responses to the texts of scripture and the spoken words of preaching and counsel. According to Greenham, this was the way God has chosen to communicate authoritative teaching to those who believed.

As in the case of false religion, Greenham's understanding of the authoritative sources of true religion reflected Elizabethan Protestantism – yet the various components of his definition found different emphases among his co-religionists. His emphasis on the centrality of sacred scripture reflected a broadly held belief among English Protestants in the period.[88] Even in the hotly contentious years of the late 1630s, William Chillingworth, who later died a royalist in the Civil War, declared that

---

[84] Ibid., fol. 60v.

[85] It is here that Greenham marked himself, like Perkins, as a Reformed theologian more concerned with justification than with sacramental grace. Breward, 'William Perkins and the Origins of Reformed Casuistry', 16.

[86] REM 524, fols 2r, 38v, 39v, 41r.

[87] Ibid., fol. 10r. See below, 151, n. 88.

[88] Collinson, *Birthpangs of Protestant England*, 10-11, 55, 95-9; Charles Cohen, 'Two Biblical Models of Conversion: An Example of Puritan Hermeneutics', *Church History*, 58 (1989), 182-96, esp. 183-6; William Perkins, *The Work of William Perkins*, ed. Ian Breward (Abingdon, Berks: Sutton Courtney Press, 1970), 38-40, 47-9, 333-4, 548-52.

'The Bible, the Bible only I say is the religion of Protestants'.[89] The emphasis Greenham gave to preaching and conferring with clergy mirrored priorities found in the writings of Bishop Jewel and others.[90] Yet this must not be overstated, for Greenham's emphasis on preaching and counsel reflected an intensity commonly associated with the godly and theologians like William Perkins, Arthur Hildersham, William Ames and Richard Rogers.[91]

Pastoral experience, however, demonstrated that even when the word of God was faithfully proclaimed, many persisted in unbelief. Referring to preaching, Greenham lamented the fact that 'the lord offereth the myne of his mercy to bee devided to them, that wil but hear, and beleev it, and no man almost regardeth it'.[92] The sayings collected by Greenham's student reflect Greenham's explanation of why some turn to God and others reject divine truth. They also illustrate his resolution of a related issue that arose out of his Reformed approach to pastoral care: how could it be that some turn to God for a time and then depart from the company of the godly?

The 'saved' and the 'damned'

The corrupt condition of human nature and humanity's inability to turn to God without divine assistance constituted the essential starting-point of Greenham's theology of conversion. In 1582, he stated this position in stark terms:

> Hee thought by nature al men bee papists, heretiques, adulterers, and in al kinds sinners, until god renued them so, that if al heresy, papistry, or ungodlines, were ceased among al men, yet in man (being left of god) is a sufficient matter, wherby al these might bee received and renued.[93]

Men and women, unaided by grace, would always turn away from God and devote themselves to all manner of corruption and false teaching. Greenham did not question God's judgement in creating a world in

---

[89] Patrick Collinson, *The Religion of Protestants: The Church in English Society 1559–1625* (Oxford: Clarendon Press, 1982), viii.

[90] See above, 61-2, 64-9.

[91] Irvonwy Morgan, *The Godly Preachers of the Elizabethan Church* (London: The Epworth Press, 1965), *passim*. For an example of tension over preaching and reading homilies see: Whitgift, *Works*, ed. John Ayre (3 vols, Cambridge: Cambridge University Press, 1851) I, 206, 539; III, 32. We wish to thank Sharon Arnoult for bringing these references to our attention.

[92] REM 524, fols 37v-38r.

[93] Ibid., fol. 21r.

which this was possible; rather he focused on the satanic temptations that spawned this rebellion. Just as the serpent enticed Eve to believe she would become like God if she ate of the forbidden fruit, 'Sathan either would have us to make ourselves our own christ, or els hee would hide from us the benefit wee have in christ'.[94] This temptation could not be overcome by good breeding or a godly environment.[95] Indeed, humanity was overwhelmed by the weight of sin and caught in the 'clawes of sathan'.[96]

While the human condition precluded any movement toward God, a way had been provided to turn away from sin and experience regeneration – or new birth.[97] God the Father was the first cause of salvation for those called to believe. Through Christ's 'covenant of the cross' and 'glorious bloodsheeding', men and women called by God received the grace needed to turn to God and seek forgiveness of their sins.[98] But Christ's work on the cross required a preparation; so the Law (the Old Testament) was given to convict men and women of sin. Greenham insisted that the Law must be preached in order to 'drive men out of themselves and send them to christ'.[99] Those who renounced their sins and clung to Christ would not be judged by him, 'beecause they judge themselves'. They received assurance that they 'are under grace and not under the law' and that they served 'christ as a conqueror' because he freed them from the burden of sin and satanic captivity.[100]

When asked in 1583 whether one received the Word first and then the Spirit, Greenham stressed that receiving the spirit of God preceded any response to the Word.[101] His answer raised important questions when wedded to his understanding of the utter corruption of human nature. Greenham and his hearers knew from experience that some heard the word of God and believed; yet many failed to respond. How could it be that some received the grace to hear and believe and others did not? Greenham acknowledged the problem and grounded his response in scripture:

> His opinion was that knowledg is in the hart, and therfore that many were justly condemned, who refused the light of knowledg in ther own harts. Besides it is said, plainly in the word of god. *The*

---

[94] Ibid., fol. 29r.
[95] Ibid., fol. 29r, 16v.
[96] Ibid., fol. 29v.
[97] Ibid., fol. 18v. The biblical texts from which the concept of 'new birth' derives include: John 3:3-8; 1 Peter 1:23; 1 John 4:7, 5:18.
[98] Ibid., fols 45r-v, 29r-v.
[99] Ibid., fol. 7v.
[100] Ibid., fol. 29r-v.
[101] Ibid., fol. 45r.

lord hath not given them an understanding hart: they erre in hart etc.[102]

The preacher served as a messenger of salvation for those who believed, and for those who did not believe he was 'an instrument of condemnation prepared for them'.[103] The elect received the spirit of God, enabling them to respond to the gospel, while others did not and were justly condemned because they had knowledge of the truth and continued to rest in their sins. This truth did not respect a person's station in life. In 1582 Greenham reportedly observed that:

> Faith in the promises of god, caused him sometyme to take children yong, and unseasoned with religion, yea and such whom, parentage, education, and frinds might rather discommend. For saith hee as good nurtures, do not help of any necessity to regeneration, so evil natures cannot hinder gods purpose in calling if the means with his mercy and blessing bee purely and painfully used.[104]

Greenham urged his hearers not to pursue this mystery too deeply:

> It is wonderful said hee, that divers hearing the same word spoken one should beleev and another not beeleev. But I am rather to thanck god that I do beleev, then to search out the reason, why others do not beeleeve, and as I am to bee thanckful for my self so I am to bee pityful for him that doth not beeleev.[105]

In this as in other matters men and women must remember that they could not stand in judgement on God's decisions. God alone was God.[106] The elect, whom God saved, were recipients of his love and mercy. The reprobate, whom he judged, were justly punished for lying in their sins.

When asked about the sin against the Holy Spirit, which scripture described as unpardonable, Greenham offered an explanation that seemed to link this sin with the reprobate.[107] Associating this sin with the knowledge of God that every human being possessed, Greenham claimed that when these sins had their source in human frailty, they were remissible. When these sins involved 'a rebellious obstinacy', they were 'void of al repentance' and 'irremissible'.[108] For Greenham the key to

---

[102] Ibid., fol. 35r.

[103] Ibid., fol. 7v.

[104] Ibid., fol. 17r. It is intriguing to note that only the last sentence of the saying is included in the published versions (First Edition, 50; Second Edition, 49; Third Edition, 29; Fourth Edition, 29; Fifth Edition, 29), suggesting that his editor(s) found the starkness of his valuation of social station uncomfortable for the time.

[105] REM 524, fol. 17v.

[106] Ibid., fol. 18v.

[107] Greenham's position reflected a common Reformed response to this issue. See: Baird Tipson, 'A Dark Side of Seventeenth-Century English Protestantism: The Sin Against the Holy Spirit', *Harvard Theological Review*, 77.3-4 (1984), 301-30.

[108] REM 524, fol. 67r.

identifying the elect rested in this fact: the godly experienced sorrow for their sins, a desire for God's forgiveness, and a longing to do God's will.

Greenham associated this altered capacity with the divine transformation of the human conscience. In this state of grace, the conscience of the believer became a supernatural faculty, superior to reason, and a reliable guide to living and acting in accordance with the will of God. Greenham gave the conscience great power in the self-examination he urged on all who came to him. He reportedly said that:

> Hee was either a prince or a peasant, either most mighty above al princes, or most vile among the sons of men. If al the monarks in the world withstand him, his own conscience comforting him, hee ruled above al. If the vilest vassal of the world, rose against him, his own hart condemning him, hee seemed to bee most miserable of al.[109]

For Greenham the pursuit of sanctification and rooting out of sin provided signs of election. Through fidelity to one's calling, frequent examination of conscience, regular recourse to the word of God, read and heard, and seeking out the company of the godly, those chosen by God could recognize in their actions and their affections the working of the Holy Spirit in their lives.

Yet pastoral experience did not permit him to rest comfortably with this neat delineation of the saved and the damned. Greenham taught that while ordinarily the saints persevere in their life of faith, some manifested signs of grace only to fall away and never return to their walk with God. In 1582 he stated that 'if hee had once seen any effectual marks of gods child in any man, hee would never, but hope wel of him, until hee had blotted them out'.[110] While Greenham always hoped for the best in observing the lives of others, experience had taught him that some departed from godly ways, never to return. This acknowledgement of the possibility of temporary faith made the search for signs of election an essential task for the godly. No one could rest secure or become complacent, for constant vigilance over thoughts and actions proved the only way to maintain assurance of election. The anxiety that often accompanied the search for assurance proved the underlying cause of the spiritual affliction which drove so many to seek out the rector of Dry Drayton.

Greenham's vision of true religion shifted the focus away from the old religion's view of human cooperation with the Holy Spirit and meritorious works toward an examination of the person's interior state in search of signs that gave assurance of election and the workings of

---

[109] Ibid., fol. 36v.

[110] Ibid., fol. 23r. Note that the printed versions of this saying edited out the concept of temporary faith. See fol. 61v for another reference to this concept.

God's grace. One scholar has referred to this as the movement from devotion to deliberation.[111] Greenham would no doubt have agreed, if this meant a movement from external observances to an interiorized religion that resulted in personal transformation and sanctification. The distinction here is crucial. Greenham, like most Elizabethan Protestants, made a direct link between papistry and reprobation. He assumed that Catholic practice was tinged with a Pelagian striving which emphasized human agency over God's grace. Greenham attempted to wean those under his care from any assumption that meritorious works played a part in salvation and to inculcate a Reformed vision of conversion. God's grace, made possible by the covenant of the cross, corrected the corrupt nature of the elect and enabled them to respond in will and action. While human activity was denied any recognition in the process of salvation, the response of the elect provided proof of the presence of transforming grace and growth in sanctification. These signs of election could be discerned by the godly and offered assurance to those who doubted the state of their soul.[112] Greenham, like other Reformed theologians, did not treat assurance as a separate theological issue, but considered it as it came up in counselling with reference to faith, election and perseverance.[113]

Just as Greenham's pastoral ministry reflected the impact and influence of Martin Bucer, so his understanding of the *ordo salutis*, order of salvation, was imbued with a Bucerian vision. Bucer described four sequential factors in the process of salvation: first, God's election of those he had chosen; second, the calling of the elect through the gift of the Holy Spirit and reception of saving knowledge of God; third, holiness of life and the 'duties of love', which made good works possible; and fourth, evidence of the glory of God in the elect, 'with which God has deemed it worthy to adorn them'.[114] Two emphases are reflected in

---

[111] Kaufman, *Prayer, Despair, and Drama*, 1.

[112] John von Rohr, *The Covenant of Grace in Puritan Thought* (Atlanta, GA: Scholars Press, 1986), 30. Also see: Joel Beeke, *Assurance of Faith: Calvin, English Puritanism, and the Dutch Second Reformation* (New York: Peter Lang, 1991), esp. chaps 3–5; Richard Muller, *Christ and the Decree* (Durham, NC: The Labyrinth Press, 1986); Wallace, *Puritans and Predestination*.

[113] Richard Muller, 'Covenant and Conscience in English Reformed Theology: Three Variations on a 17th Century Theme', *The Westminster Theological Journal*, 42.2 (Spring 1980), 319–20; Gordon J. Keddie, '"Unfallible Certenty of the Pardon of Sinne and Life Everlasting": The Doctrine of Assurance in the Theology of William Perkins (1558-1602)', *The Evangelical Quarterly*, 48.4 (October-December 1976), 236–7.

[114] W.P. Stephens, *The Holy Spirit in the Theology of Martin Bucer* (Cambridge: Cambridge University Press, 1970), 38. Also see: Jaques Courvoisier, *La Notion d'Eglise chez Bucer dans son Développement Historique* (Paris: Librairie Félix Alcan, 1933), 64–73.

this understanding of salvation. First, Bucer emphasized the limited nature of election. The necessary implication was that the means of salvation did not automatically act as agents of grace for all who received them. Second, Bucer's analysis of the order of salvation was forward looking: the elect would be called, justified, sanctified and glorified. One scholar has observed that this 'implied a necessary link between faith and love, the new birth and the new life, imputed righteousness and real righteousness'.[115] The same assessment could be made of Greenham's approach.

Greenham's understanding of predestination stood within a broad Reformed consensus among Elizabethan Protestants, shared by bishops and dissenting clergy alike.[116] While R.T. Kendall has attempted to distinguish between the experimental predestinarianism of pastors like Greenham, and the credal predestinarianism of the episcopacy, Nicholas Tyacke has effectively argued that no such division can be made.[117]

Greenham's reference to the covenant of the cross and the importance of the Law as preparation for grace also reflected ideas found in continental and English Reformed covenant theology.[118] Theologians in this tradition found in the Law of the Old Testament an explanation for humanity's failure in its covenant relationship with God, meaning the covenant of grace, a covenant made possible by the work of Christ on the cross.[119] Theodore Beza, Zacharias Ursinus, Girolamo Zanchius, William Perkins and others argued, like Greenham, that preaching the Law was essential preparation for the good news of salvation through Christ. By the Law the elect and the reprobate came to know their sins.

---

[115] Stephens, *Holy Spirit*, 38-9.

[116] Nicholas Tyacke, *Anti-Calvinists: The Rise of English Arminianism, c. 1590-1640* (Oxford: Clarendon Press, 1990), 1-3. For a useful overview of recent scholarly debate on this issue see: Green, *The Christian's ABC*, chap. 8.

[117] Kendall, *Calvin and English Calvinism*, 79-80; Nicholas Tyacke, *Anti-Calvinists*, ix. Even the avant-garde conformist, Lancelot Andrewes, who as student at Pembroke Hall may have visited Dry Drayton and conferred with Greenham, stood with Greenham in declaring predestination a mystery that defied detailed theological dissection. See: Thomas Fuller, *The Church History of Britain*, ed. James Nichols, (3rd edn, London: William Tegg, 1868), 9.7.65; Kendall, *Calvin and English Calvinism*, 80 n.3; Paul A. Welsby, *Lancelot Andrewes 1555-1626* (London: SPCK, 1958), 43-4.

[118] For recent examinations of covenantal theology on the continent and in England see: Green, *The Christian's ABC*, chap. 9; Michael McGiffert, 'The Perkinsian Moment in Federal Theology', *Calvin Theological Journal*, 29 (1994), 117-48; David A. Weir, *The Origins of the Federal Theology in Sixteenth-Century Reformation Thought* (Oxford: Clarendon Press, 1990); von Rohr, *The Covenant of Grace*.

[119] Based on the sayings, it appears that Greenham employed the concept of the single covenant – the covenant of grace, found in the works of Swiss Reformed theologians like Calvin and Bullinger and English theologians like John Bale and John Bradford. During the Elizabethan period, English Reformed covenantal theology developed the concept of

Knowledge of their sins rendered the unrepentant without excuse before the judgement seat of God. Grace, made possible through Christ's death on the cross, enabled the elect to believe, repent of their sins and turn to God.[120]

Greenham's understanding of the human conscience, and its transformation into a supernatural faculty through which God guided the elect, reflected the influence of the Christian humanist focus on the individual conscience as the true agent of reformation. Margo Todd has argued that this emphasis, found in Erasmus and other humanists of the sixteenth century, 'demanded a continuous, dynamic confrontation of the informed individual conscience with moral issues'.[121] For the Christian humanist, social station and breeding offered no inherent advantage. Each person should be judged by the exercise of self-discipline, quest for wisdom, thirst for knowledge of the scriptures, and efforts to live righteously. Respect should be given, not to the high-born, but to those who lived virtuously.[122] As this developed in the context of Reformed theology, especially in the reflections of Martin Bucer, an implicit threat to hierarchical and hereditary systems of authority emerged.[123] Greenham's reflections on these issues mirrored those of Perkins, William Ames, Laurence Chaderton and Henry Smith.[124] The implications of this proved an important factor in tensions between the conscientious godly and those who defended the establishment in the Elizabethan and Stuart periods.

This affirmation of the conscience as an agent of supernatural insight proved problematic to the godly for another reason. The recognition among Reformed theologians that temporary faith was possible,[125] raised troubling questions for tender hearts and for the scrupulous concerning the state of their souls. As in the case of the man who chopped off his leg, the consequences of afflicted consciences could be

---

the two covenants, of works and grace, which Perkins expanded and refined. For a discussion of these developments in covenantal theology see: Michael McGiffert, 'Grace and Works: The Rise and Division of Covenant Divinity in Elizabethan Puritanism', *Harvard Theological Review*, 75.4 (1982), 463-502. Also see: Richard Muller, 'Perkins' *A Golden Chaine*: Predestinarian System or Schematized *Ordo Salutis*', *Sixteenth Century Journal*, 9.1 (1978): 78-80.

[120] Kendall, *Calvin and English Calvinism*, 37-41, 59-60; Zacharias Ursinus, *The summe of christian religion* (1633), 128; Girolomo Zanchius, *H. Zanchius His Confession of Christian Religion* (1599), 47, 51; William Perkins, *Workes* (2 vols, 1608, 1609), I, 5, 79.

[121] Todd, *Christian Humanism*, 178. Also see above, Chapter 6 for a survey of this issue.

[122] Ibid., 182.

[123] Ibid., 196.

[124] Ibid., 193-5.

[125] Kendall, *Calvin and English Calvinism*, 21-5, 36, 67-75, *passim*.

dire. Perkins called the conscience both a 'little God' and a 'little hell', in both cases a source of fear and torment for those who suffered.[126] How could they know that they were among the elect? In the midst of physical, mental or spiritual anguish, how could they discern the temptations of the adversary? What were the means by which they could experience in understanding and affections the presence of the Holy Spirit in their lives? These were the questions that Greenham proved so skilled at addressing, bringing the godly to a more balanced understanding of the afflictions they experienced and fortifying them for the challenges of living as the children of God in a world menaced by Satan.

The world-view found in the Greenham sayings reflects a complex vision of life and Christian practice that conformed to broad Protestant principles, but emphasized an internalized faith and rigorously self-examined Christian practice that became a distinctive feature of people Greenham described as the godly. His understanding of the corruption of human nature, the conflict between God and Satan, and the nature and means of salvation, all reflected beliefs that were part of the Protestant ethos of the English Church. While the details of theological concepts like covenant, election and reprobation continued to evolve during the Elizabethan period, Greenham stood within a broad Reformed tradition, while exhibiting in particulars the Bucerian tradition of his formation at Pembroke Hall, Cambridge. His preoccupation with signs that provided assurance of election gave his style of ministry and counselling an orientation that identified him with the godly. This identification, so important to seventeenth-century puritans, established a legacy that continues to intrigue and puzzle historians and theologians. The question that most engages us here is: Were the claims made on his legacy by seventeenth-century puritans sufficient to label him an Elizabethan puritan, or even a puritan *avant la lettre*?

---

[126] Kaufman, *Prayer, Despair, and Drama*, 64.

CHAPTER EIGHT

Another comment concerning the name 'puritan'

Richard Greenham devoted himself to pastoral ministry, particularly to curing afflicted consciences, and avoided to whatever extent he could being a party to the divisive controversies which burdened the Elizabethan Church. His aggressively non-partisan – one might justly say antipartisan – stance has not, however, stopped historians from pitching his tent in the puritan camp. A.L. Rowse, for example, describes Greenham as puritanism's most 'choice spirit'[1] and Jerald C. Brauer begins his list of 'major Puritan divines' with Greenham.[2] While in what we have written above, we have carefully avoided the label, it is a fair question whether 'puritan' may legitimately be applied to Greenham.

Greenham was never called a puritan during his own lifetime. Even the rabidly anti-puritan Bishop Corbett, who has been cited above, did not so label him; he wrote only that puritans found comfort from reading Greenham.[3] Modern identification of Greenham as a puritan is probably a matter of guilt by association: his students and disciples were puritans, and they must have learned it from him. The fact that our first significant biography of Greenham, that by Samuel Clarke, appeared in his *Lives of Thirty-Two English Divines* has encouraged this. But it is worth noting what exactly Clarke did and said. It is true that the volume in question contains biographies of prominent Jacobean puritans. However, Greenham's biography appears fourth – following those of John Colet, Miles Coverdale and Edwin Sandys – and immediately before that of Thomas Cartwright, of whom Greenham was publicly critical. Clarke's arrangement seems designed to associate Greenham with the godly patriarchs of the church, none of whom it would even occur to us to call 'puritan'. Moreover, nowhere in the text itself does Clarke call Greenham a puritan. Indeed, he seems almost to go out of his way to avoid it.[4]

In 1717, James Peirce built on Clarke's model of including Greenham among the godly and reporting his nonconformity, but making no

---

[1] A.L. Rowse, *The England of Elizabeth: The Structure of Society* (New York: Macmillan, 1951), 479.

[2] Jerald C. Brauer, 'Types of Puritan Piety', *Church History*, 56 (1987), 48 n.25.

[3] See above, 4.

[4] 'Life of Master Richard Greenham', *passim*.

further claims. Peirce reported that Greenham was 'a man of most excellent spirit; and who, tho' he would not subscribe, or conform to the habits, yet avoided speaking of these matters, that he might not give offense'.[5] It is perhaps in 1837 that the labelling of Greenham as a puritan has its origins. Daniel Neal briefly referred to Greenham, incorrectly reporting that Bishop Cox suspended him in the 1570s, while otherwise virtually quoting Peirce word for word, with a footnote to the passage of Peirce's work, quoted above.[6] Neal, dependent on Peirce as he is, never calls Greenham a puritan either, but the title of his book - *The History of the Puritans* - made the guilt by association unmistakable. The genie was out of the bottle, and has remained out, working his taxonomic mischief ever since.

Recently, however, Professor Patrick Collinson has made some noteworthy efforts to rebottle the genie by questioning the utility of the 'puritan' label in general terms. In his Clark Library Lecture, he argued that 'all attempts to distinguish this person, or that idea, or a certain practice or prejudice, as Puritan rather than otherwise are liable to fail'. Collinson does not mention Greenham specifically, but calls into doubt the appropriateness of naming Richard Bernard, the Samuel Wards, William Whately, Andrew Willett and even William Perkins as 'puritans'.[7] He then offered a challenge which seemed particularly apposite to our study of Greenham:

> The minute examination of inert specimens, pinned out on boards, the argument of their printed works carefully dissected, should be at least supplemented with more strenuous field studies, where the specimens can be observed alive and kicking. Here the natural historians of Puritanism will find that what matters is not what people were in themselves but what they were doing to each other and saying about each other and against each other.[8]

What we have attempted above is just such a strenuous field study, and with it as a foundation we turn finally to some reflections on Greenham and the name 'puritan'.

Greenham and the name 'puritan'

Joseph Hall, whose devotional writings were much admired by

---

[5] James Peirce, *Vindication of the Dissenters* (London, 1717), 97.

[6] Daniel Neal, *The History of the Puritans; or, Protestant Nonconformists; from the Reformation in 1517, to the Revolution in 1688* (3 vols, London, 1837), I, 229.

[7] Patrick Collinson, *The Puritan Character: Polemics and Polarities in Early Seventeenth Century English Culture* (UCLA: William Andrews Clark Memorial Library, 1989), 15-16.

[8] Ibid., 16-17.

seventeenth-century puritans, was also a bishop at the time of episcopacy's greatest unpopularity, and a trenchant opponent of presbyterians and separatists.[9] As shown in Chapter 1, Hall was full of praise for Greenham. What made it possible for Hall to laud the man who trained Arthur Hildersham and Richard Rogers and was so much admired by Stephen Egerton and John Dod?

Hall found common cause with Greenham in a devotion to the unity of the church, especially in order to fight popery. Hall's sermons of the early 1620s stressed this need for unity; unity was for Hall, as Peter Lake has written, 'the essence of the Church's being'.[10] That unity rested on a set of core beliefs. Praising the English Church in 1622, Hall explained that 'we have nothing but ... the sincerity of scriptures, simplicity of sacraments, decency of rare ceremonies, Christ crucified'.[11] Hall regarded popery as extremely dangerous and used extreme language when attacking it.[12]

Lake noted an important contrast between Hall and Richard Montague on the nature of threats to the church. Although it was customary in Jacobean conformist writing to see Catholics and puritans both as threats, most writers dwelt more on one than the other. For Montague, puritanism was the greater concern; for Hall, it was popery. In Hall's 1620 court sermons, popery was heresy and as such a force to be feared and opposed. Puritanism, on the other hand, scarcely mattered; it was a collection of mistaken opinions concerning ceremonies and church government lacking doctrinal coherence.[13] Hall saw ceremonies as things indifferent and played down the importance of differences over externals in favour of similarities over doctrine. For this reason, Hall was able in 1624 to offer a list of the great lights of the church, which embraced Greenham and Hooker, Bilson and Willett, Overall and Perkins.[14] This emphasis on broad similarities was irenic, but it also had a polemical and ideological purpose. It encouraged a united front dedicated to war (literally) against popery.[15] Hall recognized in Greenham's memory a weapon not only against Catholics but also against those who would disrupt the peace of the church. Greenham's record as an ally of bishops in the fight against Catholics, presbyterians and separatists meant that Hall saw him as a fellow traveller on his *Via Media*, and with good cause.

---

[9] See above, 31, n. 1.
[10] Lake, 'The Moderate and Irenic Case', 58.
[11] Quoted in ibid., 59.
[12] Ibid., 64.
[13] Ibid., 68.
[14] Quoted in Collinson, *Religion of Protestants*, 92.
[15] Lake, 'The Moderate and Irenic Case', 78.

The broad consensus which Hall advocated, and of which he considered Greenham a part, seems in many ways similar to that which Paul Christianson describes as 'Protestant or Anglican': the

> fairly large number of people who wanted some further reformation in the Church of England, people such as those who approved of the idea of a Book of Common Prayer, but who desired some changes in the administration of the sacraments (such as standing or sitting at communion or the omission of the sign of the cross in baptism) and those who accepted the principle of an ecclesiastical hierarchy, but wished to moderate the power of the bishops ... Minor arguments over *adiaphora*, no matter how deeply rooted in theology, did not a 'Puritan' make.

Christianson argues that the more inclusive label of Anglican or Protestant 'fits the historical facts far better than that narrower notion hitherto almost exclusively employed'.[16]

Maintaining episcopacy did not separate the English Church from the larger Reformed ranks. The English Church stood on the Zurich/Berne side of the 'Dissensus Tigerinus'; Bullinger and Gualter were its allies in matters of church polity. Christianson identified as 'Puritan', in the Elizabethan sense, those who opposed the Bullingerian consensus and sought to establish a different model – a Genevan model – of government and liturgy. These puritans included Field and Wilcox, Cartwright, Fulke and Travers in the first wave, and then Thomas Brightman and 'Martin Marprelate'. Brightman in particular articulated the idea that a 'halfly reformed' church would be spewed out of the Lord's mouth.[17] Greenham was clearly not a 'puritan' by this construction of the term. He does look rather like what Christianson anachronistically terms 'Anglican'.

There is, however, a second strand of seventeenth-century evidence and scholarly discourse that merits attention here. In Professor Collinson's response to Christianson's article, he argued that 'puritans' essentially were *only* defined by their enemies and that 'Puritanism had no content beyond what was attributed to it by its opponents'.[18] Contemporary sources suggest otherwise. Peter Lake recently drew attention to godly (self-)definition, especially in the works of Joseph Bentham and Robert Bolton.[19] In 1636, Bentham explained that

---

[16] Paul Christianson, 'Reformers and the Church of England under Elizabeth I and the Early Stuarts', *Journal of Ecclesiastical History*, 31 (1980), 463-82, esp. 468-9.

[17] Ibid., 473.

[18] Patrick Collinson, 'A Comment: Concerning the Name Puritan', *Journal of Ecclesiastical History*, 31 (1980), 483-8.

[19] Lake, '"A Charitable Christian Hatred": The Godly and their Enemies in the 1630s', 145-83, esp. 150-56.

by puritans, I meane practising Protestants, such men, who daily reade the Scriptures, pray with their families, teach them the way to heaven, eschue lying, swearing, usury, oppression, time-selling, defrauding, and all knowne sinnes: spend the Lords daies holily in hearing Gods Word, prayer, meditation, conference, singing of Psalmes, meditation of the creatures, are mercifull to the poore, diligent in their particular Callings, frame their lives according to Gods will revealed in his Word, &c.[20]

One familiar with Greenham's descriptions of the 'godly' cannot fail to see a connection. Yet most of this definition could equally apply to the practice of a Reformed bishop like Joseph Hall and – if Sabbath rigour is set aside – even to Archbishop William Laud.

Lake does not focus on the particular components of Bentham's definition, but uses it to illustrate a puritan interest in the 'society of saints' or the 'visible community of the visible godly' – Christians marked out by religious practices and ethical rigour that moved beyond mere conformity to the established religious order.[21] Greenham not only incarnated the component parts of Bentham's definition, he exhibited a keen interest in the visible community of the godly.

In his 'Defining Puritanism – again?', Lake gives greater precision to this line of argument. He describes the puritan style as a 'zealous ... subset of a larger body of reformed or protestant doctrines and positions'.[22] Lake explains that he wishes

to see Puritanism as a distinctive style of piety and divinity, made up not so much of distinctively Puritan component parts, the mere presence of which in a person's thoughts or practice rendered them definitively a Puritan, as a synthesis made of strands most or many of which taken individually could be found in non-Puritan as well as Puritan contexts, but which taken together formed a distinctively Puritan synthesis or style ... [O]ur concern should not be so much to list and delimit a group of telltale Puritan opinions as to pull together a sense of the central core of a Puritan style or tradition or world view.[23]

Lake's definition of puritanism describes a voluntary religion of sociability and pious practices around which the godly organized their lives. This piety was 'aggressively word centered, dominated by a division between the godly and the ungodly, a division underwritten by the doctrines of predestination, perseverance, and election and given

---

[20] Joseph Bentham, *The Saints Societie* (1636), 29.

[21] Lake, '"A Charitable Christian Hatred": The Godly and their Enemies in the 1630s', 152-3.

[22] Peter Lake, 'Defining Puritanism – again?' in Bremer (ed.), *Puritanism*, 3-29; quoting 4.

[23] Ibid., 6.

practical expression in the forms of Puritan voluntary religion'. Centring their practice around the three scriptural ordinances of the word preached, the sacraments and the Sabbath, Lake's puritans accepted established liturgy and church government as things inherently indifferent and required by human authority. Finally, they were obsessed with the threat of popery.[24] This construction of a puritan style has a strong resonance in Greenham's life and works. His life, ministry and cure of afflicted consciences reflect precisely the values outlined by Bentham and Lake.

Was Richard Greenham, then, a puritan? He emerges from these pages as both an 'Anglican' in the Hall/Christianson construction and a 'puritan' in the Bentham/Lake model. Having undertaken precisely the sort of field study advocated by Professor Collinson, it has become clear to us that in Greenham's case, and perhaps many others, it is *une question mal posée*. Those engaged not in polemic about the ceremonies and structure of the church, but labouring in the vineyards – the parishes of Elizabethan and Jacobean England – would no doubt find the energy which modern historians and theologians have spent trying to define puritanism, and classify people as puritan or not, to have been wasted. The realities of pastoral ministry, the practical problems and needs of a parish, engendered a set of concerns which united men with a wide range of views about ceremonies and ecclesiastical government, and gave them so much in common that the label 'parish minister' transcends the party labels which have obsessed us for decades.[25] This field study suggests that endless debates over the definition and nature of puritans and puritanism should give way to more fruitful explorations of the meaning and nature of pastoral ministry itself. It was that which Richard Greenham thought was important – important enough to abandon the academic debates of Cambridge. Perhaps he still knows best.

---

[24] Ibid., 27.

[25] For a further development of this argument, see Eric Josef Carlson, 'Clergy-Lay Relations in the English Church, 1400-1700', (forthcoming). This article compares Myrk, Perkins, Herbert and Baxter on issues of parish ministry and argues for fundamental continuities which transcend differences of 'party'.

PART TWO

The sayings of Richard Greenham

Rylands English Manuscript 524, folios 1-72

Editorial Note

Every effort has been made to produce the full text of Richard Greenham's sayings, as found in Rylands English Manuscript 524, folios 1-72, in a reliable and comprehensible edition. The unabridged transcription provided here has been checked through numerous collations: nine by the principal editor of the text, Kenneth Parker, three by the co-editor of this volume, Eric Carlson, and one collation by Dr Dorothy Owen. The editorial decisions for transcribing generally follow the recommendations made by R.F. Hunnisett in *Editing Records for Publication*.[1] Michael Hunter's article, 'How to Edit a Seventeenth-Century Manuscript',[2] has also been an invaluable guide.

This edition is intended for students and scholars of early modern English history and religious thought. While the editors hope that Greenham's sayings will find a place in the classroom, it is assumed that readers can contend with the conventions of early modern English. No major modifications have been made to the spelling, punctuation, or grammatical structure of the text.[3] Certain decisions were made by the editors of this volume to produce a reliable and readable text. This manuscript is a hybrid, not a true 'notebook' and not a true fair copy, yet sharing characteristics of both. It is a notebook or journal in the sense that it appears to record sayings chronologically and contains alterations and modifications of text. It possesses characteristics of a fair copy in the quality of the script, the (incomplete) use of marginal notes, the use of distinctive calligraphy to set off or give emphasis to certain passages, and the copy of a letter appended to the manuscript. For these reasons, no clear distinction can be made concerning the 'private' (intended for

---

[1] R.F. Hunnisett, *Editing Records for Publication*, British Records Association: Archives and the User, no. 4 (London, 1977).

[2] Michael Hunter, 'How to Edit a Seventeenth-Century Manuscript: Principles and Practice', *The Seventeenth Century*, 10.2 (August 1995), 277-310.

[3] Hunter, 287.

personal use) or 'public' (intended for circulation) nature of this document – a distinction that can prove valuable in determining editorial policy.[4] The following decisions guided the editing of this text:

Inserted revisions and deleted words found in the manuscript

Inserted words and additions to the text are distinguished from other portions of the text by angled brackets ('<thus>'). Words which have been crossed out in the text, where legible, are relegated to the footnotes and presented in italics (*they said*). Explanatory comments are provided in footnotes as they are needed.[5]

Citation of printed versions of the sayings

All known printed collections of Greenham's sayings were analysed; and printed versions of sayings found in the manuscript are cited in footnotes. Although the differences between the manuscript and printed versions are at times significant, the editors considered it beyond the purview of this edition to make extensive textual comparisons, but have sought to provide scholars with a convenient apparatus to pursue such studies.[6] Footnotes referring to the five editions of the *Works* begin with the 'place', or marginal description, provided for the saying in the first edition in which it was found. Subsequent editions renumbered or moved some sayings.

Spelling

Original spelling is retained throughout, with the following exception: the use of 'i' and 'j', 'u' and 'v', 's' and 'f' or 'ff', and the long 's' and 'ff' for 'F', is modified to conform to modern British orthography.[7]

Capitalization

Original capitalization is retained throughout the transcription. In the few cases where capitalization was unclear, deference was given to modern usage.[8]

---

[4] Hunter, 288-9.
[5] Hunnisett, 23, 42-4, 45-8; Hunter, 288-9, 293-7.
[6] Hunter, 289.
[7] Hunnisett, 28-30; Hunter, 289-91.
[8] Hunter, 290.

Punctuation

Every effort was made to preserve the punctuation found in the manuscript. Where modifications were necessary to clarify the sense of the text, square brackets were inserted to indicate the addition, and the omission of any punctuation was recorded in the footnotes. The reader should be aware that in the early modern period, the full stop was sometimes used interchangeably with the colon. For this reason, the full stop is not always followed by a capital letter.[9]

Diphthongs and ampersands

Where these have occurred in the manuscript, they are silently spelled out, with no indication given in the text or footnotes.[10]

Abbreviations

Where these have occurred, they are silently spelled out in full, with no indication given in the text or footnotes. The editors found no cases in which the intended meaning was not clear.[11]

Line breaks

The line breaks of the manuscript are not duplicated in this edition, and are not indicated in the text.

Folio numbers

Each folio side is indicated in the text, marked off with square brackets with an indication of recto or verso side ('[fol. 6r],' '[fol. 28v]').[12]

Illegible, missing or omitted words

Where these circumstances occur in the manuscript, the ellipsis is used. In unusual cases, square brackets and editorial explanation are inserted in the text.[13]

---

[9] Hunter 290.
[10] Hunnisett, 30.
[11] Hunnisett, 24–8; Hunter, 291–3.
[12] Hunnisett, 50; Hunter, 297.
[13] Hunnisett, 25, 38–9.

Distinctive calligraphy

The use of distinctive calligraphy in the manuscript is represented with italics in the transcription.

Marginal notes

The marginal notes ('places') found in the manuscript are represented here with a bold typeface compared with the main text, although a distinctive difference between the two is not found in the manuscript.

Iam.
11

the acts and speaches of Mr G. 1584.

4 Rylands English Manuscript 524, fol. 52r. Reproduced by courtesy of the Director and University Librarian, the John Rylands University Library of Manchester.

1581

July 28
Haresies the
cause of them

Hee observed that as ther were in the books of the fathers dispersed sentences which as a seed lurking in them, by an evil spirit gathered together made an heresy: so the family of love have sucked out many things out of the writers, which though they of malicious purpose did not set down yet have they turned and perverted to the maintaining of ther damnable sect.[1] And ther<fore>[2] men are to watch over themselves and to take heed of the doctrine they do deliver. Likewise to stir up men to a farther love of the truth hee said, that as the gospel first began by simple fishermen to bee preached, but afterward being received in love, grew to the more learned sort: <so for not receiving the word in love but having tickling to new>[3] doctrines heresies and sects which begin but in the simpler sort and ignorant men <of> the[4] cuntry are like to invade the best learned: and god purposing to punish the wickednes of our age can as wel now send an heretical spirit not only into the cuntry people but into 400 learned preachers as hee did in times past as hee did in times past send a lying spirit into the mouth of 400 prophets[5]

September 10
Speaking against
good men

Hearing of a lerned man that made no conscience even to speake against good men, hee said, I wil not free him from heresy from poverty or sicknes, becaus hee stil goeth without the protection of the lord and is subject to bee punished either in mind or body.[6]

popish physitian
[September] 16

A godly learned man writing unto him whither a christian might use the help of a papist[7] who had been known to do many cures hee answered. Many circumstances are to bee considered and I would have these considered. first whither the man

---

[1] See Marsh, *The Family of Love*, *passim*.

[2] Altered from *they* and followed by *do deliver likewise to stir up* deleted.

[3] Replacing *so* deleted.

[4] Originally read *punish the wickednes of our age*; *punish* and *wickednes of our age* deleted, *of* inserted.

[5] 1 Kings 18:16-28. For printed versions of this saying, with its commonplace title and number see: Heresie 2, First Edition, 29; Second Edition, 28; Third Edition, 17; Fourth Edition, 17; Fifth Edition, 17. Also see: *Propositions*, [saying] 4.

[6] 'Of truth and errours, sinceritie and contempt of the word' 10, Third Edition, 445; Fourth Edition, 469; Fifth Edition, 821. Also found under: To walk uprightly, Fifth Edition, 70.

[7] For papists in the Elizabethan period see Alexandra Walsham, *Church Papists: Catholicism, Conformity and Confessional Polemic in Early Modern England* (Woodbridge, Suffolk: Royal Historical Society, 1993).

dealt before with good christians of knowledge judgement, experience faithfulnes or no. Secondly whither having asked advice of such wee have followed the same rightly Thirdly whither having used right counsel by right means wee have therwith used spiritual means of praier, fasting, searching the inward causes of our visitation Fourthly whether ther bee not some faithful and experienced man whom wee have not used in advice. Fifthly whether the dissease bee so dangerous or the party so would as asking the counsel of a papist may not bee deferred and some better means [fol. 1v] may in tyme bee required of. Sixthly whether the patient hath not his hart too greedily set on the phisition or whither hee doth more principally seek to the promises and providence of god Seventhly whether the papist bee an open blasphemour and whether hee bee a Papist of conscience or noe Eighthly if hee bee but a simple silly Papist or more obstinate whether hee useth not his phisick for a cloake of sorcery[8] Ninthly whether using the phisick hee ever healed any good professors or no. Lastly whether the patient have wisdom and strength to suffer such an one to minister unto him[9]

[September] 20 a special gift in every man Rebuking of sin how.	Hee said hee thought every man had a special gift or word or oath and that therfore yee would wish men to search them selves to that god that hath called them and to use it in prayer. But one must beeware of this if hee thinck hee may speak hee wil speak too soon if

hee thincketh hee may keep silence hee wil hold his peace too long. Again if wee look not carefully to ourselves it wil come to pas that when wee much love the persons to whom wee speak wee slake our zeale in rebuking sin if wee bee zealous against the same wee slake our love to the person[10]

October 3 Entering into the ministery without gifts not to depart therefrom if gifts bee afterward supplied	One whom god had blessed in his ministery to his people complayning to him of his want of affection and gifts when hee first entered in to his charge therby hee thought himself not to bee called of god, hee said. Seing god hath now given you some credit in the consciences of the people I advice you not to depart. for as it is in marriage that though the parties meet in

[8] It was common to blur the lines between medicine and magic, and those who practised medicine at the village level were sometimes accused of witchcraft. See Keith Thomas, *Religion and the Decline of Magic* (Harmondsworth, Middlesex: Penguin Books, 1978), 11-17, 226-7, 640-42, 653-4.

[9] *Propositions*, [saying] 73.

[10] Rebuking or Reproving of Sinne 3, First Edition, 48; Second Edition, 47-8; Third Edition, 28; Fourth Edition, 28; Fifth Edition, 28. Also found under: 'Admonition, and the

the flesh without any sanctified manner to assure themselves to bee joyned of the lord yet they are not to bee separated when god afterward giveth them grace to live holily in ther meetings wherby the lord sheweth not only that ther corrupt meeting is pardoned but that now ther meeting is blessed. So if entering into other callings for want of gifts and affections wee have no assurance [fol. 2r] at the first of a warrantable calling yet if god after both furnish us with able gifts and sanctify us with pure minds hee doth not only therby shew that one former sin is pardoned but also that hee is wel pleased with this calling wherunto hee hath so blessed not[11]

Remooving from   Hee was often laboured unto <to> remove from his
his charge pastoral place and to plant a church[12] elsewhere: hee was
       altogether unwilling unto it howbeit at length hee seemed to offer these conditions. First if they would remoove him his stipend should not bee one penny more then in his present place Secondly hee requested to have the choice of the pastor[13] Thirdly hee required such a <place>[14] as might not bee far from his charge present, beecaus hee would stil use his fatherly care to his people as to his natural childeren in the preaching of the gospel

Sadnes ⎫
     ⎬ extream   Hee had this observation that sathan under the colour
joye ⎭   of repentance did bring many into an extream sadnes
       and stricktnes in using the creatures of god: Again under pretence of christian liberty and delivery of men from extream grief, hee allureth them to an unmoderate and unsanctified mirth and intemperate use of the creatures of god. So blinding judgement hee after corrupteth affection.[15]

profiting by   When hee could not see one profit by his doctrine
preaching   presently hee wold not bee discouraged, for that hee
       <often> observed that they presently would rather murmure then profit by his speaches: after examining his speaches when

---

rules therof' 13, Third Edition, 261; Fourth Edition, 283; Fifth Edition, 635. Also see: *Propositions*, [saying] 5.

[11] Calling 3, First Edition, 6; Second Edition, 6; Third Edition, 4; Fourth Edition, 4. Fifth Edition, 4. Also see: *Propositions*, [saying] 6.

[12] In Greenham's circle a parish without preaching was not a 'church'. To go to a parish that had no preaching was referred to as 'planting a church'. The editors wish to thank Patrick Collinson for his insights on this subject.

[13] See chapter 2, 22.

[14] Replacing *church* deleted.

[15] Repentance 1, First Edition, 50; Second Edition, 49; Third Edition, 29; Fourth Edition, 29; Fifth Edition, 29. Also see: *Propositions*, [saying] 7.

ther cholar was over did much more profit by his doctrine then they that seemed at the first to receiv it very mildly, who after notwithstanding went away without al fruit or would thinck of it again

Teaching some continuance of time before the administration of the sacrament Hee thought it good for one that should have a pastoral charge to use this discipline, to stay a good while, after his coming to his people from administring the sacrament, until after a continual publique teaching by some convenient tyme and some requisite trials of the people hee may minister both some comforts, lest doing it before, hee administer to most unworthy receivers

Remembring of sermons [fol. 2v] To one that would know how to remember the things hee hard hee gave this advice, the best art of memory is to bee humble at gods threatnings and to bee comforted at his promises: for surenes that exceeding <greefs and exceeding> joyes leav great impressions in us.[16] And the best art of logique is to reason *e converso*[17] out of that saying of Paul. *Ther is no temptation hath overtaken you but the same hath overtaken others*[18] and to say, *Ther is no temptation hath overtaken <others>*[19] *but the same may overtake us* and this wil teach us to speak charitably and profitably of other mens infirmities[20]

Seing and beholding ungodly actions as interludes etc unlawful Being asked if one might not go to a place where some ungodly thing is so that our purpose bee to breed a greater detestation of that wickednes in our harts, hee said no for though some under that pretence would go to Idolatry as they said yet unles they went by motion and strength of gods spirit to cry out against idolatry they could not lawfully so do for first in so doing and so profaning in the thing not warranted in respect of our selves it is the just judgement of god that wee should learn to fal into that sin wherof before wee were ignorant beecause naturally wee are enclined to such an action. In respect of our bretheren it is lawful for that if they bee strong wee offend them if they bee weak wee mislead them in respect of gods glory, it is unlawful,

---

[16] Memorie 1, First Edition, 42; Second Edition, 42; Third Edition, 25; Fourth Edition, 25; Fifth Edition, 25. Also see: *Propositions*, [saying] 8.

[17] Technical rhetorical term meaning 'from a thing having been transposed' or 'from a thing having been interchanged'.

[18] 1 Corinthians 10:13.

[19] Replacing *us* deleted.

[20] Memorie 2, First Edition, 43; Second Edition, 42; Third Edition, 25; Fourth Edition, 25; Fifth Edition, 25. Also see: *Propositions*, [saying] 9.

beecaus such should bee our heat[21] therunto that without having heroycal spirits to speak against it wee should not so much as see such a thing[22]

[no month] 2[23]   Hee would wish some that for weakenes of conscience
Eating of meats   were abstayning to eat, for that as natural men use
                   gods creatures to stir up natural comforts so spiritual
men[24] should use them to procure some spiritual comforts and the more men should stir up godly joies in themselves [fol. 3r] for sathan seing men of a sanguine complection and sanctified, laboureth to mix with ther spiritual joyes carnal joye and so seing some of a melancholy complection sanctified to have spiritual sorrowes hee striveth to bring upon them carnal sorrowes[25]

profiting by the   To one asking counsel how hee might do to hear the
word   word with profit hee said before yee go to the church
                   humble yourselves in prayer to god that hee may
                   prepare understanding affection and memory to learn
                   and that the preacher may speak to your conscience[26]
                   after in hart with some short praier applying the same
                   threatnings and promises and instructions to your
                   own estate when you are come home from hearing,
To remember it   change al that you remember into prayer and desire
                   god that you may remember it most when you should
                   practise it and use to teach others confer of the things
                   remembred and that wil help your memory. And this
                   is a good way to remember a thing diligently to
                   remember the reason of a thing.[27]

---

[21] In the sixteenth century, 'heat' was used to refer to intensity of feeling.

[22] Ungodlines 1, First Edition, 72; Second Edition, 71; Third Edition, 41; Fourth Edition, 41; Fifth Edition, 41. Also see: *Propositions*, [saying] 10.

[23] Note that there is an apparent confusion in the marginal dates. On folio 1v 'October 3' appears and on folio 3r 'September 11' is found. It is unclear from the context whether 'September', 'November' or 'December' was intended here.

[24] This is a distinction found in the Epistles attributed to St Paul. See especially 1 Corinthians 2:14-15.

[25] Use of the Creatures 1, First Edition, 72; Second Edition, 72; Third Edition, 41; Fourth Edition, 41; Fifth Edition, 41. First portion of this saying also found under: 'Of the exercises of religion, fasting, etc. and of the carefull use of the meanes at all times' 5, Third Edition, 299; Fourth Edition, 321; Fifth Edition, 673. Also see: *Propositions*, [saying] 11.

[26] Ibid., [saying] 12.

[27] Word of God and the Hearing of it 2, First Edition, 73; Second Edition, 73; Third Edition, 41-2; Fourth Edition, 42; Fifth Edition, 42. Also see: *Propositions*, [saying] 13.

Discipline   When one complained to him of want of discipline hee said Let us bee thankful for that discipline wee have it is the lords wil even in this want of discipline to advaunce his own glory in taking that to himself otherwise wee would attribute to discipline. for besides that hee doth that by his word and praier which may bee done by discipline: it may bee, discipline would hide many hipocrites which now are discovered, and cover many christian true harts, which now are knowen. for they that are godly now are godly of conscience being a discipline to themselves. But many may seem godly in discipline which do it for fear not of love[28]

September 11   A certain man asking his advice whither for some
forsaking our   trobles [fol. 3v] hee might not depart from his calling
calling   hee said, no trobles should hinder us in our callings unles it bee in a caus of meer ungodlines: for if for every troble or for many trobles <a> man might forsake his calling hee should bee out of any calling, for-as-much as every calling hath his lets and impediments.[29]

judgements   Hee observed that although al exercises of pure
affections how   religion purely used did both strengthen judgement
gotten   and then affection yet reading and hearing and confering do most strengthen judgement and understanding and in part working an affection, but praying, singing, and meditating do most cheefly whet up affection: but in part strengthen judgement and understanding[30]

perticular sins are   Hee said for the comfort of afflicted consciences that
not punished but   the lord doth not so verily punish particular deserts
the general lying   but general fallings into sin, not smal infirmities, but
and abiding in sin   grosser presumptions: for the particular sin bringeth not wrath, but the lying in that sin, and not repenting of it bringeth wrath which drawing in other sins withal draweth in also gods displeasure: so that one sin may bee said to bee both spared and punished. Spared if being admonished wee bee humbled as David by Nathan .2.Samuel.12.[31] Josaphat by Jehu 2.Chronicles.19.[32] beecaus in

[28] *Propositions*, [saying] 14.

[29] Calling 4, First Edition, 6; Second Edition, 6; Third Edition, 4; Fourth Edition, 4; Fifth Edition, 4. Also see: *Propositions*, [saying] 15.

[30] Judgements 2, First Edition, 33; Second Edition, 32; Third Edition, 19; Fourth Edition, 19; Fifth Edition, 19. Also see: *Propositions*, [saying] 16.

[31] 2 Samuel 12:1-14.

[32] 2 Chronicles 19:1-11.

this wee seem not to draw in other sins but to bee[33] rid of this one sin punished, when notwithstanding al merciful admonitions and sorer threatnings wee stil ly in sin, and lay sin to sin, and so make a way for gods judgements to fal on us: wherfore wee may comfort ourselves for particular sins so that in the general course of our whole life wee labour truly to please god: for as a loving husband doth not take away his love from [fol. 4r] his wife though in some particulars of her obedience and dutyes shee faileth so long as shee keepeth her love wholy and truly to him: so the loving kindnes of the lord wil not cast of his children for some particular wants and faylings in special commandements so long as in sincere love of his Majestye wee stil persevere to obey him.[34]

Reverent hearing of the word in publick and speking evil of it in private
Hee observed that many would receiv the word of god publiquely preached with reverence, but being privately spoken they made no such accompt of it: therin men shewed themselves not to respect the preacher of god and of his word: but som other things: and that some (which was a fowler sin and woorthy publique reprehension) would hear a man willingly in the church and gainsay his doctrine at home wherin they bewraied[35] rather that they hard for solemnity of the place then of any devotion[36]

1582

Threatning gods judgements how it ought to bee
Hee said how in denowncing the judgement of god, either privately to one or publickly to mee, hee stil was earnestly and inwardly moved to pray that that evil which the lord had fore shewed him out of the word to fal on them might bee burned away. So far was hee from speaking in wrath that then hee most praied for them[37]

---

[33] Followed by *ruled* deleted.

[34] Matrimony 3, First Edition, 36; Second Edition, 35; Third Edition, 21; Fourth Edition, 21; Fifth Edition, 21. Also found under: Of Conscience 9, Third Edition, 276; Fourth Edition, 299; Fifth Edition, 651. Last two sentences of this saying found in: *Propositions*, [saying) 17.

[35] That is, betrayed.

[36] Preaching 3, First Edition, 44; Second Edition, 44; Third Edition, 26; Fourth Edition, 26; Fifth Edition, 26. The last sentence also found under: Of Catechizing and instruction of youth 8, Third Edition, 291; Fourth Edition, 313; Fifth Edition, 665.

[37] Preaching 4, First Edition, 44-5; Second Edition, 44; Third Edition, 26; Fourth Edition, 26; Fifth Edition, 26.

Commendation Hee being curteously saluted and <worthily>[38] commended of a religious gentle<wo>man, who said shee hard a very good report of him, answered her. The like have I hard of you but god make[39] owr after fruits of his spirit more effectual then the former or els wee shal not answer the glory of god and good opinion of his saincts commending of us.[40]

Want of occasion to good exercises When a vertuous professor in the court had lamented to him the want of occasion of good things, and the plentiful occasions of evil, hee said, Behold the wicked that dare not boldly profes iniquity redeem times sorely to commit it: even so [fol. 4v] although thou have occasions of syn, yet the caus of sin is stil in thy self seing then though you have not that strength to profes religion publiquely, yet you must redeem tyme and place secretly to frequent the exercises of godlines[41]

Dedicating a book Being purposed to dedicate a book, hee desired to bee put in mind to request earnest promis and praier that neither his name in dedicating nor thothers in accepting the book might impeach any thing from the authority of the book[42]

Zeal examined Hee said that in his most earnestnes in dealing in any matter hee was zealous over his own hart, and therfore then especialy examined and called to accompt his affections, beecaus that in such a case ther is either some special woork of god or els it is some notable work of the flesh. And wheras it is a common pedago<d>gye of the soule, that in al things wee had need to aske the government of god by his word and spirit, in that a man knoweth what hee is but not what hee shalbee in this or that action, when hee could not gage the depth of his hart, hee would impute it to the want of praier and the not traveling[43] with his hart, how to do the things in wisdom.[44]

---

[38] Replacing *earnestly* deleted.

[39] Replacing *after* deleted.

[40] Fruites of Faith 1, First Edition, 21; Second Edition, 21; Third Edition, 12; Fourth Edition, 12; Fifth Edition, 12. Also see: *Propositions*, [saying] 18.

[41] Exercise of Religion 1, First Edition, 19; Second Edition, 18; Third Edition, 11; Fourth Edition, 11; Fifth Edition, 11. This saying was restructured grammatically to create two sayings in: *Propositions*, [sayings] 19, 20.

[42] This may be a reference to Richard Greenham's *A Godlie Exhortation, and Fruitfull Admonition to Vertuous Parents and Modest Matrons* (London, 1584). It was his only publication before his death; and it did not include a dedication. The version of this work found in the First Edition has been transcribed and printed in this volume.

[43] That is, travailing.

[44] Judgements 1, First Edition, 33; Second Edition, 32; Third Edition, 19; Fourth Edition, 19; Fifth Edition, 19.

Good thoughts

Again hee said with humble thanks given to the lord that <hee> was not greatly trobled with evil thoughts but that god blessed him with good purposes, for the most part: howbeit sometimes hee was greeved that his meditations in themselves being excellent and divine were not so fit for the present tyme, place, and occasion and therfore through instant opportunity of other things they vanished away and would not bee received but as they were woonderful in conceiving and the very gifts of god: so they were marvelously in departing suddenly from him

Heavenly meditations coming and departing suddenly

Good purposes and motions presently to bee presently put in execution if it may bee

To one that being asked whether one being named to admonish an unruly party by writing, and yet doubted that [fol. 5r] it would not bee profitable should continue in that purpose and do it or noe. hee answered it was a great sin then not to do it and also a great judgement of god. god[45] often came of that sin, which was that wee should forget that good motion, or having the motion wee should want oportunity to do it: for saith hee. Let us do the thing and leave the succes to god, after wee have praied for it. And if it do so come to pas (as often it doth that though thaction[46] bee good our hart upright in doing, our affection loving and the end rightly considered bee good yet our labours and praiers bee unfruitful. Let us remember that in al those ther were secret imperfections and sins for which the lord might hinder the succes which by deferring hee might scoure away that after ward in fuller measure of his mercie when wee should bee better prepared by humility to bee thankful hee may power[47] out a more rich measure for forgetfulnes in such good motions.[48] It were good to beestow that <time> which wee have redeemed from praying and reading in putting down a note of those things in writings.

Immoderate care of outward things

To one that told him of the curious and immoderate care of a gentlewoman about outward things <hee said it commonly commeth to pas that in whom ther is such an immoderate care about outward things there are few good

---

[45] That is, good.

[46] That is, the action.

[47] That is, pour.

[48] Prayer 7, First Edition, 46; Second Edition, 46; Third Edition, 27; Fourth Edition, 27; Fifth Edition, 27. Also found under: Admonition 4, Third Edition, 256; Fourth Edition, 277-8; Fifth Edition, 629-30. Substantially modified version found in: *Propositions*, [saying] 21.

inward things> for if one have good things inward the person that hath them as they labor not for outward things somuch; but if they want that and desire them the careful seeking of them bringeth a godly neglect of careful seeking of outward things.[49]

Discerning of our company This advice hee gave to one, that it was good to discern of them who wee much receiv into our company, lest wee leese[50] the credit of the church conceived of us. For although many seem and shew themselves to bee wel disposed, yet seing ther bee so many corruptions, it is heavenly [fol. 5v] wisdom to discern of men. Wherfore it is good for us to consider with what soundnes of judgement and power of true knowledge they do speake. Many seem to lament ther affections and temptations, who lament rather for want of knowledge when they hear the word Secondly it is good to looke what sight they have of ther inward corruptions. This humility teacheth true wisdom and the sight hereof wil make us truly to know christ and him crucified. For many that have a little confused knowledge, wil much bee talking but for want of this knowledg they are not so sound Lastly see how ready they are by this soundnes of knowledg and feeling of inward corruptions to do good to others with cheerfulnes and to speak of the infirmities of others with compassion and greef. for many having those former gifts wil rather at large furiously declaime against the sins and infirmities of others, then either wisely to admonish them or brotherly to pitty them. Thes three observations are profitable for judgement, to discern men, to try whither they have good knowledge, whither they complain of ther wants and corruptions, and whither they speak with greef and compassion of the infirmities of others.[51]

[no month] 8[52] Hee being put in mind of his great zeal and fervency **Great zeal and** of speaking, that hee should leav it, said hee would **fervency of speach** not have any use it with constraint, but when the **in preaching** weightines of the thing provoked therunto and gods spirit should move unto it: howbeit when hee did some time move earnestly[53] as hee was moved by the spirit of god hee said that the fruit that came of it, though long [fol. 6r] after, did more perswade him to use it, then al the speaches of his frinds could diswade him from it.

---

[49] Care 1, First Edition, 7; Second Edition, 7; Third Edition, 4; Fourth Edition, 4; Fifth Edition, 4. Also see: *Propositions*, [saying] 22.

[50] That is, lose.

[51] Friendship 1, First Edition, 24; Second Edition, 23; Third Edition, 14; Fourth Edition, 14; Fifth Edition, 14.

[52] It is unclear from the context which month is intended here.

[53] Followed by *of it* deleted.

[no month] 11[54]   Hee[55] had most delight to frequent those places where god had made his ministry most fruitful, saying herin hee was like to a covetuous man in that ther wher he had found the sweetnes of the gain of soules thither hee desired to resort.[56]

Christian talk at   At the table, as hee was rare, either in beginning
meat   wholsome talke with modesty, or in continuing it with power and vehemency: so hee was woont to say that it was an unchristian courtesy, that men should alwaies stay for the preacher, seing they were annointed with the same spirit, though not with the like measure of like graces, and as though the minister alone was taught: therfore hee would wish others by praier to offer ther speaches to god, and to use them advisedly reverently, and not passing the bounds of ther knowledge, and if they would not speak of any thing, yet they should aske somthing: if they could not ask, yet they should speake of the Communion of saincts: if they cold say nothing yet at least they should complain of ther dul minds, which is a punished mind and even of ther dulnes and deadnes should rayse quicknes and life of speach again.

Profiting by   Hee alwaies profited if hee might bee in the place of
christian exercises   reading, praying or preaching ever of conscience to the ordinance of god, were the speaker never so wise or otherwise For if hee spake of judgement hee said hee either increased or confirmed his knowledge. If the speaker had great wants even those wants did humble him and made him inwardly to meditate of that truth wherof the speaker failed, insomuch that in that same time in hearing the wants, which things hee said hee should not have done if hee had been altogether absent, that hee cold bee as wel inabled [fol. 6v] to preach again of that text which hee hard as if hee had read some commentary.[57]

---

[54] It is unclear from the context which month is intended here.

[55] Followed by *said* deleted.

[56] Ministerie. Ministers' 2, First Edition, 42; Second Edition, 41; Third Edition, 24; Fourth Edition, 24; Fifth Edition, 24. Also see: *Propositions*, [saying] 23.

[57] Preaching 6, First Edition, 45; Second Edition, 45; Third Edition, 26; Fourth Edition, 26; Fifth Edition, 26. A common practice for 'godly' preachers was to attend and participate in local or regional exercises, often called 'prophesyings', in which the participating clergy discussed and interpreted passages of scripture. One of the primary aims of these exercises was to improve the quality of preaching in parishes by giving less able preachers appropriate pastoral approaches to scriptural passages as well as constructive criticism on sermons delivered to the group. (Greenham is observing that even when the sermon or 'lecture' was given by a poor preacher, he found some benefit in hearing it.) When Queen Elizabeth tried to suppress prophesyings, Archbishop Grindal objected strenuously, defending their orthodoxy and utility. His blunt and passionate letter

Temptation with unbeleef Unto one that was much troubled <tempted> with unbeleef hee gave this counsaile, when the temptation cometh either fal down in praier and say o lord thou makest mee to posses the sins of my youth and this temptation is of very equity[58] howbeit o lord, graunt I may by wisdom herin make this temptation an holy instruction and suffer mee to posses my soule in patience. O turn this to thy glory and my salvation I see and confes what hath been in mee a long tyme by that which now sheweth it self in mee; and that thy grace hath altogether hitherto kept under this corruption. Lord yet I beleev. Lord yet I wil beleev:[59] help lord my unbeleef thy name bee praised for this zeale of thy love and pledge of thy spirit that in this unbeleef I am greeved as in my beleef I am wont to bee comforted. And though my old and secret sins deserv that I should not only bee given over to infidelity: but also that it should bee in mee without greef and remors yet lord forgive mee my sins both old and new forgive mee myne unthankfulnes. lord increas my faith and graunt good father when thou shalt restore to mee this[60] gift <of grace> again I may use it in fear and shew it in fruits. Or if this do not prevail give yourself with al humblenes to read the word of god specialy the promises and bee stil attending upon the means waiting when the lord shal enlarge your hart. Or if this do not help go to some faithful brother,[61] confes yourself to him acknowledge your weaknes to him, and bee not ashamed to give god the glory by shaming yourself and opening your corruption to him, that so hee may pray [fol. 7r] for you, whose praier according to the promis of god made to his holy ordinance herin James 5,[62] undoubtedly shalbee hard in the appointed time.

Thus having praied by yourself and with another and used the means of reading for your recovery, though you have not present release, yet in meeknes of mind and patience of your spirit, go to your calling knowing that your praiers and the word of god being as seed must have sometime

---

to the queen in1576 led to his suspension. In spite of Elizabeth's efforts, the exercises could be found in many places in the 1580s and 1590s. The text of Grindal's letter, which gives a fine synopsis of the intent and form of the exercises, is printed in *Religion and Society*, Cressy and Ferrell, 93-9. See also Collinson, *Elizabethan Puritan Movement*; Collinson, *Archbishop Grindal*.

[58] That is, just.

[59] Mark 9:24.

[60] Followed by *good* deleted.

[61] Ministers encouraged 'godly' lay people to turn to each other for spiritual guidance, rather than relying solely on the clergy. Although Greenham uses the word 'brother', godliness and not gender determined the choice of confidant. See Willen, 'Communion of the Saints', 19-41.

[62] James 5:16.

between the sowing of them and the reaping of the fruit and increas of them. Above al things, reason not with your <u>self</u>[63] temptations, dispute not with the devil as though you could prevaile of yourself; and as I would not you should dispute with your corruption: so I wold not you should dispute it and make no account of it. for in both are extremities. If yee take it too much to hart, or marvel how yee should overcome such a temptation, it wil make you dul or desperate. If you account of it too little, and marvel how such things should come into your head, which was not wont to bee so, it wil make you strive, and you shalbee swallowed up, ere you bee aware. If you accompt of it too fearfully. sathan wil oppres you ere you begin to fight. If you accompt of it too lightly the devil needeth not to wrestle with you, you wil overcome yourself. Therfore fear in regard of yourself, fight boldly in christ: tremble for your own corruption, but rest and trust in christ your salvation. If stil you bee tempted and no body by you, write your temptation, offer it to god by praier, and promise to him you wil aske counsel of his word, at the mouth of the minister, when hee shal give you just occasion. If al this help not, comfort yourself with this pledge of election, that you are joyed when you feel your beleef [fol. 7v] and you are greeved lest you should displease god by your unbeleef, and know that as ther is a vicissitude of[64] the means of salvation which you must use: so ther is a vicissitude of temptations wherof this is one against which you must strive[65]

not weary of weldoing

When one said to him after long conference and praier Sir, I have troubled you. No my brother, not so, said hee. I never felt it by weldoing: and if I may pleasure you, it is <as> joyful to mee, as ever it was to you to receiv money, for this caus I live.[66]

Preaching of the law

Sometime hee would confes that sathan would tel his conscience that hee preached not the gospel to bring men to christ as hee ought to do, hee answered, his conscience did bear him witnes, that in these secure and semles[67] daies the preaching of the law was the nearest way to direct men by to Christ.

---

[63] 'self' is absent from the printed versions of this saying.

[64] Followed by *the means temptations* deleted.

[65] Temptations 12, First Edition, 67-9; Second Edition, 66-8; Third Edition, 38-9; Fourth Edition, 38-9; Fifth Edition, 38-9. Also see: *Propositions*, [saying] 27; *Two Treatises*, [saying 1], 192-5.

[66] Prayer 8, First Edition 46; Second Edition, 46; Third Edition, 27; Fourth Edition, 27; Fifth Edition, 27. Also see: *Propositions*, [saying] 25.

[67] That is, shameful, unfitting, unseemly.

For saith hee, by the law I drive men out of themselves and send them to christ if they wil, but if they refuse they go worthily to hel: and so to whom hee could not bee the messenger of salvation for ther unbeleef, unto them hee was an instrument of condemnation prepared for them.

Profiting by the word not presently but after some space of time Hee could not alwaies looke to the issue and effect of his doctrine, but as a good fieldsman, hee would long after hee had sowen looke for the increas, not measuring the fruit of his labor by the time present but by the tyme to come saying if hee found by experience, that they that presently seemed to embrace his doctrine unwillingly or dully, afterward when they had shaken of somewhat of that corruption and in truth before the lord had examined that doctrine in ther harts they received it thankfully and and [*sic*] imbraced it profitably.

Worldly shame [fol. 8r] Unto one that was tempted with worldly shame and thought the distemperature of his mind and body proceeded therof, hee said on this sort. first know that sathan hath no absolute power <by> <u>of</u> permission to try us,[68] against which wee must arm ourselves by faith which wil assure us that either the lord wil mitigate the temptation if our power and patience bee not great or els if hee enlarge the trial, hee wil increas our strength and retch[69] it out according to the proportion of our temptation. wee must also pray that the lord give not out the measure against his Majesty but hee would rather make sathan a surgeon to shew us our sins, then a sergeant to confound us for our sins.[70] It is the policie of the Adversary to perswade many that the weaknes of ther brain, and feeblenes of ther body proceedeth of ther temptations when indeed it cometh of ther unstaied minds, wandring too much after the motions of the devil, in that they not resting on the word, not depending on christ, not contenting themselves to bee tried, not comforting themselves by meditation attend too much and confer so often with the devils illusions and temptations, and so they complain of the effects and not of the causes of ther temptations, being much more greeved for ther present sufferings, then for ther sins past. The roote of this worldly shame is pride and hautines of mind which is a privy evil and hardly wil bee beaten into the head of them that are infected with it. But sure it is that wee would never bee so greeved for the los of a thing if wee did not too much desire it and did immoderately

---

[68] Printed version of this reads: 'Satan hath no absolute power but a power by permission to trie us ...'. Edition 1, 69.

[69] That is, stretch.

[70] Here 'sergeant' refers to the officer of a court who condemns. Thanks to Patrick Collinson for his observations on this text.

use it whilest wee had it John 12.42.43[71] which sin of hautines and pride the lord seeing in his children that they are more humbled with the los of worldly credit then with the sence of ther sins and losse of his glory, hee striketh them with that [fol. 8v] thing which is most precious to them beecaus they made no conscience of that which was most precious to him. Wherfore this is the best remedy rather to bee greeved that wee feel not our sins pardoned with god, then that wee are knowen to bee sinners amongst men and that wee bee ready to shame ourselves that god may have the glory, acknowledging shame and confusion and the whole hel of temptations to bee dewe unto us, glory praise and compassion to bee only the lords: for this is the special marke of the child of god by temptations mightily humbled, when a man is ready to shame himself for his sin, to glorify god in his mercy[72]

[no month] 16   Hee gave this advice for a general prescription of
Spiritual physick   Physick. first the parties afflicted are to labor to have
           peace of ther consciences and joy of the holy ghost
thorough the assurance of ther sins pardoned in christ. then carefully must they fly to the means, which may nourish this inward joy and peace. Thirdly they must rejoice and recreate themselves in wisdom and weldoing with the saincts of god and holy companyes. Lastly they must refresh themselves with kitching[73] Physick and a thankful using of the creatures of god.[74]

True and spiritual   Hee said with thankful humility, that his love ever
love   grew to a man as hee knew the man to grow in
           godlines and his love decaied as the graces decaied so
that first hee was greeved and then his love slaked,[75] beecaus hee cold find no more comforts in the soule of the man. So far was hee from loving or knowing any man in the flesh[76]

Unto one that asked his advice in outward things who as yet stood in greater need to bee instructed in inward hee said. If you first wil confer

---

[71] John 12:42-3.

[72] Temptations [13], First Edition, 69-70. Second Edition, 68-9. Third Edition, 39; Fourth Edition, 39; Fifth Edition, 39. See also *Propositions*, [saying] 28; *Two Treatises*, [saying] 2, 195-7. The last half of this saying paraphrased under: Of Catechizing and instruction of youth 9, Third Edition, 291; Fourth Edition, 313; Fifth Edition, 665.

[73] That is, 'kitchen'.

[74] Sicke and Sicknes 1, First Edition, 59; Second Edition, 58-9; Third Edition, 34; Fourth Edition, 34; Fifth Edition, 34. Also see: *Propositions*, [saying] 24.

[75] *Propositions*, [saying] 26.

[76] Friendship 6, Third Edition, 14; Fourth Edition, 14; Fifth Edition, 14. This saying shares characteristics found in one on fol. 23r.

with mee and establish [fol. 9r] yourself in things concerning faith and repentance, then ask mee and I wil advise you freely for your outward estate. Howbeit beecaus you seem (though I know not your hart) to bee scrupulouse in wearing a surples et cap:[77] as I wil not for al the world wish or advice you to wear them, so I would counsaile you generaly to bee wel grounded ere to leav them, lest that you shaking them of rather of light affection then sound of judgement, afterward take them againe to your shame and the offence of others.[78]

Mistrust ⎫ in　　Hee gave this advice to one, that when hee felt
　　　　　⎬ gods　mistrust of gods promises, hee should set beefore
presumption ⎭ promises him the examples of gods mercies done to others,
　　　　　　　　　that wee may bee the more assured to obtain faith: and when hee began to presume, hee should set before him the examples of gods judgements, that hee may pray for humility.[79]

Lawful use of money　A certain man that was an usurer asking him how with a good conscience hee might use his money, hee said occupy it in some trade of life and when yee can lend to the pore freely and willingly. And that you may hence forth as wel labour against covetuousnes in occupying that trade, as before ye desired to strive usury against usury, especialy use praier, the word of god and the company and conference of his children. And whatsoever yee get by lawful gain, give ever more the tenth to the pore[80]

want of means to godlines　Hee said that many now daies complain of want of means and true it is in many places. Howbeit the meanes are so plentiful and men so unthankful and slothful, that if trouble should come, wee would rather accus ourselves of want of affections then of want of means and occasion to glorify god and his word

---

[77] For Greenham's involvement in this controversy, see Chapter 2, p. 16. For a discussion of the controversy over wearing the cap, see Norman Jones, *The Birth of the Elizabethan Age* (Oxford: Blackwell, 1993), 53–65.

[78] [Saying] 5, Ceremonies, Third Edition, 491; Fourth Edition, 515; Fifth Edition 44.

[79] Unbeleef 1, First Edition 71; Second Edition, 71; Third Edition, 40; Fourth Edition, 40; Fifth Edition, 40. Also see: *Propositions*, [saying] 31.

[80] Usurie 1, First Edition, 73; Second Edition, 72; Third Edition, 41; Fourth Edition, 41–2; Fifth Edition, 41–2. For a discussion of the usury in this period see: Jones, *The Birth of the Elizabethan Age*, 7–8.

Athisme   Hee feared rather Athisme then Papism in the realm
                 for many having escaped out of the gulf of
superstition are now too far plagued and swallowed up of prophaines,
thincking either that ther is no god or els that hee is not so fearful and
merciful as his threatnings and promise commend him to bee.[81]

Praier   Hee being desired to give his judgement of a weighty
                 matter [fol. 9v] hee said Sir neither am I able to speak
nor you to hear beecaus wee have not praied. Indeed I may talke and you
hear as natural men, but wee are not now prepared to confer as the
children of god[82]

Lamentations for   Seing a woman lamenting for the sins of the people
the sins of the   hee said unto her not purposing to cause her cease
people   from soe good an action, but admonishing her to look
to her affection, you shal wel try your hart said hee, if this sorrow for sin
bee first bred for your own sins, and from yourself proceed to the sins of
others. Again the measure of your mourning must bee agreeable and
proportionable to the sin. Lastly your greef must so bee for the person as
you bee moved rather to pity and pray for him, then to hate and despise
him.[83]

Preparation before   Traveling to a certain place to preach, although hee
the hearing of the   had the testimony of his own conscience that hee was
woord   not unprepared both of praier and meditation, yet
suspecting his own affections and the want of preparation in the people,
hee said hee was afraid to speak, beecaus hee was to hope for thes causes
for the les fruit of the people by his speach,

Dispraising a   Unto one that with many words disabled himself hee
mans self   said meekly. Oh why do you seek so much your own
                     praise wherby hee bewraied[84] that privy corruption of
nature, that by too open disprais desired to stir praise and
commendation[85]

---

[81] Atheisme 2, First Edition, 5–6; Second Edition, 5; Third Edition, 3; Fourth Edition, 3;
Fifth Edition, 3. Also see: *Propositions*, [saying] 41.

[82] *Propositions*, [saying] 32.

[83] Griefe for Sinne 4, First Edition, 27; Second Edition, 26; Third Edition, 16; Fourth
Edition, 15–16; Fifth Edition, 15–16. Also see: *Propositions*, [saying] 33.

[84] That is, betrayed.

[85] Praise 1, First Edition, 46; Second Edition, 46; Third Edition, 27; Fourth Edition, 27;
Fifth Edition, 27. Also see: *Propositions*, [saying] 34.

Using physick   Hee said that it was not good to use that for a diet
<diet>   which is prescribed for phisick for then that wil not
ordinarily   woork in an extraordinary need of the body, which is
used in an ordinary course of our health.[86]

When in his meditation some good thing was offered him for to answer
as an objection which might[87] either les pertinent to the matter or not
very fitly to bee draween out of his text, hee would say, that seing what
cometh [fol. 10r] into one mans head commeth into another mans head,
at one tyme or another hee thought good to speake the thing thus
meditated of

Baptism by a   When a certain man came to have his children
negligent minister   Baptised of him, beecaus hee durst not commit them
                to the ordinary minister who had some defects, hee
answered, Brother, though your pastor bee carnal, yet I hope hee is a
Babe in christ, and though to him for administring the sacrament it is sin,
in that unreverently hee handleth the holy things of god, yet it shal not
hinder the blessing of thordinance of god on your children for as much
as the ordinance of the sacrament doth not depend ex dignitate
administrantis, sed ex fide accipientis et institutione dei.[88] When hee had
proved this by Isaachs blessing of Jacob when hee was carnally minded,[89]
by the apostle baptising being very ignorant hee added this. Go to your

---

[86] Sicke and Sicknes 2, First Edition, 59; Second Edition, 59; Third Edition, 34; Fourth
Edition, 34; Fifth Edition, 34. Also see: *Propositions*, [saying] 35.

[87] Followed by *be* deleted.

[88] 'on the basis of the merit of the one ministering, but on the basis of the faithfulness
of the one receiving and the institution of God'. This appears to be an interpretive
summary of Augustine's argument against the Donatists, that dramatically alters the
meaning of the original text, and in so doing endorses a receptionist understanding of
baptism. The Augustinian text reads, 'non propter eos a quibus ministratur, vel a quibus
accipitur, sed propter illum qui hunc Baptismum immaculatus instituit' ('not for the merits
of those by whom it is administered, or by whom it is received, but in virtue of the stainless
merits of Him who instituted this baptism'). Note that the emphasis in the text from
Augustine is on Christ and his merits alone as the basis for a valid baptism. In the
summary provided in the Greenham saying, it is not only the institution of God but the
faithfulness of the one receiving baptism that is required for validity. Augustine, 'Contra
Litteras Petiliani Libri III', in *Patrologia Latina* (Paris, 1846), 2.35.82, XLIII, 287;
Augustine, 'The Three Books of Augustin, Bishop of Hippo, in Answer to the Letters of
Petilian, the Donatist', in *The Nicene and Post-Nicene Fathers of the Christian Church*,
ed. Philip Schaff (New York: Charles Scribner's Sons, 1909), 2.35.82, IV, 551.

[89] Genesis 27:1-46. In Isaac's old age and blindness he called to his son Esau to bring
him some savoury dish in exchange for the blessing due him as the oldest son. With the
help of Rebecca, Isaac's wife, the younger son Jacob was able to masquerade as Esau, give
his father food, and receive the blessing initially intended for Esau.

pastor, and say Sir, wheras your wants in your calling, and (though otherwise I reverence both your person, your calling and your gifts) had almost scared mee from committing my children into your ministry, yet now having learned out of the word by the spirit of god through Jesus christ, that it is rather your sin then myne as I thought good to bee obedient to the ordinance of god, whose blessing only I looke for: so I am to desire you to looke to yourself lest your blood bee upon yourself, how either in this or in other duties, your negligence offendeth the sainct. if you wil hear me I shalbee glad, if not I shalbee sorry

March 4. Interogatories in Baptism[90] Unto one that asked him how hee might keep a good conscience in answering the corrupt interrogationes in Baptism, hee saied as soon I have done, you may say nothing, for as others you may make answer according to a good conscience or els you may keep your self from the action

Just obedience to an unjust commandement [fol. 10v] When one asked how they might keep certain duties to the chancellour dealing corruptly, in so corrupt dealing, hee answered to an unjust commandement wee may yeeld just obedience,[91] so it bee in things meerly outward. For when the Romans had usurped the taxes upon the people of god, Joseph and Mary went up to bee taxed[92]

Sitting or kneeling at the communion After one had asked his advice for sitting and kneeling at the lords table hee said, As for such things, Let us do as much as wee can with the peace of the church lest wee make the remedy of the evil wors then the evil it self[93]

---

[90] The 'interrogatories' were questions about faith which the minister asked of the godparents on behalf of the child being presented for baptism. Some considered these questions to be one of the flaws in the Book of Common Prayer because the godparents lacked the power to make binding promises for the infant, especially in matters of faith. In the words of John Field's 'View of Popish Abuses' (1572), 'they ask questions of an infant, which cannot answer, and speak unto them, as was wont to be spoken unto men, and unto such as being converted, answered for themselves and were baptized. Which is but a mockery of God, and therefore against the Holy Scriptures.' (*Religion and Society*, Cressy and Ferrell, 85.) See fol. 12r, below.

[91] Obedience 1, Third Edition, 25. It is significant that this saying is dropped from subsequent editions. See Chapter 4, 52-6.

[92] Luke 2:1-5.

[93] Sacraments 2, First Edition, 51; Second Edition, 51; Third Edition, 30; Fourth Edition, 30; Fifth Edition, 30. Also see: *Propositions*, [saying] 37. The Prayer Book required people to receive communion kneeling. In 1552, in response to objections raised by John Knox, a rubric was inserted which explained that kneeling was intended to avoid disorder at communion and to show humble gratitude to Christ; it was not to be construed

Possessed by the devil   Unto one that said hee was possessed of a devil hee answered as hoping that hee was the child of god, and rather deluded then afflicted. True it is that in as much as lyeth in you, you have given over your self to the devil, but it is not in your power to give yourself unto him, neither is it in his jurisdiction to posses you.[94]

Unwillingnes Conference   Hee said this was a general rule with him especialy to strive with himself to go to that place, whither to go hee findeth unwillingnes in himself. Hee said in conferring with others hee could bee as <fervent as> another, but having a godly jealousy of his corruption for the most part, hee did suppres, wherby hee felt this inconvenience, as sometyme hee abstained from many evil things: so also sometyme hee abstained even from many good things.

Rebuking of sin   Hee did use being at the table, so to rebuke sin, as hee wold reform rather then rebuke, and if a publique offence were made by a private man at tyme unconvenient, hee would rebuke the sin as zealous of gods glory, and yet correct thoffendor as pitying his brother, and that on this manner, my bretheren such a syn hath passed from this place, the giltles need not to bee offended the person gilty is to repent of it.[95]

Reprehension   Being asked how a man might reprehend, hee answered, first Looke that you have ground out of the word for reproof then looke if it stand with your calling to reproove,

---

as adoration of the bread and wine, which was condemned as idolatry. Communicants were again instructed to receive kneeling in the 1559 Prayer Book, but the 1552 rubric was not included. In 1572, John Field objected that kneeling 'hath in it a show of papistry' and also misrepresented the 'mystery' of the Lord's Supper. By sitting, according to Field, 'we signify rest, that is a full finishing through Christ of all the ceremonial law, and a perfect work of redemption wrought that giveth rest forever' (*Religion and Society*, Cressy and Ferrell, 84). Greenham objects to kneeling (the evil it self'), but suggests that the disorder of disobedience might be worse than kneeling, perhaps since it was at least possible to teach people to construe kneeling in a way free of superstition and idolatry. In many places, receiving communion sitting became the accepted practice, in spite of the Prayer Book directive. See George Yule, 'James VI and I: Furnishing the Churches in His Two Kingdoms' in Anthony Fletcher and Peter Roberts (eds), *Religion, Culture and Society in Early Modern Britain: Essays in Honour of Patrick Collinson* (Cambridge: Cambridge University Press, 1994): 182-208.

[94] Satans Practises 4, First Edition, 62; Second Edition, 61; Third Edition, 35; Fourth Edition, 35; Fifth Edition, 35. Also see: *Propositions*, [saying] 38.

[95] Rebuking or Reproving of Sinne 4, First Edition, 48; Second Edition, 48; Third Edition, 28; Fourth Edition, 28; Fifth Edition, 28. Also see: *Propositions*, [saying] 39.

[fol. 11r] afterward consider if some other may not do it more profitably then you: then looke before whom you reproov: lest yee hinder the credit of the party with his frinds and increas his discredit with his foes. again if by al occasions, of calling, person, tyme, and place the lord hath put you in the place to rebuke sin, remember you must put on the person of the offendor, that as you spare not his sin beecaus of zeale of gods glory, so you pres it not too far beecaus of compassion of a brother. Then looke that with thes your hart bee right in zeale and love, and so cal for gods assistance before you speake, for his grace, in speaking, for his blessing after your speaking: If any thing bee left out that might bee profitable, pleas not yourself in it but bee humbled for it, though some infirmities bee in you, yet they shal not do so much harm as gods ordinance shal do good.[96]

In baptism the fathers presence required   At what tyme a certain man had requested him, to preach another charge, to confirm by publique doctrine that the father ought to promis for his child, as hee was vehement in his sermon, sodainly[97] hee hard, as it were sensibly a voice saying unto him. why art thou zealous in this place, when as one shal dissanul this order, even in thyne own place, at which thing hee was astonished, and pawsed, howbeit by the grace of god hee overcame this temptation at that time. The lords day immediately following, as hee was going according to his manner to his congregation to preach, a certain man met him not very forward and said, Sir, A frind of mine meaneth to send his child to bee baptised of you, but hee himself wil not come and as hee saith hee is sick. Then cometh to mind the voice which hee had hard, in his[98] late sermon. The thing troubled his mind, stil continuing on the way to the church; reading and preaching the word, hee felt noe way how to deal in this case. Howbeit in al this his hart being before the lord, for the assistance of his spirit, in the very end of this sermon, god taught him how to doe. Wherfore coming to the font, hee looketh for the promisers[99] and [fol. 11v] father of the child, whom when hee saw not present hee desired the people to sing the 2 or 3 Psalm and openly chargeth two men the one a frind of this father absent,

---

[96] Rebuking or Reproving of Sinne 1, First Edition, 47–8; Second Edition, 47; Third Edition, 28; Fourth Edition, 28; Fifth Edition, 28. Also see: *Propositions*, [saying] 42.

[97] That is, suddenly.

[98] Followed by *way to the church* deleted.

[99] 'Promisers' refers to godparents. Many nonconformists objected to the term 'godparent' as a popish invention which lacked scriptural warrant. One solution was to use a different word, especially 'witness' (see below, fols 12r, 32v), which emphasized the acceptable dimensions of their role. Both 'promiser' and 'surety' (see above, fol. 10r, and below, fol. 12r) reflect the objectionable practice of making promises about faith on behalf of the infant. See Cressy, *Birth, Marriage and Death*, chap. 7.

thother a faithful and discreet christian on this soe, I desire you in the name of the church that ye go to this man and ask him if hee wil refuse to come, if hee were wel, and ask if hee wil come herafter, if god restore him to health. If hee graunt <to> thes things, aske him further if hee bee willing and desirous to have his child baptised; and if hee bee soe whither being absent in body, hee wil bee present in spirit if hee consent, further request, if for that hee cannot come himself and yet would have his child baptised, hee would make you his delegates, for this tyme to answer in his behalf, and afterward come himself and signify so much to the church of christ. Hee agreed to al and after they had returned his answers, the child was baptised, those men supplying the place of the father and thus his purpose through gods goodnes was dissanulled, who had thought, to have dissanulled so good an order, and the man then absent did after present himself[100]

popish baptism   A certain man talking with him, of the baptising men in tyme of papistry, hee said, for asmuch as they, even they kept the foundacion and substance of the institution that is they Baptised in the name of the father the son and of the holy ghost, ther ministry was effectual. for more prevaileth the institution of christ to do good, then the corruption of man to do evil.[101] And although no other things bee mentioned in the Apostles order then this substance yet ther might bee other circumstances of ther Baptisme

Uttering the   Hee made this rule to himself, never utter youre
temptation   temptacion but when you can have no comfort in yourself [fol. 12r] or when some stand in very great need for ther comforts. And alwaies discern to whom you speak[102]

Suspect yourself   Hee would ever learn to suspect his own opinion and affection when the case any thing concerned himself[103]

---

[100] There is no mention of the mother in this account because it was not customary for the mother to come for her churching for at least two to three weeks and thus re-enter public life. See: Adrian Wilson, 'The Ceremony of Childbirth and Its Interpretation' in Valerie Fildes (ed.), *Women as Mothers in Pre-Industrial England: Essays in Memory of Dorothy McLaren* (London: Routledge, 1990), 88-93.

[101] Of Baptisme 2, Third Edition, 267; Fourth Edition, 290; Fifth Edition, 642.

[102] Temptations 10, First Edition, 67; Second Edition, 66; Third Edition, 38; Fourth Edition, 38; Fifth Edition, 38.

[103] Affections 5, First Edition, 2; Second Edition, 1; Third Edition, 1; Fourth Edition, 1; Fifth Edition, 1.

Suretyes in
Baptism

Being demanded what his judgement was of having promisers in Baptism, hee answered in which things the scriptures give general rules, the church may use the particulars soe al bee done decently, to aedification. In regard wherof as the law commanding generally, to distribute to the pore, a man being not able to help al particularly may take upon him the releef of some special persons, who know not how to walke: and as the law commanding generally justice to defend the good and offend the evil, a man of great authority for his help herin may take some godly learned man to him, as wee cal him a cha<p>lain. I doe not see but it is a duty in Baptism to bee an assistant. Besides, If to profes our church an enemy to Arrianism wee use gloria Patri,[104] which is al one with that which in so many Psalmes is used praise yee the lord. saving that for greater light of the gospel, wee expres it more fully, then to avoid Anabaptism. It is good to have witnesses to testify to the church that wee are christianly baptised, wherof as I detest al frivilous ceremonies and pernitious reliques: so for the keeping of the peace of the church I would not have refused such holy orders as tend both aedification, to love and to comelines in the church.[105]

April 2

Telling good haps
and secret tokens
not sodainly

Hee compounded with his own soule, that when god dealed mercifully with him in his flock not to tel it in other places sodainly. Likewise when god shewed any tokens secret to him self not to utter the same before hee had praied and discerned the same to bee good for company [fol. 12v] lest it should bee so out of tyme that it might not bee delivered with some credit, lest it should either not bee beleeved, or les edify. And when soever hee did speak of any good thing hee would thinck of his sins withall that so hee might bee moved, for gods dealing being so unworthy

Joy and sorrow
for salvation and
sin

Beecaus great natural and worldly sorrow and joy wil cause a man to break his sleep at midnight, hee would try himself whether sorrow for sin or joye

---

[104] Arianism was a fourth-century heresy that denied the true divinity of Jesus Christ. Greenham refers to the liturgical formula used to affirm the divinity of the three persons of the Trinity: 'Gloria Patri, et Filio, et Spiritui Sancto. Sicut erat in principio, et nunc, et semper, et in saecula saeculorum. Amen.' (Glory be to the Father and to the Son and to the Holy Spirit. As it was in the beginning, is now and ever shall be, world without end. Amen.) For examples of its use see: *Liturgical Services: Liturgies and Occasional Forms of Prayer set forth in the Reign of Queen Elizabeth*, ed. William K. Clay, The Parker Society (Cambridge: Cambridge University Press, 1847) 15, 56, 57, 60, 61, 64, 65, 68.

[105] Of Baptisme 5, Third Edition, 268; Fourth Edition, 290; Fifth Edition, 642.

for salvation had caused him to do the like[106]

True willingnes   Hee then thought himself to bee truly willing to do any good when hee did strive al that hee might to do it, although hee could not do it as hee should[107]

Judgement rash   Hee thought al affliccions to bee pullings of him to god from[108] slothfulnes.[109] His advice was that one should not judge of any[110] action in any thing, and that one shold not judge suddainly but tarry the time, and god wil make al things known in the end, beecaus tarrying the lords leassure if wee beleev in him wee shalbee safe

Profiting   Hee thought when hee had no fear nor greef hee <cold not> profited[111] [*sic*]

Temptation   Hee being both feeble in body, and sick in mind, when hee felt the lord strengthning his sleep, and a little norishing him, as also that hee did clear his judgement and more and more gave him a mislike of evil, and likeing of good, hee knew his temptacion should go away in the lord at the end[112]

private and gentle admonitions   This hee observed as a general law that soemuch as with a good conscience might bee, hee would use private warnings before, publique dealings, and gentle and curteous speaches before vehement and sharp <u>speaches</u> and threatnings

Telling reports   Though that hee had hard hee would not speak again but when, wher, and with whom it might edify, and then also it should bee in the reverent feare of god and love unfauned to the parties.

---

[106] Griefe of Sinne 6, First Edition, 27; Second Edition, 26; Third Edition, 16; Fourth Edition, 16; Fifth Edition, 16. Also see: *Propositions*, [saying] 43.

[107] Good Workes 1, First Edition, 26; Second Edition, 25; Third Edition, 15; Fourth Edition, 15; Fifth Edition, 15.

[108] Followed by *flesh* deleted.

[109] Afflictions 1, First Edition, 2; Second Edition, 2; Third Edition, 1; Fourth Edition, 1; Fifth Edition, 1. Also see: *Propositions*, [saying] 49.

[110] Followed by *thing* deleted.

[111] Feare 2, First Edition, 23; Second Edition, 22; Third Edition, 13; Fourth Edition, 13; Fifth Edition, 13.

[112] Of Temptation 20, Third Edition, 440; Fourth Edition, 465; Fifth Edition, 817.

Zeal [fol. 13r] Hee desired to bee earnest and zealous in matters weighty concerning the lord or his people, but in smaller matters of his own affairs, and his worldly funds, hee would take heed, it were not natural or carnal, earnestnes, or not savering of the spirit.[113] Likewise would hee meditate of meeknes and other affections natural, or reformed by reason not by the spirit.[114]

Contention with men debated before god If any breach did arise between him and his frind, hee would bee careful how or ever hee debated it before other men, to debate it with himself in praier fervent, in serious meditation of gods word in a reverent fear of displeasing the lord, in true faith of his promises, in unfained purpose to pleas god, and harty love to his brother, without any flattering of himself

Prayer Hee compounded with himself three times a day to pray for thes things which hee preached: using also daily 3[115] <portions> of 119 Psalm[116]

Promise to pray for one Hee would write the names of them for whom hee promised to pray and also the name of them to whom hee should write.

Affections deceivable Hee said that when for some causes natural affections deceived him, yet the ordinance of god caused him to duties.[117]

Mirth When a certain gentlewoman boldly asked, if hee were not sometimes merry, yes saith hee wee are often merry and sometyme wee are affraid of our mirth.[118] <Whersoever he beecam if either hee did not good to others or received no good by others, hee thought al was in vain, and in speaking hee said hee most remembered those things whereof by some great joy or mirth an impression was left in him>

---

[113] Zeal in private, personal matters was unbecoming. All zeal should be motivated by the spirit, for the Lord and his people, not for personal matters and material gain.

[114] Of Zeale 3, Third Edition, 452-3; Fourth Edition, 477; Fifth Edition, 829.

[115] Followed by *petitions* deleted.

[116] Prayer 5, First Edition, 45-6; Second Edition, 45; Third Edition, 27; Fourth Edition, 27; Fifth Edition, 27.

[117] When to Suspect Affection 6, First Edition, 2; Second Edition, 2; Third Edition, 1; Fourth Edition, 1; Fifth Edition, 1.

[118] Mirth 1, First Edition, 42; Second Edition, 42; Third Edition, 25; Fourth Edition, 25; Fifth Edition, 25. Also see: *Propositions*, [saying] 30.

Seing of frinds   Hee rejoyced to see his frinds but hee was oft humbled
in this in that hee rested so much in that joye, that hee
forgot to do that good to ther salvation, or to receiv good from them to
his salvation which hee thought hee should do[119]

Fairies   One asking him what hee thought of, fayries hee
answered hee thought they were spirits: but hee
distinguished between these and other spirits, as commonly men
distinguish between good witches and bad witches[120]

Discerning men   Hee said hee praied and laboured for wisdom in
discerning men, but for charity also, that the things
which hee saw evil [fol. 13v] in them, might not come upon them

Conscience   Unto a gentlewoman that was affraid that her good
wil was suspected to her husband, being far from her
in that hee received not the letters shee sent him, hee said if your
conscience did accuse you hee could not condemn you and god wil make
known your hart unto him: if your own hart condemne you, then can hee
not excuse you, no, though hee thought very wel of you[121]

Prayers ordinary   Hee used to pray ordinarily in his ordinary place and
and extraordinary   occasions, but extraordinary, at extraordinary
occasions: and soe in his praiers did admonish many
of things in themselves which hee did not otherwise

Old sinns   When some had admonished him for making mention
of old sins, when hee was at the death of many, hee
said, first I esteem not men, as they are at the tyme of sicknes, but
ordinarily I measure them as they were in ther lives. Again they are not
gilty of old sins in deathe which repented truly of old sins in health and
life. Besides if they bee not guilty, my speach or praier hurteth not them
but profiteth others. If they bee gilty the trouble of ther minds shal turn

119 Friendship 5, Third Edition, 14; Fourth Edition, 14; Fifth Edition, 14. Also see:
Propositions, [saying] 44.

120 Witchcraft 2, First Edition, 74; Third Edition, 42; Fourth Edition, 42; Fifth Edition,
42. Also see: *Propositions*, [saying] 45. It is interesting to note that this saying did not
appear in the Second Edition, and reappeared in the third and subsequent editions with
the following marginal gloss concerning witches: 'Not for that they are good or lawfull,
but of blind people so called and reputed.' This suggests that Holland and Egerton
struggled with the position taken and how it should be handled. For discussion of these
issues see: Keith Thomas, *Religion and the Decline of Magic*, 724-34, 318-19.

121 Matrimony 2, First Edition, 36; Second Edition, 34-5; Third Edition, 21; Fourth
Edition, 21; Fifth Edition, 21.

to ther good, in that they shall find ther judgements in this world and escape the fynal judgement that is to come[122]

Holy daies fitted for fasting daies   Hee thought our civil Holidaies, to bee the fittest and most convenient times for fasting daies, both beecaus wee might then do it with lest suspicion, or offence of others, and beecaus then wee may redeem the tyme in resting from our callings[123]

Anger and greef for the godly transgressing   Hee was ever most greeved or moved with anger, (yet with love) with them whome hee tendered most in the lord, and who had given him most credit by submitting themselves wholly to his ministry.[124]

[May] 2 Profiting by speaches   [fol. 14r] Hee observed this advantage in his speaches for his encouragement first if al did not profit, so that one amongst ten profited, hee thought hee had the winings that christ had: if they profited not presently, that hee spake too, yet they might profit hereafter: if the persons to whom hee spake profited not, others standing by might profit: if none of them profited, yet hee knew the word should not bee in vain

[May] 12 A troubled conscience for sin   Hee told mee[125] in love this observation and experience, when any came with a troubled conscience for syn, wisely to discern whither they bee meanly greeved, with a general and roving sight of ther sins, or whither they bee extreamly through down, with the burden of particular sins: if so they bee, then it is good at the first to shew that noe syn is so great, but in christ it is pardonable, and that ther is mercy with god that hee might bee feared. soe on the one side shewing the mercy to come from god, but soe as they are nothing fit to receiv mercy, unles they feel ther particular and prickt sins. but if ther sorrow bee more confused in general things, then it is good to humble them more and more, to give them a terror of gods justice, for particular sins. For experience doth teach us, that this is the best way both to see sin and to bee humbled to see sin, beecaus often

---

[122] 'Of Phisicke and diet, sicknesse and health' 8, Third Edition, 419; Fourth Edition, 443; Fifth Edition, 795.

[123] 'Of the exercises of religion, fasting, etc. and of the carefull use of the means at all times' 2, Third Edition, 298; Fourth Edition, 321; Fifth Edition, 673.

[124] Anger 2, First Edition, 4; Second Edition, 4; Third Edition, 3; Fourth Edition, 3; Fifth Edition, 3.

[125] This is the first reference the recorder of the sayings makes to himself in the notebook.

men wil acknowledge greater sins they have been in, then that little <sin> they presently ly in; to bee humbled in that being thorowly thrown down, wee wil directly seek christ, and keep no stay, until wee have found comfort in him, who then is most ready to free us from our sin and to comfort us with his spirit, when wee are most cast down with our sins and <most> fear it.[126]

[May] 13
Greef for the not
profiting of the
godly

Hee protested that hee never was so moved, at the reprochings of his enemies, as the not profiting of his frinds, that is, such as hee thought the joy, crown, and glory of his ministery, for whome hee had praied and with whom hee had travailed for [fol. 14v] as thes men alone gave al the credit to his ministry in weldoing for ther salvation. so they did far more discredit him by evil doing then al others, at whose hands hee looked for no such things. And for this cause hee was not so mooved to see the common sort <of people> offend, beecaus hee marveiled not that they failed in dutyes, when others which are continually taught do so often slip, and fal[127]

True joy and
sorrow

His greatest sorrow was, when either hee spake some good thing, which was not in himself, or when hee spake some evil thing, which was in himself, and his greatest joy in the contrary.[128] Again when hee had been most vehement, and spent himself (as hee thought) that now if ever, mens harts would bee mooved: soe when hee saw no fruit it greeved him, in that men did not profit, hcc having lost more then they knew of: howbeit if this los of strength and body might bee ther gain, hee said hee was joied and not greeved

[May] 21

Hee said whensoever hee suspected, and feared some evil to come, upon another, hee ever had a desire to bee deluded, and decieved in his opinion, and that hee would bee glad to beare the shame of his gealousy, so as the person suspected might bee turned to good[129]

---

[126] Conscience Afflicted 11, First Edition, 10-11; Second Edition, 10-11; Third Edition, 6-7; Fourth Edition, 6-7; Fifth Edition, 6-7.

[127] Ministrie 1, First Edition, 42; Second Edition, 41; Third Edition, 24; Fourth Edition, 24; Fifth Edition, 24.

[128] Griefe for Sinne 7, First Edition, 27; Second Edition, 26; Third Edition, 16; Fourth Edition, 16; Fifth Edition, 16. Also see: *Proposition*, [saying] 46.

[129] Also see: *Proposition*, [saying] 48.

Trial of affection   Hee used this trial of his affections, as of anger, grief, joy or such like, on this manner, If by it hee was made les fit to pray, more unable to do the good hee should do, les careful to avoid sin, then hee thought them to bee carnall, filthy and not of god: but when his anger love and greef and other affections provoked him the more to pray, fitter to do good, then hee thought his affection sent to him to bee as the blessing of god[130]

Dulnes after   Hee said after his great joies conceived of some effec-
spiritual joyes   tual workings of god in himself, hee most commonly not long after fel into dulnes and deadnes[131]

Comforts to one   [fol. 15r] Unto one afflicted in mind hee gave thes
afflicted   comforts. first if you have knowledge to bee thanckful for it, and desire the lord to give you faith, if you have faith, which undoubtedly you may have, though not rightly discerning your self, you presently perceve not, you must wait on the lord for feeling, who often times interlineth faith with divers temptations, before hee sendeth feeling. And though it may bee you shal tarry the lords leasure long, yet surely hee wil give you it in tyme. In
Greatest faith   the mean tyme assure yourself that wher the greatest
without feeling   faith is where ther is least feeling, beecaus it is easy for one in glorious feelings, and joies unspeakable to beleev: but when a man feeling no sensible comfort in the lord, can notwithstanding beeleev on the lord, and by faith wait on him, this mans faith is most great[132]

The lord promise   Hee said the lord often gave his children no other
his children riches riches, but this his promise made unto them on which they must hang and wholly depend, until the lord seing them ready to receiv the things in the testament bequeathed unto them, shal in wisdom performe the legacies made unto them.[133]

---

[130] Affections 1, First Edition, 1; Second Edition, 1; Third Edition, 1; Fourth Edition, 1; Fifth Edition, 1. Also see: *Proposition*, [saying] 47.

[131] Dulnes 1, First Edition, 18; Second Edition, 18; Third Edition, 10-11; Fourth Edition, 10-11; Fifth Edition, 10-11. This saying in the printed version is combined with a saying that appears on fol. 20v.

[132] Conscience Afflicted 6, First Edition, 9; Second Edition, 9; Third Edition, 5-6; Fourth Edition, 5-6; Fifth Edition, 5-6. Also see: *Proposition*, [saying] 50; *Two Treatises*, [saying] 4, 198-9.

[133] Povertie 3, First Edition, 44; Second Edition, 43-4; Third Edition, 26; Fourth Edition, 26; Fifth Edition, 26.

Avoiding a thing   To one that asked his advice, whither hee might avoid
wherunto wee are   the doing of a thing, wherunto hee was called, beecaus
called because of   hee felt corruption in himself, hee said in avoiding
infirmity   society, you shal cover but not cure your infirmity,
and though you depart from men yet can you not go[134] of yourself[135]

Being with one afflicted in body and mind, unto whom the lord had
shewed many tokens of salvation, fruitfully to sanctify the present
afflictions, hee said, I fear not the tyme of the visitation of them, that
therby do grow in the gifts and graces of god but rather, I fear, the tyme
of ther deliverance, should bee overtaken with unthankfulnes, and so
woefully they should loose the fruit of that good, which they so dearly
purchased of the lord.[136]

[fol. 15v] When a certain woman was so sore trobled that 2, or. 3 held
her in her fit, hee desired that hee might deale with her alone, that is
without the hearing of others, though not without the seing the thing
done, being in an open garden for the avoiding of offence, and then hee
charged the person afflicted in the name of the lord Jesus christ, that
when the agony came, shee should not willingly yeeld to it, but in the
lord resist, beecausc experience teacheth that the overmuch fearing the
temptation before it commeth, mightily incourageth sathan: and also the
holy ghost biddeth us resist the devil and hee wil fly from us, and draw
nere unto god and hee wil draw near unto us.[137] The maid never after
was afflicted[138]

Deadness of mind   Hee gave this advice to one against deadnes of mind
                      that overtaketh the godly. First search the cause
whither it bee for some evil thing done, or for some sin seen, but not
repented of, or for some sin repented of but not thorowly or soundly.
Secondly use the remedy please not yourself in it, but raise up yourself
as from a slumber, which willingly you would shake from you, call to
mind the special greatest mercy of god and use the means. Thirdly in the
means offer yourself to god wayting humbly and patiently for

---

[134] Followed by *out* deleted.

[135] Calling 5, First Edition, 6-7; Second Edition, 6; Third Edition, 4; Fourth Edition, 4;
Fifth Edition, 4. Also see: *Proposition*, [saying] 51.

[136] Unthankfulnes 1, First Edition, 72-3; Second Edition, 72; Third Edition, 41; Fourth
Edition, 41; Fifth Edition, 41. Also see: *Proposition*, [saying] 72.

[137] James 4:7-8.

[138] Temptations 15, First Edition, 71; Second Edition, 70; Third Edition, 40; Fourth
Edition, 40; Fifth Edition, 40. Also see: *Proposition*, [saying] 71.

deliverance, neither esteem too little or too much of your affliction[139]

Prayer of faith
though not of
falling [*sic*]

Hee said to one that for want of feeling was loath to pray. you must not tarry to pray til you find feeling, but offer yourself up into the hand of Jesus christ, and so humbling yourself before him, pray on and continue in a praier of faith though not of feeling[140]

[May] 26
Others preaching
at his charg

[fol. 16r] When some would marvel at him, why hee would suffer soe many to preach at his charge, seing in some points it might seem to bee a discredit to his ministry, hee would answer that so long as his people were the better for it hee was not the wors.

[May] 27
Sence of sin
wrought by
degrees

Becaus god worketh the sence of sin by degrees in his children hee suspected them who at every sin named would shew themselves troubled forth-with[141]

[May] 28
Appetite
controuled

When hee had before him two dishes, the one better liking his stomach then the other, hee used that which best liked him beecaus hee would control his appetite

Junii 1
Hardness of hart

To one that complained of hardnes of his hart, hee said thus, you must wait for comfort, and know that now you can no more judge of yourself, then a man sleeping can judg of the things which hee did waking, or a man wandring in the dark can judge of bright colours. for as the one may whilest hee waked do excellent things, and <yet> now neither hee himself knoweth of them, nor any other, can espie them in him: and thother may bee environed, with fresh flourishing colours and yet for want of light can have no light of them his eies, nor pleasure in the objects: so you having done great good things whilest god gave you a waking hart, to put them in practise, and the light of his spirit to discern his graces in you, though now you neither have the sight nor <the> sence of them. And this is the

---

[139]Conscience Afflicted 7, First Edition, 9–10; Second Edition, 9; Third Edition, 6; Fourth Edition, 6; Fifth Edition, 6. Also see: *Proposition*, [saying] 52; *Two Treatises*, [saying] 5, 199.

[140]Feeling 4, First Edition, 21; Second Edition, 20; Third Edition, 12; Fourth Edition, 12; Fifth Edition, 12. Also see: *Propositions*, [saying] 53.

[141]Sinne 3, First Edition, 52; Second Edition, 52; Third Edition, 30; Fourth Edition, 30; Fifth Edition, 30. Also see: *Propositions*, [saying] 40.

thing that deceiveth and disquieteth many, they look for that discerning, of themselves, when the graces of god are more remis in them, which they had when gods spirit wrought, in the sweetest and fullest measure in them, and beecaus ther is some intermission, of the woork of the new birth, they thinck ther is a flat omission of the spirit of god. But as it is a token of a mind too presumptuous and infatuated, in tyme of a dead security, to perswade ourselves stil of that safety in having [fol. 16v] those graces which sometime hee had: so it is a sign of a mind abject and too much dispairing to thinck beecause wee have not a present feeling of those joies glorious and unspeakeable, which wee have had, therfore wee never had them heretofore, or that wee shal never have them again hereafter[142]

marrige   When one asked him concerning Marriage, whether it were good to Marry, seing sometimes when concupiscence prickt him, hee was much moved to it: other sometime when hee felt no such thing, hee thought hee might abstain hee answered, Many run hastily into that calling, not using the means of trying ther estate, thorowly before, as namely, whither they by praier, fasting, and avoiding al provocations of concupiscence, have the gift of chastity or no. Many use some of the means but not al. Many use al the means but a smale tyme. Therfore it is good to use first. Al these means not part of them, not for a while but long. And if it bee so that al these things wil not prevaile, then to attend upon the lords ordinance waiting when the lord shal offer just occasion, of using that estate to his glory and our comfort.[143]

Liking of religion   Hee said that being a child in Q Maries daies, hee conceived on a tyme a liking of that religion, which was true, and taught of god, why that should bee the purest religion, in so much that it wrought, in that means, upon him, as hee never had any delight in outward things. Such abundance of good meditations hee had, and so fully hee refreshed himself.

Not credulous in   When any told a thing that sounded to the dispraise
hearing others   of a man, hee as not credulous in such matters
disprais   would make weary as it were the carnal plantife

---

[142] Hardnes of Heart 2, First Edition, 28; Second Edition, 27; Third Edition, 16; Fourth Edition, 16; Fifth Edition, 16. Also see: *Propositions*, [saying] 56; *Two Treatises*, [saying] 6, 199-200.

[143] Matrimony 4, First Edition, 36; Second Edition, 35; Third Edition, 21; Fourth Edition, 21; Fifth Edition, 21. Also see: *Propositions*, [saying] 54.

in that as hee was as one not hearing, and would fence of[144] the [fol. 17r] matter a long tyme by causing him to repeat often his matter[145]

Hee said that faith in the promises of god, caused him sometyme to take children yong, and unseasoned with religion, yea and such whom, parentage, education, and frinds might rather discommend. For saith hee as good nurtures, do not help of any necessity to regeneration, so evil natures cannot hinder gods purpose in calling if the means with his mercy and blessing bee purely and painfully used.[146]

Changing ones dwelling for corruption   Unto one that was willing to change his seat for corruption of the place, where hee dwelt, hee said, whersoever hee did purpose to live for a good christian, the crosse of christ would follow him beecause in earth are some good men, and some evil, but when wee come to heaven al would bee god and therfore ther is no trouble[147]

Having received a token from a godly gentlewoman which for some inconvenience hee was willed, rather to bestow on some others then to weare it himself: Nay saith hee I wil both keep and wear the thing (though in another fashion) that so oft as I shal see her gift I may bee stirred up and put in mind to pray for[148]

Hee said that being once in a place, wher a woman through extream affliction of mind, forgetting al womanhood fel down before him, in somuch that they would have had him depart hee rather turning his face from the woman, and his back to her, fel on his knees and praied to the lord for her[149]

Comforts in reproches   Hee said although hee was subject to many and greevous reproches, yet two things did ever comfort him, thone[150] that his hart was wel and not evil affected to any man. secondly that going alone hee would humble

---

[144] That is, off.

[145] Dispraise 1, First Edition, 17; Second Edition, 16; Third Edition, 10; Fourth Edition, 10; Fifth Edition, 10.

[146] Regeneration 1, First Edition, 50; Second Edition, 49; Third Edition, 29; Fourth Edition, 29; Fifth Edition, 29. Also see: *Propositions*, [saying] 70.

[147] Calling 6, First Edition, 7; Second Edition, 6-7; Third Edition, 4; Fourth Edition, 4; Fifth Edition, 4. Also see: *Propositions*, [saying] 57.

[148] Ibid., [saying] 67.

[149] Ibid., [saying] 69.

[150] That is, the one.

himself and willingly pray to god that the authors of such reproches might bee forgiven[151]

Although hee was most sevear to his frinds and kinred in [fol. 17v] the flesh, so long as they were not reconsiled unto god, but walked ungodly, yet on a tyme being weary partly with his painful speaking to one of them, partly with the unseasonable replies of one, hee shut up the matter with a grand speach, which hee said hee had read and by gods spirit then came fitly to his memory. It is wonderful said hee, that divers hearing the same word spoken one should beleev and another not beeleev. But I am rather to thanck god that I do beleev, then to search out the reason, why others do not beeleeve, and as I am to bee thanckful for my self so I am to bee pityful for him that doth not beeleev[152]

Hee said how at his first coming to his pastoral charge hee used in his first speach this protestation. do I desire you to beeleev mee, If I promis great things I know not myself what I am or may bee therfore I pray you beeleev mee not, but look how you prove mee in tyme and so beeleev mee

Prayer for others Hee said the best way to have comfort in any of our frinds, was to pray for them and that hee never had more joy in any, then for them whom hee most praied for, and in them most, when hee praied the oftener and vehementer for them present or absent. for this is a true token of love to pray for them whom wee love[153]

Trouble in mind Hee said to one troubled in mind for a secret and yet
for a smale secret smale sin, I do not so much fear this sin in you, as the
sin pollicy of sathan by it, either in that hee wil not stick
to shew you the les sins, and hide from you the greater, or els by the quick sight of your secret and smale sins to cast upon you an open and gros sin of vain glory and privy pride[154]

---

[151] Reproches 1, First Edition, 50; Second Edition, 50; Third Edition, 29; Fourth Edition, 29; Fifth Edition, 29. Also see: *Propositions*, [saying] 58.

[152] Friendship 3, First Edition, 24-5; Second Edition, 24; Third Edition, 14; Fourth Edition, 14; Fifth Edition, 14. Also see: *Propositions*, [saying] 68.

[153] Friendship 2, First Edition, 24; Second Edition, 23-4; Third Edition, fol. 14; Fourth Edition, 14; Fifth Edition, 14. Also see: *Propositions*, [saying] 55.

[154] Conscience Afflicted 9, First Edition, 10; Second Edition, 10; Third Edition, 6; Fourth Edition, 6; Fifth Edition, 6. Also see: *Propositions*, [saying] 66; *Two Treatises*, [saying] 10, 202-3.

Reproof with inward greef of the sin

Often hee noted this in himself that when hee [fol. 18r] cold inwardly bee greeved for the sin of a man, so that hee prayed for him and wished his amendement, and yet meekly spake of his person, wounding him rather, with a loving admonition then goaring him with some intemperate and unseasoneable reprehension the lord by a secret woorking opened the hart of him, to whome hee spake towards him, that he might work the more easily upon him[155]

Unbeleef

Hee said unto a godly christian, much inveighing against his unbeleef, I do not now suspect your estate, when you seem to mee rather to have faith, then when you seem to yourself to have it. for faith being the gift of god, is the most obtained or encreased of god, when you thirsting after the increas of faith, thinck that smale measure obtained to bee no faith, or feeling no present feelings are humbled underneath the mighty and merciful hand of god for it. Rather I suspect when you say you have faith, beecaus then you can les fear and suspect yourself, and by that means ly

faith

open to unbeeleef again. And surely experience teacheth that then wee shew wee have beeleef when wee mourn for our unbeleef and then our faith may bee least when wee thinck it to bee most Besides herin you are to comfort yourself, with hope of increas of faith, beecaus faith groweth by thes two means, either by some great feelings from the lord and the spirit and humble thanksgiving adjoyned therunto, or els by humbling ourselves before the mercy seat of god for want of our faith[156]

Spiritual motions

To one that said shee had a thing told her in the spirit, which undoubtedly should come to pas, hee answered, that it might bee of god who after some great and greevous conflict comforteth them again, that are tempted: but evermore such secret woorkings are according to the word of god. And seing al such inward motions are either of god, or <wr>ought by our corruption, or sent of the devil, as an illusion, wee must try these [fol. 18v] motions by the word whether they bee for spiritual or corporal things. If they bee of god and according to his word, beeleev them for the words sake. If they agree not to the word, how pleasant soever they

[155] Rebuking or Reproving of Sinne 2, First Edition, 48; Second Edition, 47; Third Edition, 28; Fourth Edition, 28; Fifth Edition, 28. Also see: *Propositions*, [saying] 61.
[156] Unbeleefe 2, First Edition, 71-2; Second Edition, 71; Third Edition, 40; Fourth Edition, 40; Fifth Edition, 40. Also see: *Propositions*, [saying] 59; *Two Treatises*, [saying] 8, 201.

seem to flesh and blood, listen not to them, muchles beeleev them[157]

strength against When one was troubled in mind, hee gave this
temtation les after comfortable note, that although it came to pas, that
then in the after some travel in new birth, gods graces were not so
beginning of sweet, nor our sins so sower, or so greevous unto us,
Regeneration as they were at the first enterance into Regeneration,
but wee are now weaker in the les assaults having before been stronger
in the greater temptations, wee are not to dispaire, but to consider from
whence this gratious progres did come, namely of god, and not of
ourselves, who shewed himself more favourable in the beginning, both
becaus hee would not discourage us, newly coming unto him, and for
that wee suspecting ourselves with a godly suspicion in the least
temptacion, might fly unto gods help by praier, who in wisdom can hide
himself under a cloud, partly beecause, hee wil look for trial of some
strength at our hands coming to some age in new birth, partly for that
wee now les forsake or suspect our selves even in greater temptacions,
and so presumptuously wrastling with our own strength, and staying
ourselves with our own staf, wee do not cal on god for help, and not
calling do not obtain, and not obtaining help wee take the foile in the
conflict, that the lord may make known unto us; that notwithstanding
our proceedings in christianity wee are stil but men and god alone is
god.[158]

Temptacions from Hee said to one afflicted in mind that al temptations
whence they come come either of ignorance, or of want of feeling: of
                    ignorance, when sathan troubleth us with those things
[fol. 19r] which wee cannot discern, of want of feelings, when hee
tempteth us, to such things as wee cannot discern, when wee know them

Discipline in white When certain according to the order of the church of
sheets england received discipline in white sheets,[159] hee after
                    proving both of suspending, and excommunicating,
out of the scripture, this said to them The gospel is not burdened with
ceremonies beecaus it gives liberty, yet if ther in discipline must needs bee

---

[157] 'Of the word of God: and of the confirmation therof by wonders' 13, Third Edition,
449; Fourth Edition, 473-4; Fifth Edition, 825-6.

[158] Conscience Afflicted 8, First Edition, 10; Second Edition, 9-10; Third Edition, 6;
Fourth Edition, 6; Fifth Edition, 6. Also see: *Propositions*, [saying] 62; *Two Treatises*,
[saying] 9, 201-2.

[159] For 'discipline in white sheets', a common form of public humiliation used as a
penance by the church courts, see Carlson, *Marriage and the English Reformation*, 149-
50.

ceremonies, I thinck they ought to bee such as must humble us, and therfore in the law they used sackcloaths, the basest kind of attire and not sheets, which rather impart a purenes and rejoycing then impurenes, and humbling. But if <any> shal say that sheets shew the filthines of adultery, then I answer according to the diversities of sins, ther should bee a diversity of ceremonies, which the liberty of the gospel wil not permit, being free from al outward ceremonies.

To declare humbling

Hee said that to win any or continue any in the fear of god, hee would give not such things as hee loved not, but such things as hee loved most dearly, that they might know it to bee a gift of love, and not a gift of fashion[160]

Hee feeling on a tyme the grace of god assisting him, in a thing, which of himself hee dispaired, said, Oh how straight are the waies of a man, whilest the lord doth govern him and how is it beset with an hedge of thorns, when the lord doth not assist him.[161]

Hee said hee never looked for a better estate then that wherin hee was, but often prepared himself for a wors[162]

Hee thought that it were meet in the time of plagues that ther should not bee one minister both of the sick and whol, but that the people should provide either one to minister to the sick or els, such an one as should minister to the whole whilest ther[163] own pastor attended on the sick[164]

[fol. 19v] Hee said some laboured more for knowledg les for affection some more for affection les for knowledge, some busied themselves in church discipline, and were slanderly sighted in ther privy corruptions, some diligent to espy things in others abroad, and negligent to try themselves at home And therfore that it were good to match both together,[165] wherfore for the increas of judgement hee willed to use, a daily and ordinary cours of reading, but especialy of the word and that

---

[160] Feare 4, Third Edition, 14; Fourth Edition, 14; Fifth Edition, 14.

[161] Grace of God 1, First Edition, 25; Second Edition, 24; Third Edition, 15; Fourth Edition, 15; Fifth Edition, 15.

[162] Calling 7, First Edition, 7; Second Edition, 7; Third Edition, 4; Fourth Edition, 4; Fifth Edition, 4. Also see: *Propositions*, [saying] 63.

[163] Followed by *minister* deleted.

[164] 'Of Phisicke and diet, sickness and health' 9, Third Edition, 419; Fourth Edition, 443; Fifth Edition, 795.

[165] *Propositions*, [saying] 64.

in some order, with a thorough stitch for memorys sake, and for feeling to use praier and meditation, wherby it would come to pas that wee in fear of god and using the means, and applying them to our private estate should feel great abundance of matter, both of judgement and affection, whensoever the lord should cal men to any good use of them hereafter

Hee acknowledged humbly the goodnes of god in assisting him in his speaches an whole veese [sic] meekly thanked god and said hee looked for some notable dulnes to follow[166] it

Being asked what hee thought of the inclosure of ground[167] hee said hee could not say much in it. Howbeit generally hee cold not speak against it, but when it cometh to the degree that Esay speaketh of, that is, that land is joyned to land, until the poore have no roome,[168] Hee utterly condemned it according to the word of the lord.

Albeit his judgement was that hee could wish the place to bury the dead in some other place, then in the church yard, yet hee would desire whersoever it were, that it should bee kept decently and reverently in no other respect, but beecaus it was appointed for that use

Hee said how in purposing to admonish gently or coldly, hee prevailed nothing, and that many men have marveled at him, why hee would admonish his dearest [fol. 20r] frinds, with sharpest severity, howbeit hee did it for that experience, which hee had of it, that that kind of dealing did alwaies most good.

Many would marvel that hee was so jealous over mens affections, but hee thought it best to bee so zealous in the lord gods cause, and that one

---

[166] Followed by *after* deleted.

[167] In the sixteenth century, enclosure was often identified as a major social problem and cause of poverty. In one of its forms, land was removed from grain cultivation and used as pasture for sheep. This resulted in fewer jobs and higher food prices (due to reduced supply). After 1550, rising grain prices made conversion to pasture less attractive. Instead, enclosure was a way of creating more efficient, compact holdings in place of the traditional scattered strips of open field farming. In the process, the common lands on which poorer villagers often depended for survival were often reduced or eliminated. See Joan Thirsk, *The Rural Economy of England* (London: The Hambledon Press, 1984), chap. 6; *The Agrarian History of England and Wales, vol. IV: 1500-1640*, ed. Joan Thirsk (Cambridge: Cambridge University Press, 1967), chap. 4; Mark Overton, *Agricultural Revolution in England: The Transformation of the Agrarian Economy 1500-1850* (Cambridge: Cambridge University Press, 1996), 147-67.

[168] Isaiah 5:8.

should fear every least thing: and yet so loving our brethren as one should hope the best

Hee admonishing one that hee should prevent hardnes of hart betime, in his childhood, by godly and discreet correction said, that beecaus children have often the sins of ther fathers, parents in correcting should in wisdom first consider, if it were not a syn which they gave them as it were, which now they are about to correct, and finding it so that they should bee humbled in themselves, and being humbled proceed to correction, in praier in the fear of god, in wisdom, in love of ther own conversion, and with that measure as correcting ther own sins[169] <after> a sort in ther own children. For men begetting ther children without, regeneration give a natural propagation of ther sins, without some special blessing of god, for none in regeneration beegetteth any with such gifts by nature, but unles they become new born, they have no good thing in them[170]

Hee was so grounded in gods providence, that in the most abrupt and disordered speaches of his enemies or of good men, hee stil thought that god disposed ther speaches, to cause him to reap some fruit of it, and though reason presently could prompt no reason, why his enemies should so speak, yet many weeks and some moneths after, hee would make the fruit for hee was wel affected with the fact of Josiah the best king that ever was, who could not bee mooved with the speach of wicked king Pharoah but entering battel against him was slain.[171] Wherfore hee would say that no man was so good, but the lord would let him slip into some evil, for his further humbling, and no man [fol. 20v] so evil, but the lord did convey some good unto him at sometime to make his condemnation the juster[172]

Hee said after hee had received some notable and favourable pledge of gods love toward him, hee was not long after stricken with some deadnes and dulnes, and therby was humbled, so that until the lord had prepared his hart with some new grace from above hee was unfit to receiv any new mercy at the hand of the lord[173]

---

[169] Followed by *in* deleted.

[170] John 3:1-8. Hardnes of Heart 3, First Edition, 28-9; Second Edition, 28; Third Edition, 17; Fourth Edition, 16-17; Fifth Edition, 16-17. Also found under: Of Catechizing and instruction of youth 11, Third Edition, 291; Fourth Edition, 314; Fifth Edition, 666. Also see: *Propositions*, [saying] 60.

[171] 2 Kings 23:29-30.

[172] Conference 2, First Edition, 7-8; Second Edition, 7; Third Edition, 5; Fourth Edition, 5; Fifth Edition, 5. Also see: *Propositions*, [saying] 65.

[173] Dulnes 1, First Edition, 18; Second Edition, 18; Third Edition, 10-11; Fourth

Hee said howsoever worldly and carnal men accompt of ther losses, and judged of poverty, hee thought no greater los, nor any more greevous poverty, then not to find soe happy succes of his scriptures <travel> manuel [*sic*], and therfore whersoever hee had bestowed a spiritual gift, hee was a diligent watchman over the blessing of god, as one that greatly rejoyced when hee found it, and was greatly humbled when hee lost it

Hee remembered by practise the grave saying of a godly[174] father, that no cros or affliction did so much crucify and afflict a man, as his own corruptions and temptations. And therfore hee thought that al the evil which fel on david did not so much humble him as did the temtation and breaking forth of his corruption in Adultery[175]

Hee marveled at many preachers of our tyme, which would continualy invay against the flesh, and speak against the pore body, crying out that it was the enemy of the soule, when notwithstanding wee had need rather to nourish the body, as the frind to the soule for the exercise of repentance, of mortification and sanctification, and on the contrary the soul is the enemy <to>[176] the body, in using it to sin, for that ther is never any corrupt action in the body, but ther hath been first a corrupt motion and sinful affection in the soule[177]

Hee reported of himself very meekly that when [fol. 21r] hee was troubled with most greevous toothaches, and with a most lamentable *Fistula*, so as his flesh was fain to bee ript, for the finding out of tents,[178] hee felt no greater ease then in patience and sufferance, and therfore in the most bitter agonies, hee was plentiful in temptations, and would strive to reason with himself, how it was good to exercise patience timely, beecaus hee knew not what might follow after, and perswading himself how indeed ther was no patience but by tryal hee would try himself to a godly shame, and greef that having read and hard of so many precepts, and practises of patience, hee cold no longer endure. Again, who doth know whither the lord wil cal mee in this pain, or like, even as I am praying or preaching. Besides hee would say, they that

---

Edition, 10-11; Fifth Edition, 10-11. This saying in the printed version is combined with a saying that appears on fol. 14v.

[174] Replacing *learned* deleted.

[175] 2 Samuel 11:1-12:25.

[176] Replacing *of* deleted.

[177] Preaching 5, First Edition, 45; Second Edition, 44-5; Third Edition, 26; Fourth Edition, 26; Fifth Edition, 26.

[178] This was a roll of absorbent material, frequently medicated, and used to clean a wound or keep it open.

would suffer great things in persecution, must suffer smale things in peace and they that wil suffer of Papists must lern to suffer of Protestants.[179]

Hee thought by nature al men bee papists, heretiques, adulterers, and in al kinds sinners, until god renued them so, that if al heresy, papistry, or ungodlines, were ceased among al men, yet in man (being left of god) is a sufficient matter, wherby al these might bee received and renued[180]

His judgement was that violence and subtilty, were the greatest distinctions between the temptations of the devil and the temptations of the flesh. The divil especialy using these two.[181]

Hee denied this to bee a good order of discipline, first generaly to declare that a sin is broken forth, secondly to name the sin and confes the party. thirdly to name the person, after to admonish him, then to suspend him. lastly to leave him to Sathan

Hee could not abide to bee crossed in his admonitions beecause it argued a proud and a prefaract[182] spirit [fol. 21v] not that hee respected so much his private person, as that it was a thing against gods glory and truth and would have men swift to hear admonitions, slowe to crosse

One asking his advice how hee might best avoid concupiscence, hee said that a continual examination of your selves by the law, a reverent and daily meditating of the word, a painful walking in our honest calling, an holy shaming of ourselves, and fearing of ourselves before our frinds, a continual temperance in diet, sleep and apparrel, a careful watching over our eies and other parts of our bodies, a zealous geolousy to avoid al occasions, of persons, tymes and places, which might nourish concupiscence, a godly frequenting of times, persons, and places, which breed in us mortification, togither with an humbling of ourselves, with the shame of sins past, with the greefe of sins present, and with the fear of sins to come. lastly a careful using of fasting, praier and watching (when need requireth. for hee stil excepted continual fasting) are means to come to mortification herin, which being wisely and some convenient

---

[179] Afflictions 12, First Edition, 4; Second Edition, 4; Third Edition, 3; Fourth Edition, 3; Fifth Edition, 3.
[180] [Saying] 4, Naturall Corruption, Second Edition, 76; Of Naturall Corruption 2, Third Edition, 8; Fourth Edition, 8; Fifth Edition, 8.
[181] Temptations 11, First Edition, 67; Second Edition, 66; Third Edition, 38; Fourth Edition, 38; Fifth Edition, 38.
[182] 'inflexible'.

tyme used, with a moderate motion and exercise of the body, if they do not prevail it is like the lord doth call a man to the holy use of marriage. Howbeit it is to bee observed, that in fasting and watching wee are not to prefix set tymes, this day or that day but then to use when god calleth us unto it, by matter and occasion, without the which the often use of these exercises, wil breed a want of reverence of them.[183] At that speach hee gave this observation of himself, how having purposed at his first marrying to have kept a feast,[184] every last day of the week (which I suppose hee did beecaus it was both the clensing[185] of the week [fol. 22r] past, and the preparing of the lords day to come) and not performed it in the measure hee determined, hee found himself mooved on that day especialy <moved> to temptations.

Hee said hee was never much trobled for his provision, what it was, if his guests feared god: but that it was some troble to him, when hee knew them not to bee such, beecaus they might take offence. But if hee using some competent preparation did not please the other, hee thought it to bee ther sins and not his

Hee observing how sometimes the lord would translate the prais of a good worke to another, who had not laboured so in it, as hee did, would meekly say: I care not who have the praise, although an other do reap that which I do sowe, so that by any means god may bee glorified and others profited.

When one told him of certain suddain feares arising in his mind, which bread many troublesome thoughts, and yet the thing feared ensued not, hee answered, The meditations arising of those feares, beecaus they were of god were good, who in his mercy often gives us to see our own harts, in thincking of such things, as if they were indeed, and so giveth us as it were an anatomy, either of his grace woorking in us, or of our corruptions, as wee may see Jacob in fearing his brother Esau had a plain pattern of his practise,[186] which hee would have done, had the thing come to pas, which indeed not as hee feared. Besides by this fear often the lord enabeth and enarmeth us the more to suffer those things, which though presently they have not ther event, yet hereafter shal come to pas. This hee amplified both by experience in himself, and in others, in himself, in that hee felt those things, did most afflict him, which before

---

[183] Concupiscence 1, First Edition, 14; Second Edition, 13-14; Third Edition, 8; Fourth Edition, 8; Fifth Edition, 8.

[184] From the context, this appears to be a scribal error, and should read 'fast'.

[185] Followed by *of the day* deleted.

[186] Genesis 32:1-33:16.

hee least feared, and these things were benified in sufferance which hee
before suspected, which thing no doubt happened to Job.[187] In others
partly in a Lady, partly in a gentlewoman. In a [fol. 22v] lady, who in her
afflictions beeing much humbled, and in prosperity forgetting them,
much feared herself, that it would not go wel at the last. Howbeit before
her death some little space shee said to a godly preacher. now my
affections are thorowly humbled, and I shal surely never hereafter forget
the woorke of god. Therfore now draweth neare the tyme of my
dissolution, so that by her former fear shee was made fit to avoid the
thing when it came. In a gentlewoman who being long tyme exercised in
mind would often fear shee shold dy in that estate, without peace of
conscience. So as shee would open her conceived fear to her husband, a
godly christian: to whom hee would answer. As yet I fear you not, you
shal not dy in this care: afterward god graunting her the liberty of mind,
and peace of conscience, shee feared not death a whit, neither thought of
her departure: Now her husband telleth her, that shee must prepare
herself to go to the lord, for the tyme of her dissolution could not bee far,
neither indeed was it: for shortly after, shee blessedly left this life. After
in his speach hee reproved them, who measuring feares by the event,
thought ther fear to bee but frivilous, when the thing feared ensued not.
for saith hee they should rather reason to the commendable use of
fearing, beecaus the lord often breaking and humbling the hart afore
hand, deferreth the evil which otherwise might have comen upon them,
as hee often both <more> sodainly and violently bringeth more
punishments on them, who never before feared them to come. Howbeit
as in al things hee espied and met with the contrary extremities, so in this
hee willed men to beeware of immoderate feares, which rather hinder the
certainty of faith then beat down the security of the flesh, and which bee
the readiest means to pul gods wrath upon us, in that they bee the fruits
of unbeleef and such as would ty the grace[188] and promis of god to the
present danger and deliverance out of the same. The mean and middle
path [fol. 23r] is, that wee should fear and forethinck of evils to come,
not as thincking a necessity of them to fal upon us, as though god could
not or would deliver us from them but as they who being gilty in ther
own deserts do submit themselves to the hand of god, and acknowledg
themselves the heyrs of gods justice, in this and that evil, yet so as wee
meet with the lords mercy who is both able and willing even then most
of al to assist and deliver us when wee most fear, and through this godly
fear are humbled reverently underneath the hand of his Majesty. for if
natural parents know then to mittigate the stripes of ther correction to

---

[187] Job 1:13–22.
[188] Followed by *of god* deleted.

ther children,[189] when they see in them, a mild and meek submission of themselves under the hand of ther authority, and yet so fearing them as governors, as hoping for mercy of fathers. If they have that wisdome to make ther hands in correcting so much the heavier by how much the child to bee beaten is stubburner, wee must thinck this merciful medication and godly wisdome, to bee much more in the lord, from whos brightnes the other have received those sparks.

Hee said if hee had once seen any effectual marks of gods child in any man, hee would never, but hope wel of him, until hee had blotted them out[190]

Hee said hee thought it were not good at the table to bee extraordinary, either in joy or sorrow, unles it were for some special and private cause, but rather it were convenient, privately to a godly frind, or before the lord, to power out our harts and after the example of Joseph, to make our affections as little known in company as may bee[191]

Hee had a great sight of inward corruptions, and in laying out the vainnes of mens secret consciences, for which some men would thinck and say, that of al men they thought him to bee the wickedest: some said hee wrought by [fol. 23v] Spirits and magical arts: some said that other had beewrayed to him ther infirmities, and that hee spake nothing but that which hee had hard of others. But hee stil profiting by al thes false surmises, watched so narrowly over his own hart, that making an anatomy of it, hee could unrip the secret courses of sin in others

Being asked whither in the tyme of week daies assemblies, it were lawful for the buisnes of our calling to bee absent or noe, hee answered wee might, If it wer with these circumstances. first wee should consider whither the thing wee go about, might bee otherwise provided for or no, to bee done either before, or after the meeting. Secondly wee must not do it for a private gain, but when our absence furthereth some publique profit, according as our consciences before god shal tel us for if wee bee requested to bee on such a day with a man of worship can boldly deny our presence at that tyme, beecaus wee shal have to deale with a man of honor, why should wee not deny our presence to worldly buisnes, when wee have buisnes to deal with the lord of Hosts.

---

[189] Luke 11:11-13.

[190] Friendship 6, Third Edition, 14; Fourth Edition, 14; Fifth Edition, 14. This saying in the printed version is combined with a saying that appears on fol. 8v.

[191] Genesis 43:30. Company 1, First Edition, 14; Second Edition, 14.

When by the spirit of meeknes hee could not prevail in admonition used with his freinds, hee would more vehemently (but christianly) repeat his doctrine unto them willing them by praier and in humblenes of mind as before the lord to examine ther harts after ther first sleep that they might see what comfort of conscience they could find in refusing that admonition

Concerning fasting, hee was woont to say that even as men thincking to have established the Sabboth day ordained Holydaies which in the end did almost drive the [fol. 24r] true use of the sabboth out of the dores of the church: so many thincking by the twise fasting in every week to have been some furtherance, to the true fasting, have not onely missed of the pure exercise of humbling, but also have fallen into an utter abuse of the same. Others ther are who thinck wee should keep a continual sorrowing, wheras rather wee have a flat precept to the contrary, continualy to rejoyce and find in no place a commandement enjoyning continualy to sorrow

Hee said unto one afflicted in mind that men must not think that god beholdeth them as they are in one particular defect, and at one present instant, but as they are in general purpose, and as they were before. Again it is a pollicy of sathan to get us alwaies to use a vehement mourning of spirit to accuse us more freely afflicted for then wee sorrow as much for every little want, as for a great sin The devil wil use this preposterous order, as a thing to accuse us of hipocrisy afterward, in that then wee can sorrow no more in sins then in petty escapes, hee wil tel us al was but hipocrisy, wee sorrowed as much when wee committed little offenses as wee do now in the greater, wheras indeed our sorrow must bee proportionable to the sin, greater in greater sins, les in lesser sins. Again hee taught two things in a godly sorrow to bee necessary, th'one that it might bee about a right object: secondly that having a just caus wee bee in a measure. Hee added moreover, that though gods children do often sin, yet ther sin is far differing from the sining of the wicked. for as ther is a plain distinction between him that for the most part <hath his>[192] helth, sometymes having fits of sicknes, and him that for the most part is sickly having but fits of health, so also ther is a plain difference betwixt the godly, whose general cours is to please god, though sometime they have a violent fit of syn, and then that in ther whole cours syn against god and yet sometyme have [fol. 24v] ther fits in a kind of godlines

---

[192] Replacing *is sickly having but fits of* deleted.

Hee coming home from a journey and understanding of some thing not falling out wel in his family, in his absence, examined his hart and said, that surely hee praied not for them, or in praying used it as a ceremony rather then otherwise and so, said hee, was justly punished.

As hee thought repetitions in praier for the most part inconvenient, and so much the rather, for that our lord Jesus christ in his praier prescribeth such distinct matters, yet hee thought it might sometyme bee either by some great sence of sin, or some vehement feeling of our wants, or for that wee forget after, what wee said before in our praiers, either beecaus wee seing ourselves to have praied before in fashion, wee would now do it in truth, or for some such thing. And this hee wold willingly graunt, saying that if hee thought for these causes, repetitions might not bee used, his own synnes wold pursue and god would reprove him.

Hee said to avoid tediousnes in praier, hee thought it were good to pray often and briefly, as our Saviour christ in the garden, howbeit as in long praier, it is good to beeware of superstition and ambition, so in short praiers wee must bee careful, lest either carelesnes or prophainnes creep upon us.

By observation hee noted in himself, that often when hee studied painfully, and laboured exquisitely for a sermon, hee was most troubled with confusion, and could least content himself, with any comforts in bringing togither the meditations. And sufficient experience can tel that having had tyme but to pray the lord hath mightily assisted him, when hee hath spoken without any study at al

[fol. 25r] One asking him why a man fearing god, cannot find his meditation tyed to the word of god, Hee said as it was an hard thing to do it, so it sometimes came to pas; for that many that have a general good mind, to occupy ther minds in meditation, doe occupy ther thoughts confusedly, and not about some certain object, or els for that they were not thorowly perswaded in tym of ther meditations, of gods presence with them.

When one asked his advice concerning marriage, after hee had marked the man hee said, it were good to stay a while and to make longer trial of his affections, whither they were of god, or no. for beecaus of natural delight, that temptation is too impetouse, and therwithal Sathan so abuseth a mans weaknes that it is easy for a man to deceiv himself in it. Ther hee added an observation, which by experience hee had gathered of a certain man, whom hee knew wonderfully to bee <moved

to>[193] marriage, and yet attending some longer time <on>[194] the lord by fervent and continual praier, hee was delivered even from every inward motion, and titillacion therunto. which man afterward marrying had such a feeblenes in his body that hee cold not use the act of generation

Hee said this reason moved him not to bee brought under any ceremony, for that if hee should yeeld to one, it were a way to give credit to the using of more, beecause every man would by natural logique reason thus against him, that if this may bee used <then> that may bee used, and ignorant men or secret adversaries, would take advantage for the defending of ther superstitions and errors, as an old woman did, who seing the minister baptise children with a cros, thought that shee might cros herself, when shee came to pray

[fol. 25v] Hee used great patience, with a most wicked man, saying that by thes means hee kept down his enemy, to take him at every advantage, and his enemy kept stil over him in that hee cold espy no advantage, which thing if it bee thought a good pollicy among worldlings, how much more ought christians to use it for the defence of the gospel and for the credit of ther high calling.

When a certain christian had commended unto him a certain good man, departed out of this life, and told him that for love shee reserved his picture, in her sence to bee but in mind of him, hee said ther might bee a very fool like unto that picture in outward things, neither ever was it the commendation of so good a man to have such a face. But said hee if you wil truly remember him, and keep his image, call to mind by the sweet promises hee hath comforted you in the points of doctrine, and by the threatnings hee did humble you, in the points of doctrine hee did most affect you, by what means hee did especialy convert or confirm you, and by this you shal truly shew your self unto him, whilest hee was present and to remember him being absent.

Some telling him that hee looked better and that hee was far better in liking, then hee was wont, hee said, that it made him to fear himself, if it were so lest that hee were near some inward decay if hee thrived so wel outwardly.

Hee said it was an easy matter for some to wish for death, who dy not so much, for that they hastened to those joies, which by hope they lasted

---

[193] Replacing *affected with* deleted.
[194] Replacing *by* deleted.

of, as they desired to bee freed from trouble, and so after this life, not to have any being at al, either good or evil. Again hee espied, and laid out this corruption of nature, that many [fol. 26r] wil bee content to visit the sick, not so much for love to hazard ther lives, for ther brothers good: if so bee the lord shal cal them: as for that even for ther good deeds sake in visiting, they hope god wil not visit them in sicknes. Therfore hee would advise the ministers of christs truth to visit after neither of these manners, that is either beecaus they desire to bee ridd out of the crosses of this life, and in hope to beecom nothing or in hope that[195] the lord wil not take them away, beecaus they bee so faithful in visiting others. But rather that they setting the crown of glory before them, laid up in christ, and willinglie offering themselves for the life of ther bretheren should being lawfully called come with this affection. *If I live I live if I dy I dy.* Thus doing if god striketh them they had nothing but that they looked for, if the <lord>[196] spareth them they take it as an overplus of his favour: but if they should come otherwise affected woeful experience would shew that they did but deceiv themselves with a vain hope. Here hee said moreover that in tyme of a contagiouse sicknes, it were expedient in a christian congregation, that ther should bee one to minister to the whole and another to the sick. Howbeit this must bee done so that the opinion bee left free to the people to choose whether they wil have ther ordinary Pastor to minister to the whole or to the sick, and that the minister stand thus affected indifferently, that if they[197] depute him to attend on the sick, hee should exhort them to provide some other to teach the whole, or if they make choyce of him to teach the whole, that then hee admonish to get somebody for the sick. But if it bee so that the people refuse this order, then hee thought it [fol. 26v] best that the Pastor of the place should protest both his love and faithfulnes unto them and that for as much as they refused his counsel, wherin hee advised them notsomuch[198] hee in conscience canot suffer either the whol to bee untaught for any sparing of himself or the sick conscience comforted hee was ready painfully and as wisely as hee can by speaking to them a far of, to doe both dutyes.

Howbeit if any danger by this means fal among them they should stand at ther own peril for that they refused to listen to that counsel which might seem in such a case to prevent so great a danger.

Concerning recreations, hee could not away that they should bee to pas

---

[195] Followed by *god* deleted.
[196] Replacing *god* deleted.
[197] Followed by *do* deleted.
[198] Followed by *as* deleted.

away the tyme seing the holy ghost did wil us to redeem the tym: And howsoever the creatures of god may sometime of some men for some cause bee used for our refreshing: yet cards and dice hee thought altogether unlawful and that it were better that some good men would abstein even from ther pleasures lawful, then that by them evil men should take occasion to use pleasures unlawful. Howbeit above al hee thought that having such variety of exercises no man might bee dul, if in wisdom, and in ther time hee would use them and that the caus why such spiritual delights do not affect us, is beecaus men have not the word of god dwelling in them

Hee said hee would often labour to admonish and <to> reproov with some sharpnes that hee might leav the deeper impression in one.

Hee confuted a pyper saying that hee played in the church to move men to contribute ther liberality [fol. 27r] to pore folke being joyned in marriage, on this manner, Our saviour christ knew that they that sold doves and were moneychangers to help pore folks, and such as dwelt far of for ther sacrifices in the temple, might pretend a furthering of the woorship of god: and yet though thes were but in the church porch (as wee cal it) wee read hee whipt them out.[199] And Paul knew that the Corinthians might pretend the maintenance of charity, in having ther love feasts in the church after the supper of Christ, and yet hee sharply reproveth them for it.[200] Now if piping cannot bear so good a verdure, and so bright an hew as these, then thes being forbidden pyping in the church must not bee suffered

Hee said surely this long prosperity of England would breed, either heresy, or security, or some great adversity: and that howsoever, men did little fear thes plentiful daies, yet when prosperity is ful, and growen foggy and fat, so as the bowels of it bee stuft, and strout out as it were, with repletion, then must needs follow some rupture, and the abundance of welth must needs have a vent, to break out into some botch in one place or other[201]

Hee did not use to look any much in the face, unles hee loved them much for some singular graces in them, and therfore hee knew few by ther countenance, but remembred much by ther tongs, and so came to a

---

[199] John 2: 14-16.
[200] 1 Corinthians 11:17-34.
[201] Prosperitie and Peace 4, First Edition, 47; Second Edition, 47; Third Edition, 28; Fourth Edition, 28; Fifth Edition, 28.

general knowledg of them. So careful was hee in the goverment of his eies.

Hee would say, Many deceiv themselves in a bare opinion of humility, and that this were a true trial of humility If wee would willingly suffer ourselves to bee taught of our inferiours, and if wee would patiently abide ourselves to bee admonished of our[202] faults.[203]

Hee said hee thought hee did little good to any body, unles hee had a feeling, pitty and compassion on them.[204]

[fol. 27v] Hee said concerning[205] this question whether the child of god might fal twise or often into one and the same sin, that these cautions <and dismotions> are to bee observed. first whither the party bee generally called, or especialy touched. If hee bee but generally called as al christians professing the gospel, it were an easy matter to slip in that manner Secondly if the party bee[206] effectually called, it is to bee enquired whether hee bee pure in christ or no, whether hee a babe in christ or whether hee beecome to some growth in christ, for that if hee but a novace hee may twise fal so. Thirdly if hee bee growen to some good age in christ wee must observ whether the sin committed, bee a thing known to him or no. If hee know it not to bee a sin no doubt hee may also slip.[207] Fourthly if it bee in a known sin wee are to discern whether it bee in omitting good or committing evil, beecause if it[208] bee[209], bee[210] but <in> comitting[211] a[212] <good>[213] thing, hee may oft surely do it. Lastly if it come to this that it bee in committing an evil thing wee must wisely consider whether it bee of some smaller, or secret errours of this life, as slipping in thought or speach, or whether it bee a greater and presumptuous sin, for if it bee but an error of this life hee

---

[202] Followed by *selves* deleted.

[203] Humilitie 1, First Edition, 31; Second Edition, 30; Third Edition, 18; Fourth Edition, 18; Fifth Edition, 18.

[204] Feeling 2, First Edition, 21; Second Edition, 20; Third Edition, 12; Fourth Edition, 12; Fifth Edition, 12.

[205] Followed by *marriage* deleted.

[206] Followed by *so* deleted.

[207] Falling into Sinne 1, First Edition, 22-3; Second Edition, 22; Third Edition, 13; Fourth Edition, 13; Fifth Edition, 13.

[208] Followed by *come* deleted.

[209] Followed by *this* deleted.

[210] Preceded by *that it* deleted.

[211] From the context, this appears to be a scribal error. It should read 'omitting'.

[212] Followed by *n* deleted.

[213] Replacing *evil* deleted.

may oft do it, but if it bee a gros and presumptuous sin, it is not like that being effectually called, and having sound knowledge, that hee shal fal often into it

As hee was woont to profit much by the judgements of god, so one [sic] a tyme one of his people burying his wife, hee used this speach unto him, I feared god wold bury somthing from you, beecause I saw you often bury mine [fol. 28r] instructions made unto you.

Hee would often provoke one inflamed with cholar to eat, beecaus hee observed by experience, that abstinence nourisheth cholar, and a moderate receiving of gods gifts, alayed it. Howbeit hee would admonish them to beware also of immoderate eating for that also doth increase the humor, and so wee abuse the good remedy of our infirmity, to imbrace our infirmity

Hee said hee was most tenderly brought up, yet hee would labour to use his stomach to the most common diet, and that hee often would abstain from Cordial meats and drinks, for that hee was taught by experience of the lord, that extraordinary things for extraordinary purposes had ther effects, to bee remedies to cure infirmities, but when extraordinary things were made ordinary though they were never of so extraordinary vertu, yet they would do no more then ordinary meats and diets, yea so far of they were from being as medicines to help nature decaied, that they were rather as hinderances of the strength of nature, and such as did weaken a man beecaus now they had but a natural operation, the stomach being acquainted with them, as other things wherewith in former tymes the stomach or appetite was acquainted As *Sack et aqua vita*[214] take seldome and in a mood revive one and repair nature, but use them ordinarily, and they wil no more heat one then ordinary drincks, yea and that which is more, they wil much make the stomach colder. To exceed in apparel upon some special need heateth the body, but load the body continualy with it and it wil beecome no white hotter then it was having les measure, yea oft it is the more cold and perilously subject to cold. Wherfore hee prescribed it as a rule of wisdom both to himself and to others, that such physical helps of nature, should bee used but in ther [fol. 28v] necessity, and then to bee surceased again, least weakning nature too much wee should not have means to comfort it

---

[214] Sack: a light dry, strong wine from Spain or the Canary Islands. Aqua vita: whisky, brandy, or other strong liquor.

Hee said the lord passeth over many lesser sins in his[215] children, and never looks of them to impute them at any tyme unto them, and though hee imputeth ther greatest sins sometimes unto them, it is but temporally and not[216] as hee imputeth sin to the wicked, which is to punish it eternally

Hee said unto one complayning of suddain gripes and nips in the body, and of suddain fears in the mind, that wee should make our use of them, and although it wer hard to search the particular caus of them, yet it was both easy and sure, to attribute it to our failing in religion, in not doing some good which god required at our hands, or in doing it beecaus wee were too ceremonial and rested in the thing wrought. But if wee can accuse ourselves in one of these the lord doth make trial of us. Again although wee have failed in not doing, yet it may bee the lord calleth us to some thing to bee done and then are wee to look out Also by these suddaine greefs and feares, the lord wil sometime prepare a way to come unto us, not much unlike to a prince, who before his coming, hath a peal of Guns as a warning peece and then are wee to meet the lord with praier, for now is the time, now is the fit oportunity of praying becaus the lord wil shortly pas by us, and therfore wee must stir up ourselves. And having praied it is good to make hew and cry after our praiers, with a holy pursuit of them, as laying a godly claim to the promises of god, not in particular, but in general, for who knoweth but the lord what is good, in particular for our salvation. Here hee shewed by his own example to commend the use of praier how hee being once [fol. 29r] feared, with deceivable and greevous visions hee called to mind being alone in the dark night the unbeleef of the disciples on the seas when our saviour christ was a sleep,[217] then hee asked his own soule whether hee had praied, or no, or whether in praier hee made not some hast out of it, as being desirous to bee rid out of it, Then considering that hee gave himself to god, who was the lord of the night as wel as of the day, of the darknes as wel as of the light, hee praied again, and to the <praise>[218] of god hee never slept better then after hee did, so strive in faithful praier[219]

Hee said to one troubled that ther is a sincerity, in gods children which sathan laboureth to steal from them, and which they most labor to keep, wherfore wee must not bee stil groping and groveling in our corruptions,

---

[215] Followed by *people* deleted.
[216] Followed by *such* deleted.
[217] Matthew 8:23-7.
[218] Replacing *purpose* deleted.
[219] Afflictions 4, Second Edition, 2-3; Third Edition, 2; Fourth Edition, 2; Fifth Edition, 2.

which bring us to an unchearful walking, so as wee stil obscure the work of gods spirit in us which must incourage us against al fainting. For as it is in extremity most dangerous to perswade ourselves of comfort, when wee have no care to see inward corruptions: so it is a thing perilous to perswade us, that wee should have no comfort beecaus our sincere purposes, are defiled with many corruptions in our practises. Let us thinck then that Sathan either would have us to make ourselves our own christ, or els hee would hide from us the benefit wee have in christ, who forgiveth us al the errors of this life, and cannot abide that wee should account his glorious bloodsheeding, so pore and impotent and beggerly that hee having overseen the greatest sins and sinners, hee should not or would not suffer the secret sins, and corruptions of his dearest saincts, whom christ had need to save beecause they would not save themselves, whom christ wil not judge beecause they judge themselves, wee must stil know that wee are under grace and not under the law[220] (which mercy in christ if wee abuse wee are but Hipocrites) and [fol. 29v] therfore serveth christ as a conqueror to pul us out from under the burden of sin, and to rescue us from the clawes of sathan, when our sins and infirmities beat us down. Now wheras many wil say I but mee thincks my prayers mine obedience, and al is but in fashion, and that greeveth mee much herin you pray not altogether of fashion, beecaus you see and are greeved for it, sith they that indeed see it not they pray of fashion, yea and moreover this imperfection doth not so much displeas the lord, as the grief in us for our imperfections doth pleas him. And though it commeth to pas often that god doth curs a vehement praier, and doth graunt our praier when wee do pray coldly; it is not to make us either surceas from zeal or to slip to coldnes in praier (for that is the way to heresy or to prophainnes) but to teach us that wee must not on the one side trust too much to the means, as though wee would ty the lord to our praying, and to encourage us the more on thother side to use praier, when seing the lord hath hard us praying faintly, hee wil surely hear us much more when wee pray fervently[221]

When a good man was complained on for that hee used not the cros in Baptism, hee answered thus for himself, I did minister baptism and that is a sign of the cros: now to add another cros is to make the thing signifying, and the thing signified al one, and mee thincks it is against gods ordinance to make a double seal to one thing. For as I account the gospel to bee the covenant of the cros, beecaus by it wee are partakers of the cros of christ wherby hereafter wee may crucify sin in us.

---

[220] Romans 6:14.

[221] Prayer 6, First Edition, 46; Second Edition, 45-6; Third Edition, 27; Fourth Edition, 27; Fifth Edition, 27.

[fol. 30r] Hee coming to a gentlewomen long tyme afflicted, hee said that al are not to bee raised by consolations, but some by the prayers of the churches and such like. Again some are afflicted rather of ther own minds, being not able to discern ther temptacions and it is another thing to bee afflicted by gods judgement. It is one thing to bee comforted by sound judgement, when god giveth an open and understanding hart, and another thing when one is so far spent that ther must bee a continual observation what doth good, and what doth evil to the party afflicted

January 7. [1583?] Being asked whether a Magistrate being enformed of an offence might conceal it or no, hee said, If a man came to a Magistrate judicialy clayming justice, hee cold not deny punishment without offence. But if it were told him privately as to a brother in christ to sift out by his wisdome, or to exhort by his counsel, hee was not bound to open or punish it

Hee said for his own discipline, that if a man in his congregation had done evil the church not knowing of it, hee after admonition used to the person, and unpanelling his conscience with the sacrament without repentance, would not debar him of the sacrament, beecause a private evil must not deprive a man of a publique benefit, without some orderly or further proceeding in discipline, as in making thoffendors sin known to the <church>,[222] which according to the degree of <the> sin and estate of the person hee in wisdom would often do.

When hee beheld a sumptuous building, for the pore to dwel in, hee said smyling It were not a good pollicie, to build houses stately and sumptuously, but rather largely and substantially, for the pore, lest the excellency of the building shold entice, worshipful or honorable and noble personages to alter those places and taking them up to ther own private uses hinder the poore

[fol. 30v] As hee would not bee too abstaining at the table beecaus hee would not bee singular in any thing, or cause al men to looke at him, so hee would ever have some convenient tyme to reason, then meeting with sanctified speches, and that with reverence, but without contention or controversy at the table, unles it were in a matter of impiety, and then god offering extraordinary occasion to the extraordinary zeale.

Being asked whether the solemnizing of marriage in publique assembly after an holy and faithful conjunction used privately were necessary or

---

[222] Replacing *congregation* deleted.

no, hee answered it was necessary *non ad essentiam sed ad sancti-moniam conjugii*[223]

Hee said how after hee knew god, hee desired by praier two things principally, the one that hee might love the saints thother that hee might willingly and profitably behold the judgements of god in others, which as god in mercy had graunted him, so hee confessed this fruit therof, that unles hee had seen such judgements hee[224] should have fallen into many troubles[225] which now through gods grace, hee had escaped by <seing and> hearing the causes of thes troubles in others. for said hee when I see how god dealeth with others. I search mine own hart whether I have been or am such a man. I perswade my self I may bee such an one hereafter, and therfore I repented beefore gods judgement came upon mee, if ever I did the like, also by praier, and good means I was made more careful for falling into it hereafter.[226]

Being asked whether the killing of a mans own self were remissible or no, hee said have you done it; The other said I have done it: hee replied I see you have not done it: Then hee asked whither if a [fol. 31r] man in thought, had consented to it, it were remissible, as hee had attempted by eating needles points, and drincking bruised glasses to do it, as also by taking great quantities of Aqua vita. It was answered that seing that though hee would have done it, yet god had delivered him, hee should beware of it hereafter, and that hee would not now answer the question, but forwarn him of the sin: Another propounding this question, received this answer, that the jaylour in the Acts [of the] Apostles would have hurt himself, but converting and repenting his thought and purpose did not hinder him of his salvation[227]

---

[223] 'not with respect to the essence but in relation to the holiness of the union'. According to the medieval marriage law of the church, which remained in effect in England throughout Greenham's life, valid marriages were contracted when a man and woman consented to be married to each other. This could be, and typically was, done in private, with some family and friends as witnesses. Public solemnization in the parish church was expected ultimately to take place, but it was not essential (the marriage was not invalid without it). It was only necessary for the more abstract benefit of the purity or chastity (*sanctimoniam*) of the marriage. Greenham effectively summarizes the principle in this Latin phrase. While it may not be original to him, it is not specifically to be found in the church's marriage canons. See Carlson, *Marriage and the English Reformation*, 18-20.

[224] Followed by *said* deleted.

[225] Replacing *temptations* deleted.

[226] Knowledge 3, First Edition, 34; Second Edition, 33; Third Edition, 20; Fourth Edition, 20; Fifth Edition, 20.

[227] Acts 16:27-33.

Hee said to one afflicted in mind, and complayning of want of feeling, that wee must distinguish between gods spirit and his graces in us, for his spirit may live in us when his graces seem dead in us Psalm 31.[228] for as by some extream sicknes, life may bee within one, yet it cannot bee felt of the sick body: so through some great temptation the holy ghost, may bee in us, and yet wee not feel it.

Howbeit as by breathing never so short wee discern life so by the actions of the spirit never so little wee may judge of the life of god in us.[229]

Hee coming to one troubled in mind, for that shee had said shee was with child with the devil, said you doing it either ignorantly, or sodainly or unadvisedly, must not dout of pardon by repentance. Paul confesseth himself to bee a persecutor, and a blasphemer, yet in christ received forgivenes.[230] Bee not affraid of <Sathan>,[231] the[232] wicked fear him too little, the godly too much, but know of a truth that as Sathan and your corruption never told you the truth when you sinned, so they never tel you truth in accusing for sin. deal rather with <the lord>[233] then with the devil in your [fol. 31v] affliction as did Job, who knowing the devil to bee but a vassal, goeth to the principal that is to god, as if one being ready to bee executed,[234] It is not good to deal with the hangman who doth nothing but by authority, but it is good to go to the judge, who hath power to condemn and acquit, so it is safer to go to the lord by praier then to the devil who doth nothing but as the lord permitteth. Bee not affraid of temptations, it is the cours god taketh with his children: Christ was tempted without sin[235] that wee being tempted in sin, might prevaile against sin, and as sathan overcoming Adam overcame al in Adam, so hee being unable to overcome christ, is as unable to overcome them that are in christ. And christs temptations were not so much for himself as for us, that hee being tempted might succor us when wee were tempted, neither can the devil carry envy against us, but hee first pearseth christ with it. Wherfore as hee beareth a deadly food of sin against us, so must wee bear a deadly food of the word against him. And christ being our

---

[228] Psalm 31:1-24. The printed version of this saying gives this citation as Psalm 51. See First Edition, 21.

[229] The printed versions of this saying incorporates the previous saying as well. Feeling 3, First Edition, 21; Second Edition, 20; Third Edition, 12; Fourth Edition, 12; Fifth Edition 12.

[230] 1 Timothy 1:13.

[231] Replacing *temptation* deleted.

[232] Preceded by *it is* deleted; and followed by *cours god taketh with his children* deleted.

[233] Replacing *god* deleted.

[234] See the Book of Job; especially Job 31:35-6.

[235] Hebrews 4:15.

helper as wel in temptation as in salvation, suffereth the devil to cut up our corruptions that hee might heale them, wee must not then thinck it hard to last of the bitter cup of temptation, even then when wee drinck of the sweet cup of sanctification, beecaus, christ was most tempted when hee was most comforted with gods spirit. And it is gods mercy when our minds are most quiet to beeleev his justice, and it is his wil when our minds are most disquiet to beeleeve his medicine

Speaking of a learned father of the church whom the lord with some errours had buffeted in his latter times [fol. 32r] hee said Lord what shalbee my lot. Oh that men would avoid the pride of ther former weldoing, with a fear of ther after evil doing. wel if the Lord for our humbling shal a little take away his hand, blessed bee his name, that by evil reports wil so correct the pride of man, and wil give him to leav the chasticement of his peace even in this life that wee may not bee condemned in the life to come

For my part said hee, I could welbee content that as one came to Philip of Macedon with this mourning salutation. Remember Philip that thou shalt dy:[236] so one would daily say to mee. Looke to thine after fruits, and remember that thou mayest fal. Oh how much is this to bee feared seing so many of the godly kings in ther latter daies did fal so deeply, yet I have some comfort in gods graces, that among many churches mentioned in the Apocalips ther was one remained faithful, and whose after fruits were better then the former[237]

Being requested to baptise a child of a strange woman, delivered of child in his charge, hee would not suddenly refuse it, but with protestation made publickly to his people, hee desired these three condicions, before hee would minister unto it first that such woemen as were with her should answer for her honest behaviour, so far as they did or might conveniently know. Secondly lest some should take exception against him hereafter, if hee should baptise the child, the father of it not being present, hee required three, or four of some sufficient credit, in the Room of the father to promise to the church that they have caused the mother of the child faithfully to undertake, to bring up the child both as a natural mother for it outward estate, and as a christian mother for it

---

[236] This is probably an interpretive summary of the Delphic oracle Philip received when he inquired about his encounter with the Persians, 'The bull is crowned, it is ready, and the sacrificer is prepared'. Pausanias explained that it was a prophecy of his imminent death. Pausanias, *Description of Greece*, ed. J.G. Frazer (6 vols, New York: Biblo and Tannen, 1965), 8.7.6, I, 381.

[237] Revelation 3:7-13.

inward estate. Thirdly although hee thought the children [fol. 32v] of christians, might bee baptised without witnesses, yet for as much as it was the custome of the church of England to take witnesses, even of such whose parents are sufficiently known hee did judge it most convenient to have some witnesses for the baptizing of the child, the parents of it not being so wel known to the church. And although hee used great deliberation in taking it, yet hee thought if it were the child of an harlot, it might bee baptised though not for <it>[238] parents sake, yet for some of it forefathers sake, within the then said generation going before

Hee said unto one complayning of hardnes of hart, being suddenly fallen sick, this is not so good a time to try ones hart in, but then is most trial, when being freest from gods correcting hand, wee can willingly make naked our harts and make known our privy corruptions, to some faithful brother, and then to resist the caus of evil, when the effect of evil doth not constrain us to complain. Again hee observed, that as in bodily crosses, wee do not so much complain of things that bee les dangerous, though more greevous as wee do of things les greevous but more dangerouse as wee suspect more a little sicknes at the hart, then much sicknes in the belly or other parts, so gods children are much more greeved, with deadnes or dulnes of spirit, being more perilous, though then les painful, then with some strong temptation, of either anger or covetuousnes, for the time more greevous to the hart regenerate[239] but les perilous then the other of deadnes of spirit, beecaus it is the grave of many graces

Hee said this was his manner in dealing, with them that came to the communion, if they were but indifferently instructed therunto, hee by exhortation [fol. 33r] charged them to beware what they did, and hee said hee would not wish them to come, but if they came hee would not refuse them utterly, if they lay in noe sin[240]

Hee fatherly exhorted mee to labour for increas of judgement, first by reason, then by example, by reason thus without soundnes of judgement, it is a more difficult travelling for the child of god with his own hart to any fruit: again not being staied in judgement, one shalbee troubled to commit, and affraid to do many things, which indeed hee might lawfully and comfortably do, if hee had knowledg. Thirdly wee shal not without good knowledge satisfy our godly desire, in perswading or dissuading

---

[238] Followed by *the* deleted.
[239] Followed by *then* deleted.
[240] Of Sacraments 7, Third Edition, 412; Fourth Edition, 436; Fifth Edition, 788.

any, for that wee cannot do so assuredly, substantially and effectually as wee ought or would do. By example, hee exhorted mee to consider of the prophet david in his Psalm 119. how stil hee praieth for knowledg, having no one thing oftener then this Teach mee O lord thy statuits etc[241]

His manner was first to intreat generally, and more breefly of a text to his people as it were, to unbowel it before ther faces, and then with deeper meditation, and larger amplification to discours of it, as it were by several pipes, to devide it to \<them\>

When hee spake any good thing privately, hee loved to sift it deeper, but more pleasantly at the table and les seriously. And therfore as hee misliked raving and unconstant speaches, soe hee loved to dy his ears to one thing, which hee saw was the most profitable course of speaking. Howbeit if any would interrupt him in his speach, hee would willingly permit him, and carefully hear him, but with this caveat, unto the party, that hee would both insist, in the present subject of conference and yeeld him that curteously, that after hee had finished his owne speach hee would help his memory in bringing him to that speach [fol. 33v] again wherin hee had hindered him.

Hee said herein men should rightly bee condemned, in that they can so clearly see \<in\> others what they ought to do, what they should not do, and yet find no faults in themselves, for that having, this law as a judge in ther own conscience, which they contemn, they teach the lord how hee should condemn them

Hee was wise both in espying and reprooving of sin, hee would not alwaies, more sharply reproove the greater sin nor more remisly reprehend the lesser, but measuring the accidents and the circumstances of the sin with the quality and degree of the sin it self, hee did see that some appurtenances, with the sin did agravate, or extenuate it so as a greater with some circumstances, hee thought to bee les reprooveable, and some lesser sin with some accidents to bee more condemnable, even as wee see the lord did strike with death the man, that with an high hart did but gather sticks on the sabboth,[242] and yet punished not so greevously others who of infirmity did more, deeply prophane the sabboth.[243]

---

[241] Psalm 119:33-40. Judgements 4, First Edition, 33-4; Second Edition, 32; Third Edition, 19; Fourth Edition, 19; Fifth Edition, 19.

[242] Numbers 15:32-6.

[243] Rebuking or Reproving of Sinne 5, First Edition, 48; Second Edition, 48; Third Edition, 28; Fourth Edition, 28; Fifth Edition, 28.

In singing of Psalms without some special occasion[244] hee would say in company especialy such as were of some general instruction, although privately for himself according to his greef, joy or affection, hee would sing proper psalmes. yea hee thought that they that did most rejoyce might sing the Psalms, of greatest greef to put them in mind, what was or may bee in them, as also to season ther joyes with a remembrance, of the sorrowes of some of the saincts. Again those that are most thrown down, might[245] reap fruit in singing [fol. 34r] the Psalms of greatest comfort, that they may see what hath been and what is belonging to them. After they have sowen in tears, and mourned, with that holy repentance, which is not to bee repented of, also that in the mean time, they might rejoice even in them, who among the saincts do rejoyce and sometime did mourn[246]

Hee said howsoever hee would not deny duties to any inferiors, superiours, or equals, yet none ever went to his hart with an intimate love, so as hee made an inward account of him, but such as had some feeling of sin, and some greef for inward corruption. for hee cold not see how otherwise, men had any thing, but in historical knowledg. Nay hee thought wher a diversity, in professing <of> the gospel was, severed from a diversity of practise and conversation, that ther knowledge might bee more perilous then profitable. And among other gifts of god hee thought *Humility* to bee a vertue most beeseeming, the gospel, which did appear in this, in that hipocrisy did often shelter it self under it, which it would doubtles never do were it not a vertu most comendable[247]

Hee said the cause why men are les greeved for superstition heresy or Idolatry, then for thes murther, or adultery, those bee *peccata rationis*,[248] these bee *peccata affectionis, et actionis*,[249] the one go with a privy pride, under some colour of devotion, thother are ever apparent, and are accompanied with outward shame and confusion,[250] wherupon it comes to pas that many wil hang ther heads when they speak of ther filthines,

---

[244] This is an explanation of how to use psalms in different situations. When there was no special occasion, Greenham used psalms that provided general instruction. In times of joy, grief, and so on, he used psalms that spoke to those experiences.

[245] Preceded by *they* deleted, and followed by *see* deleted.

[246] The last sentence paraphrases Psalm 126:6. Of Prayer and Meditation 21, Third Edition, 402; Fourth Edition, 428; Fifth Edition, 779.

[247] Of Humilitie and pride 11, Third Edition, 338; Fourth Edition, 361; Fifth Edition, 713.

[248] 'sins of reason (understanding)'.

[249] 'sins of volition (will, feeling), and of action'.

[250] Heresie 1, First Edition, 29; Second Edition, 28; Third Edition, 17; Fourth Edition, 17; Fifth Edition, 17.

who wil after a sort brag of ther religion, when they speak of ther superstitions

His manner was when in countenance, hee was not loved or reverenced, when in speaches hee was gainsaid, hee would not once thinck to speake of it, were it done [fol. 34v] but seldome, and howsoever any dissagreed with him in lesser points of doctrine, hee stil laboured to retain love Howbeit in wisdome hee would discern such an adversary, his behaviour his manner of speaking to others his judgement in other matters, his life for the most part and manner of conversation, wherby if hee saw hee did not pretend, a malicious evil, or if hee did not speak against the cause for his person, but for weakenes of judgement, if in other things hee were sound, if his life in the general cours of it was good, hee would not as many do use once any bitter words, but with love and levity sought to reform his adversary, which thing as hee saw with some greef, to bee wanting in many ministers, so hee thought it a thing most necessary to bee laboured for, beecaus hee could not hope for a spirit of love to cover a mulitude of sinnes in dessentions, in the people and hearers, when hee saw that every little degree of disagreeing did cause such want of love often even among the teachers, yea further hee noted that many might soon agree, who for this cause disagree the longer, in that every man, is so hasty to defend his own part, that hee looketh not at al in the others, wheras both laied together the truth would soon appear

When hee was gainsaid in a general truth, beecause the caus was not his own, but the lords, hee would more vehemently reproove such a contempt of his ministry, and say. wel beecaus you bring such an open resistance to mee on whom the comfort of your salvation doth consist. I wil answer you with no other argument [fol. 35r] then this. The next time you awake in the night, when ther shal none bee by you, but god and his holy angels. and when you go to pray to the lord, consider of my speach in fear and trembling, if you can find comfort in your conscience, examine your self without hipocrisy in your bed, and do see if the lord graunt your praiers, until you acknowledg this to bee a sin, to withstand boldly and openly the preacher of gods word, let mee bear the want of credit with you hereafter, And when you see god denieth you comfort, or refuseth your praiers, yeeld to the truth.[251]

His opinion was that knowledg is in the hart, and therfore that many were justly condemned, who refused the light of knowledg in ther own harts. Besides it is said, plainly in the word of god. *The lord hath not*

---

[251] Contempt of the Trueth 1, First Edition, 13; Second Edition, 12.

given them an understanding hart: they erre in hart etc[252] And therfore hee thought that ther was never any sin in affection, which first came not by depravation of judgement, and that they had strongest affections, which had least knowledge and judgement, as wee may see in heretiques

When hee admonished any of a les sin, and saw them not profit by it, but rather that they pleased themselves in it, hee would say, I fear you are like to fal into some great sin shortly, beecaus you please yourself in the lesser sin.

His manner was, when hee preached in such places, as were not taught to speak of such texts for the most part, which might stir up the people to a careful seeking after the means of ther salvation by the word preached

Hee said in promising to afflicted minds to conceal ther [fol. 35v] secret sins, it were good to except that general and discreet kind of opening of them, to such, who not looking to hear them, as evils of any particular persons, desyre to see some secret sins, and pollicies of Sathan, either to avoid them in themselves, or to seek to comfort others being in the same sins, or by such like means wil make some use of them to gods glory

Hee said to one troubled in mind, that shee should not too much bee trobled, about particular and light sins, but that rather in greefs wee should make knowen, our harts to god the devour them privately. for if in carnal sorrowes wee find some ease, when wee make things known to our faithful and loving frinds, to our parents, our brethren etc much more are wee to thinck it an ease, to our spiritual greefs, if wee power forth our greefs into the bosome of the lord who is most faithful to conceal, most loving to take pity and most able to help us in al our greefes whatsoever[253]

Hee said that in our meatings, and feastings, wee were to look to ourselves, if good speaches bee used wee may bee thankful, if evil, sorrowful; if things not mearly evil wee are not to torment ourselves[254]

---

[252] This appears to be a conflation of texts of scripture rather than a single passage. The first phrase is from Deuteronomy 29:3 and and the second from Psalms 95:10 (or possibly the paraphrase of this psalm in Hebrews 3:10). Thanks to Professor Ben Asen for assistance in locating the text from Deuteronomy.

[253] Confession of Sinnes 1, First Edition, 13; Second Edition, 13; Third Edition, 7; Fourth Edition, 7; Fifth Edition, 7.

[254] Feastings 1, First Edition, 24; Second Edition, 23; Third Edition, 14; Fourth Edition, 14; Fifth Edition 14.

Hee never took his petty stipends for baptizing, marrying, or burying, neither his accustomed offerings, which hee said belonged as wel to the \<maintaining of the\> pore as of the minister unles hee were in some great need and necessity. howbeit, as hee avoided superstition himself, yet for that hee would not bee so injurious to his successors, hee caused the offerings to bee gathered, which as I thinck were bestowed on the pore of his chardge

Hee observed many things to bee corrupted by superstition [fol. 36r] which were good in ther first original, as, when woemen drawing near the tyme of ther deliverance,[255] do require the prayers of the church, as in a farewel commit themselves to the intercessions of the saints, partly for that they are to enter into a dangerous travel, partly for that they shalbee long without the publique means of the assembly, and therfore stand in need of the grace of god watching over them.[256] Again hee thought it civil and seemly in al sicknesses, that the bed should bee comely, adorned with whites, but especialy that this was comely in the sicknes, and after the travel of woemen, so superstition bee avoided. As for the *Chrysmes* which superstitiously are used, hee said they came of this, that men when god blessed the seed of ther body, would testify ther thankfulnes to god by giving something, to the minister, or Pastor, and the pore. Besides, howsoever foolishly, and to strictly women abuse ther liberty, yet hee thought it some equity, that after ther deliverance, they should not prophainly, bee ready to go to other places, before they had given thanks, And as they tasted of the benefit of the praiers of the saincts, both in ther gracious deliverance, and holy preservation of ther soules from evil: soe they should pray the congregation, to bee earnest in thanksgiving for them. This hee did not only require of woemen, but of men also. And yet hee observed that wemen might daily bee brought

---

[255] This is a reference to childbirth.

[256] Women in Travell 1, First Edition, 75; Second Edition, 74; Third Edition, 42-3. 'Churching' was the common name given to a controversial ceremony in the Prayer Book. Roughly one month after giving birth to a child, a woman was to end her 'lying-in' and formally re-enter the community by coming to the church to give thanks for God's protection and her deliverance from the 'great danger of childbirth'. Critics like John Field felt that the service 'smelle[d] of Jewish purification' (*Religion and Society*, Cressy and Ferrell, 87) and others called it 'hereticall blasphemus and popish foolerie', 'knavish presumption and presumptuous knaverie' and 'idle babblement' (*The Seconde Parte of a Register*, Peel, 127). It was a regular item in the menu of abuses listed by those who objected to the Prayer Book. See David Cressy, 'Purification, Thanksgiving and the Churching of Women in Post-Reformation England', *Past and Present* 141 (1993); 106-46; William Coster, 'Purity, Profanity, and Puritanism: The Churching of Women, 1500-1700', *Studies in Church History*, 27 (1990), 377-87; and Wilson, 'The Ceremony of Childbirth and Its Interpretation', 88-93.

from ther superstitious *Churchings*, but as hardly are they brought to religious thanksgivings

Hee would have men to use al good means in the tyme of peace, and before troubles come, and yet though, beecaus outward things are as a vaile, to hide gods face from us, wee cannot understand good things so easily in prosperity, or if wee understand, yet wee hardly have the feeling of them [fol. 36v] hee would stil have us use the means, in[257] hope of that fruit and comfort which commeth in the tym of affliction, unto which tyme god often reserveth, our greatest feelings, beecaus it is the most needful tyme of[258] help.[259] And if it be so that, wee have not in our prosperity, so used the means yet are wee not in adversity to dispayr of comforts, beecaus the word of god was given for mans help which needeth means not for to help god, who can comfort without means, neither are wee to bee out of hart, though our consciences told us wee used the means but in weaknes, for that the lord pardoneth our infirmities, and crowneth our sincerity in them.[260]

Hee said hee was either a prince or a peasant, either most mighty above al princes, or most vile among the sons of men. If al the monarks in the world withstand him, his own conscience comforting him, hee ruled above al. If the vilest vassal of the world, rose against him, his own hart condemning him, hee seemed to bee most miserable of al[261]

A godly minister complayning to him, that hee was troubled for pulling down certain painted glasse windowes, in his church, hee answered in my Judgement, the minister is *docere non destruere*,[262] hee is to threaten al the plagues of god against them, that should destroy such things, to lay the burden of the wrath of god upon them, but how the minister should do it alone, hee saw not, but as with consent, when by the power of the gospel hee had convinced ther consciences and by his liberality was ready to reare up new white glasse in stead of the old. For stil hee laboured that in a minister [fol. 37r] ther should bee wisdome; and love mixed with zeal, that when hee shal suffer of the world, hee might have

---

[257] Followed by *the tyme of peace and before troubles come* deleted.

[258] Followed by *health* deleted.

[259] Prosperitie and Peace 1, First Edition, 47; Second Edition, 46; Third Edition, 27; Fourth Edition, 27; Fifth Edition, 27.

[260] Prosperitie and Peace 2, First Edition, 47; Second Edition, 46-7; Third Edition, 27-8; Fourth Edition, 27; Fifth Edition 27.

[261] Conscience Afflicted 2, First Edition, 8; Second Edition, 8; Third Edition, 5; Fourth Edition, 5; Fifth Edition, 5.

[262] 'to instruct, not to destroy'.

wherwith wisely, hee might defend himself, with a sufficient warrant one of the word, and with a testimony that in a sound caus, hee even used, sound discreet, and loving means[263]

Hee said hee was often and suddenly, even in his deepest meditations trobled, with distractions of mind, which whether they were of god or no, hee tried on this manner. If they did either bring some things past to remembrance, to humble him, if it were evil, or to comfort him if it were good. If they did instruct him of any thing to come, leaving but caveat, or admonition to bee circumspect, and yet with hindering his mind in the present to roav and wander to other things, hee suspected it and fel to praier, to bee established in his present calling, from whence his corruption went about to lead him.[264]

Hee had often even in his publick ministry, besides his private conference, a suddain fayling in memory, so as by no means hee cold receiv himself, in those things which hee purposed to speak. To which infirmity or rather woork of the lord, for punishing the sins of his hearers, hee used this remedy presently, to humble his soule underneath the hand of god, and to sigh; not buisily to stand troubling or tossing of his memory beecause, hee knew and ful often had prooved, that it was the best way to help this evil[265]

So greatly hee rejoyced in troubles, that hee would not wish to bee utterly freed from his infirmities of his stomach for al the goods of the world, beecause the lord, had [fol. 37v] woonderfully, provoked him by them to examine himself often[266]

wherfore on a tyme, a special and godly frind making known his purpose unto him, in taking Physick to helpe him in a les infirmity, hee Sir your Physick may ease you of some pain, but I hope it shal not purge yow of the favor of god, for though you bee eased in this, yet for that god loveth you, hee wil meet with you in another thing[267]

---

[263] For other examples of English iconoclasm directed at stained glass windows see: Margaret Aston, *Faith and Fire: Popular and Unpopular Religion, 1350-1600* (London: The Hambledon Press, 1993), 283, 284.

[264] Rules for Meditation 19, First Edition, 41; Second Edition, 40; Third Edition, 23; Fourth Edition, 23; Fifth Edition, 23.

[265] Rules for Meditation 20, First Edition, 41; Second Edition, 40; Third Edition, 23-4; Fourth Edition, 23-4; Fifth Edition, 23-4.

[266] 'Of Phisicke and diet, sicknesse and health' 10, Third Edition, 419; Fourth Edition, 443; Fifth Edition, 795.

[267] 'Of Phisicke and diet, sicknesse and health' 11, Third Edition, 419; Fourth Edition, 443; Fifth Edition, 795.

Beecause no particular things can bee set down, how to amend exces and defect in diet, hee said this were the best rule generally to observ, so long and not les to eate, but as wee are the fitter, either to speak or to hear the praises of god, with more reverence and cherfulnes[268]

Hee said two kinds of men should have liberty to admonish him, to wit his enemies and his inferiours, these hee wold alwaies hear, beecaus hee would practise that in himself which hee taught to others

Hee said god looketh to the desire not to the deed in his children, and if wee purpose to do good, howsoever wee find ignorance, what, wher, or when to do good, god wil derect us, in occasion, tyme, and place, and in mercy wil pardon our weaknes, though wee faile in the circumstances[269]

Hee was alwaies desirous to speake some good thing after meat: among many tymes hee said to some dwelling in a place, wher the word was preached. Oh consider it is the easiest thing to hear, it is the painfullest thing to preach the gospel[270]

The sitting of one houre receiveth a fruit unto immortality. for howsoever men thinck the ministers of god to speak [fol. 38r] even whatsoever commeth into ther mouths, it is not so, they speak that, which many years they have studied for, which earnestly they have prayed for, which by woful experience they have bought, and by a painful life dearily paied for. If a prince should give out by portion a myne of money for the fetching, who would spare to go. The lord offereth the myne of his mercy to bee devided to them, that wil but hear, and beleev it, and no man almost regardeth it.[271]

Hee had a fatherly care, not onely over the salvation, but also over the diet of his wife, to which end hee using many precepts, among the rest used this to her. Bee moderate in things most which the appetite liketh of most, and check the too much greedines of an earthly thing, and you shal find this to bee a good physick to the body and an wholesome preservation for the soule.

---

[268] Diet 1, First Edition, 17; Second Edition, 16; Third Edition, 10; Fourth Edition, 10; Fifth Edition, 10.

[269] Desire 1, First Edition, 16-17; Second Edition, 16; Third Edition, 9; Fourth Edition, 9; Fifth Edition, 9.

[270] See the next note.

[271] Of Prophecie and Preaching 12, Third Edition, 396; Fourth Edition, 420; Fifth Edition, 772. In printed version, the previous saying is treated as the first part of this saying.

Hee said howsoever men might deal with outward matters, yet when greefs and fancies greev the mind, nothing could surely cure them, but onely the word of god[272]

Hee said, so often as hee was asked, of the welfare of his people, wyfe or family, hee took it as an occasion wherby god stirred him up to pray for them, to give thancks for them to examine his own hart, what means both in presence, and in absence, hee had used for ther good[273]

Hee thought that seing lords day, is a more liberal tym of the means of salvation, so our speaches in that day should bee more liberal in such things

[no month] 20 Hee observed that some speaking against eloquence, did savour much of humane spirit, in preaching which is as evil [fol. 38v] or worse. for eloquence is not simply forbidden, but when it waiteth on carnal and mans wisdome, otherwise joyned with the power of the word, it is effectual. But humane wisdome[274]

[no month] 22 Hee ever at the least bestowed an whole week, in calling his people to private conference, before the sacrament, and 2 or 3 daies before either hee would alter his text of purpose to prepare, or els hee diverted his ordinary text to that end and purpose. Neither would hee admit any, but such as either knew to examine themselves or els [blank space] and yet seem to bee [blank space] knowledge would promis to him before witnesses hereafter to bee more diligent, besides hee so examined ther knowledge, that at the next examination, hee would discern ther increas of knowledg

Hee being desirous never to make harder lawes for other mens salvation then for his own, said to one complayning, that his affliction was extraordinary. It is not so, for your affliction is far inferiour to your sins, and therfore howsoever it seemeth to you, or to any man an extraordinary affliction, yet it is with god but ordinary or les then ordinary. Besides this is a dangerous temptation, for it wil bring you to this conceit, that you shal reason thus in yourself, that an extraordinary

---

[272] Conscience Afflicted 3, First Edition, 8; Second Edition, 8; Third Edition, 5; Fourth Edition, 5; Fifth Edition, 5.

[273] Familie 1, First Edition, 20; Second Edition, 20; Third Edition, 12; Fourth Edition, 12; Fifth Edition, 12.

[274] This saying breaks off mid-sentence. A printed variation of the saying ends with: 'but humane wisedome, very barren and destitute of eloquence is evill.' Of the Ministrie 13, Third Edition, 376; Fourth Edition, 400; Fifth Edition, 752.

curs must have an extraordinary comfort, and therfore that you must look for some strange and woonderful consolation, wherby Sathan wil almost move you to contemn, or at least not so much to regard, ordinary consolations, which have helped, others, and may help you, and by this means breed in [fol. 39r] you such unthankfulnes that ere you are aware, one extraordinary affliction shalbee sent indeed[275]

Hee said[276] <hee> never durst desire to dy, howsoever his continual crosses did afford him smal desire to live, and therfore hee feared and forewarned men of ther wishes, in that they wold crucify themselves rather then bee without crosses. Because saith hee the lord heareth a man in judgement oft, though in some mercy, and when hee wisheth, this or that affliction hee layeth it on him, so that after[277] hee cannot do that good to others which to his own comfort hee might have done[278]

Hee said mens preaching grew so[279] cold and so humain, and that ther teaching was glassy, bright, and brickle,[280] that hee thought the preaching of christ simply would even grow to nothing, and mightily without gods grace decay, for in this peace, and prosperity, men are at such peace and quiet, that they have no power of godlines in them;[281] others grow so much to bee offended at this, that they run as far into another extremity, so hard it is to walk wisely in these evil daies

Hee said that when wee had some greater temptations, it were good, to seek for some <other> spiritual sins in us, beecause one shal find, that for some privy pride, or unthankfulnes, or such like, a temptation continueth longer with us. Ther is a trayn of sins and corruption, and correcting the same in us, draweth one in after another, and punisheth one with another, which if wee espy not but look only to the grosser sins wee shal hardly bee brought to yeeld with fruit into the hand of god, or profit by the admonitions of others used unto us. Again wee must use al means of help, amid al occasions [fol. 39v] of drawing on sin, and yet use every principal means at the least, for though wee avoid al occasions,

---

[275] Afflictions 11, First Edition, 4; Second Edition, 4; Third Edition, 2-3; Fourth Edition, 2-3; Fifth Edition, 2-3.

[276] Followed by *that* deleted.

[277] Followed by *ward* deleted.

[278] Death 2, First Edition, 16; Second Edition, 15; Third Edition, 9; Fourth Edition, 9; Fifth Edition, 9.

[279] Followed by *smal* deleted.

[280] That is, fragile, easily broken.

[281] Preaching 1, First Edition, 44; Second Edition, 44; Third Edition, 26; Fourth Edition, 26; Fifth Edition, 26.

and use many means, and omit but one of the cheefest god may correct that ommision in us.[282]

Hee would take these promises of them, whom first hee admitted to the sacrament,[283] and that in the sight of god and presence of some faithful witnesses, if it might bee first that beecaus the principles of religion and doctrine of beginnings were the word of god, or at least most consonant with the word and not the word of man, they would grow up in the further confirming of them, by further knowledg of the word. Secondly they promised to depart from ther former corrupt conversation, and to labour more for holines of life. Thirdly that they would make conscience to keep the sabbath wholy, and throughout in godly exercises to the lord, and as far as ther callings did permit that they would come to bee enstructed, both by publick preaching and by private conference, in the week daies fourthly that if they did fal hereafter into any sin, of disobedience, mallice, filthines, pilfery or slander, or any such like, they would suffer themselves either publickly, or privately to bee admonished of it, according to the censure and quality of the fault. fiftly they promised that if they profited not in knowledg, they would willingly bee suspended from the sacrament hereafter, until they had gotten more forwardnes in knowledg again

When a certain godly man being to preach in a solemn assembly had told him that hee was mooved to speak against many corruptions, and abuses in the church, hee said, If [fol. 40r] your motion bee of god. I dare not nor wil not prescribe you any thing. Howbeit if otherwise you ask mine advise, I answer, Seing it is the first tyme; I would wish you to preach faith and repentance from sin: and when god shal have given you some power, and credit in ther consciences, afterwards according to the measure of knowledg and of zeal, you may more safely do this. for if you speak these things now, either you may bee buffeted by yourself, or cut of from the place by others, and so never have free acces again. for if either you speak things wherof you are not fully perswaded, or if you bee perswaded of them, yet they are not sound according to truth your own conscience wil trouble you. Hee did not follow this advice, but shortly after, fel into greevous trouble of his mind and then into a phrensy

Hee said hee thought it good if men would confer more with ther Pastors saying, Even in earthly things when men cannot try gold themselves, they

---

[282] Temptations 9, First Edition, 67; Second Edition, 66; Third Edition, 38; Fourth Edition, 38; Fifth Edition, 38.
[283] That is, Lord's Supper.

know to go to the goldsmith.[284] In times past men were too far gone with *Auricular confession*, now men come too short of christian conferring. And yet herin wee must look to our harts, that wee come as willing to bee ruled for some men altogether refuse to hear som<any>thing, some wil hear somewhat, but if it come to particulars, they wil deale with the ministers as *Herod* with *John Baptist*[285] or *Zedekiah* with *Jeremiah*,[286] or els if they hear in particulars, yet they wil extenuate them in this or that thing, and deny it to bee so, as *Johanan* answered to *Jeremiah*[287]

Hee was much afraid of himself, in somuch that going to any solemn place, his wife admonishing him to beware and take heed, hee would say oh say so stil, but in reverence tel mee of it

[fol. 40v] Hee sometimes especialy on the lords daies, after his exercises before hee did eat or drinck, would humble himself in praier, and thanksgiving for himself and his people, yea so fervently in his studdy hee hath sighed and groned in his praiers, so carefully hath hee entered into meditation, and consideration of things in his bed, that hee hath sent forth many[288] sighes and grones, so as sometime his wyfe hath thought him to bee very sick, when as it was nothing but the labouring of his hart with god

Hee said hee did not like, that any questions of a mans conversation should bee had at the table, beecaus al men cannot make use of mens infirmities, neither is it meet suddenly or openly to speak of mens weaknesses

whensoever any asked a thing generally, hee would answer give generally, if particularly then hee did desire not to answer suddainly, no not untill hee had talked with the particular party, or had received some particular instructions, from the party in particular things, for that in some particular man, for special causes may bee done, which generally ought not to bee done or hard of

Hee observed some, who outwardly lived an honest and civil life, and yet hypocritically, lying in some sin, in death or before death, were constrained to utter it to ther shame which kind of judgements are most necessary, that god might shew himself to bee god, and his threatnings to

---

[284] May be an allusion to Zechariah 13:9.
[285] Matthew 14:3-11.
[286] Jeremiah 37:17-39:14.
[287] Jeremiah 43:1-7.
[288] Followed by *sins* deleted.

bee true, that the wicked might les rejoyce in ther exceeding impiety and gods children may bee raysed from ther security[289]

Hee said how having some[290] yong men in his chardg vanily disposed to ring bels,[291] hee used this discipline with them, [fol. 41r] that if they would come as early on the lords daies to bee taught and chatechized, or would continew so long late at night or in the afternoons for some profitable instructions as they did to ring, they should ring, otherwise beecause they shewed rather ther vanity of mind, then any sincerity of hart in so doing, they should not ring

Hee would wish one not to bee a witnes to any for the baptizing of his child unles the father would stand with him, being the witnes to take charge of[292] bringing up[293] the child, as also that the father should promise privately, that hee would labour in the childs godly education, and bee glad to have him as an assistant, to teach instruct and reform his child according to christian duties, yea hee seemed to make this conscience in such measure, both with the father and his fellow assistants, that beesides, hee charged these things, at the baptizing of the child upon himself, being called to a witnes hee would admit none of his godchildren to the sacrament and communion, before hee had called together the father, the child, the fellow witnesses to see how they had used some endevour for the bringing up of that child, to the means of his salvation

Unto a godly man that had his child and onely son drowned and therfore in much anxiety of mynd: hee would know whether strange corrections, bee not alwaies the staying of strange sins, hee said Albeit god did surely correct sin in the thing, yet it was not necessary that god should chiefly respect the punishment of sin in it, therfore hee willed him to consider it to bee a punishment, or a dealing with others of gods children. as the *Shunanite* had her child taken [fol. 41v] away by death[294] and that which

---

[289] Hypocrisie 1, First Edition, 32–3; Second Edition, 31; Third Edition, 19; Fourth Edition, 19; Fifth Edition, 19.

[290] Followed by *security* deleted.

[291] It was common to ring church bells to mark festive occasions as well as to mark the deaths of parishioners. Greenham (and most other godly ministers) did not object to all bell-ringing as a matter of principle. Rather, Greenham is here concerned only about young men finding time to ring bells but not to be catechized. See David Cressy, *Bonfires and Bells: National Memory and the Protestant Calendar in Elizabethan and Stuart England* (Berkeley and Los Angeles, CA: University of California Press, 1989).

[292] Followed by *the* deleted.

[293] Followed by *of* deleted.

[294] 2 Kings 4:12–37.

more is *David* a son taken away by a fearful death,[295] but that which is most of al, *Job* had al his sonnes taken away both fearfully and suddainly[296] Now one is not much to stand upon the manner of death or of the affliction. for in such outward things evils do happen, ofter to the most godly, and benefits do abound to the ungodly. But a man must store himself in the course of his life, going before, <for> his comforts, if hee had tokens of gods child. Ecclesiastes 9. *Such things happen to the good and to the wicked.*[297] Howbeit saith hee, god might correct here his security, which ever either casteth us into some sin or cros, or god might correct his too immoderate love of him or his unthankfulnes for him, in what measure hee was reformed, or his not praying for him: or the lord might take away his consolation, and withdraw his mind wholly from the[298] <world> to bee more thorowly sanctified to him self: or hee might prevent some worldlines which the father might have fallen into, or some sin which the son might have falne into, which would have been a souer trouble then his death: And yet he must stay himself on the love of god in al[299]

One asking his advice whether having a particular offence to one, hee should not before particular praier seek reconciliation, yes hee said, but in wisdome, if the offendor bee rightly affected, to ackowledg the sin, and the party offended bee in case to hear it; for opportunity when wee may best so do, for those things best please god which are best done that is, with greatest desire of gods glory. Neither yet, is that place[300] ment of private but of publick [fol. 42r] offences in Matthew 18;[301] not of unjust but of just offences, not simply to bee done, or of necessity tyme and place hindering us, but so as wee may conveniently, tyme and place and occasion given of the lord so to do. Otherwise to do it, in hart before god, and to bee ready to do it, to men when god wil

when letters commendatory, were to bee written in testimony of any christian, hee would admit it to bee done by 4 or 5 professors of same place, wher hee that was to bee commended did inhabite, and by force therof some frind might have a fuller acces to deal for him.

---

[295] 2 Samuel 18:9-15.

[296] Job 1:18-19.

[297] Ecclesiastes 9:2.

[298] Followed by *lord* deleted.

[299] Strange Corrections 1, First Edition, 62; Second Edition, 61-2; Third Edition, 35; Fourth Edition, 35; Fifth Edition, 35.

[300] Followed by *of* deleted.

[301] Matthew 18:15-17.

Hee said whatsoever natural men do wel, it is by natural wisdome, wee ought therfore much more to bee stirred up, by it to do wel in spiritual wisdome. And therfore as it is noted for a special wisdome in our Saviour christ John 2.[302] that hee did not commit himself unto al men beecause hee knew not what is in ther harts, so it is a special token of wisdom in us on the contrary rule, not to commit our selves to al men, beecause wee know not what is in ther harts.[303]

Hee said hee thought it was good for a yong man in his meat, not to bee too abstinent but somewhat liberal rather, but in his drincks to bee both moderate, and avoiding any strong drincks nor liquors

Hee said hee could not away with such as would marry too soone after they had buried ther wives, but that it were better for abstayning a tyme, to shew themselves humbled underneath the hand of god in that crosse, and to testify that it was no light love unto the parties, whom they loved in the lord for besides that it is almost unnatural to get another body in bed before the former bee rotten in the grave, [fol. 42v] it is a thing of evil report impugning common honesty, in that it may offer offence, to the frends of the parties departed, and give occasion to thinck ther love was but light, being so soon forgotten, as also for that it may give occasion, of gealousy to the parties to bee married and ther frinds, in that they may fear, that ther love wil bee as light and little to them as it was to the other before. And although any set tyme for divers circumstances cannot bee prescribed, yet usualy a year wer but sufficient for this purpose of abstinence[304]

As hee was wont to read the bible in order, not according to daies, beecause the holy ghost in wisdom hath set the best order to his own word, so hee thought it was, an unsemely thing that the book of Psalmes should bee read with questions and answers of god[305] of one following another,[306] seing that as in al places, of the word of god, so in this ther[307] is one continued, and indivisible speach set downe by the spirit of god.

Hee said it was a great corruption, in many that they thought none to

---

[302] John 2:23-5.

[303] Friendship 4, First Edition, 25; Second Edition, 24; Third Edition, 14; Fourth Edition, 14; Fifth Edition 14.

[304] Matrimonie 6, First Edition, 37; Second Edition, 36; Third Edition, 21; Fourth Edition, 21; Fifth Edition, 21.

[305] Followed by *following this so should this* deleted.

[306] Followed by *so should this* deleted.

[307] Followed by *should bee* deleted.

teach nor none to bee taught, but such as taught or were taught, such as moved or were moved by thos means, which they themselves were, wherby they shewed rather self love, and love of persons, then pure love of christ and of his trueth The remedy is, that as god hath given many callings in his church, so many kinds of administrations, in sundry callings, some excelling in one gift, some in another, some in zeale, some in judgement, some in eloquence, and al necessary, some by pyping some by mourning, some with vehemency some with mildnes, and by every one, wisdome justifying her children Now it is a godly thing if every man, could see his own gift [fol. 43r] without love of him self, and without disdain, or drawing of others to bee like himself, and also when one seeth anothers gift, how divers so ever from his own it appeareth, yet to reverence it and to give god the glory for it

Hee never used to publish any contract before the parties contracted and handfasted[308] came together before him, when they were reverently in some convenient place, with some reverent persons godlily assembled, hee demaunded of them certain questions, which being truly answered, hee proceeded to praier and exhortation meet for them, that entred so high and holy estate of gods institution. His first question is whether they are not joyned, in consanguinity or affinity, and how far they are of from it. Secondly hee asketh whether they or either of them, hath not been precontracted to any other or no: or whether they themselves had not been between themselves precontracted. Thirdly his demaund is whether they have ther parents consent or no, and of this matter hee would wisely according to tyme, place, and occasion, enquire for the truth. Lastly hee asked them whether they did purpose to continue this action publickly and with the prayers of the church to solemnize ther meeting according to the word. Al these things graunted in the presence of ther Parents or vicegerents, hee would use some exhortation for the general duties both of men and wemen, and after would contract or handfast them (as it is in the common Liturgy) in the sight of god with praier. His exhortation was first a defence of this thing to bee used, of the minister and then a breef discours of the doctrine of the law, and faith applyed to ther estate of marriage and particular callings and to ther most need. Thus of consanguinity [fol. 43v] and contract and consent the questions asked and answered with prayer and exhortation, hee left them until the further sanctimony of ther meeting.

Being asked how wee must do away the sin of an unclean person in the night, hee said <first> it were good to avoid al objects, al wandering

---

[308] Contracted or engaged by joining hands, betrothed.

thoughts, in the day, and security in praying, against it in the night, of neither the wayning of our senses nor knitting of our harts in some[309] more streight meditation of god, unto heavenly things, nor diligent prayer did remove this evil, wee must thinck god calleth us to some more earnest repentance, for this or some other sin before committed. Especialy wee are to beware of company (such especialy as may stir us up to evil) either labouring not to come into ther company at al, or having just occasion to do it in fear and praier, and doing it thus, not to tarry longer then occasion is godlily offered.[310]

Hee said hee felt often being gone to preach the word; very sharp and trembling fears in the flesh, which hee did observe to come upon him, by the very mallice of sathan, at such times as hee should either speak to humble men much, or when some more necessary doctrine was to bee delivered. Hee did not, hee durst not yeeld unto it, but would by paine and prayer resist it, speaking boldly the word of the lord to al flesh, and by that means was not only released of his fear, but also much comforted in his conscience

Although hee himself never used the spiritual himmes, or songs commonly used in our Liturgie,[311] yet hee said at the first howsoever custome and continuance hath corrupted them [fol. 44r] Hee thought they were appointed in the wisdome of the spirit: beecause whatsoever is in them, it most narrowly concerneth our redemption, wherof now being under the gospel, it beecommeth us ever to bee put in mind. And somuch the more, beecause men grow into such presumption (which is a sin far more liking to our nature, then despaire) as they wil either forget christ, or not set by him, as our daies by too woeful experience declare: for this cause *The song of Zachary*,[312] *the thanksgiving of Mary*,[313] the rejoycing of Simeon is set down,[314] which bee not things so bee used, among the jewes as hymnes, and the best kind of spiritual songs, commended to us in the new testament. And if it bee objected, that they bee such as wee cannot, so particularly apply unto ourselves. And therfore these most holy witnesses of our redemtion in christ were first brought into the church for a more continual remembrance, of those benefits, which wee

---

309 Followed by *measure* deleted.

310 Dreames 2, First Edition, 17–18; Second Edition, 17; Third Edition, 10; Fourth Edition, 10; Fifth Edition, 10.

311 The canticles of Zachariah, Mary and Simeon were used in morning and evening prayer (see biblical references below).

312 Luke 1:68–79.

313 Luke 1:46–55.

314 Luke 2:29–32.

have in christ: howsoever now custome without conscience hath rather made them odious, then conscience without custome doth continew unto them that pure use, which becommeth spiritual thanksgiving

August 7   Being asked why a man after study and laborious reading according to his calling, being desirous by meditation, to ruminate the things read, and to apply his meditations to himself, was so much interrupted, that his meditations were broken, uncontinued, intermitted,[315] with other by thoughts and violently and suddainly and unwittingly, distracted into other conceits, hee said, it was either want of preparing, and sanctifying our harts by prayer, before wee set upon so holy an exercise, for that the lord correcteth, the pride [fol. 44v] of our wits, and presumption of our harts in being so bold to work upon holy matters in our owne strength, or els for that wee resisting in a general, purpose of thincking some good thing, or at least not thincking any evil, did not fasten our minds constantly, and continually upon some particular subject, but ranging up and down, as having some part of our affections studies and meditations void for other matters, then wholly and seriously set on the thing propounded to ourselves, And this is very persuasible, and probable by reason; for that when the hart is thorowly set, it is so intent upon one thing, that it cannot bee present to moe things at that instant, especialy if they bee hinderances to the thing taken in hand.[316]

One complayning unto him for the not feeling of his corruption, which sometyme did embolden him to ty sin to sin, and to add one syn to another, as to shuffle a little sin under the repentance of a great syn, until the more general accounting tyme, when wee should sorrow for mo<r>e sinnes and for many sins, his temptation touching him on this manner, why fearest thou to commit this one syn, and this little sin, which is as pardonable by repentance as thy former synnes which are more in number and greater then this, seing thou mayest repent for this sin when thou repentest for them. Hee made this answer. In such a temptation beecause Sathan is very near, wee are to tremble under the hand of god, to fear ourselves, to strive in praier, and to mourn for the temptation wherby sathan would cause us after to [blank space] the sin not to dispute with it,[317] but suspecting [fol. 45r] ourselves to bee rather ready to add sin to sin then to repent of any sin howsoever sathan would blind

---

[315] Replacing *interrupted* deleted.

[316] Distraction 1, Second Edition, 17-18; Third Edition, 10; Fourth Edition, 10; Fifth Edition, 10.

[317] In the published versions this reads, 'whereby Satan would cause us after not to dispute with it ...'.

us with a kind of repenting wee must stay upon the power and help of god.[318]

[August] 10   Having a marriage hee had not the father of the maid
                     present for that hee was lately departed howbeit
thincking it to bee a laudable custome in the church and a tollerable
ceremony, that the father should give his daughter, both to shew his
authority over her and to witnes his consent in bestowing her, hee
certified the congregation of the fathers welliking of the thing, and so for
that matter staied himself.[319]

Hee refused not the Ring in marriage if it were offered, but took it using
thes words, to teach the man to say to his spouse I promis to bee thy faith
ful husband and to keep my body proper unto thee and to make thee
partaker of al my worldly substance. In token wherof I give thee this ring
and with a pure and sincere hart I marry thee.

When one asked him whether wee first received the word or the spirit to
the working of faith hee said wee first receiv the <spirit>[320] howbeit to
feel our faith wee must necessarily receiv the word and although the
smoak doth first, in respect of us shew that ther is fire hidden under some
close matter, yet ther was some fire before the smoak came, soe <tho>
the word first make known to us our faith, yet sure it is the spirit of god
was given us, before which wrought thus mightily by the word,[321]

One asking him, why in his usual blessing hee prefixed the grace of christ
beefore the love of god, seing that the apostle John sheweth that the love
of god the father is the cause of the grace of christ,[322] hee answered Paul
so used it,[323] and that in great wisdom of the spirit beecause, though in
respect of [fol. 45v] god the love of the father, is the original cause of our
salvation, yet in respect of us the grace of christ is the first to woork the

---

[318] Repentance 2, First Edition, 50; Second Edition, 49-50; Third Edition, 29; Fourth
Edition, 29; Fifth Edition, 29.

[319] This 10 August 1583 entry could refer to two possible marriages only: 15 July 1583,
John Boyden and Edith Bridgman or 21 July, Robert Peast and Anne Wilkinson. Neither
maiden was clearly from the parish, though another Wilkinson was married in 1597
(CRO, Dry Drayton Parish Register). This contains elements of the saying printed in the
following editions (a more complete version is found on fols 49v-50r): Matrimonie 5, First
Edition, 36-7; Third Edition, 21; Fourth Edition, 21; Fifth Edition, 21.

[320] Replacing *word and although* deleted.

[321] Faith 3, First Edition, 20; Second Edition, 19-20; Third Edition, 12; Fourth Edition,
12; Fifth Edition, 12.

[322] John 3:16; 1 John 4:9.

[323] 2 Corinthians 13:13.

assurance therof in our harts and for this cause <a> blessing being pronounced unto the people, the beginning of the blessing is used in those words which bring most assurance of the blessing.

Hee thought that al the Prophets were not called extraordinarily, but that some were called ordinarily in part as Samuel was being trained under *Ely*.[324] Again *Amos 7*.[325] the prophet protesteth to the high priest that hee was not a prophet ordinarily called so to bee, nor the son of a prophet as though hee would therfore make his authority to bee great, in that hee was immediately called of god to that dignity, being before an heardman wherin hee seemeth to make a distruction of the calling of the prophets, beecause otherwise his protestation is in vain. And the alledging of his calling had not been of such force, had it had nothing, but that which was others

Being asked if ther might now bee visions agreeable to the word, hee said they might bee extraordinary, but not to bee credible, but for the words sake, and who so is mooved with them and not with the word, wherwith a man is charged to bee mooved, and is not drawn more by the vision to the true means, that mans faith is suspicious, for as visions have been ordinary and Preaching extraordinary: so now preaching is ordinary and visions extraordinary. But if you object that the visions bee true, hee said sathan wil <speak>[326] truth and keep touch twise or thrice in les matters to get us in the learch in greater matters, at length in some contrary to the word[327]

[fol. 46r] Hee in al things would aske counsel of god by his word, by prayer thincking hee could never do good wel to other unles hee also done wel to his own soule, and hee observed, that taking in hand things more suddainly, hee either was crossed in the doing of them, or if hee had any present fruit hee saw it was not abiding, or remayning fruit,[328] wherfore hee laboured to do all things wisely for fear of offence. So that hee being sent for of many, hee would not without some good information of the cause go lest men should thinck him to bee a godly man above the rest, and some man had charged him, hee was careful also to avoid offence with the Pastor of the place whether hee went, and

---

[324] 1 Samuel 3:1–10.

[325] Amos 7:14–15.

[326] Replacing *keep* deleted.

[327] Visions 1, First Edition, 73; Second Edition, 72; Third Edition, 41; Fourth Edition, 41; Fifth Edition, 41.

[328] Prayer 3, First Edition, 45; Second Edition, 45; Third Edition, 27; Fourth Edition, 26–7; Fifth Edition, 26–7.

therfore hee would and did wish, that the pastor would signify to him the estate in particular circumstances of the party afflicted, and how hee desired his hope, that hee might have the safer warrant of his calling.

To one whom hee would have profit by the looking into the woorks of god and that no otherwise then by the word and spirit hee would wish every man to observ ther thoughts in the day ther dreams in the night, ther affections, ther enlargings, and contractions of ther harts, in joyes, greefs, teares and such like. for as in many things so in this hee excelled especially in the observation of his own actions, speeches and affections in marking what things went beefore what things followed after, what things god wrought a far of in some of his frinds at the same tyme, hee was thus and thus affected, thus or thus occupied, wherby hee stil gathered instruction of humbling, or of comfort Also hee used every night when hee awaked some exercise of prayer or meditation, beecause hee would prevent the morning watch with thincking of the word.[329]

[fol. 46v] One asking him whither hee should pay money to the commissary for coming to sermons out of ther own charge. hee said, that to go to a sermon none being at home, is lawful by act of Parliament,[330] and to give money for peace is not amis: so it bee done rather for some other thing then for going to sermon, for that were dangerous to do

Being desirous to speak to the profit of others hee said that hee observed often such a silence, as none cold wel break into it, and per often such liberty of speach as none could take hold to turn it to good: hee observed the cause of such silence either to bee some great greef or some deep meditation occupying the mind, or some deadnes of spirit, or some wordly shame, or some desire to speak and the lord staying the speach or the carelesnes of them that should hear it, in that they do not desire it. The remedy against this, is either in humility to ask some question, or to speake somewhat, and not to give place to such dulnes,[331] which if wee do both without too much fear of men, and without vain glory in ourselves, hee said surely wee should speake woonderful things and bee wel eased of our deadnes of spirit, as for himself as hee did much feel

[329] Prayer 4, First Edition, 45; Second Edition, 45; Third Edition, 27; Fourth Edition, 27; Fifth Edition, 27.

[330] The Second Act of Uniformity 1552, 5 and 6 Edward 6, c. 1, is almost certainly being referred to here. This Act left open the possibility of attending 'preachings' if they were not available in one's parish. Repealed under Mary Tudor, this provision was reinstated by the Act of Uniformity 1559. See: The Tudor Constitution, ed. G.R. Elton (Cambridge: Cambridge University Press, 1960), 397, 399-400, 401.

[331] Conference 1, First Edition 7; Second Edition, 7; Third Edition, 5; Fourth Edition, 5; Fifth Edition, 5.

himself given to that infirmity so hee saw that oftentymes without preparation and meditation, hee offering himself to god for a desire to some whom hee would profit, was much blessed, which hee interpreted, to bee, either beecaus some present, were very desirous to hear good things, whose desires the lord did answer and for that some were present, whom god by his ministery would afterwards use to do good to others. Again hee often felt a deadnes of spirit which made him untoward to doe good [fol. 47r] but also a peevishnes of mind which made him froward to any good thing, which coming was the certain forerunner unto him of some evil to come to him afterward, when hee should feel or hear of something which hee would not

when hee was to send mee to one that thought herself bewitched hee gave these advertisements, first and cheefly to beeware of sending to wissards, secondly to use prayer that sathan might bee confounded. thirdly to labour to bring the person to repent of syn, beecaus god permitteth such things to bee done, either to correct or try our faith. Lastly to perswade the party to wait for a tyme of deliverance though it were long to come, beecause though having repented of syn, yet the lord wil defer health to make a longer trial of us, whether wee wil stil trust to his help, or fly to unlawful means[332]

[September] 6   Hee thought it were good to teach children while they were yong a posterioribus,[333] such things as they have had used to them. And therfore beecause they have had the benefit of Baptism and in baptism have been blessed in the name of the Trinity, hee thought it good to teach them, things concerning the father the son and the holy ghost, that so they might bee trayned up in religion, according to that same order, which the lord Jesus himself hath both taught and practized[334]

Being once to go to a sumptuous burial of an honourable personage to whom hee thought himself a debtour in this thing, and one asking him how without hurt hee could bee at such an action, hee said, The things that are evil and greev mee, so far as I see them with greef hurt mee not.[335]

---

[332] Witchcraft 1, First Edition, 74; Second Edition, 73; Third Edition, 42; Fourth Edition, 42; Fifth Edition, 42.

[333] 'from (after) the next in order, time'. Meaning: children should be taught about the grace they have already received in baptism.

[334] Of Baptisme 6, Third Edition, 268; Fourth Edition, 290; Fifth Edition, 642.

[335] Griefe for Sinne 2, First Edition, 26; Second Edition, 25; Third Edition, 16; Fourth Edition, 15; Fifth Edition, 15.

Hee wished al men to learn this one thing which god gave him, that in saying hee ever song with affection and feeling or else hee had a mourning in his hart, that hee could not do it with affection[336]

[fol. 47v] Hee was stil desirous to keep himself from deadnes, and I tried his hart in thankfulnes by speaking somewhat after meat received to the glory of god, if god gave any good matter to his mouth, so to take it, if every one were silent, and weeping were done, then to raise up some good occasion of speaking, by reading or singing which were so used that when other things, came in place to the affore said end, they were surceased from, beecause customable sticking to any thing, bringeth les reverence and proffit. And among other things hee was very glad to speak somewhat to such whom hee thought after god might make instruments, to teach it to others more effectually, then hee could expres it, which thing hee said hee should learn of the apostle 2 *Timothy* 22.[337]

Uppon a great rain falling in a faire time, not long after the sabbath, hee had this working in hart, how one should order his affections in this estate. first in respect of god whether one should not rejoyce, seing men would not bee taught by[338] so long preaching, to keep the sabboth, that the lord by this affliction, should teach men to obey his holy ordinance. Secondly in respect of men, whether wee should not pitty <them> for that ther goods were subject to such dangers. True it is said hee that men are to bee pitied, but when the question is of piety to god and pitty to men, it were better to rejoyce that the lord wil though some hinderance of worldly things, tender the obeying of his own ordinance, then that otherwise piety should decay, and so many soules of men should perish.[339]

Hee said among other things, for the defence of the surplice and such other things, one objected this, That if the ministers did refuse to obey the queens lawes for ceremonies, they taught a way <how> others should refuse to obey [fol. 48r] other lawes, if they should not bee punished for breaking the law in this, it would bee a means that malefactors should not be punished for breaking of other lawes. It was answered that if it

---

[336] Singing 1, First Edition, 52; Second Edition, 52; Third Edition, 30; Fourth Edition, 30; Fifth Edition, 30.

[337] That is, 2 Timothy 2:2. Dulnes of spirit and of feeling 2, Third Edition, 287; Fourth Edition, 310; Fifth Edition, 662.

[338] Followed by *such* deleted.

[339] Of the Sabboth 25, Third Edition, 435; Fourth Edition, 459-60; Fifth Edition, 811-12.

bee so lamentable a case, that piety and religion cannot stand, except justice faile, that is if ther cannot bee a not punishing, of such as refuse ceremonies, but ther must bee also a not punishing of others. If justice cannot stand except piety faile, that is if malefactors cannot bee punished, unles ministers refusing the ceremonies bee punished also, the matter is dangerous, for both the church so is like to decay, and the common wealth is like to fal, for if ceremonies bee maintained, and men refusing ceremonies bee punished then the church shal receiv hurt: if malefactors bee suffered to go unpunished, then the common wealth is in some great peril. the one is in evil case for want of pure discipline, the other is in peril for want of civil justice, but surely of both it were better that civil justice should cease, then piety bee prophained

Hee observed that when Sathan would not discredit the word by some ordinary shifts, hee would cause men to use reaching, and excessive speaches to discredit the same, which do somuch the more harm, beecaus they commonly passe in zeal and are afforded for a principal mean to credit the truth. As for example, when a man shal say it is as great a sin to boute[340] on the sabbath, as to murther ones father, what is ther reason The sins of the first table are greater then the sins <against>[341] the second table.[342] Answer. It is true when like sins are compared, as Perjury is a greater sin then murder, but vain speaking is a les sin then murder, and the first sin is against the [fol. 48v] first table, and the second against the second table, but it is true of sins unequal, wherof ther is an unequal compariscon

Of one troubled in mind hee said, of al mercies of god it is a great mercy not to bee left without some favourable exercise of conscience. for if the lord saw it good for his holy Apostle and dear servant Paul, though hee was in so many watchings, fastings, exercises of humbling and praier, though hee had such an insight, into inward corruptions, that hee cryed against himself[.][343] what need have wee who either are so rare, and seldome in thes exercises, or els so cold in using of them, and yet such is our corruption, that when by exercise of mind, the lord would draw us out of our selves, wee are displeased, and to bee suffered in our sins wee are best contented[344]

---

340 That is, 'boat'.

341 Replacing *of* deleted.

342 This refers to the ten commandments. The first table refers to sins against God; The second table to sins against humanity.

343 For example: Romans 7:15; 2 Corinthians 12:7-9.

344 A version of this saying is also found on fols 64v-65r.

[September] 30   To one asking him why it came to pas, that hee found
                   himself better affected in a barren place wher the
word was not preached, then wher the means were purely and plentifully
used, hee said it was the corruption of our nature, to bee most dul in
most plentiful means. But to come nearer hee sayed first this may come,
beecause having the means, more abundantly in publique places, wee
remit our private exercises, which before wee used with great stryfe, and
continuance generally, wee do not so much reverence, and greedily receiv
the means, being often as when they bee but seldome Thirdly it may bee
the lord seeth in us a too immoderate desire and greedy affection to the
place, and therfore to correct our superstitious trusting in it, hee demeth
us some use of the place Fourthly one may promise to himself too large
a manumission, from evil beecause of the word, and before a man might
[fol. 49r] more suspect himself, being wher the word is not. fiftly sathan
hath a pollicy herin to make us to bee discontent, with our present
calling, and to hunt after a new, which more cunningly hee doth, by
shewing the inconveniences of the place, calling and tyme present, by
hiding al the profits of them and by promising and laying great benefits,
before us of the place, wher wee would bee <or>345 have been, and
hiding the inconveniences of them, Sixtly beecause it may bee a man was
or thought himself the best in an whole town, and seing nothing in
others, but corruptions pleased and provoked himself the more, in good
things, but being among many good men, wee thinck our weldoing is not
so praisewoorthy, or wee trust so securely to the goodnes of the place.
Seventhly a man may like himself better when hee is instructing others,
and more impatient of silence to hear others. Eightly a man may please
himself too much, in being glad to afford to others, but bee loath to bee
accounted such an one, as should bee inriched by any others, when as
ther is a tyme for both to gather and to spend in. Lastly a man may
thinck this is the sorest temptation, beecause it is the last, even as a man
shal thinck the last sicknes the sorest, beecaus hee feeleth the present evil,
though hee had more greevous sicknes before, but they are forgotten.
The last remedy then against this dulnes, is a careful and continual use
of private and publick exercises346

To one asking him how the angels of god watch over us, hee answered
reverently, wee are rather to pray, for the experience of this ministry unto
us, then either describe or prescribe [fol. 49v] how347 they are This is sure

---

345 Replacing *and* deleted.

346 Variant of the following printed saying (the exact version occurs on fol. 48r in the
manuscript): Variant of Securitie 3, First Edition, 51–2; Second Edition, 51–2; Third
Edition, 30; Fourth Edition, 30; Fifth Edition 30.

347 Preceded by *unto us* deleted.

if wee bee gods elect, and in the waies of god, the angels do watch over us, and yet al see it not, and when they see it, it is by the effects of ther ministry, for though ther ministry bee sure yet the manifestation of it is extraordinary[348]

October 1   When one asked him whether evil spirits did haunt, an house or no, hee said, As god and his good angels are about us, so the devil and the evil angels, <and as the good angels have not been seen but extraordinarily, so are the evil angels> and hee that depriveth himself of this meditation, weakneth his faith; for it is to our comfort and humbling, to our comfort that though wee bee in danger, and no man with us, yet god and his angels bee with us; to humble us, that though in evil doing no man can see and hurt us, yet the devil and evil spirits, hover stil over us, and therfore wee must know that as the angels have appeared to good men for special defence, so the foule spirits, do appear to some men for special sins, and when evil spirits in gods judgement arise, it is not undoubtedly, the soule of any departed, but the evil spirits in the Ayer[349]

Hee thought it to bee a good ceremony for the father to give his daughter in marriage before the congregation, if she either bee a virgin or a yong[350] widdow, to shew that shee made not her own match, but that shee made it by her fathers consent, And being asked how it should bee if the father bee dead, hee said then hee would not have the mother to do it, in the congregation, but thought it good for the father in his testament wisely to appoint some vicegerent to do his duty. If any man do this rather at [fol. 50r] the intreaty of the yong parties then at the appointment of the parents it is an abuse. Now that ther must bee in al lawful contracts the consent of the parents, hee said first children are a part of mens goods as Job 2[351] it appeareth, in that sathan having commission to set on the goods of Job, did ceaz on his children al so. Secondly if in the law a damsel might not perform her vow to the lord, her father misliking it <then much les> (as it is probable may a damsel perform a promise to a man, her father misliking it[352]

---

[348] Angels 1, First Edition, 4-5; Second Edition, 4; Third Edition, 3; Fourth Edition, 3; Fifth Edition, 3.

[349] Of Angels, Third Edition, 267; Fourth Edition, 289; Fifth Edition, 641. Also found under: 'Of Satans practises, and of Schisme and securitie' 8, Third Edition, 421; Fourth Edition, 445; Fifth Edition, 797.

[350] Followed by *maiden* deleted.

[351] The chapter is cited incorrectly in the manuscript. The correct text, Job 1, is found in the printed versions.

[352] Matrimony 5, First Edition, 36-7; Second Edition, 35-6; Third Edition, 21; Fourth Edition, 21; Fifth Edition, 21. No closure to the parenthetical comment is found in the manuscript.

Hee observed this pollicy of sathan that to provoke men to dispair hee would make them to argue thus I have not faith in this or that particular, therfore I have not faith at al in generall; <On the contrary to train men to prasumption> hee would make them reason thus; I have I hope a general faith and therfore I dout not, but my faith is sound in every particular, and both are hurtful[353]

Hee spake thus to one for advice, this is a good trial whether ones anger bee carnal, or spiritual, if our anger inkindleth us to good woorks, if it hindereth not some other holy actions, if it hindereth us not to pray with liberty of mind, if it interrupteth not our meditations, if wee cease to do no duty to the party offending us, if wee can deal with others without peevishnes,[354] though al the world accuse us, yet our consciences might in these kinds of anger excuse us

Hee would say that men must profit when having good causes in hand, they have had evil ishues, beecause it pleaseth god often to deny unto a man that most justly which men denie them most unjustly, and that either, beecause god correcteth in them some sin, wherin they live or els for that they [fol. 50v] used not prayer, and trusted too much in the means and not in god[355]

Hee said to one whom hee loved, that this was a sure experiment, whether the sin which hath often tempted us, should get the dominion in us, or bee overcome of us, if the oftener wee were tempted, the more wee were greeved, the more wee stryve against it, the more wee laboured for the contrary vertu, it should not long continue with us, <But if the first coming of sin wrought some greef in us> but the often coming made our greef les and <les and> caused to cease, from using al means to withstand it, and to bee careles in the contrary vertues, then it were to bee feared, that in tyme this should prevail against us and that wee should get no victory over it[356]

Hee said a man might know by these 3 things, whether his wyfe bee brought him of the lord or no. first if ther bee any agreeing or

[353] Despaire 1, First Edition, 15; Second Edition, 14; Third Edition, 8-9; Fourth Edition, 8-9; Fifth Edition, 8-9.
[354] Anger 1, First Edition, 4; Second Edition, 4; Third Edition, 3; Fourth Edition, 3; Fifth Edition, 3.
[355] Cause Good 2, First Edition, 15; Second Edition, 14; Third Edition, 8; Fourth Edition, 8; Fifth Edition, 8.
[356] Sinne 6, First Edition, 53; Second Edition, 52-3; Third Edition, 31; Fourth Edition, 31; Fifth Edition, 31.

proportionable liking each of other, and that in the gifts of mind concerning ther general calling, as zeal, faith, godlines, and also concerning ther particular calling. Secondly if they being thus consonant do use good means, as the word, prayer, and consent of parents in ther contract, and the good order of the church in ther meetings, and if they use no ungodly incantations, charms beastlike unhonest and unlawful means. Thirdly if ther harts bee sincerely affected to the institution according to the two former kinds, so that first they respect this end, to have an helper to gods kingdome, when each of them hath said in ther soules, I wil goe seek out one, in whom I may see mine own image, of faith zeale and holines, and who may whet up in mee, these and such like graces of god. Again when they do not marry for riches, beauty or such[357] outward things but when they desire mutually, [fol. 51r] to do the duties of one to another, Besides finding that even as it were, they desire t'hasten the kingdom of christ by fulfilling as much as in them lyeth some number of the elect: then use means against incontinency, and so wee see condemned here al marrying with old woemen being yong men, wherin ther is no hope of this thing, beecause it is the sowing in a barren ground, without hope of procreation[358]

November 14   Hee said hee could never wel comfort another when
                 hee himself was comfortles. In al places hee was
sparing in consolations, except some present did require and need them, and yet hee would both so soon check himself in his mirth secretly and moderate others, that if they saw any hurtful liberty by his mirth, hee would by and by take them down again, by some good way or other

One saying in his hearing that hee thought it might bee observed from tyme to tyme, that men have been more bountiful in furthering a corrupt religion then in releeving the professors of the word, hee answered his judgement was contrary, for that though many in popery give much, yet it is of ther abundance, but wee read in no history, that ever men sold ther <whole> possessions, and gave to the preachers, as it was done in the primitive church[359]

[November] 23   A man wel given purposing to go to a place, wher the
                   word of god is not, hee said to free mine own soule for
you, I exhort you to looke to yourself, and though neither the church,

---

357 Followed by *like* deleted.

358 Matrimony 1, First Edition, 35-6; Second Edition, 34; Third Edition, 20-21; Fourth Edition, 20-21; Fifth Edition, 20-21.

359 Of Zeale 4, Third Edition, 453; Fourth Edition, 477; Fifth Edition, 829.

nor the word bee only among us, yet to goe from the word to a place wanting the word, is the hazzarding of your salvation. And I have observed that some of mean gifts going from hence [fol. 51v] but with the choice of a place wher the word is, though in les abundance, have kept that they had, and that others of great gifts going to a place wher the word is not have lost al.

A certain yong man having without consent of frinds made a contract, hee would not marry them, until before honest witnesses, they had faithfully conditioned, that in tyme of marriage they would confes ther fault, against the glory of god, ther superiours and the whole church, which should bee done at that tyme, that the father is woont to give the virgin in marriage[360]

[November] 25   Hee observed many who being established in mind, in
                   al other things, yet in some particular things <were>
phrenetical, which was a special judgement of god for some syn

One complayning to him that hee was tempted, that ther was no god, hee said this temptation, came either to punish some other sin, or els beecause god should bee demed in these latter daies, to shew what Atheism is in us naturally, according to those prophecies. And that therfore god did here and ther pick out some of his own childeren to bee thus assaulted, both to leav the wicked world without excuse, if they wil not profit by these things, as also to humble the rest of his children herby, which naturally are subject to the same temptation

A yong man having overslipt in love, and intended to marry, without consent of governors, hee did not contract him, but admonished him <and> at the day of marriage hee used to the parties to bee married this discipline. first as they privately had confessed ther fault to the governors specialy offended, and craved pardon, so now [fol. 52r] they confessed ther fault to the church, they pronounced themselves sorrowful for offending against god and the church, they craved forgivenes they desired al to beware of the like, and praied them, to pray for them that this fault might so humble them, that they might the more warilie walk, without offence the residue of their life[361]

---

[360] 'Of Matrimonie, and of the duties which belong to that state' 9, Third Edition, 36[7]; Fourth Edition, 391; Fifth Edition, 743.
[361] 'Of Matrimonie, and of the duties which belong to that state' 10, Third Edition, 36[7]; Fourth Edition, 391; Fifth Edition, 743.

The acts and speaches of Mr G. 1584

January 11   Hee said beecause hee saw many declame against
                         mens sins and without pity of them that sinned, and
fear of themselves lest they might sin, therfore it was his manner to bring
them to retorte ther speaches to themselves and to consider of ther own
estate, and so to range ther talk

Hee observed that many would speak largely and liberally, so long as
ther speach should not bee censured, or examined of others, or made
particular cases to themselves. when ther speach might have free passage
and furtherance, of al to bee tossed[362] generaly as a ball, but when wee
come before them, that would either search the soundnes of our speach,
or recoile the edge of our speach upon our consciences and conversation,
then it was a durus[363] battel

Having to deal oft with divers troubled consciences, hee would mislike
them that could not abide to tarry the lords leasure, but nedes they
would bee helped at once, and by and by, as soon as they hard him
speak, of whom they had received a good report, and opinion and then
would thinck far worse of him, then ever they thought wel before. for
besides that hee that beeleeveth maketh not hast, this is a coming rather
as it were to a magitian, who by pronunciation of words, make silly
soules look for health, then the minister of god, whose speaches being
most[364] angelical documents comfort until and howmuch it pleaseth the
lord to give a blessing unto them, which sometimes hee doth deny [fol.
52v] beecause, wee come to men with too reverent an opinion of them,
as though they were wisemen, not unto such as using the means, yet do
look and stay for our comfort wholly from god himself[365]

A good man being somewhat vehement with him in speach[366] hee said
very mildly, Sir I knew you, though, you bee fier I wil bee water[367]

Hee marked two things wanting in the church which were neglected, hee
saw that men being in danger of death, would bee prayed for in the
church, but they would not have the church give thanks for them: again

---

[362] Followed by *of al* deleted.

[363] 'hard, tough'.

[364] Preceded by *ev* deleted.

[365] Conscience Afflicted 4, First Edition, 8-9; Second Edition, 8; Third Edition, 5;
Fourth Edition, 5; Fifth Edition, 5.

[366] Followed by *es* deleted.

[367] [Saying] 124, Vehement speeches, Fourth Edition, 742; Fifth Edition, 68.

hee saw that woemen would come to give thancks after their deliverance, but they would not beefore ask the prayers of the church. Now if any wil say that so the church would bee pestered with many things, and that Augustines complaint might bee taken up,[368] hee said, not soe; for seing it is so rare a blessing to have the fruit of the womb seing sometime the mother, sometyme the child, sometyme both dy, and that the gift and blessing of both, is a woorke passing the *sun the moon and the stars*, it were nothing superfluous, and burdenous in such cases to bee thanckful[369]

Being urged, it were not wel to dissent from the order, of the purest churches, hee said hee neither respected learned *Synodes, nor censures, nor the manner of churches*, but as they agreed with the word, and one giving him a reason of his doings, hee would lean more to him then to al the rest

Hee observed that men would make known many sins and infirmities, and yet retain one which is the most secret, and oftentimes the most chief, as moses had many reasons of his tergiversation,[370] and yet ther was one secret reason and that the greatest which hee would not utter[371] [fol. 53r] Then hee observed the great mercy of the lord, that though hee might have been displeased, specialy after such large promises for his refusal, yet hee rather pardoneth this one infirmity of fear and seeks to cure it, respecting stil his many fold good things besides then forgeting his manifold good things hee would pres him with this one want, And therfore after many reasons, the lord vouchsafeth to handle very gently his privy sore and to salve it on this manner. Nay moses ther is one thing which thow fearest most and that is thy evil intertainment with Pharoh, and the revengers of his blood whom thou sheddest, but let not this stay thee, for they are al dead.[372] This answer seemed to take away the greatest argument tergiversation, though it was last known, for presently upon this comfort hee takes his calling in hand, wherin also hee noted that how fearful soever, man is in respect of himself, yet when god

---

[368] While the saying appears to refer to a well-known concern found in Augustine's writings, no collaborating evidence from the antiquity, medieval sources or sixteenth-century writers could be found to determine the exact meaning of 'Augustine's complaint'. This phrase does not appear in the printed versions of the saying.

[369] Sicke and Sickenes 3, First Edition, 59-60; Second Edition, 59; Third Edition, 34; Fourth Edition, 34; Fifth Edition, 34.

[370] That is, forsaking, turning one's back on something in which one was previously interested or engaged.

[371] Exodus 2:11-14.

[372] Exodus 4:19.

inableth and incourageth him wee see hee shal bee invincible, even as moses against Pharoah himself[373]

It is in vain hee said to controul the outward senses without the rebuking of the hart

[January] 15   Hee observed that wher hee bestowed most labour and love, ther hee was most hardly thought of, which though it were some greef to flesh and blood yet herein hee said hee felt comfort, that even they that judged so sevearly of him in ther most need would come for him, thinck wel of him and set wel by him

Hee desired to observ cros speaches, in such as would overwhart[374] him, and would wish that ther sayings might dwel somewhat up on him, least as hee desired not presently after the manner of some greatly to bee moved either in liking or misliking, either to bee glad or to bee made sorrowful, so afterward hee would meditate of the fruit of it for tyme to come

[January] 17   [fol. 53v] Being asked how it came to pas, that in the morning or after the first sleep one should have such worldly thoughts dashed into the mind, which prevented divers better exercises, hee said hee thought it was to shew our harts, that though wee were not worldly or carnal in our lives, yet god would make known to us, that for al that our harts had corruption in them stil, and that it is profitable, both to humbling and to thankfulnes to consider those first thoughts after our sleep, beecaus they shew us stil the estate of our harts, which no dout some good men considering, have gone about to deceiv ther corruptions, by falling into prayer so soone as they awaked: howsoever since it hath growen <but> into a popish mumbling,[375] of words after sleep

[January] 18   Being asked how it came to pas, that the graces of god are sweetest in new birth, hee said wee do surely fal somewhat to the flesh again, otherwyse it is not so: and it is the work onely of the spirit, when and in what measure, although in respect of us it seemes contrary beetween us and the world for the world thincks the present pleasures sweetest alwaies, so do not the children of god, even of

---

[373] Exodus 3:1 - 14:31. Confession of Sinnes 2, First Edition, 13-14; Second Edition, 13; Third Edition, 7-8; Fourth Edition, 7-8; Fifth Edition, 7-8.

[374] That is, overthwart.

[375] Derogatory reference to Catholic prayers that Greenham believed were said by rote, with no feeling or conviction.

ther spiritual delights. Nay wee are contrary in another thing to ourselves, wee thinck our present corruptions and temptations ever greatest, as sick men alwaies thinck the last sicknes sorest: but wee thinck the present feelings of the spirit <ever> least, though it may bee they are as great as ever they were before, but who knoweth the cause of these things, seing it proceedeth wholly from god, who as a wind bloweth where and in what measure hee listeth[376]

[January] 31   [fol. 54r] Being asked how in the[377] examining of our conscience for sin, wee should find out the special sin, hee said that could not so wel bee done, for who doth understand the errors of this lyfe, but by oft examining of our selves, by acquainting ourselves with our own estate, by earnest prayer that god would reveal the sin[378], by oft reading and hearing the word, by marking the most checks of our consciences, and reprochings of our enemies, wee might bee led to the nearest sight of them[379]

Hee observed the difference of superstition and true religion in many things, and the divers estate of things in both, and namely how the devil whiles hee was made known to men onely by hornes, by huge collours, by clawes, or by an hollow voice, was woonderfully feared, but now being reveiled to bee a more secret adversary, a spiritual tempter, a privy overthrower of the soule, no man almost regards him And therfore as some have feared too superstitiously, so now it is come to the more dangerous extream, *that hee is not feared at al*, yea that which is more, when wee cannot truly beeleev the gratious help of gods holy angels unles wee beleev, the manifold, and hidden assaults of sathan, hee marked that good men, and learned did much omit this in ther prayers, that god would send his angels to them to deliver them from evil spirits[380]

It is an happy thing said hee to redeem the renuing of the inward man, even with the deny[ing] of the outward

Hee feared much the preposterous zeal and hasty runing of yong men

---

[376] John 3:8. Of Regeneration, and Sanctification' 5, Third Edition, 427; Fourth Edition, 452; Fifth Edition, 804.

[377] Followed by *opinion* deleted.

[378] Followed by *s* deleted.

[379] Conscience Afflicted 5, First Edition, 9; Second Edition, 8-9; Third Edition, 5; Fourth Edition, 5; Fifth Edition, 5.

[380] Evill Spirits 1, First Edition, 65-6; Second Edition, 65; Third Edition, 37; Fourth Edition, 37; Fifth Edition, 37.

into the ministry, beecause as judgement so stayednes, and moderation, use, experience, gravity in ordering affections, and having some mastery over his corruptions was needful in him [fol. 54v] that should govern the church. And hee observed the extream in our age to bee contrary, to that in the first, wherin men being but slenderly brought up, it was very long ere they were used in the church, but now education being bettered too hasty a trial is made of mens gifts to ther hurt that use them, and that have the use of them[381]

Hee said hee found want of judgement in men who would do and not do things without sound reason: As for himself hee would in things commanded and forbidden aske a reason, then if it were good hee would yeeld to it, otherwise hee would gainsay it, but with a reason which hee would alledge to bee tried, and offer to bee proved. And as for ceremonies i. the lesser adjuncts of religion, as sitting, standing kneeling, walking, at the receiving of the sacrament, so they were not ceremonies, of the essence of religion, and substantial ceremonies, in which sence, the sacraments may bee called ceremonies, hee would not withstand or condemn any but leav them to ther own reason, seing very good men do soe dissagree in them, or change ther opinion in them, and even say as in many other particulars, desire a reformation

But if it came to the essence of gods worship, then onely must wee bee strickt and holy: howbeit also so long as in the other ceremonies, it was free to use them as they would, it were more tollerable: but if once a common law bee made of them, that hee would not consent to: for things established by law, had need bee very sound and [fol. 55r] profitable, and not able to bee gainsaid of any, neither of caveling nor others. And for an uniformity in every particular, no common wealth under a christian goverment can bee read of, either in civil or ecclesiastical stories. And for our mixt state of the church, hee said hee could tollerate many things, as to give subsides and taxes and to suffer impropriations and such like, beecause howsoever they are demaunded, yet hee gave them by protestation, that is, though the prince should remit such things to the ministers, yet being asked asked [sic] them, hee gave not them, as to a lawful petition, but beecause hee would not break the common peace, the thing being meerly outward <and so tho the tax required of Augustus Caesar was unlawfully demaunded, yet Joseph did pay it and not unlawfully:>[382] beecause in a meer outward thing they would not break

---

[381] Ministerie. Ministers 3, First Edition, 42; Second Edition, 41; Third Edition, 24; Fourth Edition, 24; Fifth Edition, 24.
[382] Luke 2:1-5.

the peace of the church, And Christ himself refused not the tribute mony[383]

Hee thought it were good if in colledges reformation might bee made, of making them ministers, which must bee fellowes, beecaus of the inconvenience of instituting many that bee yong. And the thing at the first was popish, howsoever some object[384] it was, that for because if they might have continued in ther fellowships some yeares they would not enter into the ministry, and therfore to meet with that this was established, yet this is answered not to bee the best wisdome for that another pollicy might have been found to reform this, as that these which being fellowes and able to profit the church refused it should bee bound to repay al his former gains.

Hee thought the cause why many mens harts were hardened now a dayes was this, beecaus they saw as great gifts of tongues, learning and civil life in Papists, and heretiques, as in others of gods true servants, even as the cause of Pharaoh his obstinacy was this that being willing to bee deceived hee would not obey the lord, beecause other sorcerers of egipt by ther illusions could do as hee [fol. 55v] thought as Moses and Aaron, who as servants of god to deliver his people[385]

Hee said hee thought this to bee the cause of some to maintain the cros in Baptism, beecaus it was no part of the sacrament why then said hee, Salt et[386] oile may bee used for they are no partes of the sacrament, as Peter Lumbard himself graunteth,[387] but they bee (saith hee) added *ad honorem et decorum*:[388] wherfore if men have taken away salt and oile why do they leav stil the crosse, for abuse and beecause it was a superfluous additament, much more may the cros bee left because it is a thing as much superfluous and no les abused then the other. Besides, Baptism it self is sufficiently a significative sign of the cros, even as the gospel is sermo crucis,[389] so baptism is signum crucis.[390] Now if they wil have the cros as another sign, and so make two signes of one thing, wee dare not ordein two, seing the lord in wisdome contenteth himself with

---

[383] Matthew 17:24-7. Also, Matthew 22:17-22.

[384] Followed by *that* deleted.

[385] Exodus 7. Hardnes of heart 1, First Edition, 28; Second Edition, 27; Third Edition, 16; Fourth Edition, 16; Fifth Edition, 16.

[386] Replacing *and* deleted.

[387] Peter Lombard, *Sententiae in IV Libris Distinctae*, Liber IV, Distinctio III, Cap. 1.3 (Rome: Editiones Collegii S. Bonaventurae Ad Claras Aquas, 1981), 244.

[388] 'for honor and seemliness'.

[389] 'word of the cross'.

[390] 'sign of the cross'.

one, and so also by this means to burden the gospel with too great a multitude of ceremonies, which must not bee seing this is a difference between the law and the law and the gospel, that the law had many signes which the gospel hath not. Again whatsoever hath no good use by gods institution but hath been abused, it is better to have the thing clean taken away then otherwise, as was the serpent in the wildernes,[391] and soe would the crosse bee used which is grown into as great abuse. If they say that christians did use it Answer. they did use it in Political things, but not in things *Ecclesiastical* as it is now. Besides if the cros bee necessary why shold it not bee necessary in other things also if they say [fol. 56r] the other cros was a thing continuing, so wee say this, by the oft repeating and continual renuing of it. why did they themselves also take away in king Edwards daies the cros from the brest and bring it to the forhead,[392] which being permitted of them in the church, is used in every other solemn action, but that they wil not allow; and yet I would ask them why if they affirm it to bee good in the church, it should not also bee good at home at ther houses. Last of al the church thought good to take the cros out of their confirmation,[393] wher more edification might seem to bee, then in Baptism, beecause the children to whom it was used in confirmation had more understanding then infants receiving it in Baptism. why then it is left in Baptism wher the child for want of understanding can have no use of it at al. If they object that the church hath liberty to use some ceremonies, wee say besides, that our ceremonies bee both many in number, and superstitious in signification, which is not lawful: that is not al: for as the ceremonies under the gospel, ought neither to bee many, nor superstitious though they bee few, they must also bee such as bee comely, tending to order and christian discipline, and serving to the edification of the church. They must not bee needles or not good for whatsoever is not good is hurtful to the church for if they say the cros is for order, it is rather contrary to order: And the lovefeasts carrying a shew of order in the church were removed by Paul,[394] for that they were besides the institution, and therefore much more may the cros bee abandoned.

---

[391] Numbers 21:6-9. Just as the bronze serpent was used to heal and then taken away, the same should be done with the cross to avoid the abuse of idolatry.

[392] The 1549 Book of Common Prayer prescribed the use of the sign of the cross on the breast and the forehead at baptism. The 1552 version omitted reference to the sign of the cross on the breast. *The First and Second Prayer Books of King Edward the Sixth* (London: J.M. Dent and Sons, 1910), 237, 398. Many thanks to Professor Marion Hatchett for his observations on this issue.

[393] The 1549 Book of Common Prayer prescribed the use of the sign of the cross on the forehead at confirmation; but the 1552 version omitted reference to the sign of the cross in this rite. *The First and Second Prayer Books of King Edward the Sixth*, 251, 408-9.

[394] 1 Corinthians 11:17-34.

To one that said hee feared death hee said As I would have you to thinck
of lyfe, as being content to dy, so thinck of death as you could bee
content to live. And as for the fear of death I like as wel of them that
measurably fear it, as of them, who so joy at it; though I hope I like wel
of them also. Howbeit I soe not this in those [fol. 56v] which is in them,
and which is a thing both allowed by grace and nature that is if they
tremble at gods judgements. you wil say that notwithstanding you see
not, why you should not fear death, seing you fynd no comfort in lyfe:
to which I answer, that your lyfe hath not been without comforts,
howsoever things gone are soone forgotten, though your comforts were
not in that ful measure hoped for, and it may bee that plentiful measure
shalbee given you in death. But what if you should dy in this discomfort?
for my part as I look for no great things in my death, I would not thinck
more hardly of you, neither would I wish any to judg otherwyse of gods
children, in that estate of death: for wee shal not bee judged according
to that particular instant of death, but according to our general cours of
lyfe, not according to our deed in that present, but according to the
desire of our hart ever before. And therfore wee are not then to mistrust
gods mercy in death, bee wee never so uncomfortable, if so bee that it
hath been before sealed in our vocation and sanctification[395]

A certain man being a Papist, although not so grounded as hee desired
to bee, took a view of the life of Papists, if it were as glorious in truth as
they pretended, which when hee found <not>[396] hee turned himself to the
Protestants, and looking into their conversation hee found himself not
contented, until in the end hee met Familists in whom hee so staied
himself that hee grew in familiarity with their doctrine. The first
principle that they taught him was that there was no god, this boiled
much in him, so that hee began to add conclusions to his precept on this
sort. Surely if ther bee no god, or being a god hee is not so just and
merciful as they say: ther is <either> no heaven, nor hel, <and> if ther
bee any the joies are not so eternal, nor the pains so continual as some
men have taught; why then do I sel my certain pleasures [fol. 57r] in this
world, for uncertain pleasures in the world to come. This develish
illusion so far prevailed, that hee stoul an horse, for which hee was
apprehended, imprisoned, arained, condemned. But by the providence of
god, confering with a godly minister, hee confessed himself an Atheist,
wherupon sute was made and graunted, for his repriving until the next
assise, in hope of his conversion. In which tyme hee would willingly

---

[395] Death 3, First Edition, 16; Second Edition, 15-16; Third Edition, 9; Fourth Edition,
9; Fifth Edition, 9.
[396] Followed by *himself* deleted.

graunt al general truth taught him, with liking of his teachers, but could not by any means bee brought from his Athisme. The assise following drew near, hee is to bee executed, <the place was assigned the person needs to bee executed> who when hee should have turned from the ladder, cryed suddainly for christs sake stay my lyfe, wherupon hee spake these or the like words, wel let the world say, what they wil: doubtles ther is a god, and the same god is just for ever to his enemies, and everlastingly keeping his mercies with his children: now turn mee over, and so hee made an end both of his speach and of his lyfe[397]

Phrensy, jealousy and heresy are things most dangerous. God sheweth us oft in affliction what wee may do in our outward actions[398]

The not observing of the judgements of god maketh us so loath to love his mercies, and so slenderly to fear his judgements wee must use al exercises, of reading, hearing and confering, praying singing and meditating, but wee must not ty the woorking of gods spirit to any one particular[399]

Wee often want outward things beecause wee esteem no more of inward graces[400]

Gods children by the cros have their faith so tryed as al or some dros of sin therwithal is purged[401]

Some means may bee used before prayer, as being such as would interrupt us in prayer beecause of ther necessity, some after praier, so that wee neither neglect nor trust the means

The promises of god must bee to our prayers as a double string to our bow[402]

---

[397] Atheisme 1, First Edition, 5; Second Edition, 4-5; Third Edition, 3; Fourth Edition, 3; Fifth Edition, 3.

[398] Affections 2, First Edition, 1; Second Edition, 1; Third Edition, 1; Fourth Edition, 1; Fifth Edition, 1. In the printed version of the second sentence, the word 'affection' appears instead of 'affliction'.

[399] Exercise of Religion 3, First Edition, 19; Second Edition, 19; Third Edition, 11; Fourth Edition, 11; Fifth Edition, 11.

[400] Povertie 1, First Edition, 44; Second Edition, 43; Third Edition, 26; Fourth Edition, 26; Fifth Edition, 26.

[401] Temptations 4, First Edition, 66; Second Edition, 65-6; Third Edition, 38; Fourth Edition, 38; Fifth Edition, 38. First sentence of printed version.

[402] This is the first phrase of the first saying appended to 'Of truth and errours, sincerities and contempt of the word', Third Edition, 445; Fourth Edition, 469; Fifth Edition, 821.

As Jacob ceased not to wrastle (though his thigh was loosed) until hee had [fol. 57v] the blessing,[403] so wee must not faint in temptation, though wee bee humbled, until wee have the victory[404]

Wee must not dispair of the victory in temptation, beecaus in our striving wee had some infirmities, but rather wee must rejoyce in our will and in gods grace, wherby wee have desire to go[405]

It is a natural thing to reform ourselves whilst gods judgements <are upon us>[406]

God is more merciful to the true repentance of one then hee is just to the sins of many

It is the pollicy of sathan to lay before us the greater benefits which wee want to cause us to mourn for them, and to hyde the present benefits that wee might not bee thanckful[407]

Wee must not desyre to come out of the fire of affliction, until the lord hath purified us as pure gold for his own use, but stil thinck that the continuance of the cros, is the continual scowrer of som dros[408]

It were an happy nourcery for this church if every grounded pastor would train up both in lyfe, learning, doctrine, and discipline some toward schollar to bee his assistant in the ministry, so that after sound knowledg and discreet[409] experience, hee may commend him to the church goverment, and being happily discharged of one, to draw some other out of the university, to bee framed in like manner fit for the work of the lord

---

[403] Genesis 32:25-7.

[404] Temptations 4, First Edition, 66; Second Edition, 65-6; Third Edition, 38; Fourth Edition, 38; Fifth Edition, 38. This saying is used as the second sentence of Temptation 4 in the printed editions.

[405] Temptations 4, First Edition, 66; Second Edition, 65-6; Third Edition, 38; Fourth Edition, 38; Fifth Edition, 38. This saying is the third sentence of the printed version.

[406] 'Of the judgements of God, and how just he is in judgement, and how his promises and threatenings to Israel, appertaine to us' 8, Third Edition, 348; Fifth Edition, 724.

[407] Povertie 2, First Edition, 44; Second Edition, 43; Third Edition, 26; Fourth Edition, 26; Fifth Edition, 26. A version of this saying is used as the first sentence of Povertie 2 in the printed versions.

[408] Povertie 2, First Edition, 44; Second Edition, 43; Third Edition, 26; Fourth Edition, 26; Fifth Edition, 26. This saying is used as the second sentence of Povertie 2 in the printed versions.

[409] Followed by *repentence* deleted.

A certain maid in hempsted having a general liking of the word on atym had this meditation as shee was milking, *O lord should I thus bee found, if thou suddenly shouldest come to judgment.* Not long after shee hearing the Bel calling to the sermon, shee made hast that according to her manner, shee might go with her companions to the church, where after shee had hard, shee returned home with her said acquaintance and used this speach. *The preachers much speak against sin and earnestly denounce hel, but I doubt that* if wee go wee shal not go alone but shal have company. This speach passed, the lords judgements seemed to perce. Howbeit [fol. 58r] according to her ordinary calling shee being milking where before shee had the meditation of the day of judgement, the lord brought to her mind the graceles speach she used with her companions as shee returned from the sermon: forthwith she was taken by the arm of a whyte thing coming into her, whereat her spirits were so amazed, that shee was taken both speachles and senceles. Howbeit after three daies, in <al> which tyme shee received very little or none ordinary food, both her sense and speach was restored, so that the first words at the uncanceling of her mouth was these; I said saith shee, that if wee went to hel we should not goe alone but wee shal have company; but had not the mercy of god been above my merits, I had gone alone without company Afterward shee called for her acquaintance, and with many woords exhorted them to repentance for ungodly speaches. The mayd through gods goodnes was truly touched with this visitation and groweth as a faithful christian

It were necessary in the church of god as Josua ministred to Moses,[410] *Elisha to Elijah,*[411] *Samuel to Heli,*[412] *Gehesi to Elisha,*[413] *Baruck to Jeremiah,*[414] *the desciples to christ,*[415] *and Timothy to Paul,*[416] that likewyse every godly learned minister should trayn up some yong schollar to commend him the better, and to enable him the more to the church[417]

As when two Gentlemen ryde together in hunting, it is hard to discern each others hounds beecause they bee mingled together, which afterward

---

[410] Numbers 11:28.

[411] 2 Kings 2:1-15.

[412] 1 Samuel 2:35; 3:1-18.

[413] 2 Kings 4:12-14, 25-37.

[414] Jeremiah 36:4, 32.

[415] Matthew 4:18-22, 10:1-4; Mark 1:16-20, 3:13-14; Luke 6:12-16.

[416] Acts 19:21-2.

[417] Of the Ministrie 14, Third Edition, 376; Fourth Edition, 400; Fifth Edition, 752. A much more extensive version of this saying is found under: Ministrie 2, First Edition, 77; Second Edition, 41-2; Third Edition, 24; Fourth Edition, 24; Fifth Edition, 24.

is more easily done when the hunters are severed even so, so long as god and the world walk as it were together, it is hard to distinguish between the heires of the one and of the other, but when they are severed by persecution, it wil surely bee seen the children of god and who bee the heyres of the world[418]

Christ is not as a well locked up, or dry spring head, but an open and plentiful fountain, from whence stream on every side, tp the lowest vallies the pleasant rivers of grace[419]

[fol. 58v] many are barren in grace beecaus they are barrain in prayer[420]

As hee that had but a dimmer sight to behold the serpent in the wildernes was healed as wel as hee that saw perfectly,[421] so hee that hath but a weak faith in the son of god shal never have his faith denied[422]

This is verbatim mentioned fol. [47]   Ther is a great corruption of nature which maketh us most dul when wee have most means. This ariseth either beecause wee having the means plentifully and publiquely wee use the means more sparingly and privately or beecause wee do not esteem so highly the means ordinarily administred, as wee do when they are les familiar unto us, or beecaus the lord seing wee too immoderately desire the place wher wee are, demeth us the benefit and fruition of the place to correct our desire, or for that wee promised to ourselves too large an hope of freedome from many evils, by the means of the word it pleaseth god to proove unto us, that they bee nothing without the blessing of his good spirit. Or sathan somtimes nourisheth this apace, beecause hee would make us discontent with our present calling and to hunt after new, which hee surely doth by shewing us the inconvenience of the tyme, and place present hyding al the profits, and by shewing al the profits wher wee have been or shalbee, and hyding the inconveniences. Or beecause when wee were the best in a whole town, and saw nothing in others but corruptions, wee pleased ourselves and promised us more to good things, and being among many good men, wee

---

[418] World 1, First Edition, 75; Second Edition, 74; Third Edition, 42; Fourth Edition, 43; Fifth Edition, 43.

[419] 'Of Gods free Grace, Justice and Mercie, and how we may trie our love to God' 11, Third Edition, 320; Fourth Edition, 343; Fifth Edition, 695.

[420] Of Prayer and Meditation 20, Third Edition, 402; Fourth Edition, 426; Fifth Edition, 778.

[421] Numbers 21:6-9.

[422] Faith 4, First Edition, 20; Second Edition, 20; Third Edition, 12; Fourth Edition, 12; Fifth Edition, 12.

make not so much of our goodnes, and grow somewhat secure, and trust too much to the goodnes of the place and persons. Or in that wee like our selves wel when wee are teaching and instructing others, and more impatient of silence in ourselves and to bee taught of others, or beecause wee stil would bee getting praise by bringing out, but wee are loath to come to store up treasures new and old for tyme [fol. 59r] come, when as ther is a tyme of both, or wee more seek this, beecause the last temptation seemeth the greatest, though indeed wee have suffered as evil before, even as a man thincketh this present sicknes to bee sore<r> then any sicknes past. The best remedy against this deadnes and dulnes is continually <by> prayer, and using the means to strive against it.[423]

The[424] veiwing, familiar speaking, and touching of a woman, especialy religious, not having a just calling ther-unto, and being called, without prayer and craving for holy affections is a thing most dangerous

They are most to bee loved in whom gods graces most appeareth

The cause why wee wee [sic] are no more in credit with men is beecause wee are no more in favour with god

A certain woman saying without pitty at the birth of a poore child *here is the mouth but where is the meat,* had this saying replyed on her at what tyme shee brought forth a child which died. *Here is the meat but where is the mouth*[425]

Even as polygomy was not very hurtful, so long as it was with in Lamechs house, but when it crept into Abrahams family got great strength and prevailed much:[426] so ill opinions and heresies are then not so hurtful whilest they are among the ignorant and wicked: but when they get favour among the learned and godly they beegin to bee most dangerous[427]

Although good men need not alwaies the use of good ceremonies, yet not giving example to evil men of having them it is good to use them

---

[423] Securitie 3, First Edition, 51-2; Second Edition, 51-2; Third Edition, 30; Fourth Edition, 30; Fifth Edition 30.

[424] Followed by an illegible word deleted.

[425] 'Of parents, education of children, government of youth, and care of posteritie' 8, Third Edition, 423; Fourth Edition, 447; Fifth Edition, 799.

[426] Genesis 4:19-22; 16:1-6.

[427] Heresie 3, First Edition, 29; Second Edition, 28; Third Edition, 17; Fourth Edition, 17; Fifth Edition, 17.

God scoureth away the infirmities of his saincts through crosses yet breaketh not his holy covenants with them, but performeth it through many tribulations which they deserv and pull upon themselves[428]

[fol. 59v] A good meaning must have good means and good means a good meaning.

It is our corruption to strein curtesy with sin at the beginning, but wee run over head and eares[429] when wee are a little in wee must not as fooles stumble at the cros, but profit by the grace in it conveyed unto us, by repenting of our estate past, by giving thancks for our estate present, and fearing our estate to come.[430]

A woman seing a good minister wear a surplice said the man had Jacobs voyce but Esaus garment.[431]

The love of the creatures hinder us in good things, but the use of them further us to good things.[432]

As Iaach his intent in blessing Esau hindered not the wil of god in blessing Jacob:[433] so the corrupt intent of the Minister doth not hinder the blessing of god in the sacraments, being his own ordinances[434]

Some rejoyce so much in hearing good things preached, that they fight to bee humbled for their wants: Again some ever having an ey to some wants walk not thankfully for gods graces in them. The mean way is the safest so to[435] rejoyce in the graces of god that wee bee humbled for our wants that wee prayse god for his gifts[436]

---

[428] Last sentence of: Of Affliction 16, Third Edition, 266; Fourth Edition, 288; Fifth Edition, 640.

[429] Sinne 5, First Edition, 53; Second Edition, 52; Third Edition, 31; Fourth Edition, 31; Fifth Edition, 31.

[430] Afflictions 8, First Edition, 3; Second Edition, 3; Third Edition, 2; Fourth Edition, 2; Fifth Edition, 2.

[431] Genesis 27:1–41, esp. verse 22.

[432] Love of Creatures 1, First Edition, 35; Second Edition, 33; Third Edition, 20; Fourth Edition, 20; Fifth Edition, 20. This saying in the printed version is combined with a saying that appears on fol. 60r.

[433] Genesis 27:1–41.

[434] Sacraments 1, First Edition, 51; Second Edition, 51; Third Edition, 30; Fourth Edition, 30; Fifth Edition, 30.

[435] Followed by *walk* deleted.

[436] Grace of God 6, Third Edition, 15; Fourth Edition, 15; Fifth Edition, 15.

wee cannot bee blessed of god and of the world too, but so learn that as gods blessings are upon our head,[437] so wee must looke for the crosses of the world to bee on our backs

It is a great corruption in time of temptacion not to resist those corruptions which afterward, in tyme after our temptation wee are ashamed of, and time it self resisteth them.[438]

wee must suffer the crosses with profit to pas upon us

[fol. 60r] Ther is in many a general knowledg of the truth but when it commeth to particular practise, it is hindered in many with profits, pleasure and self love as in[439]

God correcteth immoderate love of benefits in his children as wee may see in Abraham Isaach and Jacob[440]

Some look too much to outward things and regard not inward corruptions. Some are alwaies pooring in ther inward corruptions, but see not the outward. It is good to bee exercised in both

See <how>[441] a man is in temptation and such an one[442] hee is[443]

Outward temptations do not hurt, until our inward corruption doth yeeld, beecause other<wise> temptations are as Surgeons to draw out our festred corruptions[444]

The law of god must alwaies bee interpreted to humble us

Gods children look to the spiritual use of those things which the

---

[437] Followed by s delete.

[438] Temptations 5, First Edition, 66; Second Edition, 66; Third Edition, 38; Fourth Edition, 38; Fifth Edition, 38.

[439] Printed edition omits 'as in'. Knowledge 1, First Edition, 34; Second Edition, 33; Third Edition, 20; Fourth Edition, 20; Fifth Edition, 20.

[440] Genesis 22:2; 25:28; 37:3-4. Parents 2, First Edition, 46; Second Edition, 46; Third Edition, 27; Fourth Edition, 27; Fifth Edition, 27. Printed versions refer to David instead of Jacob. For another version of this saying, see fol. 60v.

[441] Replacing what deleted.

[442] Followed by is deleted.

[443] Temptations 1, First Edition, 66; Second Edition, 65; Third Edition, 37; Fourth Edition, 37; Fifth Edition, 37.

[444] Temptations 6, First Edition, 66; Second Edition, 66; Third Edition, 38; Fourth Edition, 38; Fifth Edition, 38.

worldlings use carnally[445]

Many men would have the world to bow and bend to ther corruptions

Sathan by temptation maketh a man forget much and casteth a mist before his eies that hee cannot discern and corrupteth his tast that hee cannot judg.[446]

Long and strange temptations bee a token of long and strange sins[447]

wee must learn to bear long and strange temptations as the pleasing of gods favor.

It is good to leav secret sins to god, who wil make them knowen in tyme.

Wee must not so pres the law as wee suppres the gospel.[448]

A certain man labouring greevously of the pleurisy felt such tormentes in conscience that hee was senceles of the pains of the body. again the lord afterward changeing his mourning to rejoycing, gave him such abounding comfort of his spirit, that as before through extream anguish of his spirit, so now through most woonderful passions, of heavenly joies and assurance of his sins pardoned, hee felt no outward pains of his body though dangerously it was pained

[fol. 60v] wee cannot bee dry in the grace of god so long as wee resort to christ by prayer who hath the seven vials of[449] gold ful of his sevenfold mercies[450]

The sacraments of the jewes and of the christians differ thus, the sacraments of the jewes were like obligations to bynd them: the

---

[445] Love of the Creatures 1, First Edition, 35; Second Edition, 33; Third Edition, 20; Fourth Edition, 20; Fifth Edition, 20. This saying in the printed version is combined with a saying that appears on fol. 59v.

[446] First sentence of the fourth saying added at the end of: 'Of truth and errours, sinceritie and contempt of the word', Third Edition, 445; Fourth Edition, 469; Fifth Edition, 821.

[447] Temptations 7, First Edition, 67; Second Edition, 66; Third Edition, 38; Fourth Edition, 38; Fifth Edition, 38.

[448] Of Prophecie and Preaching 13, Third Edition, 396; Fourth Edition, 420; Fifth Edition, 772.

[449] Followed by god deleted.

[450] Revalation 2:1-5. Of Prayer and Meditation 20, Third Edition, 402; Fourth Edition, 426-8; Fifth Edition, 778-9.

sacraments of the christians are like acquittances to absolv them

wee cannot hartily bee greeved for that sin in others wherof wee have not made great conscience in ourselves.[451]

A godly minister hearing a preacher both lying unsurely, and rayling unreverently, said unto him in humble spirit Oh my brother *Spiritus dei, neque mendax, neque mordax.*[452]

Gods children cover many infirmities under one good gift in others, The ungodly bury many good gifts under one little infirmity in another[453]

wee need not go far from ourselves for monstrous and strange temptations[454]

A[455] certain man[456] complayning to *mr fox*[457] that hee was comfortles for want of feelings received this answer[458] <O brother bee of good comfort wee hold christ by faith and not by feeling>[459]

Whensoever wee are out of our calling sathan hath a fit occasion of temptation[460]

At what tyme a certain woman had accused herself of insufficient chear for the intertainment of her frinds, a godly christian and her own husband answered wyfe Gods name bee blessed: Brown bread and the peace of the gospel is good chear[461]

---

[451] Griefe for Sinne 1, First Edition, 26; Second Edition, 25; Third Edition, 15; Fourth Edition, 15; Fifth Edition, 15.

[452] 'The Spirit of God is neither false nor biting.'

[453] Covering Infirmities 1, First Edition, 12; Second Edition, 12; Third Edition, 7; Fourth Edition, 7; Fifth Edition, 7.

[454] This is the second saying appended to 'Of truth and errours, sinceritie and contempt of the word', Third Edition, 445; Fourth Edition, 469; Fifth Edition, 821.

[455] Preceded by *At what tyme* deleted.

[456] Preceded by *wo* deleted. Followed by *had excused* deleted.

[457] This may be a reference to John Foxe, the martyrologist, though no corroborating evidence could be found.

[458] Followed by *Gods name bee blessed, Brown bread and the peace of the gospel is good chear* deleted.

[459] Feeling 6, First Edition, 21; Second Edition, 21; Third Edition, 12; Fourth Edition, 12; Fifth Edition, 12.

[460] Calling 8, First Edition, 7; Second Edition, 7; Third Edition, 4; Fourth Edition, 4; Fifth Edition, 4.

[461] Prosperitie and Peace 3, First Edition, 47; Second Edition, 47; Third Edition, 28; Fourth Edition, 28; Fifth Edition, 28.

The lord hath corrected the immoderate love of parents to theire children, especialy when it was more grounded on nature then on the gifts of god, As wee may see in Abraham who so loved Ismael,[462] in Isaach who so loved Esau,[463] in david who so loved Absolon[464]

A godly physition[465] in the tyme of persecution having three [fol. 61r] pacients resorting to him to bee cured of *Aque Carkis* stud[466] sayed this strange disceas and sicknes betokeneth some strange sins and corruptions to bee in you, and therfore if you wil bee freed by mee from this sicknes reconcile yourselves to god that hee may free your sins They al at once excused themselves, wherin they bewrayed ther great ignorance. the physition unripped ther lives and at the first enquired of them, if they did not frequent the Masse. They could not plainly deny it, but covertly excused it, saying therin they did but as others which when the man of god perceived said, Have yee so highly displeased god, and know not of any sin to bee in you, go your wayes and first lern how greevous your sin is before god. for the lord having laied his rod uppon you I dare not take it of unles you shew some fruits or repentance, And thus hee dismissed them until they knowing and acknowledging ther sin, with greef returned and afterward were healed[467]

A great cause of madnes is impatience of mynd, or els the suddain wrath of god upon a man for doing something against his conscience[468]

When a certain man had put Mr fox in mind of one whom being afflicted god had blessed his ministery, and had asked him if hee were yet in his remembrance; yea said the man I forget lord and Lady but I remember such[469]

Sathan is most ready to make us most unwilling unto that wherin the lord wil most use us to the good of his church[470]

---

[462] Genesis 21:11.

[463] Genesis 25:28.

[464] 2 Samuel 18:32. Parents 2, First Edition, 46; Second Edition, 46; Third Edition, 27; Fourth Edition, 27; Fifth Edition, 27. For a similar saying, see fol. 60r.

[465] Followed by *having* deleted.

[466] That is, 'aqua carkis stewed'. Refers to a form of urine retention. We thank Dr David George for his help with this phrase.

[467] 'Of Phisicke and diet, sicknesse and health' 16, Third Edition, 420; Fourth Edition, 444; Fifth Edition, 796.

[468] Madnes 1, First Edition, 35; Second Edition, 34; Third Edition, 20; Fourth Edition, 20; Fifth Edition, 20.

[469] Of the Ministerie 11, Third Edition, 376; Fifth Edition, 752.

[470] Satans Practises 1, First Edition, 61; Second Edition, 60; Third Edition, 35; Fourth Edition, 35; Fifth Edition, 35.

It is a greater thing in a Pastor to deal wisely and comfortably with an afflicted conscience, and soundly and discreetly to meet with an heretique, then to preach publickly and learnedly[471]

No greater enemy is ther to a good cause then hee that by evil means doth handle and maintain it[472]

[fol. 61v] A certain godly woman passing over the seas with a godly preacher as hee had made a sermon and vehemently had used the threatnings of the law, said, If it bee so as yee say I am a dead woman and presently shee yeelded up the ghost

A certain woman being converted to Christian sin [sic] by a civil justice, seing him afterward slyde from the faith, and the said going about to corrupt her, which had converted her, said, Sir, I hard you speak the lord, and in hearing you, I hard you not somuch your self, but I learned of christ by you. I hard not, I say, you as a man, but I hard by you the lord our god which is invisible[473]

That is a true sorrow and greef for sin, which neither can by outward pleasures bee stolen, nor by continuance of tyme taken <from> of us but onely in Christ[474]

Afflicted consciences must not dispute too much against themselves for they cannot judg truly of ther actions: for that being displeased with their own[475] persons they cannot bee pleased with their own doings[476]

Those that are tempted are not so much to look to their estate present as on their estate to come, beecaus they that presently sow in tears, shal in tyme to come reap in joy[477]

wee are more greeved when the cros privately toucheth us, then when

---

[471] Of Prophecie and Preaching 11, Third Edition, 396; Fourth Edition, 420; Fifth Edition, 772.

[472] Cause Good 1, First Edition, 14–15; Second Edition, 14; Third Edition, 8; Fourth Edition, 8; Fifth Edition, 8.

[473] Of Repentance 17, Third Edition, 406; Fourth Edition, 431; Fifth Edition, 783.

[474] Griefe for Sinne 5, First Edition, 27; Second Edition, 26; Third Edition, 16; Fourth Edition, 16; Fifth Edition, 16.

[475] Followed by doings deleted.

[476] Conscience Afflicted 10, First Edition, 10; Second Edition, 10; Third Edition, 6; Fourth Edition, 6; Fifth Edition, 6.

[477] Psalm 126:6. Temptations 8, First Edition, 67; Second Edition, 66; Third Edition, 38; Fourth Edition, 38; Fifth Edition, 38.

publiquely it concerneth the whole church and common wealth[478]

Gods children grow not suddenly to profit and preferment, but by degree as Joseph[479]

Sometimes good outward gifts hurt the beholders, when they hurt not the possessors, as wee may see in the beauty of sarah and Joseph[480] which thing ought to humble us in the desyre of outward things and make us to bee thanckful for a mediocrity[481]

A certain man said that in our age many ministers [fol. 62r] were like to servants who had long lived under a good Master so as they had got some competent stock upon the increas wherof they did so much attend, that they neglected and forgat ther anncient care for their Mr[482]

A godly gentlewoman said that even in her ordinary labour shee tasted oft of as heavenly meditations, as if al things ordinary laid asside shee had given her whole mind to attend on the spirit of god, and of quietnes of study: shee also said that wee are like children, who need not once bee bidden to ask things necessary, but twyse to bee thanckful for mercies received[483]

The lord wil have us to beegin with smal good things the devil contrary. In evil things the lord would have us fear the first beeginings the devil contrary[484]

Bee evermore afraid of leaving good undone lest that god suffer you to fal into the contrary evil thing[485]

It is our infirmity to bee much and often in prayer: seldome and sparing in thanking

---

[478] Afflictions 9, First Edition, 3-4; Second Edition, 3; Third Edition, 2; Fourth Edition, 2; Fifth Edition, 2.

[479] Genesis 39:1-41:46.

[480] Sarah: Genesis 12:11-20. Joseph: Genesis 39:6-10.

[481] Love of Creatures 2, First Edition, 35; Second Edition, 33-4; Third Edition, 20.

[482] Of the Ministerie 12, Third Edition, 376; Fifth Edition, 752.

[483] Calling 2, First Edition, 6; Second Edition, 6; Third Edition, 4; Fourth Edition, 4; Fifth Edition, 4.

[484] Povertie 4, First Edition, 44; Second Edition, 44; Third Edition, 26; Fourth Edition, 26; Fifth Edition, 26.

[485] Feare 1, First Edition, 23; Second Edition, 22; Third Edition, 13; Fourth Edition, 13; Fifth Edition, 13.

If thou wilt ask any <benefit>[486] at gods hand begin ever with craving his favor Psalm 4 if thou wilt avoid any cros use Psalm 32[487]

Evermore bee musing, reading, hearing, and talking of gods word, and praying how to keep the purenes of doctrine and of a good conscience, and yet to wade out of the iniquity of the tyme to do good as long as may bee[488]

It is il halting before a creple;[489] when one hath been exercised with many temptations hee can discern others[490]

If thou canst not bee content to have thy sins called to remembrance thou art not thorowly mooved with them

A certain man said every day to his wyfe, hee would beeginn to study and labor, but hee never did soe

Any excessive afflictions wil bring his own punishments as our great love bringing graciousnes

[fol. 62v] To waste the creatures of god is a great sin.

Godly men are not in danger of grosly wicked woemen wherfore wee must have a greater carefulnes with ourselves, when wee are with any that pretend godlines, and so in al evils beeware of secret and colourable occasions of evil wherin wee may make a shew of good, being delivered from great offences[491]

Many are affraid to bee stricken down <for>[492] sin, for by that means they thinck they should come to dispaire

No further conscience then science

---

[486] Replacing *thing* deleted.

[487] Printed version after 'avoid any cros' reads: 'begin first with repenting and craving pardon for thy Sinne. Psal. 32'. Prayer 2, First Edition, 45; Second Edition, 45; Third Edition, 27; Fourth Edition, 26; Fifth Edition, 26.

[488] Word of God and the Hearing of it 1, First Edition, 73; Second Edition, 72; Third Edition, 41; Fourth Edition, 42; Fifth Edition, 42.

[489] Obsolete form of 'cripple'.

[490] This is the third saying appended to 'Of truth and errours, sincerities and contempt of the word', Third Edition, 445; Fourth Edition, 469; Fifth Edition, 821.

[491] Occasions of evill 1, First Edition, 43; Second Edition, 42-3; Third Edition, 25; Fourth Edition, 25; Fifth Edition, 25.

[492] Replacing *with* deleted.

It is a marvelous thing that many wil make more of a smale infirmity in another, (although they see that the whole cours of ther life is truly to pleas god) then they make at gros sins in themselves, notwithstanding they take no cours at al in their life truly to pleas god[493]

If ever wee would have the church of god to continue long among us, wee must bring it into our houshoulds, and nourish it in our families[494]

Then wee have a testimony of the love of good things and of the hatred of evil things, when no punishment or reward can draw us to evil, or withdraw us from doing good[495]

A natural dream that is coming of natural causes easily slippeth away, but if our dreams dwel longer upon us and leav some greater impression in us, they may bee thought either to proceed[496] from god or from the devil. and by these it is good to profit. If they be favourable by thincking such a thing wee might have, if wee were not unprepared for it, If it bee contrary by forethincking and fearing such an evil if the lord bee not merciful, beecause god doth often correct some sin past, which wee know not of, or doth foreshew some sin to come which wee were not afraid of. And an evil dream doth shew an evil hart either in some sin already committed, or in som sin which may bee committed[497]

[fol. 63r] It is not good suddainly to condemn a dream, nor yet too superstitiously to thinck of a dream, but to make some godly use and instruction of it. If the dream bee terrible it is good to avoid al the occasions of that evil and to give ourselves to praier. If wee give too great credit to dreams they are dangerous to weaken faith The best is neither to bee too remis nor too wyse in them, It is good to observ them, but not too much to perswade ourselves of any great things if they bee good, neither too much to fear them if they bee evil, and yet not to cast of the use which may bee made of them, seing the lord by leaving such long impressions in us doth as it were cal upon the consciences of men to

---

[493] Censures 1, First Edition, 7; Second Edition, 7; Third Edition, 4; Fourth Edition, 4; Fifth Edition, 4.

[494] 'Of Parents, education of children, government of youth, and care of posteritie' 7, Third Edition, 423; Fourth Edition, 447; Fifth Edition, 799.

[495] Love of Creatures 3, First Edition, 35; Second Edition, 34; Third Edition, 20; Fourth Edition, 20; Fifth Edition, 20.

[496] Followed by *either* deleted.

[497] Dreames 1, First Edition, 17; Second Edition, 16-17; Third Edition, 10; Fourth Edition, 10; Fifth Edition, 10.

profit by them. The like may bee said of witchery and slaunders[498]

A certain godly gentleman much acquainted with crosses being mooved for his pains which hee suffered sayd Oh blessed bee god that I suffer no more, for the same god that in mercy layeth this affliction on mee might punish mee in my soule, and in my body cast mee into hel, and might as wel and as soon taken away my life both of soule and of body as this thing[499]

To read and not to meditate is unfruitful, to meditate and not to read is dangerous for errours, to meditate or to read without praier is hurtful.[500]

A certain professor much exercised with the cros would often use this speach lord keep from us that cros which is without thy word

Rare good things are pleasaunt, but by use are les esteemed, and evil things rare are fearful, but by use are les greevous, which is when wee bring rather natural affections of joy and sorrow then spiritual meditations which are onely of the true joy and sorrow[501]

What common wealth, county, town or family the lord purposeth notably to plaugue, the same hee before notably blesseth with many benefits

It is a rare gift of gods spirit to overcome greef, and it is our common corruption that the immoderate greef of evils present stealeth [fol. 63v] from us al the remembrance of former benefits and al thanckfulnes for them[502]

A certain man some years afflicted in conscience said his continual agonies were as great as the pain of a man ready to dy, and that hee felt so smal comfort in gods countenance that hee could willingly have suffered his body to have lived in a burning fyre until the appearing of

---

[498] This is treated as a continuation of the previous saying in the printed version. See previous note.

[499] Afflictions 10, First Edition, 4; Second Edition, 3-4; Third Edition, 2; Fourth Edition, 2; Fifth Edition, 2.

[500] Rules for Meditation 21, First Edition, 41; Second Edition, 40; Third Edition, 24; Fourth Edition, 24; Fifth Edition, 24.

[501] Affections 4, First Edition, 1-2; Second Edition, 1; Third Edition, 1; Fourth Edition, 1; Fifth Edition, 1.

[502] Thanksgiving 2, First Edition, 71; Second Edition, 70-71; Third Edition, 40; Fourth Edition, 40; Fifth Edition, 40.

christ, so then hee might bee assured of gods favour towards him: yea his greatest comfort was this, that though hee should bee in hel, yet hee hoped therin of gods favour to have his torment mittigated with them that suffer least. In al which troubles notwithstanding, no world of reward, no terrour of tyrants could caus him willingly to do the least thing displeasing to god. Whom when the lord released hee would comfort himself in christ saying, that the devil would take advantage of his sorrow to make him unchearful in good things[503]

A certain man said to mee that experience taught him how sins prayed against were half slain in him

As in striving in temptacion wee shal find it both sooner to depart and to recompence the present little pain, with an after and longer pleasure: so in no resting both the temptacion doth further feed in us, and the smal present pleasing ourselves is paied with along bitter greef of conscience afterward[504]

Ordinarily and commonly no true joy is, where before in some measure hath not been some light of corruption, or humbling for temptation

Though a man have knowledg yet hee may want faith, though one have faith, yet beecause many evils and temptations come between feeling doth not alwaies follow, nor after feelings joy, nor after joy practise[505]

Many can speak four[506] things in the eares of god so long as they bee in affliction, but afterward they wil speak evil things in the ears of heaven and earth[507]

[fol. 64r] This is our comfort in afflictions that wee dy daily to the world and draw nearer to god, and as it is our greatest joy when our joy shal bee perfect that wee shal not bee mortal, so also when our sorrowes bee great that wee shal not bee immortal

---

[503] Conscience Afflicted 1, First Edition, 8; Second Edition, 7-8; Third Edition, 5; Fourth Edition, 5; Fifth Edition, 5.

[504] Sinne 16, First Edition, 59; Second Edition, 58; Third Edition, 34; Fourth Edition, 34; Fifth Edition, 34.

[505] Feeling 1, First Edition, 20; Second Edition, 20; Third Edition, 12; Fourth Edition, 12; Fifth Edition, 12.

[506] In the printed version 'four' is 'faire'.

[507] Afflictions 3, First Edition, 2; Second Edition, 2; Third Edition, 1; Fourth Edition, 1; Fifth Edition, 1.

If wee wil truly learn how to avoid sins, Let us remember oft what punishment wee have felt for sin if wee wil bee kept from unthankfulnes, wee must oft cal to mind the things that the lord hath done for our soules and his glory in us.[508]

It is a good meditation often to unfold old sins, our day sins and night sins, wee must comment, descant, and discours upon them to stir and provoke ourselves to shame and sorrow, that wee being helped by our wils, to see the height, length and depth of our sins, may see also the height, length and depth of gods mercy towards us in christ

Brought unto him from a noble man a piece of veneson to make merry with his frinds, and this present was given at such a time, as the lord threatned some plague to his church, and punishment to the common wealth answered the messenger, I pray you carry back your veneson to your lord with thanks, and signify unto him that it is a fitter tym now to fast and pray with mourning then to feast and play with mirthmaking

The more one tasteth of heavenly[509] things the les is his joy in earthly things, the more one feeleth earthly things pleasant, the les pleasure in heavenly[510]

Care in superiours and fear in inferiours cause a godly goverment[511]

A certain man afflicted in mind began through the temptation of Sathan to mislike his calling and chaunged it, afterward hee thought this calling and that calling to bee unlawful and so was almost brought to mislike al. Hee felt on a tyme a great pain [fol. 64v] in his leg, and being desirous to go from his bed to his table for booke, hee could not his leg remaining sore, then remembring that it was said in the scriptures, If thy foot offend thee cut it of,[512] hee streight way laying his foot on a block, and taking a hatchet in his hand stroke of his legg not feeling pain: the veynes being so torn hee could not but bleed to death. Howbeit hee died very repentantly. So dangerous a pollicy and so pleasant a temptation is it to an afflicted mind to leav our callings as things unlawful[513]

---

[508] Sinne 17, First Edition, 59; Second Edition, 58; Third Edition, 34; Fourth Edition, 34; Fifth Edition, 34.

[509] Followed by *joyes* deleted.

[510] Sound Joy 1, First Edition, 34; Second Edition, 32; Third Edition, 19; Fourth Edition, 19; Fifth Edition, 19.

[511] Familie 2, Third Edition, 12; Fourth Edition, 12; Fifth Edition, 12.

[512] Matthew 5:29–30.

[513] Calling 1, First Edition, 6; Second Edition, 5–6; Third Edition, 4; Fourth Edition, 4; Fifth Edition, 4.

A certain servitour purposing with the rest of the family to sanctify a fast to the lord, and yet for displeasure conceived against one, who came to a maid whom hee loved, breaking it of was forewarned of some plague of god to threaten him, hee contemning the admonition went abroad with his gun, which being charged hee held in his hand without a thomble[514] and suddenly it brast[515] the one part and the nether part falling two foot deep into the ground immediately before him, the other hinder part entering as deeply into the ground behind him. such was the providence of god for his preservation

Of al mercies of god this is a great mercy, not to bee left without some favourable exercise of our conscience for if the lord in wisdome saw it good for his holy Apostles and dear servant Paul, though hee was so
mentioned
fol. [48v]
powerful and frequent in watchings, in fastings in prayer and mourning, and had such a great light of inward corruptions that hee cryed out against himself what need have wee who either are so rare and seldome in thes exercises or els notwithstanding our using of them wee remain both cold and secure. [fol. 65r] And yet such is the corruption of our nature, that when the lord by affliction would draw us out of our sins, take us to himself and make himself familiarly known unto us wee are most displeased, but if not by afflicting us hee leav us to ourselves, suffering us to root in our sins and keepeth himself from us wee are best pleased and flesh and blood is most pleased[516]

Adversity bringeth no contention, for though in prosperity every man wil have his reason, yet in adversity the stronger wil give over his <hold>

A certain godly man found by experience that casting a deep pitch,[517] and setting an high pin[518] of <his> private exercises of humbling, hee was soe dismaid that hee could not do the like in publique exercises, that forbecause hee could not use his own manner and measure, hee could not willingly do any thing

A good man wil not rest in his liberty, or authority, that hee may or can have, but stil feareth the error of his strength, and suspecteth himself, that hee doth not the good which hee ought to do or might do.

---

[514] Variation of 'thimble', implying a protective device.
[515] Obsolete form of 'brassed', meaning burned or scorched.
[516] See fol. 48v.
[517] That is, seeking great intensity.
[518] That is, setting a high pitch, degree, step.

As the Arrowe drawen deepest pearceth most, so the praier deepest fetcht pearceth most

It is profitable to bee taught continualy though by little and little and as a stone in a continual dressling[519] to bee nourished

Patience then possesseth the soule, when whatsoever is outwardly wanting by patience is supplied[520]

One not religious hearing that the day of gods judgement was at hand, said in great boldnes, then I would I might dream of it this night, at the same night dreaming of it, hee was cast into such a terror, that hee fel into an extream fit of an Ague,[521] in which hee wished his elders, to use admonition at the first hand, and not at the second, for there is danger in delaying and that [fol. 65v] then promise of amendment bee made, that there should bee notes taken of it beecaus otherwyse they will stick to deny it

Hee never was hard to deny the use of the ceremonies yet hee used them not Hee wished that such as would refuse them would labour for sound judgement to comfort ther own consciences to assure the church, to leave the world without excuse beecause that men should not only go not after the common cours of the world but against many learned men

Hee would have this order taken in dealing with a man, first to teach him that there is a sure and certain way to bee saved if hee wil, then that ther is a way to come to salvation, and that it is by the sight of sin, and therin to cast him down is lyfe as may bee

Hee said at the reading of the Letany at this place. *O lord open thou my lips etc,* hee was made to doubt to say it, beecaus it seemed to bee in the tyme of adversity, yet afterward considering that the common wealth would waigh down the church, and prosperity would pul it down, hee thought it as necessary to say that, as at any other time, and so found great peace in his conscience

These things hee was desirous to speak to any of discretion for posterity

---

[519] That is, 'drizzling'. The phrase probably refers to the constant dripping of mineral-rich water that leaves deposits on a stone. Thanks to Dr David George for his insights in this matter.

[520] Patience 1, First Edition, 43; Second Edition, 43; Third Edition, 25; Fourth Edition, 25; Fifth Edition, 25.

[521] Followed by *he* deleted.

and wished that hee had communicated things to others, which hee did being mooved to sound and solide reasons therunto.

When one being negligent to bee taught presented his child to bee baptized, hee used this discipline with him, first hee asked him if hee were sorrowful for his negligence in coming to bee taught, Secondly whether hee was greeved for his other offences known to the church and unknown, Thirdly whether hee would promise to come to bee taught, and to reform his lyfe, and to bring up his child in knowledg and godlines To the which the party answered affirmatively, and the child was baptized

Hee observed this experience in himself, that when hee would not do a thing that was good then his own reason and the devil would easily teach him an excuse. *Lord forgive us this corruption*[522]

[fol. 66r] In good things hee would overcome his unwillingnes and sluggishnes, and prevent his delayings betimes, thinking the longer in delay the wors[523]

Hee would labor especialy in doctrine and exhortations to put men in mind that many thincking ther sins, so great, and to have fallen so oft, and so long to have continued in them, that god cannot or wil not forgive them, and by that means continue most dangerously and securely stil in sin

Hee said that the Papists were deep pollitiques who to continue their honourable memory of the Masse pinned it to every solemn feast, that so, more cunningly and closely they might convey it to their posterity

Hee said if god give us meat and drinck and cloaths it were good to bee exercised with some cros

Hee said if god had bestowed some good gifts on a man, it were good to <feel>[524] some cros to seale and season them in us[525]

Being asked what hee thought of the books of *Apochrypha* hee said the

---

[522] Of Naturall Corruption 1, Third Edition, 8; Fourth Edition, 8; Fifth Edition, 8.

[523] Securitie 2, First Edition, 51; Second Edition, 51; Third Edition, 30; Fourth Edition, 30; Fifth Edition, 30.

[524] Replacing *feel bee exercised* deleted.

[525] Afflictions 6, First Edition, 3; Second Edition, 3; Third Edition, 2; Fourth Edition, 2; Fifth Edition, 2.

jewes did esteem them as the Papists did the old schoolemen, or as wee do *Calvin* or *Beza*, and therfore by continuance of tyme they were corruptly and unadvisedly joyned to the Canonical scriptures. They contain some notable things, yet they bee mixed with errors. Our bishops of late memory writing of the histories of the church are as wel quoted, and contain as woonderful things; yet are they no more woorthy to bee made equal with the writings of the holy ghost, then other mens writings are

When hee could not bring his meditation to the pursuing of his ordinary cours hee said hee thought hee should speak of some other thing. And when hee spake extraordinarily, both in the matter and liberty of his hart, hee looked for some extraordinary touch in the peoples harts, which when hee saw not it greeved him

When one had told him that for pleasing of his frind hee had received a present, hee said I dissalow not those gifts, which come after a [fol. 66v] benefit done in token of thanksgiving, but I dissalow of them that run before hand, as a spokesman to our suits to bee handled afterward

A godly woman speaking of her temptations shee said true it is the motions are strange and greevous to the godly, but faithful is hee that hath promised, who wil not suffer us to bee tempted above our strength, but with the increas of our temptation wil also increas our faith or with the decreas of our faith, wil make our temptation to decreas also[526]

Being asked his opinion of the burial of the dead, hee said that whatsoever was not either flatly commanded, or plainly forbidden in the word, might sometimes bee used for the maintaining of love and some times bee left undone for the avoiding of superstition. And for the burial of the dead, beecaus wee read no prescript order of it. I thinck wee must follow the general rule, that is that al things bee done decently, so that ther bee neither on the one side a prophain casting of the body, nor on the other side any superstition used in the same which to avoid beecaus of the [blank space] times, it is not inconvenient, to read the word and to leav out the praying, which duties distinguish between the necessary duty of the minister in the sacraments, and his function in other les actions as also to free him from accusation of fear in the tyme of pestilence, if hee bury not, and sometimes to bee used of no private men in the daies of health and prosperity

---

[526] Tempations 2, First Edition, 66; Second Edition, 65; Third Edition, 37; Fourth Edition, 37; Fifth Edition, 37.

Hee said, that when hee considered how Noah, Moses and others fel in their latter daies,[527] and how the most excellent men have fallen, hee most earnestly prayed, that the lord would take him out of the world before that his lyfe should bring any offence to the church of god[528]

Seing a certain gentleman having his son in his arms, whom hee loved wel and tenderly, hee said Sir, there is the matter of your rejoycing, god make it also the matter of your thanksgiving[529]

[fol. 67r] Hee said in many places, that no through reformation of religion would bee in england until the lord wrought it by some notable affliction: for such is the corruption of nature that long ease and tranquility doth breed either superstition, or prophaines or heresy[530]

Unto one that thought himself to have sinned against the holy ghost hee said sathans temptations follow our affections. for if wee lightly account of sin, hee blowes[531] our eies stil with gods mercies. If wee beegin to make a conscience of sin, hee leadeth us to the judgements of god, being now as ready to aggravate the sin more then it is in itself, as before hee would extenuate it, and make it seem les then it was Howbeit I wil say unto you as samuel said to his people (I samuel.12.14.) after they had confessed themselves to have sinned against god with a great sin, True it is you have sinned a great sin before the lord, in that you made a mock at the word which you know, and yet if you turn to the lord in fear and serv him, your sin is remissible, howbeit sathan chargeth your conscience in that you have done evil against your own knowledg for although every sin against the holy ghost, is a sin against our own knowledge and conscience, yet every sin against our knowledg and conscience is not a sin against the holy ghost. for then david and Peter had sinned against the holy ghost,[532] (for they sinned after the holy ghost was come upon them, which is not true as may appear by their godly repentance afterward. Some sins are against knowledg, but[533] of[534] humane frailty:

---

[527] Noah: Genesis 9:20-29. Moses: Numbers 20:1-12.

[528] Falling into Sinne 2, First Edition, 23; Second Edition, 22; Third Edition, 13; Fourth Edition, 13; Fifth Edition, 13. Also found under: 'Of Injuries, offences and controversies' 9, Third Edition, 354; Fourth Edition, 378; Fifth Edition, 730.

[529] Parents 1, First Edition, 46; Second Edition, 46; Third Edition, 27; Fourth Edition, 27; Fifth Edition, 27. Also see: *Propositions*, [saying] 36.

[530] [Saying] 7, Church, Third Edition, 491; Fourth Edition, 515; Fifth Edition, 44.

[531] Printed versions read, 'bleeres'.

[532] David: 2 Samuel 11:3-12:15. Peter: Matthew 26:69-75.

[533] Followed by *Some* deleted.

[534] Followed by *us* deleted.

some are against knowledg of a rebellious obstinacy. These last are the persecutions of the spirit of god, as hee is the power of god. Those first are not so precisely against the holy ghost, but against god the father the son and the holy ghost, the one which may bee repented of is remissible, thother which is void of al repentance is irremissible. wherfore in that you quake and are affraid least this sin bee in you, and would rejoyce in god [fol. 67v] if you purpose to leav your former sins, and in truth henceforth turn unto the lord, I assure you that you are as yet free from this sin[535]

When a man afflicted in mind had desired his comfort, hee had this meditation, what beecause you cannot with Abraham receiv three angels[536] wil you not with lot receiv two angels,[537] or with the virgin Mary bee glad of one,[538] what beecause you cannot eate the most dainty dishes at the lords table, wil you not therfore take up the crummes that fal from his board:[539] what beecause you cannot see god face to face,[540] esteem you it nothing to see him in a mirrour

Hee could never pity any one that sorrowed not with some sight and greef of his sins.[541]

His judgement was that to have two virgins with charge was not lawful, unles the scarsity of the church were such that the estate soe required that one man should take two places, and so this should bee throughout general to al[542]

When hee should have comforted one for the los of her child, hee used this speech, Beware you cast not your sorrow of too suddainly, before you have received the true fruit of it

Hee said that though with the consent of the most godly and learned

---

[535] Tempations 14, First Edition, 70; Second Edition, 69-70; Third Edition, 39-40; Fourth Edition, 39-40; Fifth Edition, 39-40. There are significant variations between the manuscript and the printed versions of this saying. Also see: *Propositions*, [saying] 29; *Two Treatises*, [saying] 3, 197-8.

[536] Genesis 18:1-15.

[537] Genesis 19:1-16.

[538] Luke 1:26-38.

[539] Matthew 15:27; Mark 7:28.

[540] Exodus 33:11.

[541] Pitie 1, First Edition, 43; Second Edition, 43; Third Edition, 26; Fourth Edition, 25; Fifth Edition, 25.

[542] He is commenting here on the practice of pluralism, the holding of more than one parish living by one minister.

brethren hee entered into the ministry of the word, yet hee did it with this hart and purpose, that is hee would offer his service unto jesus christ that if the lord would vouchsafe him a blessing therin, hee would continue in that calling, but if the lord denying his grace and blessing would seme to refuse him, hee would publickly in the congregation to the glory of god and shaming of himself confes his unhability and[543] unwoorthines of the place and so depart

When at his preaching at a certain place a woman burst out into desperate crying, that *shee was a damned soule*, hee went down from the place to her and said thus to her, woman didst [fol. 68r] thou not come into this place to hear of thy sins and of the forgivenes of them in christ: bee of good comfort, and as thou seest thy sins so shalt thou hear pardon of thy sins; and therfore come in again, and shee returned into the church willingly and hard the word quietly, and practized it in her lyfe zealously

A certain woman said by experience that a plaistar which is made with venegar is good for ach in some part of the body. Also another said by experience that the bottom of a whyt loaf sod with a quart of running water was good for the bloody-flux

A letter against hardnes of hart[544]

I beeseech god the father of Jesus Christ give mee his good spirit in wryting to give advice, and you in reading to receiv it. Amen. Since the tyme I received Mr S. lettre, wherin hee declared his careful compassion over your estate, I have not been a little greeved; beecaus partly for want of a convenient messenger, and partly beecaus of my many fold distractions with the like occurrences and other weighty affairs I have been hindered from writing to you hitherto. And albeit I am even stil in the same case, yet conscience toward god, and compassion and love towards you forceth mee to overcome lets, which hardly I could otherwise prevaile against, And albeit I cannot wryt as I would, yet of that which I shal write, proceeding from the forenamed grounds, I look for some blessing from god through Jesus christ if you wil not too much faint in faith, and yeeld to the adversarie yea if <you> will but hope so

---

[543] Replacing *and* deleted.

[544] First Edition, 443-51; Second Edition, 413-20; Third Edition, 232-5; Fourth Edition, 870-73; Fifth Edition, 865-8. Also see: Richard Greenham, *A most sweete and assured Comfort for all those that are afflicted in Consciscience [sic], or troubled in minde. With two comfortable letters to his especiall frends that way greeued* (1595), Gx^r-Hxii^r; *Propositions*, no pagination.

wel of yourself as (in the feare of god I write it) I hope of you. first whereas it seemeth, you are sometimes greeved beecaus you tarried not stil at Cambridg according to my advice; you must know that I advised it not as a thing necessary [fol. 68v] but more convenient (as I then supposed: but yet that I advised you to obey your father, if his pleasure stil continued to have you home) wherunto <you> yeelding I cannot see how you offended, it being your fathers pleasure you should so do. And who knowes whether being here you might not have been as much troubled, theire being no priviledges for persons and places in such cases. and who knowes whether it bee the lords pleasure for the example and instruction and (I hope) the consolation of others in the end. And albeit you wil now thinck that here you were nearer the more and stronger means, yet know you and bee perswaded that god can and doth in such cases woork by fewer and weaker according to his good pleasure. Besides it is our corrupted nature to make much of such means as wee cannot have and not so to esteem those which god doth offer to us, as wee should, I beeseech you therfore in the name of jesus Christ humbly to praise god for those means which hee offereth in mercy to you, and to use them in faith accordinglie and so god shal bles you by them: and then by such conference as you may have hence by lettres; wherein If I may stand you in any stead (rather for the good opinion you have of mee, then for any great matter I am able to perform) I shalbee ready to offer any office of love unto you, as god shal inable mee, and so far forth as I shalbee instructed in your particular estate by some lettres sent from you by convenient messengers. That which I presently perceiv Mr S lettres is that you are afflicted with the blindnes of your mind, and hardnes of your hart which cannot bee mooved either with the promises of gods mercy, or fear of his judgements; nor affected with love and delite of the things which bee good, or with hatred and loathing of the evil. Great cause of greef have you I confes, but no caus of dispair dare I graunt beecause I am perswaded that your persuasion is [fol. 69r] somewhat fals, partly for want of a sound judgment of your estate and partly for some defect of faith, somewhat through your owne default. first therfore know you for a certainty, that this is no other temptation then such as divers of gods children have for a time been humbled with, and afterwards have had good ishue out of, and if it please god to move you to credit mee, I myself have known others as deeply this way plagued, as you can bee. Remember therfore that god is faithful and wil not suffer you to bee tempted above that which you shalbee able to bear etc. I Corinthians.10.13 and yet further to confirm you herein the holy scriptures do record, that this way god heretofore hath humbled his own people in whose person the prophet Esaii lamentably complaineth. 63.15. O lord looke down from heaven, and be hold from the dwelling place of thy holines and of thy glory. where is thy zeal and thy strength, the multitude of thy mercies and of thy compassions are restrayned from mee. O lord thou hast made us err from thy waies, and hardned our harts from thy fear[545] and in the next chapter verse.6. wee have been al as an unclean thing and al our righteousnes is as filthy clouts, and wee al do fade like a leaf and our iniquity like the wynd doth take us away, and there is none that calleth upon thy name, neither that stirreth up himself to take hold of thee, for thou hast hid thy face from us, and hast consumed us beecaus of our iniquities:[546] and before in the 59 chapter.verse 10. wee grope for the wall like the blinde, and wee grope as one without eies, wee stumble at the noon daie, as in the twilight, wee are in sollitarie places like dead men, wee roar like beares, and mourn like doves,[547] so complains Ezekias in the bitternes of his soule, Esay 38.14. like a crane, or a swallow so did I chatter, I did mourn as a dove[548] et psalm 51.10. when david cryeth create in mee o lord a <clean>[549] hart, renew in mee a right spirit, restore to mee the joy of my salvation.[550] Establish mee with thy free spirit doth hee not declare that his hart was unclean, his spirit crooked [fol. 69v] the joy of his salvation lost and himself subject to the spirit of bondage; so that wanting the spirit of liberty, or adoption, hee could neither cry Abba father, nor have any power against sin.[551] Thus you see how gods children may bee blynded in mind and hardned in hart, for a tyme, so that they feel in themselves the graces of the holy spirit to bee as it were perished and dead further to releev the infirmity of your judgement in this point (becaus I know it may much distres you) you must understand that there bee two kinds of hardnes of hart, the one which is not felt or perceived, thother which is perceived and felt, and that of the former there bee 2 sorts, the first which is most fearful when any doth purposely resist the motions of gods spirit, and wilfully refuse the means of their salvation, of the which the Proph Zachary. 17.11. [sic] speaketh they refused to harken and pulled away the shoulder, and stopped their ears that they should not hear, yea they made their hart as an adamant stone least they should hear the law, and the words which the lord of host sent in his spirit by the ministry of the former prophets[552]

---

[545] Isaiah 63:15, 17.
[546] Isaiah 64:6-7.
[547] Isaiah 59:10-11.
[548] Isaiah 38:14.
[549] Replacing *new* deleted.
[550] Psalm 51:10, 12.
[551] See: Romans 8:12-17.
[552] Zechariah 7:11-12.

The outragious sin of these men the Proph Esay expresseth in theise their own <fearful>[553] terms 28.15. wee have made a covenant with death and with hel are wee at agreement, though a scourge run over, and pas thorough it shal not come at us, for wee have made falsehood our refuge, and under vanity are wee hid,[554] this was a fearful estate indeed, yet for al that no man can say, but some of those having soe hardned their harts, might bee, and were afterwards converted

Thother kind of hardnes of hart which is not felt <nor>[555] perceived, or if perceived, yet not felt (which albeit is les fearful, yet is dangerous inough) is in such as although they wilfully resist not gods spirit in good means, yet securely carelesly and willingly, they ly in sin without <any> remors of it or true taste of good things. Such was davids estate by the space of a year before Nathan the prophet came to reproov him, and rouse him from his lulled sleep[556]

Both these kinds I am perswaded you are free from, otherwise then in temptation sathan may sometimes move you therunto. The other [fol. 70r] kind of hardnes of hart which may bee perceived and felt is of two sorts, the one in them that are desirous of means wherby they may bee releeved, although they do fynd smal or no ease in themselves for a time, Of this kind the Prophet Esay 63[557] 15[558] in the name of some of gods people complained and such was davids estate after that Nathan had reprooved him <and gods spirit began to woork with him> yet cryeth hee out (as I said before) of the los of graces. And when hee saith god wil accept of noe sacrifices, bee they never so many nor precious, without a contrite hart and broken spirit[559] hee sheweth that for a time, (even after the prophet had reproved him) hee wanted both. This is your case and therfore you are in the estate of salvation, for david was in this case, even after hee had confessed his sin and had received absolution and pardon from god by the ministry of Nathan, although hee neither felt joy thereof nor true greef for the other yet becaus in truth of hart hee confessed his sin (as my trust is you do) and was certainly persuaded of the pardonablenes of it by gods mercies, as you must bee if you wil have mercy (although hee was far of from feeling it and applying it to his

---

553 Replacing *filthy* deleted.
554 Isaiah 28:15.
555 Replacing *and* deleted.
556 2 Samuel 12:1–12.
557 Followed by *19* deleted.
558 Isaiah 63:15.
559 Psalm 51:16–17.

woful conscience) his state was good and very wel to bee hoped of:[560] and you must know and bee perswaded that those things which are written of gods saincts, as namely of david and Peter[561] and such others are ensamples for us, if wee wil stay ourselves upon the word of god in the ministery of his servants, and wait upon the lords good time, until hee come nearer unto us by his spirit, nearer I say for hee is already come unto you or it may bee hee never went from you, beecaus to bee greeved and humbled with blindnes of mind and hardnes of hart to beeleev certainly the truth of gods promises in general, and to reverence the servants of god which bring the glad tidings of salvation, and to long after comfort, using the means of the word of praier, and of the sacrament of the supper, and the company of gods [fol. 70v] children, contrary to hope under hope yea without any present feeling, al this is a certain argument that gods spirit is with such and therfore with you. This estate though it may bee very greevous yet it is never dangerous much les fearful, unles any bee so wilful, that they wil persevere and continue in desperate refusing al good means, unles they persevere I say, for that through the subtil sleight of the spiritual adversary and his forcible power wherby god suffereth him sometimes for a season to winnow them as wheat, they are so bewitched and intoxicated that they are carried by violent force of temptation to wax weary of, or to refuse al means of comfort by fits, yea almost <to have> no desire at al unto them, yea somtimes even to speak evil of them. But all this is but in temptation, and therfore god wilbee merciful unto them for christs sake. Thus job cursed the day of his birth, and wished to bee strangled,[562] Jeremy almost repented that ever hee preached in the name of the lord; both scarsely abstayning from blasphemie.[563] David moved with the spirit of ambition, though dutifully admonished, willfully went on in numbring the people.[564] Peter also vaingloriously presuming of his own strength, being most wisely and effectualy premonished of his weaknes even by our lord jesus, yet wittingly rusheth as the horse into the battail, and then very cowardly yeeldeth, yea doubtly demeth yea strengthneth his sin with a threefold coard, and fastneth it with banning and cursing.[565] And yet al these obtained mercy most bountifully for why as sathan had desire to winnow them, so our lord jesus christ prayed for them, that their faith though it was greevously assaulted, yet that it should not bee[566]

---

[560] 2 Samuel 12:13-23.
[561] Matthew 26:69-75; Mark 14:66-72; Luke 22:54-62.
[562] Job 3:1-12; 7:15.
[563] Jeremiah 20:7-18.
[564] 2 Samuel 24:1-10.
[565] Matthew 26:69-75; Mark 14:66-72; Luke 22:54-62.
[566] Followed by *destroyed* deleted.

overcome; although it was battered, yet that it shold not bee destroyed
and though it was sore oppressed, yet that it should not bee
extinguished. And here bee you fully perswaded, that tho Luc 22.32 the
words seem to run as belonging unto Peter only *viz I have prayed for
thee, that thy faith should not faile* [fol. 71r] yet that hee praied as wel
for the rest of the Apostles yea for al the faithful it is evident. for first hee
saith not Simon sathan hath desired to winnow thee,[567] but you, why
then saith hee I have prayed for thee, verely beecaus hee should more
greevously offend then the rest (although there offence was very great)
therfore his and our most blessed saviour applied to him the promis, but
did not impropriate it to him alone and restrain it from the rest.
Compare with this place John 17.20. and you shal see that the heavenly
verity affirmeth that hee prayed not onely for the Apostles, but for al
those that should beeleev through their word. yea further our lord jesus
Christ was yesterday, is today, and shyal bee for ever, and as the
forefathers were baptized into him, and did eat his flesh and drinck his
blood, so was his praier effectual even to them under the law, much more
to us under grace

And when you can find testimony of your hart, that when you would do
wel evil is present with you, and that you do the evil that you would not,
then do not you it but sin in you when it leadeth you captive Romans
7[568] much more then when sathan woorketh withal buffeting you assure
yourself that god hath pittie on you that the vertu of his power shalbee
perfect in your weaknes 2 Corinthians. 12.9. If you beleev, according to
your faith it shalbee done unto you

But you wil say you cannot beeleev that this vile and crooked hardnes of
hart, can bee remitted and renewed, and this was the second point,
which in the former part of my letter I gave you to understand was the
cause of your excessive distres. I beeseech you and charge you in the
name of our lord jesus christ that you wil not willingly lie, nor offer
injury to gods spirit, nor to your self who have received it: tel mee what
is the reason why you thinck you have no faith, verely beecause you have
no feeling nor no other fruits therof as you thinck[569] wel first then agree
with mee herein (as you must if [fol. 71v] you wil not disagree from the
truth) that feeling is but an effect and a fruit of faith, and therfore ther
may bee faith without feeling, as wel as the caus without the effect, and
the tree without any appearance of fruit, yea of sap for a season, and as

---

[567] Luke 22:31.
[568] See especially Romans 7:13-15.
[569] Followed by *have no feeling* deleted.

a man sore wonded and disceased, may for a season bee deprived, almost of al operations of natural lyfe to the outward shew, and his own judgement and feeling, so may a spiritual man bee so sore wounded by sathan, and disseased by present sight and feeling of his sinful corruptions specialy in temptation, that hee may thinck, yea and may appear to others, that the life of the spirit is not in him. Thus Peters faith did not wholly faile (as you have hard) or els the prayer of our saviour prevailed not.[570] Thus when david Psalm 51.12.[571] declared that his hart was unclean and his spirit crooked or unstable et Psalm. 14.[572] that hee had lost the joy of his salvation and spirit of liberty or adoption yet verse 13.[573] hee praieth that god would not take his holy spirit from him, therfore hee was not deprived of the spirit of sanctification: here seemeth repugnance but their is none: hee was deprived for a season, of the graces of the sanctifying spirit, but not of the holy ghost where with hee was sanctified, with graces as god restored unto him, so I am perswaded hee wil do unto you, yea I dout whether you are deprived of them, but onely that partly melancholy and partly sathan working therwith, make you do injury unto your self, and to the graces of the spirit in you, which I beeseech you take heed of. But the messenger cannot stay, therfore I cannot write as I would, of this or of the remedies you should use, which hereafter I wil, as god shal enable mee. And I pray you let mee understand (as I requested in the beginning) of your estate in particular, somewhat more, and that by this bearer if you can, beecaus hee is of your acquaintance, and wil bring it unto mee faithfully. Onely I add now unto that I have written of [fol. 72r] hardnes of hart at large that you must diligently observ the word (*Create*) which david useth psalm 51.[574] declaring how hee had no feeling of his hart: to this joyn that which the Prophet Esay 57.23.[575] speaketh in the person of god. *I create the fruit of the lips to bee peace, peace, as wel to him that is far of as to him that is neare*

---

[570] Luke 22:31-2.

[571] The following editions incorrectly cite this as Psalm 5:12: First Edition, 449; Second Edition, 419; Third Edition, 235. Fifth Edition, 868, gives an indecipherable citation: 'Psal.51.3.10'. Fourth Edition, 873, cites this as 51:12. The most appropriate verse for this reference is Psalm 51:10.

[572] The following editions cite this as Psalm 5:14: First Edition, 449; Second Edition, 419; Third Edition, 235. Fifth Edition, 868, cites it as Psalm 51:11. The Fourth Edition, 873, cites it as Psalm 51:14. The correct citation for this reference is Psalm 51:12.

[573] The following editions cite this as Psalm 5:13: First Edition, 449; Second Edition, 419; Third Edition, 235. Fifth Edition cites it as Psalm 51:12. Fourth Edition, 873, cites Psalm 51:13. The correct citation for this reference is Psalm 51:11.

[574] Psalm 51:10.

[575] This passage is incorrectly cited in manuscript and Fourth Edition, 873. First Edition, 450 and Second Edition, 420, incorrectly cite this as Isaiah 64:2. Third Edition, 235, and Fifth Edition, 868, correctly cite this as Isaiah 57:19.

Therfore in faith you may as wel pray with hope to obtain as did david: therfore say with him often and with gods people Esay 96.12.[576] *O lord thou art our father, wee indeed are clay, but thou art our maker and wee are the woork of thy hands etc*, know you that god can cause, wolves, lyons, Leopards etc dwel safely and lovingly with lambes. Calves, kine[577] etc Esay 11.6.[578] And that which is impossible to men is possible to god, even to caus a cable rope to go through the ey of an needle;[579] that is to change the hard hart of the unbeleeving covetuous wretched man; much more yours, yea know you that al things are possible to him that beleeveth; cry then I beeleev, O lord help my unbeleef, and I dare promis you in the name of our lord jesus Christ if you shal have your harts desire in goodnes. Thus abruptly I must make an end. I commend you unto god and the word of his grace, which is able to build you up, and give you the right of inheritance among them that are sanctified. And the very god of peace sanctify you throughout, that your whole spirit and soule and body may bee kept blameles, until the coming of our lord jesus christ faithful is hee which called you which wil do it.[580] Amen. I pray you pray for mee, and I trust, as I have, so I shal pray for you and much more.

Yours in Jesus christ to use in

any need R.G.

---

[576] This passage is incorrectly cited. The correct citation is Isaiah 64:7.

[577] That is, cows.

[578] Isaiah 11:6.

[579] Matthew 19:24-6.

[580] This sentence is a close paraphrase of 1 Thessalonians 5:23-4.

PART THREE

Selected texts from Greenham's *Works* (1st edn, 1599)

Selected texts: an editor's introduction

One of the goals of this volume is to make available to scholars and students a reliable and convenient introduction to published texts attributed to Richard Greenham. Using Greenham's fame as an 'experimental divine' as a guiding principle, we chose works that emphasized pastoral issues and provided the reader with a variety of literary forms found in the published works. Four of the five texts appear unabridged and complete. 'A large treatise of the Sabboth' has been edited down to its essential arguments and conclusions. Space prevented the inclusion of his lengthy exegesis of biblical passages in support of his theological conclusions.

Philippa Tudor and Ian Green[1] have made scholars aware of the neglect of sixteenth- and seventeenth-century catechizing, which ministers found increasingly necessary as a prelude to successful preaching. Many ministers wrote their own catechisms to aid in their efforts, but virtually none are available in modern editions. Greenham proved deeply committed to a systematic programme of catechizing in his parish.[2] This (unfinished) text, 'A short forme of Catechising', provides an interesting example of how catechisms were conceived and written by a godly pastor.

Recent books by Kenneth Parker and John Primus,[3] as well as numerous studies of sabbatarianism in other books and articles, illustrate that issues of Sabbath doctrine and observance are far from resolved in current scholarship. Greenham's 'A large treatise of the Sabboth', described by contemporaries as the most influential work on the subject, figures prominently in these studies. While its length made an unabridged edition impossible here, this edited version should prove a major service to students and scholars interested in the Elizabethan debates on Sabbath doctrine and practice.

One aspect of Greenham's restructuring of parochial ministry that

---

[1] Philippa Tudor, 'Religious Instruction for Children and Adolescents in the Early English Reformation', *Journal of Ecclesiastical History*, 35 (1984), 391–413; Green, *The Christian's ABC*.

[2] See below, 265–97.

[3] Parker, *English Sabbath*; John Primus, *Holy Time: Moderate Puritanism and the Sabbath* (Macon, GA: Mercer Press, 1989).

deserves careful attention concerns marriage. Eric Carlson's recently published volume on marriage in this period highlights important changes in this 'estate' during the Tudor period.[4] In Greenham's 'A treatise of Contract' we have a short piece on betrothal and marriage that illustrates his practical effort to deal with perceived problems in marriage law and practice.

Exhortations to read and meditate on the scriptures proved a core principle in Greenham's advice to the godly. In his 'A profitable treatise containing a direction for the reading and understanding of the holy Scriptures', we have a brief piece which illustrates his vision for lay education and spirituality, as well as the relationship between reading and preaching.

In his sermon, 'Of the good education of children', Greenham provided a typical example of Elizabethan social theology. It is unique among Greenham's works because it was published during his life.

While the voluminous collections of Greenham's 'works' are far richer than any small selection could adequately reflect, the editors hope that this representative sample will inspire the reader to explore in greater depth the 'practical divinity' of Richard Greenham. His pioneering work in the restructuring of Elizabethan parochial life points toward many fresh avenues of research on this period.

---

[4] Carlson, *Marriage and the English Reformation*.

A short forme of Catechising

Whereas all men desire to be blessed and the most men are deceived in seeking blessednes: tell me which is the true way thereunto?

To know God to be my father in Jesus Christ by the revelation of the Spirite according to his worde, and therefore to serve him according to his will, and to set forth his glorie; beleeving that I shall want nothing that is good for me in this life, and that I shall enjoy everlasting blessednes in the world to come.

How know you this?

By the working of the holy Ghost, and by the meanes of Gods word.

What call you Gods word?

It is the revealed will of God set forth unto us in the holy Scriptures.

Which call you the holy Scriptures?

The bookes of the olde and new Testament, commonly called Canonicall.

Are all things, that are necessarie for us to know, conteined in them?

Yea: for God beeing full of all wisdome and goodnes, would leave out nothing that was requisite for us to know.

Is it lawful for to adde or to take any thing from Gods word?

No: for God hath flatly forbidden it, and hath pronounced greevous curses upon those that doe it.[1]

Why is it so grievous a sinne?

Because it is a verie great sinne to alter the last will of a mortall man: therefore much more grievous a sinne it is to change the last Testament of the eternall God.

Why is it requisite that the will of God should be set forth unto us?

That wee might have pure rules of his worship, and sure grounds of our salvation.

Is it not lawfull to repose any part of Gods worshippe or of salvation in the doctrines and doing of men?

No: for all men by nature are lyars, and defiled with sinne.

What followeth hereof?

That all mens doctrines and doings are mingled with lyes and corruptions.

---

[1] Revelation 22:18–19.

How farre are wee bound to their doctrines and doings?

So farre forth as they bee agreeable to Gods word.

May all read the Scriptures?

Yea, all that be of age able to discerne betweene good and evill ought to encrease in knowledge for their furtherance in salvation, as they encrease in yeeres.

Why must all such read the Scriptures?

1. First, because every one must be able to proove and trie himselfe whether he be in the faith or no.

Why else?

2. Secondly, because every one must be able to proove and examine mens doctrines and doings by the scriptures, that they be not in their salvation by them deceived.

3. Thirdly, because every one must bee able as his calling requireth to teach, admonish, exhort, & comfort one another.

4. Fourthly, because every one must be able to make an account of the faith and hope that is in him.[2]

What if men cannot read?

Then they must use the helpe of others that can read.

Is it enough to read the scriptures privately, or with others?

No: for God hath also commanded to heare them read publikely in the Church.[3]

And is it enough to heare them read publikely in the Church?

No: for he also hath ordained preaching to be used.[4]

Why must preaching be joyned with reading?

Because it is the most principall and proper meanes to beget faith in us.

Why must faith be mixed with the word read and preached?

Because otherwise the word profiteth us nothing.

How many things are requisite to bee in every one that will come to heare the word read and preached?

Amongst others, foure are necessarie.

What is first?

1. First, a trembling feare of the Majestie of God.

2. Secondly, an assured faith in Christ.

3. Thirdly, an earnest endeavor to frame our lives thereafter.

4. Fourthly, they must pray for the holy ghost to be given them, to enlighten their mindes, and to write all these things in their hearts.

Which be the principall parts of Gods word?

The Lawe and the Gospell.

---

[2] 1 Peter 3:15.
[3] 1 Timothy 4:13.
[4] Acts 10:42; 1 Corinthians 1:17.

What call you the Lawe?

It is that part of the worde that commandeth all good and forbideth all evill.

What if wee could keepe the Law?

Then we should be blessed.

What if we breake the Law?

Then wee are subject to the curse of God, and so to death and damnation.

What call you the Gospell?

It is that part of the word which containeth the free promises of God made unto us in Jesus Christ without any respect of our deservings.

What doth that worke in us?

It worketh in us a true and lively faith in Jesus Christ, whereby wee lay holde of the free remission of our sinnes in him, and the true repentance of them.

What must we learne by the whole word of God?

Two things:
1. first, to make a right and sound entrance to our salvation.
2. secondly, how to encrease and continue in the same unto the end.

What is required for our right and sound entrance to our salvation?

Three things are required
1. first, to know and to be perswaded of the greatnes of our sinnes, and the miserie due to the same.
2. secondly, to know and be perswaded how we may be delivered from them.
3. thirdly, to knowe and be perswaded what thankes wee owe to God for our deliverance.

How shall wee come to the right sight of our sinnes, and a sound perswasion of the greatnes of them?

By the spirit of God leading us into the true understanding of the law, and a due examination of ourselves thereby.

Where is the law set downe?

It is written in many places of the scriptures, but the summe thereof is contained in the ten Commandements.[5]

Rehearse them.

I am the Lord thy God, thou shalt have none other Gods but me.

How are they devided?

Into two principall heads or tables, as they be called.

What doth the first table teach us?

It teaches us our dutie towards God, and is contained in the foure first

---

[5] Exodus 20:1-17; Deuteronomy 5:6-21.

Commandements.

What doth the second teach?

Our dutie towards our neighbour, and is contained in the sixe last Commandements.

Why are the duties towards God set downe before the duties towards our neighbour?

Because the love of God is the ground of the love of our neighbour.

What followeth hereof?

That none can rightly love his neighbour except hee first love God.

Why are the duties towards our neighbour joyned to our duties towards God?

Because the love of our neighbour is the proofe of our love towards God.

What ensueth hereof?

That none can love God aright, except he also love his neighbour.

Why are the Commandements set downe in ten partes, and not in generall?

Because God is not pleased with doing our duties in generall or in some part, but he will be wholly served in all and every one of his Commandements.

Why are they set downe singularly or to every one?

Because every one must doe his own dutie though none goe before him.

What followeth of this?

That every one must beare his owne burden, and none shall have excuse by the example of others.

Are there not some rules which serve for the better understanding of every one of the Commandements?

Yea, there be foure which have special uses:

1. First, in every Commandement where evill is forbidden, there the contrarie good is commanded.
2. Secondly, many moe evils are forbidden and many moe good things are commanded in every commandement, than in word are expressed.
3. Thirdly, because God is a Spirite, therefore his commandements are spirituall, and require spirituall obedience.
4. Fourthly, in every commandement where evill is forbidden, there the occasions of the evill is forbidden; & where good is commanded, there also the occasions of good are commanded.

Rehearse the first Commandement.

Thou shalt have none other gods but me.[6]

---

[6] Exodus 20:2-3; Deuteronomy 5:6-7.

What evill is here generally forbidden?
Even that which the words doe import.
What good is commanded?
To have God to be my only God, and to be alwayes in his presence.
What is it to have God to be our onely God?
To give him all things proper and peculiar to his Maiestie.
Which be those that properly concerne God, and therefore be the speciall things commanded?
They be very many.
Rehearse the summe of them, whereby the rest may bee understood.
I am bound to beleeve in God, to love God, to feare and obey him, to pray unto him and praise him.
After what sort must you performe these duties of faith, love, feare, obedience, prayer, and thankesgiving?
With my whole mind and understanding, with my whole heart and my whole strength.[7]
Which be the peculiar sinnes herein forbidden?
To faile in giving to God any of these or the like forenamed good things, in any part or in any respect.
what els is particularly forbidden?
To give any of the fore named good things to any creature, or any other thing whatsoever, whereby my heart may bee withdrawen from God in any part or in any respect.
Which be the occasions of the breach of this commandement?
1. First, the vaine desire of the pleasures, riches, and glorie of this world.
2. Secondly, a negligent and carelesse use of the meanes of serve God his providence.
Are not the contrarie good things to these commanded?
Yea.
which are they?
1. First, a heart contented with any estate, and using things of this world as though we used them not.
2. Secondly, a reverent & diligent use of the meanes to serve Gods providence.
Rehearse the second commandement.
Thou shalt not make to thy selfe any graven Image, nor the likenes, &c.[8]
What evill is expresly forbidden in this commandement?

---

[7] A reference to Jesus's summary of the law in Matthew 22:37.
[8] Exodus 20:4-6; Deuteronomy 5:8.

I am forbidden to make any image either to represent God or to worship him by.

What evill is generally forbidden?

I must avoid all inventions and devises of men in the outward worship of God, which be contrary or beside the written word of God.

Which be the speciall evils forbidden?

There be some which we must necessarily avoid, unlesse wee will fall into superstition and idolatrie; and they be these:

1. First, to joyne the false parts of worship with the true worship of God.
2. Secondly, to be present in body at idolatrous and superstitious service.
3. Thirdly, the reservation of some speciall monument of superstition and idolatrie.

   Which be the lesser occasions forbidden, and yet, so wee have the speciall grounds of Gods worshippe, we must and may tollerate them when we can not helpe them?

1. First, all vaine, idle, and superstitious ceremonies.
2. Secondly, all keeping company with false worshippers.

   Is not the evill in heart also forbidden?

Yea, so far forth as I lust in my heart to have any of them prevaile or be established.

What good is generally commanded?

All the outward means of Gods worship, which be agreeable to his written word.

What is specially commanded?

I must use such doctrine, prayers, sacraments, and discipline of the Church, as be agreeable to Gods word in the substance.

What occasions of good be here commanded?

1. First, to have and use good bookes of the doctrine and historie of the Church, written according to Gods word.
2. Secondly, erecting and maintaining schooles of learning, as nurseries of the ministrie.
3. Thirdly, sufficient provision to be made for the Ministers of Gods word.
4. Fourthly, building and maintaining Churches and all things belonging thereunto.
5. Fiftly, I must use all good ceremonies and orders agreeable to the word of God.
6. Sixtly, all familiar companie with the true worshippers of God.

   What good in heart is commanded?

I am commanded to use the meanes of gods worship not only outwardly, but also in spirit and truth.

What is meant by these words: For I the Lord thy God am a jealous God, &c.

That God will punish false worshippe in the false worshippers, and in their posteritie unto the fourth generation.

What is meant by these words: And will show mercie unto thousands, &c.

That God will blesse his true worshippe in the true worshippers and their posteritie unto the thousand discent.

What is the use of these?

The use is to make false worshippe more vile, and his true worship more pretious in our eyes.

Rehearse the third Commandement.

Thou shalt not take the name of the Lorde thy God in vaine, &c.[9]

What evils be here forbidden?

1. First, all perjurie, banning, or cursing, enchanting, or conjuring.
2. Secondly, all swearing by false Gods, or naming them with reverence.
3. Thirdly, all customable swearing or speaking of God without reverence.
4. Fourthly, to cause Gods name to be dishonoured by false doctrine or ungodly life, either in my selfe or in others.

What good is herein commanded?

1. First in matters concerning Gods glorie, I must be sweare by God onely in $\begin{cases} \text{justice.} \\ \text{judgement.} \\ \text{trueth.} \end{cases}$

2. Secondly, I must endeavour from my heart to grow up in true knowledge, and a godly life, that so Gods name may be praised in my selfe and in others.

What is meant by these words: For the Lord will not hold him guiltlesse, &c.

That God will certainely punish the dishonouring of his name in any sort.

What is the use of this?

The use is this: to make us more fearefull to dishonour him, and more carefull to glorifie his name.

Rehearse the fourth Commandement.

Remember the Sabboth day to keep it holy, &c.[10]

What is here generally commanded?

I am commanded to make it my whole delight, to sanctifie the holy Sabboth of the Lord from morning to night.

---

[9] Exodus 20:7; Deuteronomy 5:11.
[10] Exodus 20:8-11; Deuteronomy 5:12-15.

What is particularly commanded?

1. First to use all the publike meanes of Gods worship in the congregation of Gods people.
2. Secondly, to rejoyce to use all such private exercises as may make the publike meanes profitable to my selfe and to others.

Which be those private exercises?

1. First, the examining of my sinnes and wants, private praier, reading of the Scriptures, singing of Psalmes, conference with others, and applying all things to my selfe with a care to profite others.
2. Secondly, relieving the needie, visiting the sicke, and them that be in prison, comforting them that be in any miserie, reconciling them that be at variance, admonishing the unruly, and such like.

What is especially commanded?

The spirituall beholding of the creatures of God, thereby to provoke my selfe and others to praise him.

What else is?

A diligent searching of my heart with a like care to find it out, and to reape some profit of the forenamed meanes, so that I may be the better for and through them.

What is then particularly forbidden?

1. All such labours and pleasures in thought, word, and deede and forbidden, as may hinder me and others for using of, or profiting by the same meanes.
2. Secondly, the leaving unused and of those publike means or private exercises.

What is here generally forbidden?

The using of either of those publike or private meanes in ceremonie without some good fruit in my selfe, or care of fruit in others.

Rehearse the fift commandement?

Honour thy father and thy mother, that thy dayes may be long in the land, etc.[11]

Whome doe you understand by father and mother?

By father and mother I doe not understand onely my naturall parents, but also those whome God hath set over me for my good, as magistrates, ministers, masters, and such like.

What duties doe children owe unto their naturall parents?

Children ought reverently and obediently to receive the instructions, commandements, and corrections of their parents, to succour them, and to pray for them.

What are they forbidden to doe?

To refuse or murmure at the instructions, commandements, and

---

[11] Exodus 20:12; Deuteronomy 5:16.

corrections of their parents, or to neglect any dutie belonging to them.

How may they trie their love by these duties?

They may trie whether their love be right three wayes.

First, if they be as desirous to doe all these duties to their parents, as they be as desirous to doe all these duties to their parents, as they would have their parents to doe all duties unto them.

What is the second?

Secondly, if they be as desirous to doe all duties to their parents, as they would have their children hereafter to honour them.

What is the third?

Thirdly if they be as willing to doe all these duties to their parents, as they would receive long life or any other blessing at the hands of God.

What duties doe parents owe to their children?

Parents ought to teach, correct, pray, and provide for their children.

How may they trie their love by these duties?

They may trie their love two wayes.

What is the first?

First, if they be as carefull to doe all duties to their children as they would have had their parents in times past to have performed all good duties unto them.

What is the second?

Secondly, if they be as carefull to doe duties to their children, as they would have their children hereafter to be dutifull unto them.

What be the duties of servants to their masters?

Servants ought in feare & trembling to submit themselves to the instructions, commandements, & corrections of their masters, and to doe no eye service to them.[12]

What if parents and masters doe not their duties to their children and their servants?

Yet they must obey them for conscience to Gods ordinance.[13]

What if they commaund unjust things?

Then they must obey God rather than men, and submit themselves to their corrections.[14]

Why are these words added: That thy daies, &c.

They are added to allure us more carefully to keepe and willingly to obey this commandement.

And shall not disobedience be punished?

Yea: it shall be rewarded with a short and miserable life.[15]

---

[12] See Ephesians 6:5-9.
[13] Romans 13:5.
[14] Acts 5:29.
[15] Exodus 20:12; Deuteronomy 5:16; ephesians 6:1-3.

How may they trie their love by these duties?
They may trie it three manner of waies.
What is the first?
First, if they be as desirous to doe all these duties to their masters, as they woulde have their masters doe the dutie of masters unto them.
What is the second?
Secondly, if they bee as carefull to doe all these duties to their masters as they would have their servants to be dutifull unto them when they shall be masters.
What is the third?
Thirdly, if they be as willing to do all duties to their masters as they would be glad to receive long life or any blessing at the hand of God.
What duties doe masters owe to their servants?
Masters ought to teach and correct their servants, and to pray for them.
How may they trie their love by these duties?
They may trie their love in two waies.
What is the first?
1. First, if they be as desirous to doe all these duties to their servants, as they would have their masters deale with them if they were servants.
What is the second thing?
2. Secondly, if they bee as carefull to doe all these duties to their servants, as they would be to have their servants to do all duties unto them.
Rehearse the sixt Commandement?
Thou shall doe no murder.[16]
How many things are here forbidden?

Foure especially:

1. first is forbidden, by weapon or poison to kill our brother.
2. secondly, by wounde or blowe, or any other means to shorten the life or empaire the health of any man.
3. thirdly, by worde, countenance, or gesture, to mocke, grieve, or contemne any man.
4. fourthly, we are forbidden all anger, hatred, or envie, whereby wee may be brought to revenge our selves upon our brother.

What good is here commanded?
1. First, we are commanded to have peace with all men, as much as is possible and in us lyeth.[17]

---

[16] Exodus 20:13; Deuteronomy 5:17.
[17] Romans 12:18.

2. Secondly, we are commanded in thought, word, & deed, to seeke the preservation of the health of our brother.

Rehearse the seventh Commandement.

Thou shall not commit adulterie.[18]

How many things are here forbidden?

Three things are forbidden.

Which is the first?

First all outward actions are forbidden whereby the bodie is defiled; as adulterie, fornication, uncleannesse.

How many wayes is uncleannesse committed?

Two wayes:
- first, either against:
  - our owne bodies, which is unnaturall; or,
  - the bodies of other creatures; which is monstrous.
- Secondly, by marrying one
  1. of false religion;[19] or
  2. of no religion at all.[20]
  3. within the degrees of forbidden.[21]
  4. without the consent of parents.[22]
  5. it is committed by using the marriage bed intemperately.[23]

What is the second thing forbidden?

Secondly, all instruments and occasions are forbidden, whereby this sinne is raised up or strengthned in us, and they be all contained in this word *Wantonnesse.*

How is wantonnes seene?

In 2. things:
- first, when either
  1. the whole body is abused in idlenes, or vaine sports: or,
  2. any parte of the body, as the eye, the eare, the tongue, the nose, the hand or foot are abused.
- secondly, when wee doe intemperately abuse meate, drinke, sleepe, or apparell, or use any inconvenient company, time, or place.

What is the third thing forbidden?

Thirdly, all inward settled lustes are forbidden, whereunto the heart doth give consent.

---

[18] Exodus 20:14; Deuteronomy 5:18.

[19] 2 Corinthians 6:14-15.

[20] Atheism was not a concern in biblical times. Marriage to an atheist is not explicitly forbidden, but would be precluded by 2 Corinthians 6:14-15.

[21] Leviticus 18:6-18.

[22] This is not specifically forbidden in scripture.

[23] Hebrews 13:4.

What good is commanded?

1. First, I am commanded to keepe my selfe pure and chast both in body and soule.

2. Secondly, to use those meanes carefully, which may keepe us chast.

Which be the meanes of chastitie?

Continuall sobrietie in meat, drinke, sleepe, and apparell.

Continuall painfulnes in our calling.

Fasting and watching so often as need requireth.

What if by these meanes we cannot be kept chast?

3. Then thirdly we are commanded to marrie, and in marriage to use those meanes carefully whereby the marriage bed may be kept pure and undefiled.[24]

Rehearse the eighth commandement.

Thou shalt not steale.[25]

How many evils are herein forbidden?

1. First, all these outward acts are forbidden, whereby stealth is committed.

How many waies is stealth committed outwardly in act?

Two waies, either

by our selves and this is 3. wayes:

1. first, all secret filching & open robbery, be it of never so small a thing, for never so great a need.
2. secondly, all extortion or violent wrong, all oppression & unmercifull dealing.
3. all deceit in buying and selling or exchanging, in restoring things borrowed, found, given to be kept, and such like.

by others, either

by commaunding or councelling others to steale.
by keeping counsell.
by consenting any way to them when they steale.

Which are the second evils forbidden?

2. Secondly, all outward occasions of stealth are forbidden.

Which be they?

All idlenes, wastfull spending of goods, living in an unlawfull calling, all false:

waightes.
measures.
coynes, and such like.

---

[24] Hebrews 13:4.
[25] Exodus 20:15; Deuteronomy 5:19.

What is thirdly forbidden?

Thirdly, all inward stealth of the heart is forbidden.

Which is that?

The setled will or desire of our neighbors goods, although we can not get them, or for feare, shame, or some other respect we doe not take them.

What is here commanded?

1. First, to restore goods evill gotten, or wronfully kept.
2. Secondly, to labour faithfully in a lawfull calling, to be sparing of that we get, and to helpe others as their neede requireth.

Rehearse the ninth Commandement.

Thou shalt not beare false witnes, &c.[26]

What is forbidden herein?

Wee are forbidden not onely to beare false witnesse our selves, but also to be partakers with false witnes bearers.

How many wayes doe men beare false witnesse?

2. wayes:
- 1. outwardly — and against — others; & that is — in judgement, or, out of judgement.
- 2. inwardly — or themselves — when they deny that to be in them which is indeed: or when they take upon them that which belongeth not unto them, whether it be good or evill.

In Judgement, when they give or receive false information, pronounce or write any false sentence.

Out of judgement,
1. when any raise up, spread abroad, or listen after false reports.
2. when any report the faults of others without care of their credit, or when with flattering hearts they commend any man.

2. Inwardly either
1. in suspition without just cause,
2. in Judging falsely or hardly of any man.

Which be the occasions of false witnes bearing?

They be fleshly hatred of our enemies, the carnall love of our selves or of our friends, to get the things we love, and to avoid the things we feare or hate.

---

[26] Exodus 20:16; Deuteronomy 5:20.

How are we partakers with false witnes bearers?
If we either command or counsell it to be done.
If we mislike it not, staying it if we can.
   What is here commanded?
1. First, in judgement to further righteous causes so farre forth as my
   calling requireth.
2. Secondly, to speak the truth from my heart to every man, so farre
   forth as it is requisite for him to know it.
3. Thirdly, to be as carefull of the credit of my neighbour as of mine
   owne, both in his presence and absence, so far forth as the nature
   of his offence will permit.
4. Fourthly, to hope and beleeve the best of every man.
   Rehearse the tenth Commandement.
Thou shalt not covet &c.[27]
   Are all motions and desires evill?
No: for the desire to meate, drinke, sleepe, and such like are naturall,
and in their owne nature good, unlesse through our corruption they
become sinfull.
   What motions be evill?
Those motions be evill, which $\left\{\begin{array}{l}\text{God; or,}\\\text{our neighbour.}\end{array}\right.$
   are either against
   Are all those forbidden in this Commandement?
No: for all those which are against God are forbidden in the first
Commandement: but those motions are only here forbidden, which are
against our neighbour.
   Seeing in the former commandements wee are forbidden to hurt
   our neighbour in heart, how doth this differ from the former?
In the former commandements the setled desires of the heart are
forbidden, but the motions are onely here forbidden whereunto the heart
doth not consent.
   Whereof doe these motions arise?
They either arise from our owne corruption, or are offered be Sathan
or by men.
   Are all these motions sinne in us?
All that arise of our corruption are sinnes in us; but they that be
offered by Satan or men are not sinnes, unlesse we be infected with them.
   How are wee infected with them?
1. When we take pleasure in them.
2. When we be intangled with them.
3. When we suffer them to tary in our mindes, though our hearts doe
   not give consent.

---

[27] Exodus 20:17; Deuteronomy 5:21.

How is this commandement broken?

Three wayes:
1. first, when evill motions arise of our corruption mooving us to hurt our neighbours.
2. secondly, when we be infected with those motions which Satan or evill men doe put into our minds.
3. thirdly, when we doe not with like affection desire the good of our neighbour as we doe our owne.

What is then commanded?

I am commanded to love my neighbour as my selfe.[28]

Who is your neighbour?[29]

Every one that is neare me & standeth in need of my helpe, and it lyeth in me to helpe him, though otherwise hee be a stranger unto me, or my foe.

Why judge you so?

Because of the Image of God in him, and that he is mine owne flesh in respect of our first parents.

Doth the law of God prescribe the perfit rule of righteousnes?

Yea: for there is no good thing in deed, word, or thought, but here it is commanded, and likewise no evill but here it is forbidden.

Can everyone keep the law of God perfitly?

They that are not borne againe of God cannot keepe it all nor in any one point, as pleasing God thereby in respect of themselves.

Who so?

Except a man be borne againe of God hee cannot see the kingdome of heaven, nor enter therein,[30] neither can he keepe the commandements of God: moreover, all men by nature being borne and conceived in sinne are not onely insufficient to any good thing, but also disposed to all vice and wickednesse.[31]

What punishment is due to the breakers of Gods law?

In this life the curse of God, and death, with manifold miseries both of body or soule, or both.[32]

What else?

Where this curse is not taken away, everlasting death and damnation both of bodie and soule in the world to come.

But God is mercifull.

He is indeed full of mercie, but he is also full of righteousnes, which

---

28 Matthew 22:39.
29 See Luke 10:30-36.
30 John 3:3-6.
31 Psalm 51:5; Romans 7:17-20.
32 Romans 6:23.

must fully be discharged, or els we cannot be partakers of his mercie.

And cannot wee by our selves make satisfaction for our sinnes?

We cannot by any meanes, but rather from day to day encrease our debt.

But doth not God wrong to man, to require of him that he is not able to performe?

No: for God made man so, that he might have performed it, but hee by his sinne spoiled himselfe and his posteritie of those good gifts.

Can any creature in heaven and earth which is onely a creature, make satisfaction to his righteousnes?

No, none at all: for first, God will not punish that in another creature, which is due to be paid by man: and beside, none that is onely a creature can abide the wrath of God against sinne, and deliver others from the same.

What manner of man is to be sought out to be our mediatour and deliverer?

Hee which is indeed a verie man and perfectly righteous, and more mightie than all creatures, that is he which also is verie true God.

Why must he be man, and perfectly righteous?

Because that the righteousnesse of God requireth, that the same nature that sinned, should paye and make amends for sinne.[33]

Why must he be God withal?

Because that by his godly power he may abide the burden of Gods wrath in his flesh, and may get againe and restore to us the righteousnes and life which we have lost.

Who is that mediator which is verie God and verie man, and perfectly righteous withal?

Our Lorde Jesus Christ, who was made unto us wisdome, righteousnes, sanctification and redemption.[34]

What is the use of all that hitherto hath been taught?

The use is to bring us to a sound perswasion and feeling of our sinnes, because they have deserved so grievous punishment, as either the death of the sonne of God or hell fire.

Are they onely delivered from the curse of the Lawe, and made partakers of the merites of Christ that are truely humbled?

Yea: for heaven and earth shall passe away, but one jotte or tittle of Gods Lawe shall not faile till all be fulfilled.[35]

---

[33] Romans 8:3–4.
[34] 1 Corinthians 1:30.
[35] Matthew 24:35.

How is the truth of Gods Law fulfilled?

It is fulfilled in
- 1. Gods children, because it bringeth them to be truely humbled in themselves for their sinnes, and then sendeth them to Christ in whome it is fully fulfilled.
- 2. the wicked; because it declareth to them their just confusion, when to the end they either presume of despaire.

Is sorrow for sinne sufficient to bring us to salvation?

No: for we must also have a true faith.

What is that true faith that saves us?

It is a true perswasion of the mercies of God merited by our Lord Jesus Christ.

How shall we attaine to this true faith?

By the Spirit of God giving us the true perswasion of the gospell.

Where is the Gospel declared unto us?

It is generally declared unto us in the holy Scriptures: but the Church of God hath gathered out of them a certaine summe thereof.

Which is that?

The Articles of our Christian faith, commonly called the Creede.

Rehearse the Articles of our Christian faith.

I beleeve in God the father Almightie maker of heaven and earth, &c.

Into how many parts are the Articles devided?

Into two
- the first is of faith of God.
- the second is of faith concerning the Church.

What are you taught to beleeve in the first part?

In the first part I declare that I beleeve in God the
- father.
- sonne.
- H. ghost.

Why say you, I beleeve in God, and not in Gods?

Because there is but one onely true God upon whome my faith is wholly stayed.

Seeing there is but one God, why name you three, the
- *Father.*
- *Sonne.*
- *Holy Ghost?*

Because that God has so opened himselfe in his worde that these sundry persons are but one true & everlasting God.

Why say you, I beleeve in God, and not rather, that there is a God?

By saying, *I beleeve in God*, I declare that I put my whole trust and assurance in God, whereas the Devils and wicked men believing *that there is a God*, yet cannot put their whole trust and confidence in God.[36]

---

[36] James 2:19.

Why say you, I beleeve, and not, We beleeve?

Because I must be saved by mine owne faith, and not by the faith of another.

Why call you God, Father?

Because he is the Creatour of heaven and earth, and so is the father of all creatures.

Why call you God Creatour of heaven and earth, and not, Maker of heaven and earth?

Because hee created all things of nothing; for to create, is to make a thing of nothing, but to make, is to make a thing of that which was something before.

Why call you him Almightie?

Because as he created all things of nothing, so does he preserve and guide them by his almightie power, wisdome, justice, and mercie.

What comfort doth this article minister unto you?

It ministreth unto me foure notable comforts:

1. First, that all good Angels of God shall watch over me,[37] & pitch their tents about me.
2. Secondly, that neither the devill nor man shall have any power to hurt mee, but when and as farre foorth as God does give them leave.[38]
3. Thirdly, that I shall have a profitable and convenient use of all Gods creatures.[39]
4. Fourthly, though I suffer hurt by Sathan, or want of the creatures, yet all this shall turne to my good in the end.

How can this be?

Because God can doe it as an Almightie God, and will doe it as a most mercifull and loving father.

True it is that by creation we had this benefite, but we have lost it, and are become the children of wrath: how then can God become our father, and shew his mercy unto us?

He is become our father by faith in Jesus Christ the sonne of God.

What beleeve you of God the son?

1. First, I beleeve that he is able to worke my salvation.
2. Secondly, I beleeve that he hath wrought it indeed after that manner that is set downe in the Creede.

How can you beleeve that he is able to worke your salvation?

I doe beleeve it, because he is both God and man, and hath an office from God the father to worke my salvation.

---

[37] Psalm 91:11.
[38] Job 1:9-12; 2:4-6.
[39] Genesis 1:26-30.

By what words in the Creed doe you beleeve Christ to be God?

By these wordes, *His only sonne*, I declare that I beleeve in Christ the only begotten sonne of God, begotten of his father before all worldes, God of God, light of light, very God of very God, begotten not made, being of one substance with the Father, by whome all things were made.

Why call him the onely begotten Sonne of God?

Because he is the alone sonne of God, by nature.

How can this be, seeing Adam, the Angels, and we also be the sonnes of God?

Adam was the sonne of God by creation, which we have lost, but yet we be the sonnes of God by regeneration.[40]

Why was it requisite that he should be God?

Because nothing but God was able to abide & overcome the wrath of God and the punishment due unto sinne.

What comfort have you by this, that Christ is God?

Hereby I am sure, that he is able to save me by reconciling me to the father, that he may make me the child of God.

By what wordes in the Creede doe you shewe that you beleeve Christ to be man?

By these wordes, *Borne of the virgine Mary*, I doe shewe, that Christ is borne of the virgin Mary as others be, and subject to all infirmities of man, sinne only excepted.

Why are these words added; Conceived by the Holy Ghost?

To shew, that Christ by the holy Ghost was conceived in the wombe of Marie, she continuing still a pure Virgine, and that he was borne holy and without sinne, whereunto all other men by nature are subject.

Was it needfull that Christ should be without sinne?

Yea: for otherwise the Godhead and Manhood could not be joyned together: and againe, if hee had been a sinner, hee could not have satisfied for the sinnes of other men.

Why was it requisite that Christ should be man?

Because the righteousness of God requireth, that the same nature which had sinned, should also pay and make amends for sinnes.

What comfort have you by this, that Christ is man?

Hereby I am assured, that Christ is fit to suffer the punishment of my sinne, and being man, himselfe is also meet to be more pitifull and mercifull unto men.

What fruit have you by his holy conception?

I am assured that his holy conception has covered the corruption of my nature, and that his pure conception shall be imputed unto me.

---

[40] The reference to Adam as the son of God is an allusion to Luke 3:38. Also see: 1 Corinthians 15:22; Romans 8:1–17, esp. verse 14.

What comfort have you by this, that he is both God and man?

By this I am most certenly assured, that he is able most fully to finish my salvation, seeing that he is man he is meet to suffer for sinne; as he is God, hee is able to beare the punishment of sinne, and to overcome in suffering, and therefore he is called JESUS.[41]

What does Jesus signifie?

It doth signifie a Saviour.

Why doe you call him Jesus?

I doe call him *Jesus,* (that is, a Saviour) because he saveth me from all my sinnes, & because there is none other means whereby I may in part or in whole be delivered from them.

What comfort have you by this?

My comfort is even the same which I have said, and the rather, because God from heaven gave him his name, and the Church on earth hath subscribed thereunto.

What signifieth Christ?

It signifieth *Annointed?*

Why is he so called?

Because hee was anointed to be a ⎰ Prophet ⎱ Priest ⎰ King ⎱ for all his people and so for me.

How gather you this?

By the annointing of Prophets, Priests, and Kings, which were figures of him.

Was Christ annointed with materiall oyle as they were?

No: but he was annointed with all giftes of the holy Spirit without measure.

Why doe you call him Prophet?

Because he was, he is, and ever shall be the onely teacher of the Church.

What were then the Prophets and Apostles?

They were his disciples and servants, and spake by his spirit.

What comfort have you by this?

Hereby I am sure, that he will lead me into all truth, revealed in his word, needfull for Gods glorie and my salvation.

Why call you him Priest?

Because offering up himselfe a sacrifice once for all, he hath satisfied for all my sinnes, and maketh continuall intercession to the father for me.[42]

What comfort have you by the Priesthood of Christ.

---

[41] Matthew 1:21.
[42] Hebrews 7:24-5; 9:26.

Hereby I am assured that he is my mediatour, and that I also am made a Priest.

How are you made a Priest?

By him I have freedome and boldnes to draw neare and offer my selfe and all that I have to God the Father.

Why call you him King?

Because hee doth guide and governe me unto everlasting life by his word and spirit.

What comfort have you by this?

Hereby I am assured, that by his kingly power I shall finally overcome the flesh, the world, the devill, death and hell.

Why call you him Lord?

Because not with golde nor silver but with his precious blood hee hath purchased us to be a peculiar people to himselfe.

What comfort have you by this?

Seeing he hath paid so precious a price for me he will not suffer me to perish.

What is the second thing wherein the faith of Christ consisteth?

Secondly, I beleeve that he hath wrought my salvation indeed after that manner that is set downe in the Creed.

After what manner hath he wrought your salvation?

1. First, by his most painefull sufferings for sinne.

2. Secondly, by his most glorious victorie and triumph over sinne.

In what words are his most painfull sufferings expressed?

In the words; *Suffered under Pontius Pilate, was crucified, dead and buryed, he descended into hell.*

What is the generall meaning of these wordes?

By them I shewe my selfe to beleeve, that Christ endured most grievous torments both of body and soule.

What comfort have you by this?

I am freed from all those punishments of body and soule which my sinnes have deserved.

How then commeth it to passe, that wee are so often afflicted with grievous torments both in body and soule?

Our sufferings are not by desert any satisfaction for our sinnes in any part, but being sanctified in the most holy sufferings of Christ they are medecines against sinne.

Why are these words added; Suffered under Pontius Pilate?

Not onely for the truth of the storie, but also to teach that he appeared willingly and of his owne accord before a mortall judge, of whome hee was pronounced innocent, and yet by the same he was condemned.

What comfort have you hereof?

That my Saviour thus suffering, not any whit for his owne sinnes, but wholly for mine and for other mens sinnes before an earthly judge, I shall be discharged before the heavenly judgement seate.

What is meant by this, That he was crucified?

That he died not onely a common death, but such a death as was accursed both of God and man.

What comfort have you by this?

I am comforted in this, because I am delivered from the curse which I have deserved by the breach of the law, & shall obtaine the blessing due unto him for keeping of the same.

What is meant by this, That he dyed?

That his soule was separated from his bodie, so that hee died a corporall death.

Why was it requisite that he should die?

Because by sinne came death into the world, so that the justice of God could not have beene satisfied for our sinnes, unlesse death had bene joyned with his sufferings.[43]

Why is it farther added, That he was buried?

To assure us more fully that he was truely dead.

What comfort have you by his death and buriall?

1. I am comforted, because my sinnes are fully discharged in his death, and so buried, that they shall never come into remembrance.
2. Secondly, my comfort is the more, because by the vertue of his death and buriall sinne shall be killed in me, and buried, so that henceforth it shall have no power to raigne over me.
3. Thirdly, I need not to feate [*sic*] death, seeing that sinne which is the sting of death is taken away by the death of Christ, & that now death is made unto me an entrance into this life.

What is the meaning of this, He descended into hell?

This is the meaning, that my Saviour Christ did not onely suffer in bodie, but also in soule did abide most unspeakeable vexations, griefes, painfull troubles, and feare of minde, into the which both before, and most of all when he hanged upon the crosse he was cast.

What comfort have you by this?

I am comforted in this, because in all my grievous temptations & assaults I may stay & make sure my selfe by this, that Christ hath delivered me from the sorrowfull griefes & pains of hell.

What beleevest thou in this Article, He rose again from the dead?

I beleeve that Christ in his manhood hath suffered for me, and that he did in the third day rise again by his own power from the dead.

---

[43] Romans 5:12-21.

Wherein doth this Article minister comfort unto thee?

In 3 things:
1. His resurrection doeth assure me, that his righteousnesse shall be imputed to me for my perfect justification.
2. It comforteth me because it doth from day to day raise me up to righteousnes & newnesse of life in this present world.
3. It ministreth unto me a comfortable hope that I shall rise againe in the last day from bodily death.

What beleevest thou in this Article, He ascended into heaven?

I beleeve that Christ in his humane nature (the Apostles looking on) ascended into heaven.

What comfort have you thereby?

1. I am comforted in this, that Christ has prepared a place for me in heaven which now I feele by faith, and hereafter shall fully enjoy.
2. I am comforted by his intercession to the father for me.

What fruit have you by his intercession?

1. First, it doeth reconcile me to the Father for those sinnes which I doe daily commit.
2. Secondly, being reconciled in him, I can pray to God with boldnes, and call him Father.[44]

What is the meaning of the Article, He sitteth at the right hand of God the Father?

I beleeve that Christ in mans nature was advanced by the Father unto that high authoritie whereby he ruleth all things in heaven and in earth.

What comfort have you thereby?

1. I am comforted because I shall receive from him all things needfull for me under his gratious government.
2. By his power all my enemies shall be subdued and troden under my feet.

What beleeve you in this Article, From thence he shall come, &c.

I beleeve that Christ shall come in his majestie to pronounce sentence upon all those that were dead before, and upon them that then shall be found alive.

What comfort have you by this?

1. I am comforted in my greatest miserie, knowing that Christ will come one day and rid me out of all.
2. I am sure that hee will give sentence on my side, and take me to glorie with him.

Why say you, I beleeve in God the holy Ghost?

Because he is God equall with the father and the sonne.

---

[44] Galatians 4:6; Matthew 6:9.

Why call you him Holy?

Because he is the authour of all holines.

What fruit have you by this?

1. The holy ghost doth assure me, that I am the child of God by making me to call him *Abba* father.[45]

2. He assureth me by the death & resurrection of Christ, that sinne dieth in me, and I am raised up to holines of life.

3. The holy Ghost leadeth me into all truth needfull to Gods glorie and my salvation.

4. He comforteth me in all my troubles, and in death assureth me of a better life in this same body and soule.

What is the meaning of this Article, I beleeve that there is a Catholike Church?

That God hath a certaine number of his chosen children, which he doth call and gather to himselfe.

Why say you, I beleeve that there is a Catholike Church?

Because that the Church of God cannot be alwaies seene with the eyes of man.

Why call you the Church, Holy?

Because the Church on earth though in it selfe it is sinneful, yet in Christ the head it is holy, and in the life to come shall be brought to perfection of holines.

Why doe you call it Catholike?

Because God in all places & of all sorts of men had from the beginning, hath now, and ever will have a holy Church.

What is the meaning of this article, The communion of Saints?

The whole Church communicateth with Christ and every member one with another.

What comfort have you by this article?

1. I am comforted, because I am justified by that faith where by Adam and Abraham were justified, which is tyed to no time, or place, and excludeth no person.

2. I am comforted, because I am made partaker of Christ & all his mercies by faith, and of all the blessings of the Church by love.

What beleevest thou is this Article, I beleeve the forgivenes of sinnes.

I beleeve that God for Christs sake doth freely forgive me not only all my sinnes, but also the punishment that I have deserved by them.

What say you, I beleeve the forgivenes of sinnes?

Because no reason can perswade me, but the holy Ghost onely must worke the assurance of it in my heart.

---

[45] Galatians 4:6; Matthew 6:9.

What comfort have you hereby?

1. First, I am comforted, because all the sinnes I have and daily commit, shall never be laid to my charge.
2. Secondly, I am comforted, because that the weakenes and wants of all my duties are covered and supplied in Christ.
3. Thirdly, I am comforted, because God will heare me praying for others, that they may have faith to feele the forgivenesse of sinnes.

What beleevest thou in this Article, the resurrection of the bodie unto life everlasting?

I beleeve that this bodie after it shall be dissolved into dust shall be raised up againe at the last day, and my soule shall live in everlasting glorie.

What comfort reape you hereby?

1. I am made comfortable and chearefull in well-doing, seeing my labour shall not be in vaine.
2. I am made to despise the pleasures and glory of this world, and with patience to suffer all troubles that are laid upon me in this present life.
3. It comforteth me over the death of my dearest friendes, & maketh me chearefull in death, knowing that I shall have a part in the resurrection of the just.

What fruit have you when you beleeve all these Articles?

All do come to this end, that being justified by faith, I am righteous in Christ before God.

What be the severall fruits?

1. First, I am at peace with God, although in my selfe for my outward sinnes which I daily commit, and my inwarde corruption which remaineth, I am accused.
2. I get strength to fight against my outward sinnes, to subdue my corruption, to doe outward good workes, and to delight in the law of God in the inward man.
3. I have a right to all Gods creatures, so that the use & want of them shall turne to the furtherance of my salvation.
4. I am assured of the glorification of my soule and bodie in the heavens, because I am made an heire of everlasting life.

Why is this given wholly and onely unto faith?

Not because faith doth deserve it, but because the merits of Christ can be laid hold on and applied to my selfe by none other meanes but by faith alone.

Can not our good workes in some part justifie us before God?

No: for the righteousnes which is able to stand in the judgement of God must be perfect in all respects.

Are not our good workes perfite?

No: for in many things we sinne all: and againe, the best workes we doe are defiled with sinne, and therefore can deserve nothing at the hands of God.

Why then doth God promise a reward unto them?

The reward that God doth promise, is not for the desert of workes, but of his owne grace and mercie.

Will not his doctrine make men carelesse of well doing?

No: for they that be ingrafted into Christ, must needes bring forth good workes.

Why is it needfull that they should doe good workes?

1. First, that we may by them shew our selves thankefull unto God for all his benefits.
2. That we may be assured of faith & election by good works.
3. That by our good workes we may edifie others.

How maist thou edifie others?

1. First, by encouraging & strengthening those that are good.
2. Secondly, by winning those that are not come unto God.
3. And then by stopping the mouthes of the wicked.
4. The fourth ariseth of the former, and that is the glorie of God, which is advanced by them.

Are good workes so needfull, that without them we cannot be saved?

Yea: for although good workes doe not worke our salvation in any part, yet because they that are justified are also sanctified, they that doe noe good workes declare that they neyther are justified nor sanctified, and therefore cannot be saved.

Then they must much more bee condemned which committe sinne & lie in it?

Yea: for such are not onely pronounced to be accursed by the law, but also the gospell hath denounced that they shall not inherite the kingdome of heaven.[46]

Can everyone doe good workes?

None can doe good workes but they that are borne againe.

How can they that are thus borne againe doe good workes?

They that are thus borne againe, and carrie in them the Image of God, have repentance wrought in them, from whence good workes doe proceed.

What is repentance?

Repentance is a turning of our selves to God, whereby we crucifie and kill the corruption of our nature, and reforme our selves in the inward

---

[46] 1 Corinthians 6:9; Galatians 5:21.

man, according to Gods will.

What is it to crucifie the corruption of our nature?

It is truely and with all my heart to be sorie that I have angerd God with it and with my other sinnes, and everie day more and more to hate it and them, and to flie from them.

How is this sorrow wrought?

It is wrought in me partly by the threatnings of the lawe, and the feare of Gods judgement, but especially encreased by the feeling the fruite of Christ his death, whereby I have power to hate sinne and to leave it.

How is this reformation of our selves wrought in us?

Onely by the promises of the gospell, whereby wee feele the fruit of the rising againe of Christ.

What doth ensue hereof?

Hereby we are raised up into a new life, having the Lawe written in our hearts, and so reforme our selves.

Hereby it appeareth that none can repent of themselves or when they will?

Yea: for it was said before, that it is the gift of God given unto them that are borne againe.

By this it is also evident that Gods children stand in need of repentance, so long as they live?

Yea: for there is none of Gods Saints but alwaies carrying this corruption about them, they sometimes fall and are farre from that perfection of goodnes which the Lorde requireth.

Seeing it was said before that good workes did proceed from repentance, what properties are required of workes?

1. First, that they be such as God hath commanded in his Lawe.
2. Secondly, that they that doe them be such as be ingrafted into Christ and continue in him.

What say you then of the good workes of them that be not in Christ?

They doe no good workes, because they neither are as yet members of Christ, nor doe offer them to God in the name of Christ.

3. The third propertie of workes is, that they may be to glorifie God, and to assure our selves of our salvation.

Is it not lawfull to seeke our owne praise and merit by our owne good workes?

No: for all our good workes are imperfect, and salvation is onely merited by the death of Christ, as was said before.

We have heard that the lawe worketh the knowledge of our sinnes and feeling of our miserie, what meanes hath God ordained to worke faith in us?

He hath ordained
- 1. The Gospel
- 2. Prayer   } to beget and breed it in us.
- 3. Sacraments
- 4. Discipline   } to confirm it in us.
- 5. Affliction

What is the Gospell?

It is that part of Gods word whereby the holy ghost worketh in us a lively faith to apprehend the free remission of sinnes in Jesus Christ.

How many kinds of faith be there?

Two, a
- Generall faith, whereby I beleeve God to be true in all his workes.
- Special, & this is either
  - whereby I beleeve God to be just in his threatnings, & so am made penitent: *or,*
  - whereby I beleeve him to be made merciful in his promises, and so come to repentance.

What difference is there betweene penitence & repentance?

Penitence is a sorrow for sinne wrought by the law: Repentance is a recovering ourselves from sin wrought by the gospell.

Is there such difference betweene the Law and the Gospell?

Yea: for the Law differeth from the Gospell in 4.things.

1. First, the Law revealeth sinne, rebuketh us for it, & leaveth us in it: but the gospell doth reveale unto us remission of sinnes, & freeth us from the punishment belonging thereunto.
2. The law commandeth to do good & giveth no strength: but the gospell inableth us to doe good, the H. ghost writing the law in our hearts, and assuring us of the promise.
3. The law is the ministery of wrath, condemnation & death; but the gospell is the ministery of grace, justification, & life.
4. In many points the law may be conceived by reason; but the gospell in all points is farre above the reason of man.

Wherein doe they agree?

They agree in this, that they be both of God and declare one kind of righteousness, though they differ in offering it unto us?

What is that one kind of righteousnes?

It is the perfect love of God and of our neighbour.

What thing doth follow upon this?

That the severe law pronounceth all the faithfull righteous.

How doth the law pronounce them righteous?

Because that they have in Christ all that the law doth aske.

But yet they remaine transgressours of the law?

They are transgressors in themselves, and yet righteous in Christ, and in their inward man they love righteousnes and hate sinne.

What then is the state of the faithfull in this life?
They are sure in Christ, and yet fight against sinne.
    What battaile have they?

They have battle both { within, the battle of the flesh against the spirit.
and
without, the temptations of { Satan. the world.

    How shall they overcome?
By a lively faith in Jesus Christ.
    What call you the flesh?
The corruption of our nature wherein we were borne and conceived.
    Doth that remaine after regeneration?
Yea: it dwelleth in us and cleaveth fast unto us so long as we carrie the outward flesh about us.
    How doth the flesh fight against the spirit?
By continuall lusting against the spirit.
    How is that?
1. By { hindering or corrupting } us in the good motions, words, and deeds of the spirit.

2. By continuall mooving us to evill { motions. words. deeds.

    What call you the Spirit?
The holie Spirit which god in Christ hath given us, wherby wee are begotten againe.
    Doe we not receive the spirit in full measure and in perfection at the first?
No: but first we receive the first fruits, and afterward daily increase of the same unto the end,[47] if the fault be not in our selves.
    How doth the spirit fight in us?
By lusting against the flesh.
    How doth it lust against the flesh?
1. First, partly by rebuking and partly by restraining in us the evill motions and deeds of the flesh.

2. By continuall inlightning and affecting us with { thoughts words deedes } agreeable to gods will.

    What call you the world?
The corrupt state and condition of men, and of the rest of the creatures.

---

[47] Romans 8:23.

How doth the world fight against us?
By alluring and withdrawing us to the corruptions thereof.
What meanes doth it use?

1. It allureth us by false $\left\{ \begin{array}{l} \text{pleasures} \\ \text{profit \&} \\ \text{glorie} \end{array} \right\}$ of this world from our obedience to god.

2. It allureth us otherwhiles by $\left\{ \begin{array}{l} \text{paines} \\ \text{losses and} \\ \text{reproches} \end{array} \right\}$ to distrust gods promises.

How shall we overcome the pleasures, profite, and glorie of this world?

1. By a true faith in Jesus Christ, who despised all these things to worke our salvation, and to make us overcome them.
2. By faith in gods word that feareth us from[48] doing anything that is against his will.

How shall we overcome the $\left\{ \begin{array}{l} \text{paines} \\ \text{losses, and} \\ \text{reproaches} \end{array} \right\}$ *of this world?*

1. By a lively faith in Jesus Christ who suffered all those things to worke our salvation, and to inable us to suffer them.
2. By a stedfast faith in Gods promises and providence that wee shall want no good thing, and that all things seeming hurtfull shalbe turned to the furtherance of our salvation.

What call you Satan?
The adversarie or enemy of god and his people.

How doth he fight against us?

1. By subtiltie alluring us to sinne, and therefore he is called a Tempter, or Serpent.
2. By laying fearefully to our charge our sinnes committed, and therefore he is called the Devill an accuser.
3. By seeking by manifold inward terrors and outward troubles to swallow us up, and therfore is called, a roaring Lion.[49]

How shall we fight against Satan and his tentations?

1. By faith in Jesus Christ, who overcame all his tentations in his owne person, that so we might overcome in him.
2. By resisting the inward motions & outward occasions of sin.

How shall we doe that?
By beleeving that wee are baptized into the death and resurrection of Christ.

How shall we overcome Sathan and his accusations?

---

[48] That is, makes us afraid of.
[49] 1 Peter 5:8.

1. By faith in Jesus Christ, who hath justified us from all the sinnes for the which he can accuse us.
2. By all those comfortable promises of forgivenes of sinnes which in Christs name are made unto us.

   How shall we overcome him in our terrors and troubles?
1. By faith in Jesus Christ who was heard in all his troubles to give us assurance that we shall not be overcome in them.
2. By faith in gods providence, whereby we know that he can do no more unto us then the Lord doth direct for our good.

   We have heard that the word is the first and chiefe meanes not onely to beget, but also to strengthen & increase faith in us: what is the next principall meanes?

Praier is the next principall meanes serving for the strengthening and encreasing of faith.

   What is Prayer?

It is a lifting up of the mind and a pouring out of the heart before god.

   Is there any prescript rule of praier left us in the Scriptures?

Yea: even the praier which our Saviour Christ taught his disciples, called The Lordspraier.[50]

   Is it lawfull to use no other forme of words?

We may use an other forme of wordes, but we must pray for the same things and with like affection that is prescribed in that praier.

   How is that praier devided?

It is devided into the $\left\{\begin{array}{l}\text{Preface, or entrance to the praier.}\\\text{Praier it selfe.}\\\text{Conclusion, or shutting up of the praier.}\end{array}\right.$

   Which is the Preface?

Our Father which art in heaven.

   What doth the Preface put us in mind of?

1. First, of him to whome we pray.
2. Secondly, of our owne estate in praier.

   To whome doe we pray?

Onely to God the $\left\{\begin{array}{l}\text{Father.}\\\text{Sonne.}\\\text{Holy ghost.}\end{array}\right.$

   Why doe you here name the Father?

Because discerning the persons, wee pray to the Father secretly understanding it, that we doe it in the mediation of the Sonne, by the working of the holy ghost.

   Why must we pray to the Father in the mediation of Christ his Sonne?

---

[50] Matthew 6:9-13.

Because god beeing displeased for sinne, wee can have no dealing with him, but only by the meanes of his sonne, in whome he is well pleased.[51]

Why is it required that we pray by the working of the H. ghost?

Because the Holy ghost assureth us that he is our father; and whereas we know not what to pray, nor how to pray, the holy ghost doth teach us both.[52]

What must we be perswaded of, and how must we be affected in prayer?

Partly concerning —

ourselves

1. we must be truly humbled, which is wrought in us two wayes:
 1. with a perswasion of our sinfull miserie and unworthiness to be helped.
 2. with a certaine persuasion of the glorious majesty of God in heaven that must helpe us.

2. wee must have a certaine confidence we shal be heard, and this is wrought in us.
 1. by faith, being perswaded that God loveth us as his own children in our Lord Jesus Christ.
 2. by faith, being perswaded that our father being God, he is able to doe whatsoever hee will in heaven and in earth.

others

1. That all Gods people pray for us.
2. We must be perswaded, that it is our bounden duty to pray for others as well as for our selves.

How are the petitions divided?

Into two partes; for
1. wee make request for those things that concerne Gods majestie.
2. For those things that concerne our own welfare.

Which be those that concerne Gods majestie?

The 3. first
1. hallowed be thy name.
2. thy kingdom come.
3. thy will be done in earth as it is in heaven.

---

[51] Luke 3:22.
[52] Romans 8:26.

What is meant by the names of God?

1. The names and titles of God, as *Jehova, the Lord of hostes,* and such like.

2. The
$$\left\{ \begin{array}{l} \text{1. wisdome} \\ \text{2. power} \\ \text{3. mercie} \end{array} \right. \left. \begin{array}{l} \text{4. goodnes} \\ \text{5. truth} \\ \text{6. righteousnes} \\ \text{7. eternitie} \end{array} \right\} \text{of God.}$$

Why be these called the names of God?

Because as names serve to discerne things by, so God is knowne to be God by these things.

What is meant by the word Hallowed?

We pray, that as God is glorious in himselfe, so he may be declared and made knowen unto men.

How shall Gods name be declared to be holy and glorious?

1. First, we pray that his wisdome, power, goodnes, mercie, truth, righteousnes, and eternitie, may more and more be imparted unto us and other of Gods people.

2. Secondly, we pray, that according as we know these things, so the fruits of them may appeare in ours and all Gods people lives, that so Gods name may be honoured & praised.

What doe we pray against in this petition?

1. First, wee pray against all ignorance of holy things wee should knowe, and want of good workes, whereby God wants of his glorie.

2. We pray against all false religion, wickednes, and ungodlines, whereby Gods name is dishonoured.

FINIS.

A large Treatise of the Sabboth

IT is written, Exod.20.8. *Remember the Sabboth day to keepe it holie, &c.* Dearely beloved in the Lord, there is no commandement of Gods part more urged, and of our parts lesse observed, than this one of the Sabboth: wherefore with zeale to Gods glorie, and love unfained unto your selves, I have indevoured in that measure and maner that God hath inabled me to intreate of this argument. The necessarie use whereof we shal more plainly perceive, if we doe wisely consider either the lamentable inconveniences which accompanie the want of the pure understanding thereof: or the manifold commodities, which ensue the right embracing of the same. The inconveniences are partly to bee observed in the wicked, and partly to be noted in the children of God. In the wicked who either are seduced by false doctrine, or else which are carelesse of true doctrine. They that are deceived by false religion, bee either Papists on the one side, the Families of love[1] with such like heretikes on the other side: whereof the one, that is the Papists, make the Sabboth day but an ordinance, and ceremonie of the Church, and therefore observe it, but as a thing taken up and reteined by the Church of Rome: as also they doe many other holy daies in the yeere. The other seeing no further into it, then as it is an ordinance and ceremonie, and thinking it to containe nothing morall, crie out against it, as willing to have it wholly abrogated, seeing all ceremonies have had their end in Christ: alleadging, though nothing to the purpose, that God is a spirit, and will bee worshipped in spirit and in trueth: and therefore the observation of a day is nothing availeable to his worship. Againe, what credit it hath in them that are carelesse of religion, all men may see. Tush (say these men) the Sabboth is too Jewish and full of superstition: and therefore unto them it is all one with other common holie daies, saving that peradventure they had rather have it, then want it; not for any love of religion, but for easing of their flesh, and the more in glutting themselves with carnall pleasure: by means whereof they make it a day of the world, not a day of the Church; a time rather dedicated to the pampering of the flesh, then sincerely consecrated to the building up of the soule and spirit. In the children of God otherwise well instructed, have also risen many scruples concerning this matter, how it is ceremonious, and how it is not: which kinde of men keepe the Sabboth not as grosse heretikes, and yet not as carefull observers, by reason that

---

[1] For Greenham's conflation of Papists and Familists, see above, pp. 18-19.

they are not thoroughly taught in it, nor fully perswaded of it. Wherefore wee may see how needfull this doctrine is, yea although we had no care of them, that are not in the Church, yet in respect of them of whom we have most care, being in the Church of God with us. And this necessitie we shall also observe, if in trueth wee marke the several commodities, which proceede from the right understanding hereof. For seeing the Sabboth day is the schoole day, the faire day, the market day, the feeding day of the soule, when men purely knowing the use of it, separare it wholly from other daies, they shall see how they may recover themselves from sinnes already past, arme themselves against sin to come, grow in knowledge, increase in faith, and how much they shall bee strengthened in the inner man. Wherefore in the booke of God, when the Lorde will urge the observation of the whole law, hee often doth it under this one word of *keeping the Sabboth*.[2] Againe, when the Prophets sharply rebuke the people for their sinnes, they particularly lay before them, how the Sabboths of the Lord are broken.[3] And to speake the trueth, how can a man lie long in the liking of sinne, who embraceth this doctrine in conscience, who willingly would have his sinnes discovered, his conscience unripped, the judgements of God against his sinnes threatned, wherby he might come to a loathing, and grow to a further misliking of his sinnes daily? Sure it is indeede, that as in other thinges, so in this the ceremoniall use little availeth. Howbeit, if for the ceremoniall use of the Sabboth, because many so use it, therefore wee should leave it, wee might as well by the same reason put out of the doores of the Church the administration of the Sacraments, the making of prayer, the preaching of the word, because the most part of men use these things for a fashion: neither is it the question which we have in hand, what men doe, but what they ought to doe in the observation of the Sabboth. In the setting downe whereof, this order doth offer it selfe to be observed: first to speake of the commandements it selfe, and then of the reasons thereof. The commaundement as we see, is delivered both affirmatively and negatively, whereas all other the commandements are but either affirmatively, or negatively expressed: so that where it is said, *the Sabboth day keepe holy*, the holie use of the Sabboth is flatly and streightly urged: where it is added, *in it thou shalt not doe any worke*, the irreligious breach of the same is plainly restrained.[4] The reasons be in number foure. The first is included in the worde *remember*, and is drawne from the ende, which is thus much in effect; Wilt thou worship me purely, and love thy neighbour unfeinedly? then observe this one thing, which I have therefore placed indifferently betweene those commandements which

---

[2] For example, Exodus 20:8.

[3] Isaiah 58:13-14; Jeremiah 17:21-3.

[4] Exodus 20:8-11.

concerne mine owne honour, and the comfort of thy brethren. The second reason is derived from the authoritie of the law-giver, whereby the Lorde urgeth our obedience, and is expressed in these wordes, *the seventh day is the Sabboth of the Lord thy God*. The third is inferred of the equitie of this law: wherein the Lord dealeth with men as it were by conference, and disputeth by plaine reason, that justly we cannot deny him the seventh for his owne glorie, who hath not denied us sixe daies to travaile in our owne affares. And this is gathered when he saith, *sixe daies shalt thou labour and doe all thy worke: but the seventh day, &c.* The fourth and last reason is borrowed from proportion of the Lords owne example, that as in sixe daies he made all things, and in the seventh ceased from creating, though not from preserving them:[5] so in sixe daies wee may have a naturall use of the creatures of God, but on the seventh day wee ought to have a spirituall use of them. Under these may be touched another reason derived from the time, wherein the Lord first commaunded the Sabboth, which was in mans innocencie: so that if before transgression it was an effectuall meanes to keepe out sinne, then after mans fall it must needes bee of force to withstand sinne. It may seeme the best way to some, first to intreate of the commandement it selfe, and then of the reasons. Howbeit, because the Lord his wisedome sometime prefixeth the reason, as in the first commandement, and seeing it is a thing of small effect to urge the use to them who are not grounded on the doctrine, and it is hard to overmatch the affection untill judgement be convinced: wee will first arme the matter with reasons, and then shew both how this law is kept, and how it is broken. This order is commended unto us by the holy Ghost, 2.Tim.2.16. and for want of this order, many excellent Sermons have little effect: and where judgement, by the trueth is not convinced, their many exhortations fall to the ground: for which cause also the holy use of the Sabboth so little prevaileth with many, in that they are not grounded with judgement in the true knowledge of the same.

But before wee come to the particular discourse of the reasons, generally let us consider why this commaundement is in words larger, in reasons fuller then any other commandement. If wee take a view of the whole law, we may observe how the Lord hath set downe sixe precepts in many words, and foure nakedly in bare wordes, as the 6. the 7. the 8. and the 9. why then are the first five commandements so apparelled with reasons, and the last so dilated by a speciall amplification: the other foure being so briefe and so naked? Certainly the Lorde and law-giver foresaw, that unto these men would easily bee brought to yeeld: and wee see how the very Heathen have freely granted them, the Philosophers

---

[5] Genesis 2:2–3.

have fruitfully written of them, all civill righteous men doe earnestly maintaine them: and to bee briefe, common honestie counteth him no man that wil murther, he is thought beastlike that defileth his bodie, outward civilitie condemneth a theefe, and the common sort of men mislike a backbiter and slanderer. Againe, he knew in his eternall wisedome, how they would neither in reason so soone be admitted, nor in affection so easily embraced: and therefore to meete with the subtiltie of mans nature, and corruption of mans heart, they are set downe more pearcingly. This wee shall see in the first and last commandements of the second table. In the first, when the Lord had commanded honour to be given to parents, he enforceth his commandement with annexing a promise of long life, and why even judgement herein is much corrupted. For many there are who granting the inconveniencie and vilenes of murther, adulterie, and false witnesse bearing, yet deny the necessitie and the excellencie of Magistracie. Yea, and albeit in judgement many men yeeld to the reason therof: yet is not the equitie thereof so soone in affection embraced: for experience of all ages proveth, that the corrupt nature of man is most hardly brought to bee subject, and these last miserable daies can witnesse the same more especially, wherein men are growne to bee without naturall affection. Not without cause therefore is this precept fenced with reason.

In the last (where God laieth a more precise rule and straighter charge to the conscience of man, then flesh and blood would willingly beare, because men thinke it some rigorous dealing to have their least affections arraigned, and their secret thoughts condemned, as willing to have their thoughts not to be called into any court, to hold up their hand at the barre of judgement) he is constrained as it were by particular branches and severall articles to set downe the law, that wee might not finde some starting holes to creepe out at, and so wring our selves out of the precincts of the same. Yet more evidently doth this appeare in all the commaundements of the first table, because they are more contrarie to the judgement of man meerly naturall, although he be otherwise never so wise, and the word of trueth must only trie them: for in the first commandement, the reason is prefixed; in the second, third, and fourth commaundements, the reasons are annexed. But here may arise this quesiton, to wit, why the second and fourth precepts, are so amplified in words, and strengthened with more reasons, then any of the other? Surely herein the Lord declareth, how he plainly foresaw, how among the rest these two commaundements would finde least intertainment, and most be refused. But what shall we say of the Papists, Familists, and Heretikes among us in these daies: and of other men also otherwise of sound judgement, which affirme that as well the second as the first commandement is ceremoniall: whereof the one would bring into the church Images, the other prophanenes. Wherefore the Lorde in his wisedome foreseeing these cavilling wits, preventeth their purposes: so that if either they yeeld not, or make resistance to the trueth so manifest, they oppose themselves to the knowne and open trueth, and so make themselves the more inexcusable. We see to acknowledge, that there is a God, to honour father and mother, to abstaine from blood, not to defile our flesh, not wrongfully to oppresse, not to bee a notorious slaunderer; every Papist and naturall man guided but by the light of reason, will easily grant. For the wonderfull order of the heavens, the continuall course of the Sunne, Moone and Starres, the outgoings of the mornings and evenings declare there is a God. Reason perswadeth how the things in the world must needes bee governed, and that wee owe love unto him by whom they be guided. Nature teacheth that mens lives must be maintained: common civilitie abhorreth adulterie, oppression and backbiting. But if ye aske how this God is to bee worshipped, and what times we must sanctifie to that use: wee shall see how many countries, so many religions; how many men, so many devises. Thus wee see how necessarie it was that the Lorde should provide for his owne glorie, and captivate al mans inventions, seeing all these commaundements doe most fight against the reason of man, and by reason have most been oppugned. So in the pure observing of these, consisteth the sincere keeping of the rest of them. For how shall we know how to walke in pure worship with an upright heart before the Lord? how shall wee give him the honour due unto his glorious name? how shall we be instructed rightly, and reverently to deale with the dignitie of our brethren, faithfully with their lives, purely with their bodies, righteously with their goods, or tenderly with their credit: but by those waies and rules which the Lorde hath prescribed in his word? and when should we learne those rules, but as such times as he himselfe hath appoynted and sanctified for that purpose? Againe, where these two commaundements are not rightly understood, there true religion goeth to wracke. For admit that we should not carefully follow the word of God, how many religions would then start up? Let this bee granted, that every man should have what day he would for the worship of God, and then see how many daies men would bestow on the Lord.

But let us come to the reasons, whereof the first is drawne from the end of the law, and is partly signified by this word *remember*, and partly by this word *sanctifie*, *Remember the Sabboth day to keepe it holie*. For this word *remember*, which is here prefixed, is set downe this word *observe*, in Deuteronomie:[6] wherein wee are forewarned to watch the more diligently, and attend more carefully upon this commandement. In

---

[6] Deuteronomy 5:12-15.

which poynt wee may observe, that whereas all other commaundements
are simply set downe and directly propounded, this alone hath a preface
prefixed, which is thus much in effect. Wilt though learne sincerely to
worship me according to that substance, manner and end, which I have
prescribed? and wilt thou truly trie thy love to me, by exercising the
duties of love to thy brethren? then forget not to keepe holie the Sabboth,
wherein I shall teach thee both how thou shalt walke uprightly in the
worship due unto me, and also live obediently in duties concerning man.
Againe, the nature of the word importeth thus much, that this law was
not onely graven in the hearts of our forefathers, as were all the other:
but also in expresse words injoyned unto Adam and Eve in paradise, and
manifestly practiced of the Israelites in the wildernesse, Exodus 16. and
that therefore in this common promulgating of the law, they should
especially remember this, which is not newly given, as are the rest, but
rather renued as being given out before. True it is, that before this
solemne publishing of the law in mount Sinai, this, and all the other the
commaundements were written in the harts of our forefathers, as we may
see in the booke of Genesis. For the first we reade how the Lord said
unto Abraham, Gen.17. *I am God all sufficient,* walke before me, and be
upright.[7] Concerning the second, Gen.31.19. Rachel is said to steale her
fathers idols. Gen.35.2. Jacob reformeth his household, and cleanseth it
from idolatrie. For the third, wee may see how religious they were in
swearing.[8] Concerning the fift, what authoritie exercised Jacob towards
his children? what duties yeelded they to him both in life and death?[9]
How they hated murther, it is manifest in that historie.[10] Both Josephs
continencie, and the punishment threatned to Abimelech declare, how
hainous a thing adulterie was unto them.[11] Concerning theft, Laban his
quarelling with Jacob,[12] and Joseph his accusing of the brethren,[13] do
shew that it was a thing unlawfull. Lastly, Abimelech the king
reprehendeth both Abraham, Genes.20. and Isaac, Genes.26. for bearing
false witnes in denying their wives.[14] Thus we see what efficacie is
couched in this preface, in that it sheweth both by the precept, and
practise given and yeelded of our first fathers, how this commandement
alone, was given in expresse words: as also that this one precept is the
schoole of all the other commaundements. But to what end? to keepe it

---

[7] Genesis 17:1.

[8] Genesis 21:22–31; 26:28–31; 31:43–54; 47:29–31.

[9] Genesis 42:1–4; 49:1–33.

[10] Joseph's brothers were tempted to kill him, but did not: Genesis 37:19–22.

[11] Genesis 39:6–20; 20:1–18.

[12] Genesis 30:25–31:2.

[13] Genesis 44:1–17.

[14] Genesis 20:9–10; 26:9–10.

as ceremoniall? No, to sanctifie it as morall, for the end of the Sabboth consisteth in these two things: first in the moral: secondly, in the figurative, ceremonial, or shadowish observation of it: as wee take the shadow here for a figure, because a ceremonie is more then a shadow. That I call morall, which doth informe mans manners either concerning their religion to God, or their duties unto man: that I meane figurative, which is added for a time in some respect to some persons for an helpe to that which is morall, as Deut.5.15. *Remember that thou wast a servant in the land of Egypt.* Howbeit, that this first morall end is here understood, the first words declare, where it is said, *sanctifie the Sabboth day.* For where mention is made of the ceremonie, it is said to keepe, and not sanctifie the Sabboth. Now what is it to sanctifie the Sabboth day, but to put it apart from all other daies for a peculiar use of Gods worship: for otherwise wee must know, that all other daies are sanctified: so that to sanctifie, it is to do that thing on the Sabboth for which it was commanded: but of this wee shall speake more largely by the grace of God in the last reason. In the meane time let us briefly observe this, that as our first parents did sanctifie the Sabboth in viewing the creatures of God, for to praise him: so wee sanctifie it in using the meanes, which he hath appointed for his worship. So that first we using the exercises of religion, whereby we may bee sanctified, and then joyne with them the spirituall use of the creatures, whereby we may bee furthered in our sanctification, should after use the exercises of love, wherby we may shew that we are sanctified. Our first fathers needed not ordinarily the ministrie of the word: but had the great bookes of Gods works. We have neede of the word both publike and private, and therefore must learne it, that having learned it, we might the better exercise the duties of love: so then, that which was first to Adam, is now the last to us, to wit, the beholding of God in his creatures, and the praising of him for the same. In the Psalme 92. which was appoynted to bee sung of the Church on the Sabboth, is set downe as the chiefest use thereof, the singing of Gods mercie, the shewing of his righteous judgements, in rewarding the godlie, though afflicted, in punishing the ungodly, though here they bee advanced, as also in learning to know God in his worship and in his workes. Againe, Psal.95. wee shall not see any ceremoniall use of the Sabboth: but that it should be used in praying to God, in praising of God, and hearing of his word. This is confirmed, Exod.31.13. *Speake unto the children of Israel, and say, Notwithstanding keepe ye my Sabboths: for it is a signe betweene me and you in your generation, that ye may know, that I the Lord do sanctifie you.* As also Deut.5.12. *Keepe the Sabboth day to sanctifie it, as the Lord thy God hath commanded thee.* And Ezechiel 20.12. *I gave them my Sabboths to be a signe betweene me and them, that they might know, that I am the Lord that sanctifie them.* In which places, as the reason is adjoyned of keeping the Sabboth: so wee must understand, that where it is called a signe; it is meant a document, and not a figure (for every figure is a signe, but every signe is not a figure, as we may see in the Sacraments) which are not figures or shadowes of things to come: so that, in that the Lorde saith, *my Sabboth is a signe betweene me and you,*[15] it is as much in effect, as if he should say: my Sabboth is a common instruction betweene you and me; of me as the Creator, Redeemer, and Sanctifier; of you as created, redeemed, and sanctified: so that the Sabboth is a document and pledge of Gods will, whereby we should know, what he is unto us, and wherein wee should learne what we should doe to him. In which respect this commandement is no more ceremoniall, then the first, where the Lord propoundeth what he is to us, and secretly includeth what we should bee to him. No marveile then though this bee the principall end, which was not begun to the Jewes, but first injoyned to Adam and Eve. Wherefore wee may thus reason both safely and soundly: Whatsoever is the first end, is the chiefest end: but to sanctifie the Sabboth is the first end, because it was ordained so to Adam in time of his innocencie, at what time it could not be a figure, because by the judgement of all sound learned, whereof I have read some, there were no figures untill sinne came into the world, from which our parents were yet free: but a meane to keep them in innocencie, in that notwithstanding their excellent creation they were subject to falling: therefore this end must bee the chiefest. This was not onely given to the posteritie of Abraham, but to the whole posteritie of Adam: and therefore it was not proper to the Jewes, being first begun in paradise, and then afterward renewed in Mount Sinai. So that this morall end was the first ende, and common ende: and although as the Jewes had a more speciall cause of worshipping God, in that they had received a more peculiar deliverance, when they could have no rest in Egypt, they on this day did remember their rest: yet neverthelesse this was not the end, but rather a reason why they did keepe the Sabboth: as wee may see also Exod.23.12. where the Lorde commaundeth the seventh day to rest, adding as a reason, not as an end *that thine oxe, and thine asse may rest, and the sonne of thy maide and the stranger may bee refreshed.* Where this sparing of the beasts is added as a reason drawne from that humanity, which is in the law, not as a thing for this speciall end in this precept commanded, which is proper rather to the sixt commandement, and but accessarie unto this. For which cause this ceremonie being but accessarie, cannot take away the principall, and being the latter, it cannot take away the former. It is no good reason, that the accessarie being taken away, the principall

---

[15] Exodus 31:13.

should also be abrogated: but rather on the contrarie, the accessarie removed, the principall may remaine, the more peculiar appertinance being past, the more generall substance may continue: and though the latter be disanulled, the former may bee unabolished. Wherefore though the ceremoniall end, which was but an accessarie, and added afterward as a thing peculiar to the Jewes, is gone with them, to whom this law was made: yet the morall end, which was the principall, and first given out as a thing generall to all, appertaineth still unto us. Lastly, whatsoever severeth either God from man, or man from man, the same is abrogated: the law morall, which is free from all ceremonies, and through Christ requireth nothing but a sincere, though not a perfect obedience, as being voide of all rigour, and exempted from the curse, therefore the law morall is not abrogated. For nothing is disanulled, but the rigour and curse of the law, which made a divorcement between God and man and the ceremonie of the law, which made a separation betweene man and man, that is, betweene the Jew and the Gentile, as we may gather, Coloss.2. and Galat.4.[16] Wherefore we affirme, that as it was peculiar to the Jewes as concerning their deliverance, that Sabboth is ceased: but as it is common to us with them, and all others to bee preserved in the meanes of true worship, the Sabboth is to be observed: so that not the doctrine and sincere obedience of the Sabboth, but the curse of the law, and rigorous keeping of the Sabboth is abrogated. When one thing hath divers ends, if one thing be removed, the other may remaine. For as the Sacraments in the time of the law had two ends: the one to foreshew that Christ should come, the other to assure them what they should have in Christ when he came: and in that they did foreshew Christ to come, they are gone, as they assured us what we have in Christ, they remaine still with us. And as for one example wee may see in the Sacrament of Circumcision two ends; the one a signe of the circumcision of the flesh, which is now ceased; the other a seale of repentance and faith: and so it is unto us remaining a token of imitation, though not in the same manner of administration that is in circumcision, yet in the same matter of that effect, to wit, in Baptisme: so likewise the Sabboth having two ends, the one morall, the other ceremoniall: as it was ceremoniall and was given to the Jewes, as they were Jewes, it was proper to the Jewes: but as it was morall, not given to the Jewes alone, but to our first fathers before the Jewes, and to the Gentiles after the Jewes, it remaineth no lesse to all men, after the Jewes ceased to be a peculiar people, then the comming together to one place doth yet appertaine unto us. For although in that the Jewes came together to one place, as it represented the Church of God, it is taken away, because God is present with us in all places: yet as

---

[16] Colossians 2:13-15; Galatians 4:1-7, 21-8.

they had it to establish them in their worship, and we need as necessary helps for religion as ever they needed, the same remaineth with us. Now, if the Sabboth were but a signe of spirituall rest, as some have phantastically thought, and not rather an holie schoole to teach us the worship of God, we would grant it ceremoniall: but seeing this is according to the first institution, and that ceremony but in time and for a time was added unto it, though wee have not their day, yet wee have a resting day, as though we have not their seales, yet we have seales, and though the accessarie be gone and ended with them, yet the principall continueth to us, and remaineth after them. Wherefore we conclude this first reason, that as the Sabboth is morall, we must keepe it in trueth, though in weakenes, knowing that the rigour of the law being gone with the curse and ceremonie, we have a promise to have our weakenes and defects herein forgiven us in Christ, as we have in all other things.

Now let us come to the second reason, drawne (as wee have shewed) from the equitie of the lawe, and contained in these words: *Sixe daies shalt thou labour, and doe all thy worke: but the seventh day, &c.*[17] This appeareth to bee no hard law, nor burthensome, but easie, and such a one as all may yeeld unto it. For seeing the Lord hath given us six daies for our calling, then let us not thinke it strange or streight, that hee hath reserved and taken up the seventh day to himselfe: who, if he had commanded one day to worke, and another to be bestowed in his worship, for the glorious profession of his name, might justly have challenged it. This reason then is such, that for justice and equitie cannot but provoke our obedience, and more forcibly chargeth us, if we bee disobedient. This kinde of argument is usuall in the booke of God, as Genes.3.2.3.[18] where our mother Eve frameth this reason to the Serpent very well, had she stood to it: *We eate of the fruit of the trees of the garden: but of the fruite of the tree, which is in the middest of the garden, God hath said, Ye shall not eate of it, &c.* Wherein as she commendeth the mercie of God in giving them so largely the use of all the trees, excepted onely one: so from the law of equitie she exaggerateth their sinne, if having so bountifull an use of many trees lawfull, they should eate of the one tree that was forbidden. The same reason alleadgeth Joseph to restraine his mistresse of her lewd and lothsome purpose, Genesis 39.8.9.[19] *Behold, saith he, my master knoweth not what he hath in the house with me, but hath committed all that he hath to mine hand. There is no man greater in his house then I: neither hath he kept any thing in his house, but only thee because thou art his wife: how then can*

---

[17] Exodus 20:9-10; Deuteronomy 5:13-14.
[18] That is, Genesis 3:2-3.
[19] That is, Genesis 39:8-9.

I doe this great wickednesse, &c. In which place as he on the one side commendeth his masters liberalitie: so on the other side he sheweth how his sinne should even by the rule of justice bee more hainous and horrible, if not contenting himselfe with his masters curtesie, he should intrude himselfe into his own possession. Againe, from hence Job reproveth his wife, and sheweth her blasphemie, Job.5.10. *Thou speakest (said Job) like a foolish woman: what? shall we receive good at the hand of God, and not receive evill?* Thus by the square of righteousnes the man of God proveth her offence to bee the greater, in that having received so many blessings, she could not away once to taste of the crosse. Out of the mouthes of these two or three witnesses we may gather how hainous an evill it is, that not contenting our selves with the large measure of six daies travaile, wee should bee so bold, as to invade the Lorde his seventh day reserved for himselfe.

Thus we see how the Lord granteth us six daies for our bodies, and the seventh day for our soules: not that we must thinke, that other daies are to be separated from this use, but that this day must bee wholly severed from other for that use. For if it were possible, or could bee convenient either in respect of our calling, or the places where we dwell, twice to meete every weeke day, as it is yet used, though more of custome and fashion, then in faith and of conscience in most places, it were nothing but equall. For looke what proportion is from six daies to the seventh, the same may be gathered from nine, or rather twelve houres to the tenth: whereby the tithe at the least may bee affoorded for the Lorde. And herein is the onely difference betweene the six dayes and the seventh, that the worship of God must in the six dayes bee used at such seasons, as in wisedome are so separated and divided to that ende, without any hinderance of our lawfull and necessarie callings, as it doth not take up the principall, but shreds and overplus of our vocation: but on the seventh day we must make such a separation from other dayes, that what wee did but in part, or the weeke, or working dayes, we may doe in whole on the seventh and Sabboth daye. True it is, that this equitie of twice meeting every day, is more convenient for Cities and populous townes, where many dwell together, then in other places and situations, which for distance off, have not the congregation so dwelling together.

Here our common distinction of calling the weeke dayes working dayes, and the Sabboth dayes holie dayes, taketh away their frivolous assertion, who thinke that every day should bee our Sabboth daye, as though wee should confound and shuffle together our working dayes and resting dayes.

Now if the permission of the six-dayes appertaine to us, is not the sanctifying of the Sabboth daye also commaunded to us? And if those thinges bee permitted us, which concerne our calling; are not much more those thinges commaunded, which respect our sanctification? Wherefore if any say, the commaundement is ceremoniall, may not the same say the permission is ceremoniall? For who so affirmeth the one, may affirme the other: but both falsely. If we should admit these daies were to be restrained in some respects, and for some speciall causes, wee affirme this restraining must bee for a time, but not continuall: and that when the reasons of the exceptions should cease, then the exceptions themselves should cease also. But some will say: What will you not allow some day of rest for humbling and fasting, or allowing some daies for humbling? will you not allow one also for thanksgiving and rejoycing? To this I answer, that concerning fasting when there is a speciall neede of a day appoynted, this is no commandement of man, or of the Church, but of God himselfe, who as he hath laid upon us the neede of the remedie: so hath he also commanded us to use the remedie. And as for the day of rejoycing, I thinke it may bee put on the Sabboth, which we make our daies of thanksgiving. For as the Jewes used the Sabboth as a day to remember with thanksgiving their creation: so we may use that day for a thankfull remembrance of our redemption, because in it we may meditate of all those benefits, which our Saviour Christ by his nativitie, circumcision, passion, resurrection and ascension, hath purchased for us. But if any man obiect, that this is too niggardly and sparingly, because as God is extraordinarie in mercie, so we should bee extraordinarie in thanksgiving. I graunt that Christian Magistrates may for necessarie occasion, in wisedome of the spirit, alter the times, and appoynt some seasons for that purpose: so it bee done for awhile, and continue not as perpetuall: for in sixe daies, as we taught before, wee must chiefly labour in our callings, and bestow some part of times in God his worship: and on the Sabboth day wee must chiefly waite on God his worship, and bestow no time on other things but upon necessitie, because we are no lesse charged on the Sabboth to worship God, then we are permitted on the other day to follow our ordinarie callings.

Now let us proceede to the third reason, taken from the law-giver, or author of the commandements. For it thus followeth, Exod.20.vers.6. *But the seventh day is the Sabboth of the Lord thy God, &c.* This argument we know to be used severally in the three precepts going before. In the first it goeth before the commandement: in the second it commeth after: in the third it is more neerely adjoyned. And here it is called *the Lords Sabboth*: which proveth that therefore it must bee wholly spent upon the Lorde. Now were it ceremoniall, then it should followe that there were but nine commandements, seeing (Deut.4.13.) Moses affirmeth, that the covenant which the Lord commanded his people to doe, were tenne commandements: where we see, that not the Church, but the word of God setteth downe this computation. And albeit the ceremonies be also the commandements of the Lord, neverthelesse wee must wisely distinguish betweene the one and the other. The commaundements were immediatly given out by the Lord himselfe, the ceremonies were given immediatly to Moses from the Lord: but immediatly from God to his people by the ministrie of Moses. For it is said, Deut.5.22. *These words the Lord spake unto all your multitude in the mount out of the middest of the fire, the clowdes, and the darknes with a great voyce, and added no more thereto.* In which place the man of God speaketh of the tenne commandements, which a little before he had repeated, as they were published, generally to all by the Lord himselfe, which therefore are perpetuall to all people, nations and languages, not only to the Jewes, but also to the Gentiles. The ceremonies, as we know, were not universall, but beginning with the Jewes they ended with them: neither were they perpetuall, but in Christ his comming were abrogated. This difference is yet more plainly set downe, Deut.4.13.14.[20] *Then the Lord declared unto you his covenant, which he commaunded you to doe, even the tenne commandements, and wrote them upon two tables of stone. And the Lord commanded me the same time, that I should teach you ordinances and lawes, which ye should observe in the land, whither ye goe to possesse it.* Where Moses maketh a flat difference of those lawes, which God gave in his owne person, and them which were given by his ministrie. By this word *ordinances*, which is in this verse, are signified, as some affirme, those lawes, whereby the Jewes did differ from other people. Thus we see how Moses was the minister of the ceremoniall law, which was given but unto some, and lasted but for a season: but the morall law, which appertaineth to all men, and it is in vertue forever, the Lord himself did give it forth. Now as we answer the Papists in defending against them the second precept as morall, and not ceremoniall: so we likewise stand against them in this. For looke what straying and unstaied minds were in the Jewes concerning the worship of God, the same also is in us by nature: and what helpes soever they needed therein, either to bee put in minde of their creation, or to the viewing of God his workes, or sacrificing to the Lord, the same are as needfull for us to helpe us in our sacrifices: for wee neede a perfect rule as well as the Jewes, to preserve us from idolatrie and heresie. Againe, seeing wee have as great neede of a solemne time for these things, werein wee may give our selves wholly to hearing, praying, and receiving of the Sacraments, as they had for their worship: wee are subiect to as great distractions of minde in our callings, as they were, and being with them of a finite nature, can no more then they doe infinite things. It is as requisit for us as for them to have a law,

---

[20] That is, Deuteronomy 4:13–14.

as well for the time, as for the manner of worship: wherein laying aside our ordinarie workes, wee should chiefly and principally wholly give our selves to those exercises of religion, and duties of love, which only in part wee did before, and so more freely espie our sinnes past, eschue our sinnes present, and strengthen ourselves against the sinnes to come. Wherefore to shut up this argument, we affirme against the wicked heretikes of our time, that so long as we stand in neede of corporall meanes, as meate, drinke, apparell, and sleepe, for the continuing of our corporall estate: so long we shall also neede the spirituall meanes, as the word, the Sacraments and prayer for the continuing of our soules. And as it is not ceremonial for these considerations to use these means: so it is morall to have a time commanded and observed, wherein these things should be practised.

It remaineth to speake of the fourth and last reason, drawne from the proportion of God his owne example, as may appeare in these words, Exod.20.11. *For in sixe daies the Lord made the heaven and the earth, the sea and all that in them is, and rested the seventh day: therefore the Lord blessed the Sabboth day and hallowed it.* Wherein we have thus much in effect, as the Lord made the creatures in sixe daies: so wee in sixe should have a naturall use of them. And as he sanctified, that is, put a part the seventh day to his owne worship, and blessed it with a peculiar blessing given to his worship appointed: so we also setting this day apart from the ordinarie workes of our calling, should wholly and only consecrate it to the worship of God. So that as God made all things in sixe daies: so wee may use them sixe daies, as Adam did in the garden: and as the Lorde rested from his workes of creation, though not from his worke of providence and administration; so must we set apart this day, to looke for a speciall blessing and speciall benediction of God his worship, because of his own promise and institution. Why did the Lord this to our first father? he beheld the workes of every day, and blessed every day? We must note, that he gave a speciall blessing above the other daies, unto this day. Now therefore admit that a man should grant this much to our heretike, that we should bee as perfect as Adam in his innocencie: (which is a manifest heresie) yet they must grant, that we stood in need of the word and Sacraments, the use wherein they doe deny, seeing Adam had need of the use of these things, being yet without sinne. Wee therefore oppose thus much unto them, that so long as they will acknowledge a neede of corporall helpes, by calling for meate, sleepe, and apparell: so long their soules stand in neede of spirituall meanes, as of the word, Sacraments and prayer, because their soules must as well be preserved, as their bodies nourished. Our first father then had a Sabboth to be put in minde of the Creator, and that without distraction he might the better bee put in minde of the glorious kingdome to come, that more freely he might give himselfe to meditation, and that he might the better glorifie God in sixe daies. As the heretikes then deny the necessitie of the word, prayer and Sacraments: so we looke for a new heaven, and a new earth, and then we hope and acknowledge, that we shall keepe a continuall Sabboth. But in the meane time, seeing the Sabboth which wee now have, was before sinne, wee since sinne came into the worlde, have much more neede of it, because that which was to continue Adam in innocencie, is to recover us, and to continue us in our recoverie. The Lorde then having sanctified this day, it is not our day but the Lord his owne day.

But some will say: How? is God better served on the Sabboth, then on any other day? I answere, not that we put religion in that day, as it is a day, more then in any other: but that on that day wee are freer from distractions, and set at more libertie to the worshipping of God, then we are on the other sixe daies, wherein wee are bound to our ordinarie and lawfull calling. Wherefore as we put no holines in the creatures of water, bread and wine in the Sacraments: but acknowledge all inward grace to proceede from God his blessing and institution: so wee promise unto our selves on the Lord his day a greater blessing, not for any thing in the day it selfe, but by reason of God his owne ordinance, and promise of a blessing to the same. And as wee denie not a blessing from the Lord on private prayer, reading and conference, but acknowledge a greater blessing to bee due even by the Lord his owne promise, to these exercises publike in comparison of the other: so wee deny not the grace of God to bee upon those houres redeemed from our outwarde callings, and consecrated to the Lord: but confesse a more speciall blessing from God to belong to that whole day, which the Lord hath taken up to himselfe alone, and that for his owne promise sake unto all them, which come with simple hearts to obey his holy commandement.

Thus having confirmed the doctrine of the Sabboth by the holie Scriptures, and proved that there is a morall use of the same, as well for us as for the Jewes: ... it followeth now according to our first division, that wee should speake of the observation of the Sabboth it selfe, shewing how it is kept, and wherein it is broken. For both these are expressed in the Commandement: wherein is set downe the affirmative, to teach how to keepe it; and the negative, to shew how we breake it. The affirmation is in these wordes: *In it thou shalt doe no manner of worke, &c.*[21] First then wee will shew, how the Sabboth ought to be

---

[21] Exodus 20:10; Deuteronomy 5:14.

kept: then afterward we will declare how it is broken. Where it is said in the beginning of the precept, *Remember to keep holie*:[22] and in the end thereof, *the Lord hallowed the Sabboth*:[23] so that it is not simply said, Remember to keepe; but, *to keep holie*: neither is it simply mentioned, that the Lord left the seventh day, but *blessed the seventh day and hallowed it.* Hereby is insinuated unto us, that in this day wee should grow in love towards God, and tender affection to our brethren, wee are taught that then wee keepe the Sabboth aright, when we use it to that end for which it was ordained, that is, when wee use in it (as wee have before shewed) those exercises, whereby wee may bee the more sanctified, and God the more glorified both on this, and in the other daies of the weeke. These exercises be such, as are either private or publike. The publike exercises are twice at the least to be used euery Sabboth, and they bee these. First the word read and preached: then prayers fervently made with thanksgiving, singing of Psalmes, reverent administring of the Sacraments.

And first for the reading and preaching of the word we reade, Nehem.8.8. *And they read in the booke of the Law of God distinctly, and gave the sense, and caused them to understand the reading.* Also we may see this in the practise of the Apostles, Act.13.vers.15. *And after the lecture of the Law and Prophets, the rulers of the Synagogue sent unto them, saying, Ye men and brethren, if ye have any word of exhortation for the people, say on.* And as the Ministers did reade and preach the word, so it was the practise of the Church to heare, as Eccles.4.17. *Take heede to thy faste, when thou entrest into the house of God, and bee more neere to heare, then to give the sacrifce of fooles.* And it is said, Nehem.8.3. *The eares of all the people hearkened unto the booke of the Law.* And concerning praying; thanksgiving, and singing, the Prophet of God useth a vehement exhortation to the Church, Psal.92.1. *Come* (saith he) *let us rejoyce unto the Lord: let us sing aloude to the rock of our salvation.2. Let us come before his face with praise: let us sing loude unto him with Psalmes.* And Psal.65.1. *O God, praise waiteth for thee in Sion, &c.*

Now for the Sacraments generally we are to marke, that as in the time of the Law the sacrifices were most used on the Sabboth day: so our Sacraments succeeding the sacrifices are then most to be frequented. As for the Supper of the Lord, it appeareth Act.18, I.Corin.II. (as it seemeth) that it was administred every Lords day, although now adaies the ministers may not so doe, for the great ignorance and carnall securitie of people. For the administration of Baptisme, although there be no

---

[22] Exodus 20:8; Deuteronomy 5:12.
[23] Exodus 20:11.

expresse places of the Scriptures shewing the practise of it on this day:
yet there are many good reasons agreeable to the word, which will prove
the same. First, wee know Circumcision was used on that day, and
therefore Baptisme which is come into the place of Circumcision, is to be
used on the Sabboth day. Againe, Baptisme is a publike action of faith,
whereby a member is to be received into the Church, and therefore the
prayers of the whole congregation ought to bee made for it: all must bee
hereby put in minde of the benefits which they have reaped by Baptisme,
and so make a double profit of their presence hereat.

Now seeing old and yong, men and women, masters and servants,
fathers and children, cannot so generally and conveniently meete on the
weeke daies, by reason of their callings, as they can on the Lords day,
their busines set apart: it seemeth by good reason that the Sabboth is the
fittest day for this Sacrament. Againe, if the Lord in his infinite wisedome
and goodnes commaunded Circumcision to be used on the eight day,
both for the avoyding of superstition, if any tied the grace of God to the
outward signe, as also for a sufficient time, wherein the children might
gather some strength to the cutting of their flesh; why were it not a thing
requisite, that Baptisme should bee deferred to the Lords day, both for
the removing of their superstitious opinion, who thinke the children
dying unbaptized to bee but damned; and also for the better enabling of
the childe to be dipped in the water, according to the ancient manner and
pure nature of Baptisme? Wherefore for these causes Baptisme cannot
bee denied to be a publike dutie of the Sabboth. Concerning private
exercises on the Sabboth, they are either going before the publike, or
following after, or comming betweene. The duties going before are either
in examining our selves, or stirring up of our selves. The examination of
our selves consisteth partly in surveying our estate past, and partly in
considering of our present condition: in surveying our estate past, wee
are to call to minde either what sinnes the weeke before we have
committed, to the more humbling of our selves in prayer: or wee must
remember, what graces of God in our soules, what benefits of God on
our selves or in our friends we have received, to the better provoking of
our selves to thanksgiving: in considering of our present condition, wee
are to examine how wee stand affected, what measure of faith,
repentance and godliness is in us: if there be any speciall want or
occasion of publike prayer, we must crave the prayer of the Pastour and
congregation: if any peculiar cause of a solemne thanksgiving bee
offered, wee must give the preacher and people word of it: as also if there
be occasion of some want, we are to pray for the minister, that his mouth
may bee opened, to make some happie and holy supply by the worde of
it. How requisite this examination is, our civill practises may declare.
Wee see worldly thriving men, if not everie day, yet at the least once in

the weeke they search their bookes, cast their accounts, conferre with their gaine their expences, and make even reckonings, whereby they may see whether they have gained, or whether they have lost, whether they are before hand or come short: and shall not wee much more, if not once a day, which were expedient yet once in the weeke at the least, call our selves to a reckoning, examining what hath gone from us, what hath come towardes us, how wee have gone forwarde in godly proceedings, or how wee have gone backward, that if we have holie increases, wee may give thankes and glorie to God; if we come short, we must humble ourselves, and endevour the weeke following, to travaile with our selves the more earnestly to recover our former losse. This examination had, we are further to stirre up ourselves before wee come to the publike exercises. This consisteth in reading, meditating and praying, whereby we may provoke a spirituall appetite the more hungerly, desirously, & lovingly to resort to the congregation. How necessarie this is, the long and woful experience of non proficients in the schoole of Christ, doth lamentably shew. For what is the cause why in the prayers of the Church wee so little profit? what causeth the word to be of so small power with us? whereof commeth it that the Sacraments are of such slender account with us? Is it not because we draw neere to the Lord with uncatechised hearts, and uncircumcised eares, without prepared affections, and unschooled senses: so that we come unto and depart from the house of God with no more profit, then wee get at stage-playes, where delighting our eyes and eares for a while with the view of the pageants, afterward we vainly depart? If we at any time are to entertaine some special friend or stately guests, it is civilitie to avoide all things noysome, and to procure all things handsome in our houses: and shall we not thinke it Christianitie at such times as the Lord hath made speciall promise to visit us, and to become our friendly guest, to purge the loathsome affections of the heart, and dispose our soules in some holy order for his entertainment? Are wee so diligent to present our selves on the Sabboth in our best attire, because then wee shall come before the whole congregation: and shall wee be negligent to attire our soules, seeing wee are to appeare before God and his Angels? Doe wee outwardly professe this day to bee a more solemne time then any other day of the weeke: and shall we inward practise denie the same? Wherefore in his holy preparing of ourselves, wee are to imitate the wisedome of worldly men, who having a sute to the prince, or some noble personage, which hath not that happie successe and issue, which was hoped for, by and by begin to call themselves to account, to consider with themselves in what circumstance they failed, whereby lesse circumspectly, and lesse advisedly they attempted their enterprise, accusing themselves of folly, and unconsiderate dealing in their cause, whereby, as wofull experience teacheth them, their request fell to the ground. Unto these men herein wee must not be unlike, when in dealing with the Lord we profit not so much by hearing reading, praying, or any other publike exercise, as wee should: neither must we sticke to reason with our selves, and to condemne our selves as faultie, either in omitting something to bee done, or committing something to bee undone, before wee addresse ourselves to our publike duties.

Now that this examining and stirring up of ourselves may the better bee done it is requisite (contrary to the long and lothsome practise of the most part of men) that wee rise early on the Sabboth day. We see yong men will rise early to resort to mariages, to feastings, to goe a maying, to ringing of bels, or such like vanities: the Papists will breake their sleepe, that more timely they may have their Masses, and popish practises: the heretikes also to attend on their vaine revelations, will recover some time by early rising: all which are to our shame, that for holy and heavenly exercises, to serve the Lord in spirit and trueth, will redeeme no time, whereby the Lord his Sabboth may be the better sanctified: but on the contrary, by bathing our bodies in our beds on that day more then on any other, as perswading our selves too great a libertie therein, wee make it a day of our rest, and not of the Lords rest.

The Israelites are said to have risen very early to their idolatrie: the Prophets are reported to have stretched out their hands betimes in the morning.[24] Wherefore for shame of the one, for the imitating of the other, let us stirre up our selves more early on the Lord his day, as making the Sabboth our delight, Esay 58.[25] whereby wee may bee no lesse carefull to bestow the first fruites of the day and the sweetnes of the morning in the pure service of God, then Idolaters in their idolatrie, young men in their vanities, worldly men in their covetousnes, and heretikes in their heresies use to doe. If we thus shall examine our selves in our sinnes committed, and gifts of God received; if we shall humble our soules for the one, and be thankfull for the other; if we shall survey our wants, pray for our pastours, prepare our selves, and use all these exercises in wisedome, and rising early, unlesse upon some special cause or weaknes, requireth rather our holy keeping of our beds, then our uprising, let the experience of the after fruites and good increases of the publike exercises speake, and let triall report, if the word be not more precious, our prayers more powerfull, our receiving of the Sacraments more effectuall, more profitable unto us. Now concerning those exercises which follow after, or come betweene those publike meanes, they are

---

[24] Isaiah 5:11; Micah 2:1.
[25] Isaiah 58:13-14.

either for the increase of faith and repentance to make the publike meanes more profitable to us, or the exercises of love, whereby wee may shew some fruite of the other. The exercises of faith and repenteance are reading, comparing of things heard, examining and applying them to our selves, praying, thanksgiving, and meditating.

Now it remaineth to intreate of the duties of love, because the Lord his Sabboth is not a day of knowledge alone, but of love; not only of hearing the word by preaching, but also of doing the word by practising: and these duties either respect the persons of our brethren, or they concerne such things as are about our brethren. The things concerning their persons, are either in regard of their soules or of their bodies: the exercises respecting the things that are about them, are either appertaining to their goods, or to their credit. The duties unto the soules of our brethren, are to teach the ignorant, to bring sinners to repentance, to binde up the wounds of them that are afflicted in spirit, to comfort the weake, to strengthen the hands that fall downe, and the knees that are readie to faint, to stirre up them which bee dull, to admonish the unruly, to confirme the faith of them that beleeve, to encourage them in weldoing, which have begun well, and to rebuke the wilfull offenders. And though these should be the exercises of every day, yet especially they belong to the Sabboth, wherein we make a supply of the wants, which wee have on the weeke daies. The duties of love required to the bodies of our brethren, are the visiting of the sick, the relieving of the imprisoned, the helping of the poore and miserable, the feeding of the hungrie, the cloathing of the naked, the comforting of the distressed, the bestowing of our goods on them that are needie.

Furthermore, in all these exercises both publike and private, both concerning faith, and the duties of love, both with our selves and with others, two things especially of us must bee observed. First, we must at night trie our hearts, with what truth, with what care, and with what sinceritie we have done these things: because as God abhorreth hypocrisie in every thing, so especially he cannot abide it in his owne worship. Secondly, we are to examine our selves, with what profit either to our selves or to others, with what comfort, with what increase of good things wee have been conversant in these duties, that we rest not in the worke wrought, but that we may offer up the fruits of our holy increase in a good conscience to the Lorde.

The Sabboth (wee say) is broken either by generall impediments and lets, whereby wee cannot sanctifie the day: or else by those evill fruites, which follow the not keeping of the same. For as there be two things commanded, to wit, rest, and sanctification of the rest: so two things are forbidden, namely, labour and travaile, so farre as either they hinder the sanctifying of the Sabboth, and the prophaning of the Sabboth rest. First of the impediments of sanctifying of the Sabboth, which in their owne nature are indifferent, we must know, that as the furtherances of this sanctification are commanded, so the hinderances are forbidden: and as rest is so farre commanded, as maketh to the sanctifying of the day: so our workes are not simply forbidden, but so farre forth as they bee hinderances to the holy observation of the same. And these bee either lawfull workes, or lawfull recreations and pleasures. And therefore, as wee say in the Commandement going before, that all vaine, light, usuall and accustomed othes are forbidden, and yet affirme, that all such othes are commanded, as are taken up in the defence of God his glorie, our brethrens welfare, or in any other cases of waight and importance, when the things must needes be knowne, and otherwise then by an oth cannot be knowne: so wee say in this precept, all usuall affairs on the Sabboth are here forbidden, and we grant, that if these fall out for the glorie of God in the preservation of his creatures necessarily to be done, or so, as they may enable us the more to any duties of the Sabboth, then they are not onely not forbidden, but also more straightly enjoyned us. And therefore as no otheres creeping under pretence are allowed, but such as are waightie, likewise wee permit no works of pretended necessitie, but such as in that they cannot bee done the day before nor the day after, are for the former considerations necessarily required. And whereas the Lord doth not onely give leve to draw the oxe or the asse out of the ditch to preserve their lives, but also to leade them to the water to make their lives more comfortable to them: we permit not onlie things needfull to the life of man, but also things convenient to the use and comfort of man, as the dressing of convenient meats, whereby a man may bee made more cheerfull in the duties of sanctification: so that both in using them we refresh and not oppresse our selves, and in preparing them wee use the time before, after, or betweene the publike exercise. But as God hath permitted this leave: so we on our parts are to take heede that we abuse not his libertie.

This moderation prefixed, let us sift more narrowly the things that are forbidden. These are either the workes of our calling, or lawfull recreations. The workes be such, as either are more usuall in the sixe daies, or being but at certaine speciall times in the moneths or yeeres used lesse usuall. First concerning the workes having their ordinary course in the weeke daies, as plowing, sowing, using of handicrafts, and such like, there is no question, and the most prophane person will not call them into question, but it is taken as granted, that these workes must give place to the worship of God, that men being freed from them may bee the more sanctified.

But some will pretend a more usuall necessitie in certaine and peculiar callings, of which as they say, standeth a further question, as among makers of coale, and iron, Heardmen, Sheepheards, Carriers, Drovers, and traffique men, all which indeed have great and laborious callings: yet must wee say, and hold this ground, that in these and like ordinary callings, the ordinance of the Lord doth not hinder the good order of man, but they are so subordinated the one to the other, as if wee give to each of them their time and their place, the workes of man may bee used, and yet the worship of God preferred: because as our callings serveth to Gods worship, so Gods worship sanctifieth our callings. True it is, that the Lorde requireth not onely the worship of the Sabboth day, but also of other weeke daies either privately at the least, or publikely, if our callings so permit: and howsoever we deny not unto these men some larger libertie on the sixe daies, yet they must not be exempted from the duties of the Sabboth day, which generally is laid upon all men, and especially on these men, whose labours as they are the more troublesome and continuall in the weeke daies, so they ought the rather to rest on the Sabboth daies. And seeing they will not discharge themselves of the like graces with other men concerning their creation, redemption, and sanctification, if they make not a supply on the seventh day for their libertie in the sixe daies, they are inferiour to the condition of beasts: for the beasts on that day have their rest, and they have not. Besides in pretending such excuses, they openly bewray their want of spirituall wisedome. For there is no such calling: but if they were as wise to God, as they are politike in increasing their riches, they could tell how to divide their times and seasons for the easing of their bodies, and refreshing of their soules on the Sabboth. And here men are to be charged with looking to their servants. For the commandement is flat and expresse: even *thou and thy servant*.[26] It is not sufficient for men to come to the Church themselves, but they must bring their servants also. The Lord saw how men would be ingenious in deceiving their own

---

[26] Exodus 20:10; Deuteronomy 5:14.

soules, by not bringing their charges and families with them to the congregation: who not withstanding being created, redeemed and sanctified, are as highly indebted to the worship of God as the masters. But let them not beguile themselves, for the blood of their soules shall be required at their hands, who being too lordly & tyrannous governours, make their servants either equall to beasts, or worse then beasts, caring for nothing but for the world, never thinking on hell, whereunto they are hastening.

[A]s for Faires and Markets, which by politike, wise, and worldly men on the Lords daies are maintained, it argueth the want of godly wisedome where they be used, because without any prejudice to the worship of God they may not conveniently bee observed. For if no necessitie, profit, nor pleasure could cause the Papifts to have their Faires on their Christmas day, Easter day, holy Thursday, and Corpus Christi day; then it is a shame for us, that in trueth and zeale ought to goe before them, to defile the Lords day herewith: yea I adde, it is intolerable, because a firme statute and civill law enforceth a plaine inhibition of all such worldly convents and assemblies on that day. These Faires are for the most part either solemne marts and of greater continuance, or petie markets and of lesse resort: if they be more solemne markets, then the continuance of the gaine in the weeke daies may easily affoord the Lord his right on the Sabboth daies: if they be the petie markets, then they are within the compasse of seven daies, and they may be used on the sixe daies betweene the Sabboths, not charging the Lords day with them.

Concerning seeding time and harvest, we have heard them on the Sabboth by expresse words forbidden in Exodus.[27] And here one thing maketh me to marveile, why men pleade rather for the libertie of the harvest, then of the seeding time, when the time is for the one and for the other, and he that restrained the one, restraineth the other: yea and there is more of wisedome and lesse labour required in the seeding, and there is lesse neede and more labour used in the reaping time. And yet many thinke it strange to sow and plow on the Sabboth day, who make no conscience to mow, reape, and cart it on that day. But here to the commaundement let us joyne the promise. If we be carelesse to provide for the worship of God, the Lord will ease himselfe of caring for us. But, if we first seeke the kingdome of God, and his righteousnes, al these things shall be given unto us.[28] And in trueth the necessitie of the harvest

---

[27] Exodus 34:21.
[28] Matthew 6:33.

rather chargeth us with many moe duties on the Lords day, then dischargeth us of any one. First the labour of the sixe daies at that season is so great, as men cannot conveniently give themselves to the worship of God either publikely or privately, and in that respect especially in that time they are to make conscience of the Sabboth, wherein they must endevour to make some godly supply for their former defects. Under this wee may couch another reason. Although greater possessors have larger libertie in the workes of this calling, yet have they servants and cattell, which at harvest time especially labour: for whose good and ease seeing the Lord hath provided in every Sabboth, we can not without unmercifulnes to the creatures, and the controlling of God his ordinance, in these busie times especially, denie our servants and cattell their rest, because they had then most need to cease on the Sabboth day, when they most travaile on the weeke daies. Secondly, experience teacheth us, that if the weather in this quarter of the yeere bee more unseasonable, men are then most readie to unclaspe their hold on Gods providence by their carnall diffidence. Againe on the other side, if the times are more temperate, and the fruites of the earth more abundant, then we securely hide our hearts in the earth, and tying our affections to our enlarged and full fraught barnes, wee vomit out our surfeting conceits with the rich man, and say, O *my soule take they rest, though hast store laid up for many yeeres:*[29] and so we burie our soules in the abundance of our increase. But what is it to have a handfull of corne, and to gaine therewith a viall of the wrath of God? What doth it helpe, when the Lord either to correct our sinnes, or make triall of our faith, doth send foule weather, that a man should blot out the print, and rub out the marke of Gods work with such contemptuous disobedience? Ought wee not rather in such a scarcitie, as the Lorde appointeth by Joel,[30] to erect a new Sabboth in prayer and fasting, then to pull downe the old Sabboth by toyling and labouring, that the Lord seeing our repentance, might stay the windowes of heaven, and surceasing from his punishment might leave some blessing behinde him? Now therefore to cure our diffidence, to helpe our impatience, and to correct our covetousnes, as also to witnes our subjection to the blessed will of God, the Lord often sendeth this triall in the time of harvest.

And thus having spoken of the workes of our callings, now we are to speake of the workes of our pleasures. Concerning the lawfull

---

[29] Luke 12:19.
[30] Joel 1:13–14.

recreations of this life, which Christianitie doth permit and not forbid (for of unlawfull pleasures being alwaies out of season, and especially on the Sabboth, wee have nothing to say) whether they may have place and time on the Lords day or no, here is the question. In this part of the treatise, I say, we doe not speake of prophane and idle pleasures, but of them which bring some further use after they bee used, and which are permitted by the word of God, so measure in them may be used, and they bee sanctified unto us by the word and by prayer. And yet even for these wee dare not give the time consecrated to God, unto playing and pleasures. Neither are we curiously to frame any exquisite division in this matter, but first wee will consider of the feasts and bankets accustomed on this day, and afterward of other recreations and exercises at that time frequented and used, which though in their time, place and persons they are not unlawfull, yet at this time on the Lords day we denie them to be lawfull. As for feasts, wee may part them into love feasts, Church feasts, and sumptuous feasts, which carie with them some further expences and larger liberalitie, as are those which are used at mariages, at the admitting of men into their civill offices, or else are taken up some special benefits received, or some extraordinarie judgements removed, or some other causes like unto these, as when men carying some port and countenance in the common wealth, according to their degrees and callings, at some times doe ordaine.

Touching these solemne and sumptuous feasts, thus much we affirme briefly. Such as on the Lords day institute such solemnities, and stuffe every office, and bumbast every corner of the house with men and women, are to be admonished duly to consider of that, which is reported to David both in the historie of the Kings, and in the booke of the Chronicles, who having a vaine desire and superfluous appetite, would not deferre, but longed to taste of the water in the well of Bethlehem a welfenced citie, and from whence water could not be conveied by hand, without some jeopardie to them that fetcht it. Wherefore three of his most worthie men have this business assigned them, to the compassing whereof their lives were hazarded. At their returne, grace making his after fruites better then the former, after better deliberation used, he powred forth the water on the ground, saying, God forbid that I should drinke the blood or the lives of these three men: shewing thereby both his offence in sending them, and the free mercie of God in saving them.[31] Wherefore (excepting the estate of princes) for as much as these pompous preparations cannot conveniently be used on the Sabboth without the hazard of mens soules, as in that divers offices in noble families require divers persons to performe divers duties, and so that

---

[31] 2 Samuel 23:13-17.

which is a day of rest, is made a day of toyling. The equitie of the not kindling of a fire must binde Christians, although the sanction doth not constraine them. Whereas the Israelites of an inch of libertie would take an ell, for a childish instruction this thing was restrained them. And although we have a further libertie to kindle a fire, for as much as we are in colder countries then the Israelites were: yet the equitie of the law must teach us, that wee ought not to turne this libertie to bee a servant of our wanton desires, or to foster carnall licentiousnes, and hinder the worship of God.

If it be demaunded, whether this day be fit for mariage or no: I answere, it is, because on that day as it is a day of rejoycing, there is a more lawfull libertie of speech, and a more liberall use of cheerfull behaviour. Howbeit, let them not on that day, if they marrie, make their solemne cheere: but seeing they may have a convenient companie some other day, let them either both marrie and feast some other day, or marrie on the Lords day, and feast another. And if it be demanded, whether lovefeasts may be kept on this day or no. I answere, there is difference betweene lovefeasts and solemne feasts. And if men were as wise, as they were in the times of Poperie, they would be politike to finde out some meanes to provide for the glorie of God, and yet not altogether neglect the convenient furniture for their table. I am not to appoint, neither doe I undertake to prescribe how meate should be prepared, or how offices should be divided: yet by experience I can give testimonie of some, who for their religion bare credit in the Church, and for their authoritie carie some countenance in common wealth, and yet on the Lords day have their tables both Christianly and worshipfully furnished without any hinderance of the worship of God at all, notwithstanding the number of their daily retinue and ordinary familie is great. It is one thing to provide feasts of intertainment more then competent, and another thing to use love feasts nothing lesse then is conveient, the one oppressing and disabling us to holy exercises, the other refreshing and enabling us to the duties of religion.

Now concerning the exercises and pleasures of the bodie, leaving all vaine pastimes at all times unlawfull, but most especially on the Sabboth, and to speake of such recreations, as in themselves are lawfull, and may lawfully bee used of the children of God in their time and place; as those of shooting, training up of souldiers, and such like, all which their pleasures carie a profit either present, or in time to come, to the Church or common wealth, wee denie not simply then their places, but thinke them convenient and commendable with the testimonie of the holy Ghost: 2.Sam.I. where Jonathan is commended of David for his shooting. Howbeit, the Sabboth day is no fit time for these uses, which we will shew briefly. First wee must know, that the Lord having forbidden the workes of our ordinary calling, which carie with them a more speciall promise of profit and warrant of reward in their time, forbiddeth also lawfull pleasures: because if the use of those is forbidden, being lawfull and necessary for the upholding and maintaining of mans life, then these things not so needfull, though convenient for creation, are much more inhibited. And this we shall see more plainly, if wee remember that rest is so farre commanded, as it is an helpe and furtherance to sanctification, and labour so far is forbidden, as it is an impediment of the same. In regard whereof, if pleasures bee no lesse lets and impediments to the hallowing of the Sabboth, then bodily and ordinary labours, then pleasures have no more libertie on the Lords day then our outward workes. Furthermore, we must be circumspect not to rest in any drowsie or sleepie securitie of the flesh: but in what measure soever we detract from the ordinary workes of our calling, in that proportion must we adde to the sanctification of the day: not much unlike to good Christians, who bestow on their soules whatsoever they take from their bodies. Which wisdome and diligence though wee use most carefully, yet for as much as we shall leave as many duties unperformed, as we shal have performed, I see not what leisure wee can lawfully lend to recreations. If any carnall professor shall presse this thing more vehemently, me thinketh he may blush at the defence of it, seeing this kinde of keeping holie daies in pleasures and playing was used even of the Heathen, *who sate downe to eate and drinke, and rose up to play*,[32] first balacing their bellies with feasts, and then refreshing themselves with play. Wherefore as we now denie Church-feasts as imitations of the Heathen: so doe we deny holie day playes, as remnants of ancient prophanenes.

But if it bee here objected, that the Jewes had ther solemne feasts, musicall instruments, and exercises of pleasure, yet the men always by themselves, and the other sexe by themselves; not with that monstrous mixture of men and women, which is a chiefe sinne and arch enemie to religion of our age, and that with holie Psalmes made by David and Moses, not with vaine minstrelie used of prophane Atheists: I answere, as Paul speaketh I.Cor.13. of his owne person, that they being as children spake as children, they understood as children, they thought as children, being but in the rudiments: but we becomming men, must put away childish things. Againe, the superstition of the Papists checketh this abuse, who would admit none outward exercises on their Easter, Whitsontide, and holy Thursday, at what times they thought a bird would scarcely build her nest. Did not the Papists breake their superstitious holie daies, and shall we so prophanely pollute the Lorde

---

[32] Exodus 32:6.

his Sabboth? Our Easter day, our Ascension day, our Whitsontide is every Lordes day: and therefore wee ought to make a speciall care of sanctifying of this day. What shall I say of the zeale of worldlings, which may controle by contraries the securitie of our sins? For all worldy men seeke never for pleasure, whilest profit doth drop: as wee may see in them that live on Faires and Markets, as Chapmen and Inholders. So long as they hope to gaine a penie, how waite they, how diligent are they, how little play they, how busie are they? And why? Forsooth it is their harvest, it is their market, which (they say) they must attend upon whilest occasion lasteth. Beholde the policie and painfulnes of the world may teach us, what we ought to do for our soules. Is not the Sabboth the harvest time and the market day for the soule, wherein wee should gather in whilest the Sunne shineth, wherein wee should be very diligent, whilest our gaine is promised, wherein wee must provide for a living and maintenance, and lay up store, laying all pleasure aside untill the time to come?

It remaineth in the last place to shew, how the Sabboth is prophaned either in thought, in word, or in deede. For there is a difference betweene the not sanctifying, and the plaine prophaning of the Sabboth, in that the one is not altogether desirous to breake it, the other hath no desire at all to keepe it. Neither is the Sabboth only broken by prophanenes, but also by idle works, and not carefull keeping of it. Some prophane the Sabboth by corrupt judgement, as Heretikes: some by a corrupt life, as carnall professors; the one a high malice of Satan, the other a dangerous deceit of the divel. When men too worldly minded, make the Lords day a day of riddance, a packing day, a counting day to make oddes even with all men, but even things odde with God. And it is the lamentable sin of our age, to presse the Lords ordinance and appointed day with all relikes of law matters, with the dregs of ancient quarels, or new broched brawlings, with posting to Justices; not to be reconciled but to be avenged; not to finish, but to revive controversies, and to rub old injuries untill they bleed: so as that day that is sanctified and ordained for love, is a day of hatred, of a day of reconciliation, it is made a day of dissention, and this cannot but proceede from a prophane stock. Others as seeming more favourable, though they make not this day a time of pampering the flesh (which is a time of purging the flesh) yet they make it a day of palpable darknes, which should be a day of bright shining light: by hunting of beares, by haunting of playes, and such like, that if they begin the day in the spirit, they will end it in the flesh, receiving some good motions in the morning, they burie them in the evening, and giving the Lorde the forenoone, they recompence the divell with the afternoone. Yea in some place the Lords day is the divels day, being fraught with so many fraies, stained with such filthie fornication, & burthened with the sinnes which their ordinary callings on the weeke daies spue out, in that on those daies they cannot bee frequented for want of companie. Now whether we speake of the not sanctifying, or of the prophaning of the day, we affirme the Sabboth to be broken in thought, word and deede. For the whole law being spirituall, Rom.7. and this being a principall part of that law, it must needes bee that this precept, as well as the rest, taketh up as well the inner as the outward man. Besides, it is a generall rule in the law, that whatsoever is unlawfall to be done, the same is unlawfull to bee thought or spoken of: and looke in what measure the wicked actions of men are forbidden, in the same maner is the wicked affection and communication forbidden also. Many have not withstanding made such proceedings in sinne, that when they should recken with their soules, they recken with their servants, and when they should make even with their conscience, they strike even with their chapmen, and yet perswade themselves of small breach of the Sabboth, because (as they say) they doe but speake a little with their tongue, and scribble with their pennes. Then wee must know, that as what wee may doe, that wee may talke of: so what wee may not doe, that may wee not talke of. Wherefore laying aside our filthie songs, our table talke of worldly matters, our carnall devises and worldly compasses, which we are fetching in our thoughts, whilest wee sit in the congregation, our privie discourses of our successe in our callings, and our politike disposing of our weeke following; all which shut out of the doores better things, and overquell the vigour of good things. Wherefore as the nourishing of ill thoughts is at al times unseasonable: so to harbour them on this day is most abominable. Many will temper their tongue, & stay their hands, but yet will give some libertie to their hearts: as though the Lord condemned not as well the hypocrisie of the one, as the wickednes of the other. Now we must remember to every generall point to joyne our particular practise, that wee may obtaine the blessings laid up for the obedient, and avoide the curses laid up for the disobedient: which the Lord assist us in, for Christ his sake our Lord and Saviour.

FINIS.

A Treatise of a
Contract before Mariage

After prayer he spake as followeth:

That none of us might doubt whether there be just occasion of this manner of our meeting or no: wee are to call to minde even from the Heathen, that the light of nature taught them, that there was a solemne promise to bee made of the parties that should be maried before they were to be joyned in mariage, and that was called their espousage: and therefore we were the more to bee blamed, if we should neglect so good a custome, especially being commended by the chosen people of God, as we may gather of his words: for we reade that the Lord God made a law concerning the espoused persons, that if they were unfaithfull of their bodies, they should be condemned as adulterers, even as well as the maried parties.[1] Mary also was affianced unto Joseph, before the solemnifying of their mariage.[2] And the use of the Church standeth with good reason: for that the neglect of it is an occasion that many are disappoynted of their purposed mariages, because some of them through inconstancie goe back. It is very meete also, that they should have some instructions given them concerning the graces and duties that are required in that estate, that they may pray unto the Lord, and so be prepared and made fit to be publikely presented to the congregation afterwards.

Now further as concerning the nature of this contract and espousage, although it bee a degree under mariage, yet it is more then a determined purpose, yea more than a simple promise. For even as hee which delivereth up the estate of his lands in writing (all conditions agreed upon) is more bound to the perfourmance of his bargaine, then hee that hath purposed, yea or made promise thereof by word of mouth, although the writings be not yet sealed: even so there is a greater necessitie of standing to this contract of mariage, then there is of any other purpose or promise made privately by the parties. These things observed, I purpose as God shall give mee grace to give some lessons, how you must prepare your selves to live in the estate of mariage. I will

---

[1] Deuteronomy 22:22–4.
[2] Matthew 1:18.

for the helpe of your memorie deale in this sort and order: first briefly going through the Articles of your faith, and then through the Commandements, noting some especiall duties fit for this purpose.

As concerning your beleefe in God the father, you know brethren you must beleeve in him, as being creator of all things, and also the governor and preserver of the same: you must also understand that he created man according to his owne image, and gave him the preheminence and government of the woman, for the helpe of the man, that he might bee furthered in the service of his God. So you must much more looke that you be not hindered from the Lord by your wife: for there are many whilest they desire marriage, so long as their hope is deferred they are carefull in the discharge of their dutie: but afterward once injoying those things they looked for, they waxe more negligent then they were before, greatly dishonoring God by their unthankfulnes. And it may be the onely fault of man, if he bee not helped by his wife to grow in godlines: for I thinke that even Evah in moving her husband Adam to eate of the forbidden fruite,[3] had beene an helper unto him, to bring him acquainted with the malitious enmitie of Sathan against them both, if according to the great measure of graces he had received from the Lord, he had been more faithfull in obeying the will of God, and had wisely rebuked his wife. And againe, although the woman was the occasion of sinne: yet the force of sinne to the corruption of mankind came into the world by the sinne of the man, For so the Apostle saith, Rom.5. *As by one man (meaning Adam) sin entred into the world, & death by sin: and so death went over all men, for as much as all men have sinned, So much more the grace of God, and the gift of grace, which is by one man Iesus Christ, hath abounded unto many.*[4] And in the 3. of Genesis wee reade, that the eyes of the woman were not opened untill the man had eaten of the fruite: but so soone as he had eaten, the eyes of them both were opened, and they knew that they had sinned.[5] Therfore I gather thus much, that rebuke should have prevailed more to convert her, then her moving of him to transgresse, should have been able to pervert him. I speake not to excuse the woman, for I know the Lorde was displeased with her, and for that cause hath laid a speciall punishment upon her, in the painfull bringing foorth of children.[6]

But that I might shew the great charge that lieth upon the man, to stay the corruptions of the woman, by reason of the authoritie which the

---

[3] Genesis 3:6.
[4] Romans 5:12, 15.
[5] Genesis 3:1–7.
[6] Genesis 3:16a.

Lord hath given him over her:[7] which I would have you brother[8] diligently to consider of. And you my sister must take profite, by calling to minde, that this was one end of your creation, that you should glorifie God in being an helper to your husband:[9] therefore take heede that you bee not a hinderer unto him, to trouble him or to vexe his heart, whereby hee should be lesse fruitfull in his calling: but be you cheerfull towards him, so that although he should have little comfort in all other things, yet he may finde great cause to reioyce in you. And this you must know, that as it is required of your husband to seeke for wisedome to be able to governe you: so the Lord requireth of you to be subiect unto him, remembering also that as God hath injoyned you silence in the congregation, so you must seeke for instruction at his mouth in your private chamber.[10]

Another thing I would have you both to consider of in this poynt of your beleefe, is faith in Gods providence. And marke that well I shall say unto you: for it is a special thing, and I know it shall doe you good, if God blesse it unto you: for if you be assured in your hearts that it was the Lord who in his gratious providence brought you thus together, you shall bee comforted against all troubles and hinderances that shall by any meanes bee raised up against you. For this is the nature of Satan to bring men and women to this doubt: and when they once yeeld unto it, what trouble and what strife doth he work betwixt them? For whereupon ariseth that impatiencie of spirit that wee see to be in many, in murmuring, in chiding, in cursed speeches, and much like unquietnes? doth it not come of this, because they have not a reverent perswasion that the Lorde in his providence as by his owne hand joyned them in that neere bond and conjunction together? Therefore my good brother and sister, as you would continue and increase in much love and peace one towards another, marke I say this poynt diligently: for it shall bee a very comfortable stay unto you both, whatsoever should fall out afterward, contrarie to that you looked for: as if there should bee any disagreement in your severall dispositions and natures: or if you should fall into sicknesses, into any diseases, or such like trials, you remembring that this was the Lords doing, you may bee more assured that yet for all this, it shall be well in the end, if you be constant in prayer, calling upon God the father through faith in Jesus Christ. Now that you may prove unto your owne hearts that the Lord hath knit you thus together, you must consider that it must needes bee the Lord who hath moved the hearts of

[7] Genesis 3:16d.

[8] Not literally his 'brother'; Greenham uses 'brother' and 'sister' throughout this sermon in the inclusive Christian sense.

[9] Genesis 2:20.

[10] 1 Corinthians 14:34–5.

your Christian parents to give their lawfull consents unto you in the same, and God in mercie shall give you greater assurance of it, if you marke his dealings with you from time to time.

Now as touching your faith in Jesus Christ, understand that mariage is holie unto them onely, whose hearts are sanctified by faith in his name. And although God will alwaies approve his owne ordinance, yet it must needes prove hurtfull in the end unto them, who call not for his blessing upon the same: and without repentance will turne to their further condemnation. Therefore you are both to examine your selves diligently herein: and you brother. _A_. must learn hereby so to love your wife, as Christ Jesus loved his spouse his Church: that is to say, even as our Saviour Christ is very patient towards it, and by little and little purgeth, washeth and cleanseth away the corruption of it.[11] So must you in like manner in all wisedome use the meanes, and with a patient minde waite for the amendment of any thing that you shall finde to be amisse in your wife, and that the graces of Gods spirit may daily increase in her. Therefore I charge you in the sight of God and his Angels, and as you will answere unto me and the parents of this my sister, before the judgement seate of Christ, that as you receive her a virgin from her parents, so you neglect no dutie whereby her salvation may bee furthered, that you may present her pure and blameles, as much as in you lieth, unto Jesus Christ when he shall call you to account. And doe not think that this is a harder charge, then is meete: for seeing that God hath promised a blessing unto those husbands that are faithfull to the converting of their unbeleeving wives, how much more than shall you prevaile with a Christian daughter, and one, I hope, that hath received the faith as well as your selfe? And you my sister, must likewise take heede, that you refuse not to obey your husband, in all things agreeable to Gods most holie word. For you must by his ordinance bee subiect unto him, even as the Church is subiect unto Jesus Christ.[12] And as the Church should bee but a strumpet, and be unworthie of Christ, and those blessings which he bringeth with him for her, if she would not receive and acknowledge him as her head: so could you not looke for any benefit from your husband, unlesse you should submit your selfe unto him, according to the commaundement of God. Neither doe I thus charge you with any obedience but in the Lord: for if he should require any such thing of you, as should cause you to depart from Christ, I would have you in any case remember that you are principally espoused unto Christ. And herein also you must consider, that there will be speciall graces of obedience and modestie and godlinesse looked for of you: not

---

[11] Ephesians 5:25-8.
[12] Ephesians 5:22-4.

onely in respect of your good education, but also because of that helpe which is now offered unto you. And when the holy Ghost in his Scriptures telleth you, that the beleeving wife may (through his blessing) winne the unbeleeving husband, if so bee she walke Christianly in godly conversation with modestie and feare before him:[13] let this incourage you to hope for better successe, by all meanes of dealing towards one that is faithfull, and I trust will be willing in all good things to comfort you.

Now thirdly, in that you are taught to beleeve in God the holy Ghost, it admonisheth you to pray for his teaching, that you may by him bee led into all trueth, and further instructed and drawne unto every Christian dutie, from time to time. The duties are very many to be gathered out of every article, as also out of the severall Commaundements: but I will onely give you a taste, and touch only some one dutie, required of you in every one of them. In that you beleeve that there is an universall Church and communion of Saints, you must bee diligent to approve your selves one to each other, that you are parts and members thereof: and further the graces that God hath bestowed upon either of you, must be common in the use thereof to each other: so againe you must sustaine the infirmities one of another. Finally, you must provoke and stirre up one another, that your faith may be strengthened, and your selves comforted against all other griefes, by the assurance you shall have wrought in you concerning the forgiveness of sinnes, wherein your happines doth consist: as also in the hope of the resurrection of your bodies, and the continuall meditation of eternall life.

We will come now to the Commandements: and first for the former commandement, which requireth all spirituall service of you that is due unto the Lord, that you stedfastly beleeve in him, love him with all your hearts, and with feare and reverence to call upon his name, in all things giving thankes, as to him which is the author and giver of every good and perfect gift unto you. You must make the profit of this commaundement, that if you will look in trueth of heart, to bee faithfull, loving and dutifull one to the other, these graces must spring from the other, as being the fountaine and welspring of all life and trueth unto them. For contrariwise, if you bee unmindfull of God, he will not suffer you to finde the benefits of trueth one by the other.

The second Commandement, which requireth of you to worship God after the true manner, that he appoynteth in his word, teacheth you thus much, that you must nourish your love in this estate, by the practice of things whereby hee is worshipped and honoured of us: namely, by hearing and reading of his holy word, and by the use of the Sacraments. For that love that is stirred up and nourished by this meanes, is most

---

[13] 1 Peter 3:1-6.

pure and will longest endure, when fleshly love soone vanisheth and vadeth away.

In the third Commandement, as you are trusted with the glorie of God: so you are charged brother that you abuse not his name, if you bee faithfull unto the Lord, in seeking his glorie and the advancement of his trueth, and of the kingdome of Jesus Christ, preferring it in all things as is meete; then farely will the Lord blesse you, and prosper your waies: but if you fall away and slide into any heresie, and so dishonour his Maiestie; then will God certainly plague you in his wrath, and hee will make that which you desire to have greatest comfort in, turne into a curse upon you. And I would have you remember to this ende, how God the Lord dealt with wicked Amaziah, who for the prophaning of Gods glorie and worship, had the heart of his wife drawne from him, and so to his great reproach became a notorious whore.[14] So likewise my sister, that you dishonour not God, as being a meanes of withdrawing your husbands heart from the duties of his calling, but nourishing faith and a good conscience in all things with him: so will the Lord for his owne names sake blesse you together. For you shall finde it true which he hath spoken: *Them that honour me I will honour, and them that despise me shall be despised.*[15] But beware (I say) that you give no occasion of falling away, or backsliding unto your husband, least God also bring shame upon you by him, by giving him over to some sinne. I speake not this as though I doubted these things in either of you both: for I hope for better things of you: but in speaking to you, I admonish my selfe, wishing that wee all take heed, that we fall not as the wicked and sinners into the hand of God: for he will not hold him guiltles that taketh his name in vaine.[16]

I will speake nothing of the fourth Commaundement, onely referring you to that I taught publikely this day, concerning the conscience wee ought to have, in the true and spirituall keeping of the same.

The fift Commandement teacheth you to be obedient, and to relieve and obey your husband. And marke this sister I shal now say unto you: if you had never so many gifts, if you had the wisedome of Abigael,[17] and all other graces which are in any woman: and yet if you wanted obedience to your husband, I tell you true that you are nothing worth and you could have no part in Jesus Christ: who denieth himselfe to bee the governour of any, that will not acknowledge their husband to be their

---

[14] Amaziah was king in Judah, 796–767 BCE. See 2 Chronicles 25; 2 Kings 14:1-20. Greenham's source for the story of Amaziah's wife Jecoliah becoming 'a notorious whore' is unclear; it cannot be found in the accounts in 2 Kings or 2 Chronicles.

[15] 1 Samuel 2:30.

[16] Exodus 20:7; Deuteronomy 5:11.

[17] See 1 Samuel 25.

head. Therefore sister, let others doe as they list, but be you in the number of those that doe feare God, and as the daughter of Sara by doing well; who yeelded reverence to Abraham, and is commended in the Scripture for her dutifull speech she used alwaies unto him, calling him Lord, or Sir.[18] Now brother, remember that you must so governe, as you must give account of the maner of your government even unto God himselfe. Besides, where there is greater dignitie, there must you know that there is greater graces required: and in ruling well there are many speciall duties to bee performed. Therefore you must behave your selfe wisely, least you dishonour your selfe by abusing your authoritie: for it is a daughter of Israel that is committed unto you, and one that is fellow heire of the same grace in Jesus Christ with you. Againe, you must consider that a woman is a very fraile creature, and may soone be discouraged; when as there ought to bee more constancie, and staiednes on your part. Therefore in the sixt Commandement, God forbiddeth all churlish behaviour, all lumpishnes, and all unkindness and discurteous speeches; charging you also to beare with many weaknesses, to the end they may bee most quietly reformed. And you sister are forbidden all solemnes, and that you also for your part take heede of all bitter speeches, and of naughtie names which wee heare throwne out of some women of unquiet spirits: and if you wil have your infirmitie cured by gentlenes, then deale you in like manner towards your husbands. For it cannot be but occasions of unquietnes will sometimes be offered in either part: and therefore in many things you must willingly beare each others burthen. Besides this (sister) there is a dutie required in this commandement, that you take care of the health of your husband, in dressing meates holesome for him. And this shal be a meanes that his heart shall be more bent in all loving affection towards you.

In the seventh Commandement there are many things to bee noted, but I can but touch some one or two at this present for want of time: the speciall use and substance of it is thus much, that you live chastly in this estate, and that you keep the mariage bed undefiled, and let mee give you both this warning, that you take heede in the beginning, marke what I say, least that which ought to be a meanes to further chastitie, should turne to the hinderance of you. Therefore pray to God to give you grace that you may bee soberly affected in all things, and namely in the use of mariage: and repent of that which is past, if you have any way offended the Lord in this behalfe. For many failing in repentance for their former sinnes, fall afterward unto their uncleannes againe. As for you brother, true love towards your wife, will be a notable stay from all corruptions:

---

[18] 1 Peter 3:6; A difficult case to sustain in light of Sarah's sharp speech to Abraham in Genesis 16:5.

this we reade of Isaac, Gen.24.67. because he loved Rebecca very dearely, he had no more wives but her; albeit in those daies (it was a grievous sinne) even amongst many of the faithfull, they had at once more wives than one. Therefore when you are from her abroad, make a covenant with your eyes, and let not your heart wander after any other, but thinke upon your owne wife, and delight your heart in her continually, and pray earnestly unto God for her, and so will the Lord increase your love unto her, and moue her heart also to delight and long after you. So must you doe sister, that the same blessings may overtake you: as surely if you imbrace his feare, and walke in his waies, he will blesse you as well in bearing of children, as in other his manifold graces which he hath in store to bestow upon you.

Here also I must by the way admonish you of one other thing, which I had forgotten before, and that is this; your love must spring from that reverence and feare that you must yeeld unto your husband: for true love is mixt as it were with these two: and this is a speciall dutie, and often repeated in the Scripture, that the wife must feare the husband. So that you see sister, that you must not looke to have your husband at your becke for your love: but you must render due benevolence unto each other. For as the bodie of the husband is not his owne, but his wives: so is not the womans her owne, but her husbands: for they are both one flesh, as the Scripture doth teach.[19]

Now, if any doe object, that this is the way to bring women into bondage, and to bee as drudges to their husbands, if they should in this manner be subject unto them, No, no, it is not so, but the most readiest way to procure unto themselves grace, peace of conscience, and more sweete libertie; whilest they live in obedience to God, and his holy ordinances. And therefore the spirit of God admonisheth all women, that they be not afraide of any such vaine terror.

Now further my brother and sister, that you may keepe your bodies pure and chaste, one for the other, I would counsell you to beware of being alone with any, when there is feare of temptation unto evill: but bee carefull, that you may alwaies have witnesse of your Christian behaviour: and in keeping companie convenient, chuse unto your selfe such as bee most sober and faithfull. Well, although there bee many more duties, yet I will content my selfe to goe one thing further, that is, that as you seeke for continuance and increase of love, so you take heede of jelousie: for although that true love is very earnest, and mixt with godly jelousie; yet there is a wicked jelousie, and that moveth causeles suspitions, which worketh great woe unto such as give credit unto them. Take heede therefore my brother and sister of this, yea though there

---

[19] 1 Corinthians 7:3-4.

should seeme to bee some just cause, yet give not too speedie credit unto them. Now, if you desire to know in your heart, which are ungodly suspitions, know them by this token: for they will make you more negligent in praying one for another, and more slacke in performing all other duties of love one to another.

In the eighth Commaundement you are charged brother, to use all lawfull meanes to provide for the maintenance of your wife in honest estate: else were you worse than an Infidell. But I charge you to take heede, least through distrust in the providence of God, you make shipwracke of a good conscience, using any unjust or unlawfull meanes. And you sister are commanded to be a good huswife, and to keepe those things together which you have, and so increase them, as you may from time to time bee helpfull unto others. For if you should consume and waste things unprofitably, you should grieve and trouble the minde of your husband, who ought to bee eased of that care by you. And further, if it should please God to call either of you to suffer persecution in time of triall, the weaker must for the Lords cause give place to the stronger, and desire the Lord to give greater strength: for we must labour for grace, that we may be willing for the Gospell, to forsake all things whatsoever we have.

Out of the ninth Commandement I will give you this rule, that neither of you blaze abroad the infirmities of each other: it is a great enemie to pure love. But if there bee neede of counsell and helpe in any matter, then chuse a faithfull friend with consent, that may be an indifferent judge betwixt you. And againe, in any case tell the trueth one to another: for it is a thing diligently to bee regarded in these our daies, when as men and women are so full of policies and subtill fetches, that there is almost no simplicitie to be found in any.

In the last Commandement, which concerneth wicked motions and thoughts, although there bee no consent given unto them, you are to consider that your nature will never be freed from them in this life: therefore you must prepare to prayer, and other heavenly exercises of faith, to strive continually against them.

Thus I will end, beseeching God for Christ Jesus sake to give you of his spirit, that may teach you in these things, and inable you to further duties agreeable to his holy will, to the glorie of his name, and your everlasting comfort.

O Lord God deare father, for they welbeloved sonne our Saviours sake, make us thankfull for this thy gracious providence towards us. Oh Lord forgive us all our sinnes, and keepe us pure both in soule and bodie: for thine owne name sake write these instructions in our hearts, and give us grace to make practise of them in the whole course of our lives: guide us in al things deare father by the grace of thy good spirit, and let the mercifull eye of thy fatherly providence watch over us continually, that we may bee comforted in thy waies, and quickened alwaies to give thee immortall praise, and that through thy deare sonne Jesus Christ, our Lord and only Saviour, Amen.

After the exhortation and prayer, he asked the parties to bee contracted these two questions:

1. Of their consent of parents.

After their answere of their parents consent to make a faithfull promise of mariage one to the other, at such time as their parents could agree upon it, they were charged to keepe themselves chast, untill the mariage bee sanctified by the publike prayers of the Church: for otherwise many mariages have been punished of the Lord for the uncleannes that hat been committed betwixt the contract and the mariage.

2. Whether they were ever precontracted?

Then he charged them saying: I charge you, as by authoritie from Jesus Christ, in whom you looke to bee saved, that having the consent of your parents, and received these precepts, that (I say) ye labour to grow in knowledge, and in the feare of God. And now as in the sight of God (without all such levitie as of others is used) you must make before the Lord a contract, which is farre more then a promise: and that on this manner their hands being joyned. I R. doe promise to thee.F. that I will be thine husband, which I will confirme by publike mariage, in pledge whereof I give thee mine hand. In like manner doth the woman to the man. Then after prayer the parties are dismissed.

FINIS.

A PROFITABLE TREATISE,
CONTAINING A DIRECTION

for the reading and understanding of the
holy Scriptures: by Master G.

Those things which God hath joyned together, no man may sever asunder. Therefore preaching and reading of the holy Scriptures being of God joyned together in the worke of our salvation, may not bee severed asunder. In all sciences, arts and trades, teachers and masters are requisite ordinarily for the sound learning and practising of them: we must bee perswaded much more that it is necessary to have guides to goe before us in the way to salvation. That preaching is the most principal means to increase and beget faith and repentance in Gods people, must be granted, Deut.18.18.33.10. Levit.10.11. Mal.2.6.7. 2.Chro.36.15. Esay 50.4.5.7.8.53.1.55.10.11.57.19. 58.1. 61.1.62.15.6.7. Mal. 13.3.28.19.20. Ephe.4.11.12.13.14. Rom.10.14.15. 1.Cor.1.21. I. Pet.1.23. 25.[1] And where this ordinary means of salvation faileth, the people for the most part perish: Pro.29.18. Hos.4.6. 2.Chro.15.13. Esay 56.9. Mat.15.14. Luk.11.52. But that the reading of the Scriptures publikely in the Church of God, and privately by our selves, is a speciall and ordinary meane, if not to beget, yet to increase faith in us. It is likewise proved, Deut.6.6.11.18. Psal.1.2. Joh.5.39. Matth. 14.15. Rom.15.14. 2.Pet.1.19. Nehem.8.8. Act.13.15.15.21. The manifold fruit which comes of the reading of the Scriptures prove the same.

Reading rather establisheth, than derogateth from preaching: for none can bee profitable hearers of preaching, that have not beene trained up in reading the Scriptures, or hearing them read. Many inconveniences come from the neglect of reading, as that the people cannot tell when a sentence is alleadged out of the Canonicall Scriptures, when out of the Apocripha, when out of the Scriptures, when out of other writers, that they cannot discerne when he speaketh his owne, or a sentence of the Scripture.

Againe reading helpeth mens judgements, memories and affections,

---

[1] We have retained all references as they are given in the original published text. The run-on references can be converted into modern citations as follows: Deuteronomy 18:18 and 33:10; Malachi 2:6-7; Isaiah 50:4-5 and 7-8, 53:1, 55:10-11; 57:19; 58:1; 61:1; 62:1, 5-7 (the original text printed '62.15' for '62.1.5'); Matthew 13:3; 28:19-20 (the original printed 'Mal.' for 'Mat.'); and so on.

but especially it serveth for the confirmation of our faith: which may be proved by the example of the men of Berea, Act.17.13. it serveth to discerne the spirits of men, I.Joh.4. to make sounder confession of our faith, to stop the mouthes of our adversaries, and to answer the temptations of Satan and the wicked.

But because men sinne, not only in neglect of hearing and reading, but also in hearing and reading amisse: therefore the properties of reverent and faithfull reading and hearing, are to bee set downe, which are these that follow: they be eight in number.

1. Diligence.	5. Conference.
2. Wisedome.	6. Faith.
3. Preparation.	7. Practice.
4. Meditation.	8. Prayer.

The three first goe before reading and preaching. The foure next come after them. The last must go before, and be with them, and come after them.

1 If diligence be necessarie in reading profane authors, then much more in reading the Scriptures. Diligence maketh a rough way plaine and easie, and of good taste, which otherwise is hard and unsavourie. In our diligence we must keepe an even course, and not to be like those who upon some sudden good motion, or by reason of some good companie, or by reason of some good action draweth neere, or for feare of danger, etc. reade for a time, and soone after give over againe. Reade Pro.2.1.2. Mat.13.44.

2 With diligence must be joyned wise-dome, which is in choise of

{ Matter. Order. Time.

For want of wisedome, in the matter they reade, many sinne in studying other bookes before the Scriptures, and in the Scriptures in searching things not revealed, and pretermitting things revealed, as John and James sought should sit at Christs right hand, and left hand: but they sought not to come thither. And his Disciples said, Act.1. *Wilt thou at this time restore the kingdome to Israel:*[2] not asking the meanes to come to the kingdome of heaven. And in things revealed many will curiously and busily search for things not profitable, as genealogies, and carelesly neglect the things that are to be searched. And some ignorant how to reforme themselves, will be talking of reforming the Church. And if the preacher must give milke to the weake, and stronger meate to the stronger Christians: if he must thus apply his doctrine to the hearers,

---

[2] Acts 1:6.

then much more the hearers themselves must apply their owne reading to their owne capacities.

Wisedome is in order: as that men must bee fast grounded in the principall points of doctrine: first wee must lay the foundation and build upon the same: also wee must keepe an order in our readings, and not bee now in this place, now in another: for order is the best helpe for memorie and understanding: he that readeth little after a good manner, profiteth more then hee that readeth much otherwise: as he that limpeth in the way, doth better then he that runneth in another way, or out of the way. Therefore for want of order many reade much, but profit little.

Wisedome must be used in discerning the times: for we must not reade alwaies, and doe nothing else, as some offending in the one extreme, are after driven by Satan to the other. The Sabboth is wholly to be spent in such exercises: on other daies, in the morning, at noone, and in the evening, that is, when we may redeeme the day from the workes of our calling, as David and Daniel did pray at these three times,[3] under which is contained all the worship of God. We must doe as much as we can every day, and no day must passe without line. *God hath made every thing beautifull in his time.* Eccle.3.11.

3 Preparation followeth: If any man goe away without any profit, and either understandeth not, or understandeth amisse, want of preparation is the cause.

Preparation is { 1. In feare of God his majestie.
2. In faith in Jesus Christ.
3. In a good and honest heart, with a greedie desire to eate up Gods word.

In all apparitions God alwaies sent feare before, as his apparitor, it ingendreth teachablenes, and meeknes of minde, as we see in Isaac, who (as it is said) feared, and then he said, *I have blessed Jacob and he shalbe blessed.*[4] We see it also in the woman of Samaria, Joh.4.7. and in the men Act.2. From want of this reverent feare, commeth all checking of God his word, and that men dare bee so bolde with it: but they that feare *will be swift to heare, and slow to speake*, Jam.1.19. and will *lay up his word in their heart*[5] with the Virgin Mary. Though they understand it not, though they kick at the word and spurne against it, yet if God once teach them with his feare, then will they acknowledge it to be the blessed word of God.

Feare commeth upon men sometime they know not how: and if then

---

[3] Psalm 55:17; Daniel 6:10,13.
[4] Genesis 27:33.
[5] Luke 2:19,51.

they goe to God they shall finde some excellent blessing; either in having their understanding inlightened, or some good affections put into them.

This feare is in respect of God his majestie and our owne corruption, to correct the pride of reason, and to controle our affections: and experience will shew, that when our reason and affections are tamed by miserie, calamitie, sicknes, and inward griefe, then wee are very teachable. And when men erre, then the pride of their reason is punished, as in Heretikes and prophane persons. Contrarily, God his good spirit resteth upon the humble to cleere their understandings: but they first crucifie their understanding and affections, and offer them up in a sacrifice to God.

Faith in Christ is the second thing in this preparation, we must bring that with us when we come to reade, looking on him as on the Messiah, that must teach us all things: he is *the lion of the tribe of Juda, to whom it is given to open the booke of God.*[6] He opened the hearts of the Disciples going to Emaus.[7] Preachers build hay and stubble, because they doe not only glorie in him, but doe seeke credit and preferment by preaching themselves.[8] All Heretikes differ among themselves, yet they all agree in this that they erre from Jesus Christ.

A heart prepared to learne is required, Pro.17.16. Wherefore is there a *price in the heart of a foole to get wisedome and he hath none heart?* Our Lord Jesus Christ saith, that those that brought forth fruite (when they had heard) some thirtie, some sixtie, some an hundred fold, they were such as received the word *with a good and honest heart*, Luk.8.[9] Here saith a godly and learned man, men are shut out because they come without a heart.

Now followeth the properties that must follow our readings: whereof the first is meditation, the want of which makes men depart without fruite, though they reade or heare diligently. Meditation makes that which wee have read to bee our owne. *He is blessed which meditates in the law day and night.* Psal.1.[10]

Meditation is either of the { Minde and understanding.

Heart and affections.

Meditation of the understanding, is when reason discourseth of things read, or heard, which the wise of the Heathen call, the refining of judgement, the life of learning. They that want this, how much soever

---

[6] Revelation 5:5.

[7] Luke 24:13-35.

[8] 1 Corinthians 3:12.

[9] Luke 8:15; See also Matthew 13:23.

[10] Psalm 1:2.

they have heard or read, yet shall they never have sound and setled judgement. And for this cause it is said, that the greatest clarkes are not the wisest men.

Meditation of the affections, is when having a thing in judgement, wee ever digest it and make it worke upon our affections. It is a continuall searching of our selves, and labouring to lay up all things in the treasures of our hearts. The other will goe away except this bee joyned with it: for judgement will away except we frame our affections unto it.

Meditation in judgement goeth before: then this must follow, that wee may bee sound in judgement before wee either feare or cheere up our hearts, least we have false feares or false joyes. Many are of sound judgement, and yet have not their hearts purged and touched: they can give counsell to others, but cannot follow themselves, because they joyne not affection with judgement. Meditation without reading is erronious, and reading without meditation is barren.

The next thing is conference. In naturall things man standeth in neede of helpe, then much more in spirituall things he standeth in need of others. And as *iron sharpneth iron: so one friend another*, Prou.27.[11] And as two eyes see more, two eares heare more, and two hands can doe more then one: so this is a speciall communion of Saints, and God hath promised, that when two or three are gathered together in his name, that he will be present with them by his spirit,[12] as he was corporally with his Disciples going to Emaus.

Conference is either with { Ministers of God. / Our equals. / Or others.

This rule must bee kept, that conference with our equals must be of those things which we heard of our Ministers, as it must bee kept also in meditation, which is a conference with our selves. We must for a time like babes hang at the mouthes of the Ministers, because wee cannot runne before wee goe: nay we cannot goe without a leader. No man may presume to understand above that which is meete to understand, but labour to understand according to the measure of sobrietie, as God hath dealt to every one the measure of faith: and when they have laid the foundation, then build the walles and pillers. The Eunuch would not interpret the word without a guide, but he layd it up in his heart, as the Virgin Mary did.[13] For want of true humilitie conference is slaundered, because it is used after an evill manner, as before they bee surely

---

[11] Proverbs 27:17.
[12] Matthew 18:20.
[13] Acts 8:26–38; Luke 2:51.

grounded in principall points of religion, to talke of other matters. Secondly, wee must come in love without anger, envie, or desire of victorie: therefore in conference wee must use the preparation spoken of before: the want of which maketh much janglings and wranglings in companie.

Lastly, wee must procure things honest before men, that it may bee done wisely, without confusion and destruction: and not by too great a multitude, that wee may affoord our doings before men; not with the doores shut, least any man shoulde heare. This is the difference betweene the conference of the godlie and religious, and the conventicles of Heretikes.

The next thing is faith: The word must bee mixed with faith: Heb.4.2. *The word which they heard, profited them nothing, because it was not mixed with faith*. But all have not faith: therefore the Prophet Esay said, *Lord who will beleeve our report?*[14] And Luke 18.18. *Suppose ye that the Sonne of man when he commeth shall finde faith on the earth?* All the former must bee used to refine faith: for as gold before it bee pure is seven fold tried in the fire, so faith which is much more precious then gold, must goe through all these meanes.

Faith here is an increase of all that in preparation. A Marchant must have something before he be a Marchant, but he occupieth to increase and get more: so wee must beleeve in Jesus Christ by a generall faith going before: but we must use all the forenamed meanes to increase our knowledge and faith in all particulars. One may be a faithfull person generally, and yet an unbeleever in particulars. As Christs Disciples to whom he said, *If you had faith but as much as a graine of mustard seede, etc.*[15] As Abraham, Rebecca, and Zachary had.

There is a difference between faith and opinion or knowledge: for our knowledge and opinions vanish away in afflictions. But as golde is tried in the fire, so faith will abide the fire of affliction. Sathan winnowed Peter, but his faith failed not: for Christ failed not, for Christ prayed for him, and for his Disciples, and for all beleevers, that their faith should not faile.[16]

Next followeth practise: That wee have a desire that the word may bring foorth increase of faith and repentance. Psal.119.98. *By thy commandements thou hast made me wiser then my enemies, for they are ever with me*. The practise of Infidels is nothing, because it is not joyned with faith. But Christ saith, *Blessed are they which heare and doe*.[17] And

---

[14] Isaiah 53:1.
[15] Matthew 17:20.
[16] Luke 22:31-2; John 17:6-26.
[17] Luke 11:28.

so saith James, that this is that assureth us that wee have faith.[18] He that doeth this, is compared unto him that buildeth his house upon a rocke, and our workes are not the foundation of the house, but then wee have builded upon Christ.[19] When wee joyne the fruits of our faith with knowledge, they will speake for us, to our consciences, and to others. Our Saviour Christ saith, that that servant that knoweth the will of his master and doth it not, shall be beaten with many stripes: for it is worse to offend of knowledge then of ignorance.[20] And why should he give us any more, if we practice not that we have? For to him that hath shall be given, but from him that hath not shalbe taken away, etc.[21] Why do many hearing the word, either continue or increase in their blindnes, but because they would not practice that they knew, and also even that they had is taken from them? If a good conscience be not joyned with faith, faith shall be taken away and errors succeede. If then wee bee forgetfull, wee must confesse that the want of practice is the cause thereof. The rule of reason in all things is, that the best way of learning is by practice: then how much more if wee practice will God increase our talents.

The last thing is prayer, which must be used both in the beginning, in the middle, and in the end. Prayer must be in all the former meanes: for without it we can never use them, nor have nay blessing by them.

Prayer containeth under it, { Prayer.

{ Thanksgiving.

For prayer, that it must bee used when wee reade, it is plaine I.Cor.2. *The eye hath not seene, etc.*[22] meaning not only the joyes contained in the kingdome of heaven, but even those that are contained in the word. And againe in the same place, *As no man knoweth the hart of a man, but the spirit of man:*[23] so no man knoweth the meaning of the Lord in his word, except God give him his spirit to declare it unto him. And if we must pray when we come to our meate and drink, that God may giue nourishment to us by them then how much more must wee pray God to nourish us by his word: for else we cannot profit thereby. And as no man dare touch meate and drinke before he pray, and wee have no title to it before it bee sanctified to us by prayer: so how impudent are they that dare touch Gods booke without prayer, or thinke that otherwise they have title unto it? *Paul may plant, and Apollo may water, but God giveth*

[18] James 2:14–26.
[19] Matthew 7:24–7.
[20] Luke 12:47–8.
[21] Luke 19:26.
[22] 1 Corinthians 2:9.
[23] 1 Corinthians 2:11.

the increase[24]: so if any be senselesse still, and yet have heard long, it is because God hath not revealed his will unto them. Men may bee diligent, yet they shall erre if God give not his spirit: and though they meditate and conferre, yet they shall be punished for giving libertie to their roving braine and to their tongue, except they pray for Gods spirit.

Many rest in knowledge, and want faith, because they want prayer: and we rest in knowledge, and never practise, because we pray not to God to write his law in our hearts by his spirit, that now, not we, but he may worke in us. They that take any thing in hand without prayer, howsoever they say they abhorre Poperie, yet they practise it, because they take upon them to have some power in themselves.

For thanksgiving, if we be bound to praise God when he hath fed our bodies, how much more when hee hath fed our soules? And shall God be justly offended with us, if wee thanke him not for our refreshing, with meates, sleepe, etc? and shall wee not tremble for feare of revenge, if wee have not praised God for any light, or any good motion that hee hath put into us? For want hereof, after some lightning followeth some darknes, and after much feeling commeth deadnes: and by this meanes Satan goeth about to take all Gods graces from us. David saies, *Blessed art thou Lord, O teach me thy statutes.*[25] This sheweth that we must ever praise God before we come to reade. Many are fervent in asking, but cold in giving thankes. And if we would give thankes to God, it would much ease us in asking, and God would not punish us in taking his graces from us.

FINIS.

---

[24] 1 Corinthians 3:6.
[25] Psalm 119:12.

OF THE GOOD EDUCATION OF CHILDREN

The sixt Sermon.
Proverbs 17.21.

He that begetteth a foole, getteth himselfe sorow, and the father of a foole can have no joy.

The holy Ghost speaking in the Scripture of foolish sonnes, (*as that hee that begetteth such a one, getteth himselfe sorow, and that the father of a foole hath no joy*) meaneth it not so much of naturall idiots, and such as are destitute of common reason: although it is true that this is a lamentable judgement of God, and a heavines to the parents of such a childe, as of wicked children, such as are either ignorant in the word, not knowing how to order one right step to the kingdome of God: or else having some knowledge of God, ungodly abuse it, to maintaine their carnall lust and appetite. For this cause as it would grieve parents to have naturall fooles to their children, or such as either through some imperfection of nature are dismembred, or deformed, and misfigured in the parts of the bodie: so much more should it grieve them to have such children, as either for want of knowledge and heavenly wisedome, cannot walke in the feare of God: or abusing the knowledge given them, prostitute themselves to all sinne and wickednesse.

It is marvellous to see how greatly parents can bewaile the want of one naturall gift proceeding of some imperfection, and how easily they can passe over without any griefe, the want of all spirituall graces, springing from corrupt education. In like manner, it is straunge that men can take the matter so heavily, when their children breake into such offences, as either have open shame, or civill punishment following them, and yet can make no bones but post over such sinnes as are against the majestie of God, accompanied with everlasting confusion and unspeakable torments: wherein what doth most part of men bewray, but their great hypocrisie, in that neither their joy nor their griefe is sound to their children, and that they love themselves more in their children, then either their salvation, or the glorie of God? The tender love and care whereof no doubt did increase the sorow of David for the death of his sonne Absolom, who was not so much grieved for the loss of a sonne, as for that untimely end of his sonne.[1] Let us learne therefore to correct our

---

[1] 2 Samuel 18:9–19:7.

affections to our children, and be grieved for their ignorance, impietie and sinnes: whereof either our carnall compassion, the not lamenting of our owne naturall corruption, the want of prayer for an holy seede, or prophane education armed with the wrath of God, may bee a most just occasion. Can a man hope for a holy posterite? or doe wee marveile if the Lord crosse us in the children of our bodies, when wee make as bold and brutish an entrance into that holie ordinance of the Lord, as in the meeting of the neighing horse with his mate, when being joyned in that honourable estate of matrimonie, either a meere natural men without all knowledge of God we beget our children: or as too carnall men without the feare and reverence of the Lord, neither bewayling our corruption which we received of our forefathers, nor praying against our infirmities which may descend to our posteritie, wee abuse the mariage bed? Lastly, when having received the frute of the wombe, we have no care by vertous education to offer it to the Lord, that our childe by carnall generation may be the childe of God by spirituall regeneration? Surely no. And yet men without all looking up to Gods providence and secret counsell, without all bethinking themselves of their corrupt nature, from which their children are descended, without all looking back into their wicked and godlesse bringing them up, wil fret against their sins, and fume against their children: yea often they wil correct them, and that to serve their owne corruptions, not so much grieved for that they have sinned against God, as that they have offended them. Christians therefore must know, that when men and women raging with boyling lusts meete together as brute beasts, having none other respects then to satisfie their carnall concupiscence, and to strengthen themselves in worldly desires, when they make no conscience to sanctifie the mariagebed with praier, when they have no care to increase the Church of Christ and the number of the elect, it is the just judgement of God to send them monsters, untimely births, or disfigured children, or naturall fooles: or else such as having good gifts of the minde and well proportioned bodies, are most wicked, gracelesse, and prophane persons. Againe on the contrarie side, we shall finde in the word of God noble and notable men commended unto us for rare examples of vertue and godlinesse, whose children were asked and obtained of God by prayer. Our first parents Adam and Eve being humbled after the birth of their wicked sonne Kaine, obtained a righteous Abell, of whom when by his bloodie brother they were bereft, they received that holy man Seth.[2] Abraham begetting a childe in the flesh, had a cursed Ishmael: but waiting by faith for the accomplishment of Gods covenant, hee obtained a blessed Isaac.[3] Jacob not content with

---

[2] Genesis 4:1-8; 5:3. In the examples in this section, Greenham reads a good deal into the text which is not explicitly there.

[3] Genesis 16; 17:15-22; 21:1-7.

one wife, according to the ordinance of God, was punished in his children: yet after being humbled, he received a faithfull Joseph.[4] Elkanah and Annah praying and being cast downe, had a prophet that did minister before the Lord.[5] David and Bethsheba lamenting their sinnes, obtained Salomon a man of excellent wisedome.[6] Zacharie and Elizabeth fearing the Lord, received John the Baptist and forerunner of Christ.[7] Looke what sinnes we have received naturally without Gods great blessing, without prayer and humbling of our selves, we shall conveigh them to posteritie: and although the Lord doe grant sometimes naturall gifts unto the children of carnall and naturall men, yet for the most part they receive their naturall sinnes withall. But if the children of God by regeneration doe see into themselves, and lament their sinnes of generation, praying that their naturall corruptions may be prevented in their posterities, they shall see the great mercie of God in some measure freeing their posteritie from their sinnes.

Now when thou shalt see such sinnes to be in thy children, enter into thine owne heart, examine thy selfe, whether they are not come from thee, consider how justly the hand of God may be upon thee, and when thou wouldest bee angrie with thy childe, have an holy anger with thy selfe, and use this or such like meditation with thy owne soule: Lord shall I thus punish mine owne sinne, and that in my childe? Shall I thus prosecute the corruptions of my auncesters? Nay I see O Lord, and prove that thou art displeased with me, for the too carnall desire of posteritie. I lay then in some sinne, I asked it not of thee by prayer; be mercifull unto me O God, and in thy good time shew some pittie upon my childe; thus thinking when thou goest about to correct the corruption of nature in thy childe, which he could not helpe, arming thy selfe with prayer, repenting with Jacob, thou shalt be so affected, that as thou art desirous to draw thy childe out of sinne, so yet to doe it with the mildest meanes, and with least rigour. And one thing is most wonderfull that some will teach their children to speake corruptlie, and doe wickedly whilest they are young: and yet beate them for it when they be come to riper age. Againe some will enboulden their children to practise iniquitie towards others, which when by the just judgement of God, they afterward practise against their parents themselves, they are corrected for it. And yet deal with these and such like men, for the evill education of their children, and they will answere, doe not we as much as is of us required? We send our children to the Church to be instructed of the pastor, and to the schoole to be taught of the maister, if they learne, it will bee the better

---

[4] Genesis 29-30.
[5] 1 Samuel 1:1-20.
[6] 2 Samuel 12:15-25.
[7] Luke 1:5-25, 57-8.

for them, if not, they have the more to answere for another daye, what
can wee doe more? But remember O man, consider O woman, who
soever thus speakest, that for thy sinnes sake, and thy want of prayer,
there may bee a plague upon the pastors paines, and a curse upon the
teachers travaile: if parents would have their children blessed at Church
and at schoole, let them beware they give their children no corrupt
example at home, by any carelessenes, prophanenes, or ungodlinesse;
otherwise parents will doe them more harme at home, then pastors and
schoolemaisters can doe them good abroad. For the corrupt example of
the one, fighteth with the good instruction of the other, which is so much
the more dangerous, because that corrupt walking is armed with nature,
and therefore more forceably inclineth the affections of children to the
side. And further, experience teacheth us, that children like or mislike
more by countenance, gesture and behaviour, then by any rule, doctrine,
precept, or instruction whatsoever. Some there by also, that will not have
their children taught, untill they be ten or twelve yeres olde: because as
they say, before that age, they have but an apish imitation. To whom I
answer, that although indeed they cannot then deepely discerne, nor
profoundlie conceive things; yet how many things before those yeeres
both will they receive and remember? And I demaund, if children being
apish in imitating evill whilest they be yong, which they will have the
habit of when they bee old, why may they not much more better doe
apishly good when they are yong, which they may doe carefully when
they are old? Besides, let them so goe untaught, and they will grow so
headstrong, that they will sooner be broken then bended. And sure it is,
that one stripe or two words will doe good to a childe in the beginning,
then a hundred stripes afterward.[8] And here let parents bee admonished
of their undiscreete correction, who doe their children more harme in
shewing a merie countenance after their discipline used, then they doe
good by their chastising, although in their anger they be corrected.
Neither doe I purpose to take away naturall affections, and a Christian
kinde of compassion in all our censures: for it is my great complaint of
the brutish unmercifulnes of many parents herein; but I would wish
Christians to correct their undiscreete affections herein by heavenly
wisedom. Neither am I so Stoicall as to denie a more milde and affable
kinde of speech, to be both lawfully and conveniently used to children:
but yet I wish it to be voyde of all unseemelie levitie, and without all
shew of foolish, vaine and unnecessarie behaviour. To bee briefe, how
needfull household government is towards our children, it may appeare
by the slender thriving and small profiting of religion or vertue, either in
the Church or Common-wealth. For complaine men, and preach they

---

[8] On beating, see e.g., Proverbs 17:10; 20:30.

never so much abroad, unlesse they will begin to reforme their owne houses, and give religion a roome at home, especially in their owne hearts, they shall travell much, and profit little. And surely if men were carefull to reforme themselves first, and then their owne families, they should see Gods manifold blessings in our land upon Church and Common-wealth. For of particular persons come families; of families townes; of townes provinces; of provinces whole realmes: so that conveighing Gods holy trueth in this sort from one to another, in time, and that shortly, it would so spread into all parts of this kingdome. Well I say, let there be never so good lawes in cities, never so pure orders in Church, if there bee no practise at home, if fathers of families use not doctrine and discipline in their houses, and joyne their hands to Magistrate and minister, they may indeed, but most unjustly (as many have done) complaine that their children are corrupted abroad, where indeede they were before, and still are corrupted at home. Alas, if parents to whom the comfort of their children well brought up, is a precious crowne, will not informe and reforme their children in the feare of God, whom it doth chiefly concerne; how should hope sustaine these men, that others will performe this dutie for them, to whom the charge doth farre lesse apppertaine? Lastly, let parents remember, that therefore oftentimes they have disordered and disobedient children to themselves, because they have been disobedient children to the Lord, and disordered to their parents when they were yong; whereof because they have not repented, the Lord punisheth their sinnes committed against others, with the like sinne in others against themselves.

Wilt thou know thou father how thou maist have that blesing, to bee the blessed father of a blessed seede? Wilt thou know O mother how to avoyd that curse, to be the cursed mother of a cursed seede? then bring thy children within the covenant, endevour to make thy sonne by nature, the sonne of God by grace; and thy daughter by nature, the daughter of God by grace: and remember that God which on his part protested to our father Abraham, that he was all sufficient for the accomplishment of his promise, in giving him a blessed seede, required also of our father Abraham for his part, that he should walke before him and bee upright.[9] Wilt thou then have the one part of this covenant, that is, that God should blesse thee in thy seede? then remember thou also the other part, that is, that thou walk before the Lord and be upright. Wilt thou have thy children as the blessed seede of Abraham? teach them with Abraham the commandements of God, pray for them with Abraham that they may live in the sight of the Lorde; bee readie to offer them with Abraham, that they may be an holie sacrifice to the Lord. It is thou O man, O

---

[9] Genesis 17:1.

woman, that maist doe thy childe the greatest good and the greatest harme: if thou praiest for him, and repentest for thy selfe, the Lord will blesse thy care, the pastors paines, and the teachers travaile. But if thou despisest these duties, the Lord will denie thee those blessings, and the curse of God will be upon thy childe at home in thy house, abroad in the Church and in the schoole. And seeing the Lord hath promised that hee will bee thy God and blesse thy seed, if thou be faithfull: thou maist both hope, that thou art of the faithfull, if thou haue a blessed seede, and feare that thou hast not as yet the blessing of the covenant, when thy seede is cursed.

But some will say, had not Jacob wicked children,[10] and David godlesse sonnes?[11] And doth not daily experience teach us, that wicked men have godly children? Yes: for besides the secret counsell of the Lord herein, wee must know that neither the promise of the Lord is so universall, that every particular childe of a faithfull man should be within the covenant: for if of many there be but one blesssed, the promise is performed. Yea which more is, though that a faithfull man have never a good childe, yet if unto the thousand generation there bee but one good, the covenant is not broken. Neither must wee tie the Lords worke so much to man, that a good man may not have an evill sonne, seeing though the Lord visit not his sinnes, yet he may visit the sinnes of some of the forefathers, to the third and fourth generation going before.

To the second I say: that an evill father having a good childe, though the Lord shew not mercie to that particular man therein, yet hee may remember his promise to some of the forefathers in the thousand generation going before. And though that evil man have no cursed childe, yet the curse may bee accomplished in the third and fourth generation following. Wherefore not speaking of election or reprobation, which wee leave onely to the Lord to make good or bad, according to the good pleasure of his owne will, I exhort parents to use the ordinarie meanes to bring up their children, so, as they either by some good tokens may see them the children of God, and heires of the covenant: or at the least be comforted in their own consciences, if the Lord refuse their children for some cause unknowne, in that to their abilitie they have used all good meanes to bring them up well, and offered them to God. And if parents have cause to bee grieved, when thus travailing in good education, they cannot see good in their children; how much more cause of griefe may they have, when they have used no labor at al to bring them up in the feare of the Lord. And yet many will be grieved for the one, that will not be grieved for the other. Wherefore let us learne (if we

---

[10] Genesis 34:13-31.
[11] 2 Samuel 13:1-29.

will conveigh Gods blessings to our posterities) to use all holy duties thereunto: and on the contrarie, if wee will bee loath to conveigh Gods judgements to our children, let us carefully avoyd all meanes that leade unto it. And surely as it is a blessed thing in the houre of death with Simeon to depart in peace,[12] leaving our wife, children and servants spouses to Christ, children to God, and servants to the Lord: so in death no one thing will be more grievous unto a man, then the Lorde having given him the charge and dignitie of so many soules, to be furthered to salvation, that his owne tormented conscience shall presse him, how, in as much as he could, he hath helped them forward to their damnation; and so which is more fearefull, he shall have them spuing and foming out in his face continuall curses, in hell accusing him for ever to be the murtherer of their soules. Howbeit, I do not exempt children from all blame, so charging the parents, as though the children were free from all guiltines herein: for I am not ignorant that as in the time of Ezekiel, so in our daies, youth is ready enough to take up this proverbe, *The father have eaten sowre grapes, and the childrens teeth are set on edge.*[13] But I affirme, that though the occasion be offered of such wicked parents, yet the cause of destruction is still in the children themselves. And besides that, it is sure that the soule which hath sinned shall dye the death. Seeing also there bee some yong men, who notwithstanding the great prophanenes of the most, the manifold corruptions offered abroad, the ungodly examples abounding at home, are so mightily preserved by the seede of grace, that they escape safely in an holy course of life, lamenting when they see the least occasion of evill, rejoycing in the least occasion of good things: the rest who please themselves, and hope to shelter their sinnes under their parents defaults, are plainly left without excuse, and are justly guiltie of the blood of their owne soules. Labor therefore ye yong men to wipe away the teares of griefe from your fathers eyes, and stay the sorowfull spirits of your tender mothers, and consider with your selves if you have any good nature in you, and have not buried the use of common reason, what a shame it is to bee a shame unto your fathers, to whom ye ought to bee a glorie: and thinke ye wanton wits that have not cast off all natural affections, what a contempt it is to be a contempt unto your mother, to whom ye have offered as it were a despightfull violence, in that ye are as it were a corosive unto her heart, when as ye should have been a crowne unto her head.

The end of all this briefly is thus much, that parents having children not walking either in knowledge or in a good conscience, must make some use of so just a cause of griefe, examining themselves, and accusing

---

[12] Luke 2:25-35.
[13] Ezekiel 18:2.

their owne soules before the Lorde; either for that their meeting was prophane to so holy an estate; or brutish, because they desired rather a seed like unto themselves in flesh and blood, then such as might be like to Christ by grace and new birth; or that they begat their offspring, as meere naturall or very carnall men; or because they either prophanely neglected all education, or monsterously misliked that in their children which they liked in themselves, and punished in them their owne corrupt precepts; or for that they suffered injuriously their children to doe evill unto others, which they could not suffer them to doe unto themselves; or untaught that at home which was taught abroad; or in that they doe lie in some sinne unrepented of; or else because they never made conscience to bring their posteritie within the covenant of salvation: but still loved their flesh in their children, and not their soules. And children must here also learne, that it is one speciall propertie of a liberall and ingenious nature, to bee carefull so to live, that in time they may be a glorie to their fathers, and a joy to their mothers: which the Lord grant to us all for his glorie, and our everlasting comfort: through Jesus Christ our Lord and onely Saviour.

FINIS.

PART FOUR

Appendices

Richard Greenham's printed works

This appendix is designed to assist those who wish to study Greenham's printed works and could benefit from a guide through the bewildering array of titles. It does not replace the *Short Title Catalog*, which should be consulted for information on the printers of Greenham's works and on the current locations of copies of the various volumes. However, we hope to make using the *Short Title Catalog* easier since Greenham's works are scattered throughout it due both to misattributions and anthologizing. Each entry below indicates the *Short Title Catalog* (STC) number. Since most readers will use Greenham's works on microfilm, we also give the reel number from the UMI 'Early English Books 1475–1640' series. There follows a brief guide to the contents of each volume and notes on special features which may be of interest. The main listings maintain the numerical ordering of the *Short Title Catalog*; a chronological listing of Greenham's published works is given at the end of the appendix.

I. Omnibus collected works

STC 12312; Reel 1102. *The Works of the Reverend and Faithfull Servant of Iesus Christ M. Richard Greenham, Minister and Preacher of the word of God: Examined, Corrected, and published, for the further building of all such as love the trueth, and desire to know the power of godlines: By H.H.* 1599. (A facsimile of this edition was published in 1973 by Theatrum Orbis Terrarum Ltd, of Amsterdam, and Da Capo Press Inc., of New York.) This volume includes a dedicatory letter; preface to reader; epigrams; 'Grave Counsels and Godlie Observations; Serving Generallie to direct all men in the waies of true godlines, but principally applyed to instruct and comfort all afflicted consciences'; 'Seven Godly and Fruitfull Sermons, upon Sundry Portions of Holy Scripture: With very profitable obseruations and meditations of the 4. and 14. chapters of the Proverbs', which begins with a separate title page and epistle by Henry Holland, and contains sermons on quenching the spirit, murmuring, zeal, a good name, humility, the education of children, and repentance and true sorrow for sin; 'Godly Treatises of Divers Arguments, Tending Principally to Comfort and cure soules afflicted', also with separate title page, and epistle by Holland and containing 'The First Treatise for an afflicted Conscience'; 'The Second Treatise, Belonging to the Comfort of an Afflicted Conscience'; 'The Markes of a Righteous Man'; 'Sweet and Sure Signes of Election, to them that are brought low'; 'A Treatise of a Contract before mariage'; 'A Treatise of the Sabboth'; 'A Profitable Treatise, Containing a Direction for the reading and understanding of the holy Scriptures'; and 'A Short Forme of Catechising. With Certaine godly Letters for the instruction and comforting of some friends afflicted', which begins with a separate title page (giving Richard Bradocke as printer) and contains an incomplete catechism, 'A Letter against hardnesse of heart', 'An other comfortable Letter by Master R.G. to Master M.', and 'A Letter Consolatorie, written to a friend afflicted in conscience for sinne'.

STC 12313; Reel 245. 1599. Different printer; contents same as above.

STC 12313.5; Reel 1817. *The Workes of the Reverend and Faithfull servant of Iesus Christ M. Richard Greenham, Minister and Preacher of the Word of God: The Second Edition, Revised, Corrected, and published, for the further building of all such as love the trueth, and desire to know the power of godlines: By H.H.* 1599. Contents are the same as in the first edition.

STC 12314; Reel 244. 1599. Different printer; contents same as STC 12313.5.

STC 12314.5; Reel 1852. *The Second Part of the Workes of the Reverend and Faithfull Servant of Iesus Christ, M. Richard Greenham, Minister and Preacher of the word of God. Collected and Published, for the further building of all such as love the truth, and desire to know the power of godlinesse. By H.H.* 1600. A commonplace book of 75 chapters, arranged alphabetically, compiled by Holland from additional manuscripts received after the publication of the earlier volume. Holland wrote in the dedicatory letter: 'The first part of these works ... being accepted of many, both learned and truely religious: I was the rather incouraged to seeke out the rest carried about in written copies from hand to hand, and dispersed into divers parts of this land. And what I have found, I have set in the best forme and frame I could, for the edification and comfort of Gods people.' In his letter to the readers, he repeated this basic theme, adding 'that some part of these collections were taken from [Greenham's] mouth when he preached, the rest written ... with his owne hand, but no part revised or corrected by himselfe with intent and purpose to be published'. Holland wrote that he omitted what he 'thought lesse pertinent, or not so sutable to the rest of his works'.

STC 12314.7; no film. 1600. Different printer; contents same as STC 12314.5.

STC 12315; Reel 1307. *The Workes of the Reverend and Faithfull Servant of Iesus Christ M. Richard Greenham, Minister and Preacher of the Word of God, collected into one volume: Revised, Corrected, and Published, for the Further Building of all Such as love the trueth, and desire to know the power of godlinesse: By H.H.* Third edition, 1601. Holland added a new letter stating that controversial writings to confute the enemies of the gospel are sometimes beneficial but at other times 'rather fill the heads and hearts of men with a spirit of contradiction and contention'. Greenham's goal, according to Holland, was 'to edifie the heart and conscience [and] to stirre up the heart, and to quicken affections to embrace true godlinesse ...'. The epigrams are not included in this edition. The first part essentially duplicates the first edition with only minor changes, including some additions to the 'Grave Counsels'. After the treatise on the Sabbath, there is a brief section of 24 sentences on the theme of the upright heart, probably the 'Short precepts and rules for the afflicted', which was listed in the table of contents in the first edition as appearing between the Sabbath treatise and the rules for bible reading, but which did not in fact appear. The catechism includes a new dedication to Mistress Anne Bowles and Mistress A. Stevens ('I am well assured you remember Master Greenham's great care and love towards you, which was unfained, because of the good experience he had of your unfained faith in Christ, and love towards him'), urging them to use it to educate their children 'as Eunice and Lois did' and to give themselves joy by being able to 'have his owne very words written and set before your eyes, which you have heard often to your great joy sounding in your eares ...' (p. 210). The catechism ends with the following editorial note: 'I cannot as yet finde any more of this Catechisme; If any man have the rest in his private use, he shall doe well to communicate the same unto the Church for the good of many' (p. 231). This is followed by the second edition of the second part (that is, of STC 12314.5), with its own title page ('Godly Instructions for the Due Examination and Direction of Al Men, to the Attaining and Retaining of faith and a good conscience'). Finally, there is a section of previously unpublished material with a new title page: *The Third Part of the Works of the Reverend and Faithfull Servant of Iesus Christ, M. Richard Greenham, Minister and Preacher of the word of God: Collected and Published, for the Further Building of all such as Love the trueth, and desire to know the power of godlinesse.* It begins with a table of contents, dedication and letter to the reader. Next are treatises on the Resurrection, examination before the Lord's Supper, the fear of God, and hypocrisy; 113 'grave counsels, which came lately to my hands from a godly preacher', identified as John Brodley of Sowerby, near Halifax; treatises on anger, blessedness and fasting; and a long section of meditations on Psalm 119.

STC 12316; Reel 1025. Variant of STC 12315, also of 1601. Restores the epigrams, including a new one in praise of Holland.

STC 12317; Reel 1547. *The Workes of the Reverend and Faithfull Servant of Iesus Christ M. Richard Greenham, Minister and Preacher of the Word of God, collected into one volume: Revised, Corrected, and Published, for the further building of all such as love the trueth, and desire to know the power of godlinesse. The Fourth and Last Edition: in which is added, sixe severall treatises of the same Author, never before published: by H.H.* 1605. This is the first edition published after Holland's death. In a new letter, Holland's widow Elizabeth wrote to King James I that she presented the book to him partly because of the author, 'a man renowned for his rare pietie and paines, and for his singular dexterities in comforting afflicted consciences', and partly because her late husband 'straightly and many times charged me upon his death-bed to present and dedicate the whole unto your Highnes, as a pledge which hee desired to leave unto the world, of his most dutifull affection, and earnest desire to doe your Maiestie all the honour, and the Churches within your Highnes dominions, all the service that he could'. The contents are largely the same as those of the third edition, although the separate title pages are changed to reflect the new year of publication. In the First Part, there are three new sermons on Matthew 13:44 added, which had been published separately in 1604 (STC 12324.5; see below). The Third Part includes some relatively minor additions, notably in the meditations on Psalm 119. The new general editor, Stephen Egerton, added a new section: *The fourth part of the Works of the Reverend and faithfull servant of Iesus Christ, M. Richard Greenham, Minister and Preacher of the word of God: Collected and Published, for the further building of all such as love the truth and desire to know the power of godlinesse. By H.H.* In the dedication to Sir Marmaduke Darrell and Sir Thomas Bloother, surveyors-general for the victualling of the navy, Egerton wrote that Virgil, asked why he read the writings of Ennius, said: 'I gather gold out of Ennius his dunghill.' So, wrote Egerton, 'if one heathen man could gather gold out of the writings of another, how much more may we (being Christians) gather not gold only, but pearles and pretious stones out of the religious and holy labours of Master Richard Greenham (though not all polished by his owne penne) being a most godly brother, yea more than a brother, even a most painefull Pastor, zealous Preacher, and reverend father in the Church of God, of whom I am perswaded that for practicall divinity (which ought worthily to have the preheminence) he was inferiour to few or none in his time'. This new Fourth Part contains: 151 aphorisms and commonplaces entitled 'Grave Counsels and Divine Dierctions [sic], for the Attaining and Retaining of Faith and a Good Conscience'; a sermon on Ephesians 6:10-12; 'A Godly Exposition of the XVI. Psalme'; observations on Genesis 42:9,12-15, 21; a sermon on Hebrews 13:17 on the subject of ministry; fragmentary notes of a sermon on confession of sins; a sermon on Galatians 6:14-15 discussing the enemies of the church; a sermon on Galatians 6:15; an additional set of 'Godly Observations, Concerning Divers Arguments and Common Places in Religion', arranged according to 24 very mixed headings (conscience, order, hearing the Word of God, 'who be swine and who be dogges', unmercifulness, works, against policy, the Epistle to the Hebrews summarized, three notes of the truly righteous man, sabbath, discipline and excommunication, of means, names of the devil, contempt of the ministry, shame, justification, parables and similitudes, God's providence, seeking God, sin, profit and pleasure, Christ's power, Ecclesiastes summarized and temptation); a treatise on Acts 2:14-17 entitled 'Of the Sending of the Holy Ghost', which was a vehicle for attacking the Family of Love and other enemies of the church; 'A Short Treatise of Prayer, upon the words of the Prophet Ioel, chap.2.32: alleaged by Peter, Act.2.21'; and a series of letters of spiritual direction entitled 'A Short Direction in Three General Rules, for one troubled in Minde', 'A Letter against hardnes of heart' to a Master S., 'A Letter Consolatorie to Mistris Mary Whitehead'; and a letter, probably to William Cecil, 'Master Greenhams care for the poore Schollers of Cambridge'.

STC 12318; Reel 1174. *The Workes of the Reverend and Faithfull Servant of Iesus Christ M. Richard Greenham, Minister and Preacher of the Word of God, collected into one volume: Revised, Corrected, and Published, for the further building of all such as love the trueth, and desire to know the power of godlinesse: by H.H. The Fift and Last Edition: In Which Matters Dispersed Before Through the whole booke are methodically drawne to their severall places, and the hundred and nineteenth Psalme perfected: with a more exact Table annexed.* 1612. Egerton completely rearranged the contents into a more rational structure. The first part contains most of the collections of Greenham's 'sayings' and the catechism; the second contains seventeen treatises (all eight from the first edition, and those on the Resurrection, the Lord's Supper, God's fear, hypocrisy, anger, blessedness, fasting, the Holy Ghost and prayer); the third contains the seventeen sermons; the fourth includes meditations on Psalm 119 (with some new material supplied by Dr Robert Hill) and Proverbs 4 and 14, and the summaries of Hebrews and Ecclesiastes. The final part is a miscellany, containing 'Godly instructions for the due examination and direction of all men, to the attayning and retayning of faith and a good conscience' (that is, the 75 chapters of the Second Part of earlier editions); 'other divine arguments, and common places in religion' (that is, the 'Godly Observations' of the Fourth Part, without the summaries of Hebrews and Ecclesiastes); Greenham's pastoral letters and the letter about poor scholars; and 'Maister Greenehams Prayer'. This final item is the only entirely new item. Unfortunately for William Welby, he did not own the rights to print the prayer; the rights belonged to Roger Jackson, and on 11 October 1613, the Stationers' Company fined Welby (*Records of the Court of the Stationers' Company 1602 to 1640*, ed. William A. Jackson [London: The Bibliographical Society, 1957], p. 62). Although rearranged, most of the epigrams and epistles from earlier editions appear in this edition as well. The various sections have separate title pages.

II.   Single works and partial collections of individual works

STC 4296; Reel 1510. *A Briefe and necessarie Catechisme, concerning the principall poynts of our Christian Religion. Written for the good of all such as seeke after consolation in Christ.* 1602. The title page gives the author as 'R.C.' but this should read 'R.G.'. The contents are the same as those of the catechism printed in the omnibus volumes.

STC 11503; Reel 638. *A godly Exhortation, and fruitfull admonition to vertuous parents and modest Matrons. Describing the holie use, and blessed institution of that most honorable state of Matrimonie, and the encrease of godlie and happy children, in training them up in godly education, and houshold discipline.* 1584. Listed in STC under 'R.G.'. This is the only one of Greenham's works published during his lifetime, but there are no indications of his involvement in its publication. The main text is that of the sermon 'On the Good Education of Children', which is printed in all of the omnibus volumes. In addition, there is a list of seven thoughts from scripture about children and parents (p. Aii) which does not appear elsewhere.

STC 11503.3; Reel 1987. Variant, also of 1584. This contains some material not in STC 11503 or in the omnibus volumes. First is an epistle headed 'To Christian parentes, and Housholders, grace, and mercie in Christ'. This is clearly separated from the rest of the volume by blank sheets (both sides) at the beginning and end. The letter argues that 'the great blessinges sent of God, the lawes made by the Prince, the woorde preached by the Ministers, take small effect, and bring foorth little fruite: because parentes and maisters shew such examples of loose liberties in them selves, and throwe the raines of licentiousnesse into the neckes of others' (A2). Following this letter is a single sheet entitled 'These are the orders which I have sene observed in a Christian Gentlemans house, to the profit of his houshold, example of others, comfort of Gods children, & honor of God'. It describes the routine of household devotions: 'while they had a minister' the household was at church twice on the Sabbath and once each weekday, 'but since the restraint of their Minister' they have prayers at home kneeling in the parlour; confession of sins 'with morning prayer for private householdes' and prayers for the church and the queen, the Lord's Prayer and the Confession of Faith, 'all which prayers are in the booke of Common Prayer' (A5v).

STC 12319; Reel 1988. *A fruitful and godly sermon; containing necessary and profitable doctrine, for the reformation of our sinfull and wicked lives, but especially for the comfort of a troubled Conscience in all distresses.* 1595. This and STC 12323 are the two works not originating in London. Both were printed in Edinburgh by Robert Waldegrave, the printer of the Marprelate tracts, who had fled to Scotland. This piece is the same as the sermon on Proverbs 18:14, which appears in the 1599 *Works* as 'The First Treatise for an afflicted Conscience'.

STC 12321; Reel 1239. *A most sweete and assured Comfort for all those that are afflicted in Consciscience [sic], or troubled in minde. With two comfortable letters to his especiall frends that way greeved.* 1595. This contains the sermon on Proverbs 18:14 in STC 12319, 'A Letter against hardnesse of heart' (attributed to Robert [sic] Greenham), 'An Other Comfortable Letter by Master R. G.', and 'Sweet and sure signes of Election, to them specially that are brought low'. All appear in the 1599 *Works*.

STC 12322; Reel 298. *ΠΑΡΑΜΥΘΙΟΝ. Two Treatises of the comforting of an afflicted conscience, written by M. Richard Greenham, with certaine Epistles of the same argument. Hereunto are added two Sermons, with certaine grave and wise counsells and answeres of the same Author and argument.* 1598. The editor is known from the dedicatory letter only as 'H. C.'. The table of contents lists a number of treatises which are not actually in the volume as well as 'A great number of grave and wise counsels and answers, gathered by Master John Hopkins and others that attended him for that purpose', likewise absent. The actual contents are the first, second and fourth treatises in the 1599 *Works*; the three pastoral letters from the 1599 *Works*; the first and seventh sermons from the 1599 *Works*; and 'Certaine wise and grave counsels and answers, made by the same author, of the former argument', which are fifteen items found in the 'Grave counsels' of 1599.

STC 12323; Reel 639. *Propositions Containing Answers to Certaine demaunds in divers spirituall matters, specially concerning the Conscience oppressed with the griefe of sinne with an Epistle Against hardnes of heart, made by that worthie Preacher of the Gospell of Christ, M. R. Greenham Pastor of Drayton.* 1597. This was also printed by Robert Waldegrave in Edinburgh. Something bearing virtually the same title was registered to Ralph Jackson on 17 Febuary 1597/8, but no separate English edition is known to exist. Contents are 'Certaine demaunds answered by M. Greenham a learned man' (a set of 107 unsorted 'sayings') and the ubiquitous 'A Letter Against hardnes of heart'.

STC 12324; Reel 1687. *Short rules sent by maister Richard Greenham to a gentlewoman troubled in minde, with directions for a christian life.* 1612. Unique among Greenham's printed works, this is a broadsheet. It is perhaps compiled from STC 21204.5 and 21213.1 (see below): the 'Short rules' appear in the former (based on 'A Short Direction' in the 1605 *Works*) and the 'directions for a christian life' are in the latter.

STC 12324.5; no film. *Three very fruitfull and comfortable sermons on the 13. Chap. of S. Matthew. Verse. 44.* 1604. These are the three sermons added to the 1612 *Works*.

STC 12325; Reel 710. *Two learned and godly sermons, Preached by that reverende and zelous man M. Richard Greenham: on these partes of Scripture folowing. The first Sermon on this text. A good name is to be desired above great riches, and loving favour above silver and golde. Pro. 22, 1. The second Sermon on this text. Quench not the spirit. I.Thessa. 5, 19.* 1595. Both sermons appear in the 1599 *Works* under the same titles.

III. Anthologies containing Greenham material

STC 5694; Reel 1684. Thomas Cooper, *The Christians daily sacrifice: Containing a daily direction for a setled course of Sanctification. Expressing The scope of the seven Treatises of Master Rogers, as also the summe of Master Greenham his spirituall observations, with some further increase tending to perfection.* 1608. Also 1609 editions (STC 5694.5; Reel 647) and 1615 edition (STC 5695). This work contains Cooper's distillation of Rogers and Greenham rather than any specific works of either divine.

STC 6938; Reel 1349. John Dod and Robert Cleaver, *Foure Godlie and Fruitful Sermons: Two Preached at Draiton in Oxford-Shire, At a Fast, enjoyned by authoritie, by occasion of the pestilence then dangerously dispearsed. Likewise Two Other Sermons on the Twelfth Psalme. Whereunto is annexed a briefe Tract of Zeale.* 1611 (second edition). See also 1610 (first edition): STC 6937.5. The last item is not Greenham's sermon on zeal which appears in the 1599 *Works.* According to Dod and Cleaver's editor John Winston, the 'Tract of Zeale ... is a collection of divers rules which I heard & read touching that subject, principally of such as were scattered heere and there in Maister R. *Greenham* Workes: which being exceeding usefull, I thought good to gather them into one ... for the ease and helpe of those that are well affected, especially of such whose abilitie will not reach to the price of that great volume of M. *Greenhams* labours.'

STC 6944; Reel 1446. *Seven godlie and fruitfull sermons. The six first preached by Master John Dod: the last by Master Robert Cleaver. Whereunto is annexed, A briefe Discourse, touching, I. Extinguishing of the Spirit, 2. Murmuring in affliction.* 1614. The annexed pieces are severely abridged from Greenham's sermons on the same topics in the 1599 *Works.*

STC 6944.4; Reel 1813. *Ten godly and fruitfull sermons preached upon severall places of scripture. By J. Dod, R. Cleaver. Whereunto is annexed a briefe treatise of zeale.* 1610. See STC 6937.5 above.

STC 13589; Reel 1416. Henry Holland, *Spirituall preservatives against the Pestilence. Or seven lectures on the 91. Psalme. First Printed in Anno, 1593. And now revised, corrected, and published, as generally for the instruction of ignorant people: so specially for the confirmation of the weake servants of Jesus Christ, describing the most divine and most soveraigne Preservatives against the pestilence. Hereunto is added a sweete prayer of M. R. Greenhams, never before published.* 1603. This is the first appearance of the prayer which was added to the 1612 *Works.*

STC 21204.5; Reel 1692. *A Garden of Spirituall Flowers. Planted By Ri. Ro. Will. Per. Ri. Gree. M. M. and Geo. Web.* 1609. Many subsequent editions also listed in STC. Contains 'Short Rules sent by M. Richard Greenham, to a Gentlewoman troubled in minde, for her better direction and consolation; as also very necessary for every Christian to be exercised withall', an incomplete version of 'A Short Direction' in 1605 *Works.*

STC 21213.4; Reel 1824. *A Garden of Spirituall Flowers. 2 Part. Yeelding a sweet smelling savour in the Nosthrils of each true-hearted Christian.* 1612. Many other editions listed in STC. 'A score of wholesome Precepts, or Directions for a Christian life' appear in 1612 as the third column of the broadsheet STC 12324 (see above).

Greenham's works in chronological order of publication

STC 11503 *A godly Exhortation ... Describing the holie use, and blessed institution of that most honorable state of Matrimonie ... 1584.*
STC 11503.3 Variant, 1584.
STC 12319 *A fruitful and godly sermon; containing doctrine especially for the comfort of a troubled conscience 1595.*
STC 12321 *A most sweete and assured comfort for all those that are afflicted in consciscience [sic]. 1595.*
STC 12325 *Two learned and godly sermons. Pro. 22, 1. 1. Thessa. 5, 19. 1595.*
STC 12323 *Propositions Containing Answers to Certaine demaunds in divers spirituall matters ... 1597.*
STC 12322 ΠΑΡΑΜΥΘΙΟΝ. *1598.*
STC 12312 *The Works ... 1599.*
STC 12313 Variant; also 1599.
STC 12313.5 *The Workes ... 1599.*
STC 12314 Variant; also 1599.
STC 12314.5 *The Second Part of the Workes ... 1600.*
STC 12314.7 Variant.
STC 12315 *The Workes ... 1601.*
STC 12316 Variant.
STC 4296 *A briefe and necessarie catechisme. 1602.*
STC 13589 H. Holland, *Spirituall preseruatives ...* (Greenham's prayer). 1603.
STC 12324.5 *Three very fruitfull and comfortable sermons ... 1604.*
STC 12317 *The Workes ... 1605.*
STC 5694 Thomas Cooper, *The Christians daily sacrifice ... 1608.*
STC 21204.5 *A Garden of Spiritual Flowers. 1609.*
STC 6944.4 Dod and Cleaver, *Ten godly and fruitfull sermons ... 1610.*
STC 6938 Dod and Cleaver, *Foure Godlie and Fruitful sermons ... 1611.*
STC 12318 *The Workes ... 1612.*
STC 12324 *Short rules sent by maister Richard Greenham to a gentlewoman ... 1612.*
STC 21213.1 *A Garden ... 2 Part. 1612.*
STC 6944 Dod and Cleaver, *Seven godlie and fruitfull sermons ... 1614.*

Comparison of 'Grave Counsels' and Rylands English Manuscript 524

For the posthumous first edition of Greenham's *Works*, editor Henry Holland prepared a section of Greenham's aphorisms and godly advice arranged in the form of a commonplace book, with sayings grouped under topics, arranged alphabetically. This is the 'Grave Counsels, and Godlie Observations; Serving Generallie to direct all men in the waies of true godlines, but principally applyed to instruct and comfort all afflicted consciences' with which the volume begins. Holland expressed his anxiety that readers might think Greenham guilty of 'pride or singularitie' for having produced pages of his own wise counsel. Instead, he reported, 'such observations ... were collected and taken by others, and not set downe by himselfe'. The sayings were supplied, according to Holland, by someone identified only as 'Hopkins.'[1] There is clearly some relationship between Rylands Manuscript 524 and the manuscript which Hopkins sent to Holland. The table below documents that relationship.

Column I lists the categories into which Holland arranged the 'Grave Counsels' (spelling modernized); column II gives the total number of separate items in each of those categories. In column III, we indicate the items which also appear in Rylands Manuscript 524 ($\sqrt{}$ = all). In column IV, we indicate the items which cannot be located in Rylands Manuscript 524. Over two-thirds of the 'Grave Counsels' can also be found in Rylands Manuscript 524.

---

[1] John Hopkins must be Holland's source. ΠΑΡΑΜΥΘΙΟΝ. *Two Treatises of the comforting of an afflicted conscience, written by M. Richard Greenham, with certaine Epistles of the same argument. Hereunto are added two Sermons, with certaine grave and wise counsells and answeres of the same Author and argument* (London, 1598) contains 'A great number of grave and wise counsels and answers, gathered by Master John Hopkins and others that attended him for that purpose' (A4r). Although there are some minor textual differences, and the order is rather different, many of the sayings found in *Two Treatises* share a common source with the 'Grave counsels' printed in the First Edition.

I. Categories in 'Grave Counsels' (Works 1599)	II. No. of items	III. Items in Rylands MS 524	IV. Items not in Rylands MS 524
Affections	6	1, 2, 4, 5, 6	3
Afflictions	12	1, 3, 4, 6, 8–12	2, 5, 7
Anger	2	√	
Angels	1	√	
Atheism	2	√	
Calling	8	√	
Care	1	√	
Censures	1	√	
Conference	2	√	
Conscience afflicted	15	1–11	12–15
Covering infirmities	1	√	
Contempt of the truth	1	√	
Confession of sins	2	√	
Concupiscence	1	√	
Company	1	√	
Cause good	2	√	
Despair	3	1	2, 3
Death	3	2, 3	1
Desire	1	√	
Dispraise	1	√	
Diet	1	√	
Dreams	2	√	
Dulness	2	1	2
Doctrine	1		1
Exercises of religion	3	1, 3	2
Experience of our corruption	1		1
Faith	4	3, 4	1, 2
Family	1	√	
Feeling	6	1–4, 6	5
Fruits of faith	2	1	2
Falling into sin	2	√	
Fear	3	1, 2	3
Feastings	1	√	
Friendship	4	√	
Grace of God	5	1	2–5
Godliness	2		1, 2
Good works	1	√	
Grief for sin	8	1, 2, 4–7	3, 8

Continued on next page

I. Categories in 'Grave Counsels' (*Works* 1599)	II. No. of items	III. Items in Rylands MS 524	IV. Items not in Rylands MS 524
Hardness of heart	3	√	
Heresy	3	√	
Heart	1		1
Haste how it argueth unbelief, and watching and waiting	1		1
Hearing of the word	1		1
Humility	3	1	2, 3
Hypocrisy	1	√	
Judgements	4	1, 2, 4	3
Sound joy	1	√	
Knowledge	3	1, 3	2
Love of the creatures	4	1–3	4
Madness	1	√	
Matrimony	6	√	
Meditation (including Rules for Meditation)	22	19–21	1–18, 22
Ministry, ministers	3	√	
Mirth	1	√	
Mercy	1		1
Memory	2	√	
Occasion of evil	1	√	
Patience	2	1	2
Pity	1	√	
Poverty	4	√	
Preaching	6	1, 3-6	2
Prayer	8	2-8	1
Praise	1	√	
Parents	2	√	
Prosperity and peace	4	√	
Rebuking or reproving of sin	6	1-5	6
Regeneration	1	√	
Repentance	2	√	
Reproaches	1	√	
Riches	2		1, 2
Reading	1		1
Sacraments	2	√	

Continued on next page

I. Categories in 'Grave Counsels' (*Works* 1599)	II. No. of items	III. Items in Rylands MS 524	IV. Items not in Rylands MS 524
Security	3	2, 3	1
Singing	1	✓	
Sin	17	3, 5, 6, 16	1, 2, 4, 7–15, 17
Sick and sickness	4	1–3	4
Satan's practices	4	1, 4	2, 3
Superstition	1		1
Strange corrections	1	✓	
Solace	2		1, 2
Salvation	1		1
Speed in good things	1		1
Sermons	1		1
Schism	1		1
Surveying of our selves	1		1
Spirit of God	1		1
Evil spirits	1	✓	
Temptations	15	1, 2, 4–15	3
Thanksgiving	2	2	1
Unbelief	2	✓	
Ungodliness	1	✓	
Use of the creatures	1	✓	
Unthankfulness	1	✓	
Visions	1	✓	
Usury	1	✓	
Word of God and the hearing of it	3	1, 2	3
Witchcraft	2	✓	
Worship of God	1		1
World	1	✓	
Women in travail	1	✓	
Word preached	1		1
Supplementary: Marks of the children of God	1		1
Ministry	1	✓	

Select bibliography

Manuscripts

British Library	Add. MS 5813
Cambridge University Library	
Ely Diocesan Records	A/5/1
	B/2/3
	B/2/6
	B/2/11
	D/2/8
	D/2/10
	H/1/3
Cambridgeshire County Record Office	Dry Drayton original parish register
Guildhall Library, London	MS 9163
Gonville and Caius College, Cambridge	MS 53/30
Greater London Record Office	DL/C/335 (Liber Vicarii Generalis, 1590–95)
John Rylands Library, Manchester	Rylands English Manuscript 524
Prerogative Court of Canterbury	41 Fenne
Public Record Office	PROB 11/119
St Bartholomew's Hospital, Archives Department	Ha 1/3

Secondary Books

Aston, Margaret, *Faith and Fire: Popular and Unpopular Religion, 1350–1600* (London: The Hambledon Press, 1993)

Beeke, Joel, *Assurance of Faith: Calvin, English Puritanism, and the Dutch Second Reformation* (New York: Peter Lang, 1991)

Blatchly, John, *The Town Library of Ipswich, Provided for the use of the Town Preachers in 1599: A History and Catalogue* (Wolfeboro, NH: Boydell & Brewer, 1989)

Bolgar, Robert, *The Classical Heritage and its Beneficiaries* (Cambridge: Cambridge University Press, 1954)

Bushnell, Rebecca, *The Culture of Teaching: Early Modern Humanism in Theory and Practice* (Ithaca, NY: Cornell University Press, 1996)

Carlson, Eric Josef, *Marriage and the English Reformation* (Oxford: Blackwell, 1994)

Cohen, Charles, *God's Caress: The Psychology of Puritan Religious Experience* (New York: Oxford University Press, 1986)

Collinson, Patrick, *Archbishop Grindal 1519-1583: The Struggle for a Reformed Church* (Berkeley and Los Angeles, CA: University of California Press, 1979)

———, *The Birthpangs of Protestant England* (London: Macmillan Press, 1988)

———, *The Elizabethan Puritan Movement* (London: Jonathan Cape, 1967)

———, *The Puritan Character: Polemics and Polarities in Early Seventeenth Century English Culture* (UCLA: William Andrews Clark Memorial Library, 1989)

———, *The Religion of Protestants: The Church in English Society 1559-1625* (Oxford: Clarendon Press, 1982)

Cooper, Charles Henry and Thompson Cooper, *Athenae Cantabrigiensis* (2 vols, Cambridge, 1858-61)

Cope, Esther S., *The Life of a Public Man: Edward, First Baron Montagu of Boughton, 1562-1644* (Philadelphia, PA: The American Philosophical Society, 1981)

Costello, William T., *The Scholastic Curriculum at Early Seventeenth-Century Cambridge* (Cambridge, MA: Harvard University Press, 1958)

Courvoisier, Jaques, *La Notion d'Eglise chez Bucer dans son Développement Historique* (Paris: Librairie Félix Alcan, 1933)

Crane, Mary, *Framing Authority: Sayings, Self, and Society in Sixteenth-Century England* (Princeton, NJ: Princeton University Press, 1993)

Crane, William, *Wit and Rhetoric in the Renaissance, The Formal Basis of Elizabethan Prose Style* (New York: Columbia University Press, 1937)

Cressy, David, *Birth, Marriage and Death: Ritual, Religion and the Life Cycle in Sixteenth and Seventeenth Century England* (Oxford: Oxford University Press, 1997)

———, *Bonfires and Bells: National Memory and the Protestant Calendar in Elizabethan and Stuart England* (Berkeley and Los Angeles, CA: University of California Press, 1989)

Curtis, M.H., *Oxford and Cambridge in Transition: 1558-1642* (Oxford: Clarendon Press, 1959)

Duffy, Eamon, *The Stripping of the Altars* (New Haven, CT: Yale University Press, 1992)

Elrington, C.R. et al. (eds), *A History of the County of Cambridge and the Isle of Ely* (9 vols to date, London and Oxford: various publishers, 1938-)

Elsky, Martin, *Authorizing Words: Speech, Writing, and Print in the English Renaissance* (Ithaca, NY: Cornell University Press, 1989)

Ferguson, Arthur, *The Articulate Citizen and the English Renaissance* (Durham, NC: Duke University Press, 1965)

Fincham, Kenneth, *Prelate as Pastor: The Episcopate of James I* (Oxford: Clarendon Press, 1990)

Grafton, Anthony and Lisa Jardine, *From Humanism to the Humanities: Education and the Liberal Arts in Fifteenth- and Sixteenth-Century Europe* (Cambridge, MA: Harvard University Press, 1986)

Green, Ian, *The Christian's ABC: Catechisms and Catechizing in England c.1530-1740* (Oxford: Clarendon Press, 1996)

Greenblatt, Stephen, *Renaissance Self-fashioning: From More to Shakespeare* (Chicago, IL: University of Chicago Press, 1980)

Greimas, Algirdas J., *Du Sens: Essais Sémiotiques* (Paris: Editions du Seuil, 1970)

Haller, William, *The Rise of Puritanism* (1938; reprint, Philadelphia, PA: University of Pennsylvania Press, 1972)

Hasler, P.W., *The House of Commons 1558-1603* (3 vols, London: HMSO, 1981)

Hunnisett, R.F., *Editing Records for Publication*, British Records Association: Archives and the User, no. 4 (London, 1977)

Jenkins, R.B., *Henry Smith: England's Silver-Tongued Preacher* (Macon, GA: Mercer University Press, 1983)

Jones, Norman, *The Birth of the Elizabethan Age* (Oxford: Blackwell, 1993)

Kaufman, Peter Iver, *Prayer, Despair and Drama: Elizabethan Introspection* (Champaign, IL: University of Illinois Press, 1996)

Kearney, H., *Scholars and Gentlemen: Universities and Society in Pre-Industrial Britain 1500-1700* (Ithaca, NY: Cornell University Press, 1970)

Kendall, R.T., *Calvin and English Calvinism to 1649* (Oxford: Oxford University Press, 1979)

Kinney, Arthur, *Humanist Poetics: Thought, Rhetoric, and Fiction in Sixteenth-Century England* (Amherst, MA: University of Massachusetts Press, 1986)

Knappen, M.M., *Tudor Puritanism: A Chapter in the History of Idealism* (Chicago, IL: University of Chicago Press, 1939)

Lake, Peter, *Moderate Puritans and the Elizabethan Church* (Cambridge: Cambridge University Press, 1982)

Lechner, Joan Marie, *Renaissance Concepts of the Commonplaces* (New York: Pageant Press, 1962)

Leedham-Green, E.S., *Books in Cambridge Inventories. Book-Lists from Vice-Chancellor's Court Probate Inventories in the Tudor and Stuart*

Periods (2 vols, Cambridge: Cambridge University Press, 1986)

Lewis, C.S., *English Literature in the Sixteenth Century* (Oxford: Clarendon Press, 1954)

Lysons, D. and S. Lysons, *Magna Britannia*, (2 vols, Cambridge, 1808)

Marsh, Christopher W., *The Family of Love in English Society, 1550–1630* (Cambridge: Cambridge University Press, 1993)

Martin, Jessica, *Recollected Dust: Izaak Walton and the Beginning of Literary Biography* (Woodbridge, Suffolk: Boydell, forthcoming)

Mason, H.A., *Humanism and Poetry in the Early Tudor Period* (London: Routledge and Kegan Paul, 1959)

Morgan, Irvonwy, *The Godly Preachers of the Elizabethan Church* (London: The Epworth Press, 1965)

Morgan, John, *Godly Learning: Puritan Attitudes towards Reason, Learning, and Education, 1560–1640* (Cambridge: Cambridge University Press, 1986)

Moss, Ann, *Printed Commonplace-Books and the Structuring of Renaissance Thought* (Oxford: Clarendon Press, 1996)

Muller, Richard, *Christ and the Decree* (Durham, NC: The Labyrinth Press, 1986)

Neal, Daniel, *The History of the Puritans; or, Protestant Nonconformists; from the Reformation in 1517, to the Revolution in 1688* (3 vols, London, 1837)

Ong, Walter J., *Interfaces of the Word: Studies in the Evolution of Consciousness and Culture* (Ithaca, NY: Cornell University Press, 1977)

——, *The Presence of the Word: Some Prolegomena for Cultural and Religious History* (New Haven, CT: Yale University Press, 1967)

——, *Ramus: Method, and the Decay of Dialogue* (Cambridge, MA: Harvard University Press, 1958)

——, *Rhetoric, Romance and Technology: Studies in the Interaction of Expression and Culture* (Ithaca, NY: Cornell University Press, 1971)

Outhwaite, R.B., *Inflation in Tudor and Early Stuart England* (2nd edn, London and Basingstoke: Macmillan, 1982)

Overton, Mark, *Agricultural Revolution in England: The Transformation of the Agrarian Economy 1500–1850* (Cambridge: Cambridge University Press, 1996)

Page, Frances M., *The Estates of Crowland Abbey: A Study in Manorial Organization* (Cambridge: Cambridge University Press, 1934)

Parker, Kenneth L., *The English Sabbath: A Study of Doctrine and Discipline from the Reformation to the Civil War* (Cambridge: Cambridge University Press, 1988)

Pearson, A.F. Scott, *Thomas Cartwright and Elizabethan Puritanism,*

1535–1603 (Cambridge: Cambridge University Press, 1925)

Peirce, James, *Vindication of the Dissenters* (London, 1717)

Porter, H.C., *Reformation and Reaction in Tudor Cambridge* (Cambridge: Cambridge University Press, 1958)

Rowse, A.L., *The England of Elizabeth: The Structure of Society* (New York: Macmillan, 1951)

Rozett, Martha Tuck, *The Doctrine of Election and the Emergence of Elizabethan Tragedy* (Princeton, NJ: Princeton University Press, 1984)

Seaver, Paul, *The Puritan Lectureships: The Politics of Religious Dissent, 1560–1662* (Stanford, CA: Stanford University Press, 1970)

Seiler, Friedrich, *Das Deutsche Sprichwort* (Strassburg: K.J. Trubner, 1918)

Sheldrake, Philip, *Spirituality and History: Questions of Interpretation and Method* (New York: Crossroads, 1992)

Slack, Paul, *The Impact of Plague in Tudor and Stuart England* (London: Routledge & Kegan Paul, 1985)

Spufford, Margaret, *Contrasting Communities: English Villagers in the Sixteenth and Seventeenth Centuries* (Cambridge: Cambridge University Press, 1974)

Stachniewski, John, *The Persecutory Imagination: English Puritanism and the Literature of Religious Despair* (Oxford: Clarendon Press, 1991)

Steig, Margaret, *Laud's Laboratory: The Diocese of Bath and Wells in the Early Seventeenth Century* (Lewisburg, PA: Bucknell University Press, 1983)

Stephens, W.P., *The Holy Spirit in the Theology of Martin Bucer* (Cambridge: Cambridge University Press, 1970)

Taylor, Archer, *The Proverb* (Cambridge: Harvard University Press, 1931)

Thirsk, Joan (ed.), *The Agrarian History of England and Wales, vol. IV: 1500–1640* (Cambridge: Cambridge University Press, 1967)

————, *The Rural Economy of England* (London: The Hambledon Press, 1984)

Thomas, Keith, *Religion and the Decline of Magic* (Harmondsworth, Middlesex: Penguin Books, 1978)

Todd, Margo, *Christian Humanism and the Puritan Social Order* (Cambridge: Cambridge University Press, 1987)

Tyacke, Nicholas, *Anti-Calvinists: The Rise of English Arminianism, c. 1590–1640* (Oxford: Clarendon Press, 1990)

Valor Ecclesiasticus (6 vols, London, 1817)

Venn, J. and J.A. Venn (eds), *Alumni Cantabrigienses, Part I: From the earliest times to 1751* (4 vols, Cambridge: Cambridge University Press, 1922–27)

Von Rohr, John, *The Covenant of Grace in Puritan Thought* (Atlanta, GA: Scholars Press, 1986)

Waddington, John, *John Penry, the Pilgrim Martyr, 1559-1593* (London, 1852)

Wallace, Dewey D., Jr, *Puritans and Predestination: Grace in English Protestant Theology* (Chapel Hill, NC: The University of North Carolina Press, 1982)

Walsham, Alexandra, *Church Papists: Catholicism, Conformity and Confessional Polemic in Early Modern England* (Woodbridge, Suffolk: Royal Historical Society, 1993)

Weimann, Robert, *Authority and Representation in Early Modern Discourse*, ed. David Hillman (Baltimore, MD: The Johns Hopkins University Press, 1996)

Weinstein, Rosemary, *Tudor London* (London: HMSO, 1994)

Weir, David A., *The Origins of the Federal Theology in Sixteenth-Century Reformation Thought* (Oxford: Clarendon Press, 1990)

Welsby, Paul A., *Lancelot Andrewes 1555-1626* (London: SPCK, 1958)

Essays and articles

Booty, John E., 'Preparation for the Lord's Supper in Elizabethan England', *Anglican Theological Review*, 49 (1967), 131-48

Boulton, Jeremy P., 'The Limits of Formal Religion: The Administration of Holy Communion in late Elizabethan and early Stuart London', *London Journal*, 10 (1984), 135-54

Bourgeois II, E.J., 'The Queen, a Bishop, and a Peer: A Clash for Power in Mid-Elizabethan Cambridgeshire', *Sixteenth Century Journal*, 26 (1995), 3-15

Brauer, Jerald C., 'Types of Puritan Piety', *Church History*, 56 (1987), 39-58

Bremer, Francis and Ellen Rydell, 'Puritans in the Pulpit', *History Today* (September, 1995), 50-54

Carlson, Eric Josef, 'Clerical Marriage and the English Reformation', *Journal of British Studies*, 31 (1992), 1-31

————, '"Practical Divinity": Richard Greenham's Ministry in Elizabethan England', in Eric Josef Carlson (ed.), *Religion and the English People 1500-1640: New Voices/New Perspectives*, Sixteenth Century Essays and Studies (Kirksville, MO: Thomas Jefferson University Press, 1998)

Christianson, Paul, 'Reformers and the Church of England under Elizabeth I and the Early Stuarts', *Journal of Ecclesiastical History*, 31 (1980), 463-82

Cohen, Charles, 'Two Biblical Models of Conversion: An Example of Puritan Hermeneutics', *Church History*, 58 (1989), 182–96

Collinson, Patrick, 'A Comment: Concerning the Name Puritan', *Journal of Ecclesiastical History*, 31 (1980), 483–8

———, '"A Magazine of Religious Patterns": An Erasmian Topic Transposed in English Protestantism', in his *Godly People: Essays on English Protestantism and Puritanism* (London: The Hambledon Press, 1983)

———, 'A Mirror of Elizabethan Puritanism: The Life and Letters of "Godly Master Dering"', in *Godly People*

———, 'The "Nott Conformytye" of the Young John Whitgift', in *Godly People*

———, 'Shepherds, Sheepdogs, and Hirelings: The Pastoral Ministry in Post-Reformation England', in W.J. Sheils and Diana Wood (eds), *The Ministry: Clerical and Lay, Studies in Church History*, 26 (Oxford: Blackwell, 1989)

Condren, Conal, 'More Parish Library, Salop', *Library History*, 7 (1987), 141–62

Coster, William, 'Purity, Profanity, and Puritanism: The Churching of Women, 1500–1700', in W.J. Sheils and Diana Wood (eds), *Women in the Church, Studies in Church History*, 27 (Oxford: Blackwell, 1990)

Cressy, David, 'Death and the Social Order: The Funerary Preferences of Elizabethan Gentlemen', *Continuity and Change*, 5 (1989), 99–119

———, 'Purification, Thanksgiving and the Churching of Women in Post-Reformation England', *Past and Present*, 141 (1993), 106–46

Cross, Claire, 'An Example of Lay Intervention in the Elizabethan Church', *Studies in Church History*, 2 (1965), 273–82

Donagan, Barbara, 'Godly Choice: Puritan Decision-Making in Seventeenth-Century England', *Harvard Theological Review*, 76:3 (1983), 307–34

Eales, Jacqueline, 'Samuel Clarke and the "Lives" of Godly Women in Seventeenth-Century England', in W.J. Sheils and Diana Wood (eds), *Women in the Church, Studies in Church History*, 27 (Oxford: Blackwell, 1990), 365–76

Eire, Carlos M.N., 'Major Problems in the Definition of Spirituality as an Academic Discipline', in Bradley C. Hanson (ed.), *Modern Christian Spirituality: Methodological and Historical Essays* (Atlanta, GA: Scholars Press, 1990)

Enssle, Neal R., 'Patterns of Godly Life: The Ideal Parish Minister in Sixteenth and Seventeenth Century English Thought', *Sixteenth Century Journal*, 28 (1997), 3–28

Fox, Alistair, 'Facts and Fallacies: Interpreting English Humanism', in Alistair Fox and John Guy, *Reassessing the Henrician Age:*

Humanism, Politics and Reform 1500-1550 (Oxford: Basil Blackwell, 1986)

Frankforter, A. Daniel, 'Elizabeth Bowes and John Knox: A Woman and Reformation Theology', *Church History*, 56 (1987), 333–47

Gittings, Clare, 'Urban Funerals in Late Medieval and Reformation England', in Steven Bassett (ed.), *Death in Towns. Urban Responses to the Dying and the Dead, 100–1600* (Leicester: Leicester University Press, 1992)

Green, Ian, '"For Children in Yeeres and Children in Understanding": The Emergence of the English Catechism under Elizabeth and the Early Stuarts', *Journal of Ecclesiastical History*, 37 (1986), 397–425

Grey, Hanna, 'Renaissance Humanism: The Pursuit of Eloquence', *Journal of the History of Ideas*, 24 (1963), 497–514

Haigh, Christopher, 'The Continuity of Catholicism in the English Reformation', in Christopher Haigh (ed.), *The English Reformation Revised* (Cambridge: Cambridge University Press, 1987)

————, 'Puritan Evangelism in the Reign of Elizabeth I', *English Historical Review*, 92 (1977), 30–58

Hunter, Michael, 'How to Edit a Seventeenth-Century Manuscript: Principles and Practice', *The Seventeenth Century*, 10/2 (August 1995), 277–310

Jardine, Lisa, 'The Place of Dialectic Teaching in Sixteenth-Century Cambridge', *Studies in the Renaissance*, 21 (1974), 31–62

Kahn, Victoria, 'Humanism and the Resistance to Theory', in Patricia Parker and David Quint (eds), *Literary Theory/Renaissance Texts* (Baltimore, MD: The Johns Hopkins University Press, 1986)

Kaufman, Peter Iver, '"Much in Prayer": The Inward Researches of Elizabethan Protestants', *Journal of Religion*, 73 (1993), 163–82

Keddie, Gordon J., '"Unfallible Certenty of the Pardon of Sinne and Life Everlasting": The Doctrine of Assurance in the Theology of William Perkins (1558-1602)', *The Evangelical Quarterly*, 48/4 (October–December 1976), 230–44

Kristeller, Paul O., 'Humanism and Moral Philosophy', in Albert Rabil, Jr (ed.), *Renaissance Humanism: Foundations, Forms, and Legacy* (3 vols, Philadelphia, PA: University of Pennsylvania Press, 1988)

Lake, Peter '"A Charitable Christian Hatred": The Godly and their Enemies in the 1630s', in Christopher Durston and Jacqueline Eales (eds), *The Culture of English Puritanism, 1560-1700* (Basingstoke: Macmillan, 1996)

————, 'Deeds Against Nature: Cheap Print, Protestantism and Murder in Early Seventeenth-Century England', in Kevin Sharpe and Peter Lake (eds), *Culture and Politics in Early Stuart England*, (Stanford, CA: Stanford University Press, 1993)

————, 'Defining Puritanism – again?', in Francis Bremer (ed.), *Puritanism: Transatlantic Perspectives on a Seventeenth-Century Anglo-American Faith* (Boston, MA: Massachusetts Historical Society, 1993)

————, 'Matthew Hutton – A Puritan Bishop?' *History*, 64 (1979), 182–204

————, 'The Moderate and Irenic Case for Religious War: Joseph Hall's *Via Media* in Context', in S.D. Amussen and M.A. Kishlansky (eds), *Political Culture and Cultural Politics in Early Modern Europe. Essays Presented to David Underdown* (Manchester: Manchester University Press, 1995)

————, 'Robert Some and the Ambiguities of Moderation', *Archiv für Reformationsgeschichte*, 71 (1980), 254–79

McGiffert, Michael, 'Grace and Works: The Rise and Division of Covenant Divinity in Elizabethan Puritanism', *Harvard Theological Review*, 75/4 (1982), 463–502

————, 'The Perkinsian Moment in Federal Theology', *Calvin Theological Journal*, 29 (1994), 117–48

Muller, Richard, 'Covenant and Conscience in English Reformed Theology: Three Variations on a 17th Century Theme', *The Westminster Theological Journal* 42/2 (Spring 1980), 308–34

————, 'Perkins' *A Golden Chaine*: Predestinarian System or Schematized *Ordo Salutis*', *Sixteenth Century Journal*, 9/1 (1978), 69–81

Owen, Dorothy, 'The Enforcement of the Reformation in the Diocese of Ely', in Derek Baker (ed.), *Miscellanea Historiae Ecclesiasticae. III, Colloque de Cambridge, 24–28 Septembre 1968*, (Louvain: Publications Universitaires de Louvain, 1970)

Owen, H. Gareth, 'Tradition and Reform: Ecclesiastical Controversy in an Elizabethan London Parish', *Guildhall Miscellany*, 2 (1961), 63–70

Porter, Stephen, 'From Death to Burial in Seventeenth-Century England', *The Local Historian*, 23 (1993), 199–204

Primus, John H., 'Lutheran Law and Gospel in the Early Puritan Theology of Richard Greenham', *Lutheran Quarterly*, new series 8 (1994), 287–98

Principe, Walter, 'Toward Defining Spirituality', *Studies in Religion/Science Religieuses*, 12/2 (Spring 1983), 127–41

Rechtien, John, 'John Foxe's *Comprehensive Collection of Commonplaces*: A Renaissance Memory System for Students and Theologians', *Sixteenth Century Journal*, 9/1 (1978), 83–9

————, 'The Visual Memory of William Perkins and the End of Theological Dialogue', *Journal of the American Academy of Religion: Supplement*, 45/1 (March, 1977), 69–99

Schneiders, Sandra M., 'Spirituality in the Academy', *Theological Studies*, 50 (1989), 676–97

Screech, M.A., 'Commonplaces of Law, Proverbial Wisdom and Philosophy: Their Importance in Renaissance Scholarship (Rabelais, Joachim du Bellay, Montaigne)', in R.R. Bolgar (ed.), *Classical Influences on European Culture A.D. 1500–1700* (Cambridge: Cambridge University Press, 1976)

Sharpe, J., '"Last Dying Speeches": Religion, Ideology and Public Execution in Seventeenth Century England', *Past and Present* 107 (1985), 144–67

———, 'Scandalous and Malignant Priests in Essex: the Impact of Grassroots Puritanism', in Colin Jones, Malyn Newitt and Stephen Roberts (eds), *Politics and People in Revolutionary England* (Oxford: Blackwell, 1986)

Solly, Edward, *Notes and Queries*, 6th ser., 8 (21 July 1883), 55

Steere, Dan, '"For the Peace of Both, For the Honour of Neither": Bishop Joseph Hall Defends the *Via Media* in an Age of Extremes, 1601–1656', *Sixteenth Century Journal*, 27 (1996), 749–65

Tipson, Baird, 'A Dark Side of Seventeenth-Century English Protestantism: The Sin Against the Holy Spirit', *Harvard Theological Review*, 77/3–4 (1984), 301–30

Todd, Margo, '"An act of discretion": Evangelical Conformity and the Puritan Dons', *Albion*, 18 (1986), 581–99

———, 'Puritan Self-fashioning', in Francis Bremer (ed.), *Puritanism: Transatlantic Perspectives on a Seventeenth-Century Anglo-American Faith* (Boston, MA: Massachusetts Historical Society, 1993)

Tyacke, Nicholas, 'Popular Puritan Mentality in Late Elizabethan England', in Peter Clark (ed.), *The English Commonwealth* (Leicester: Leicester University Press, 1974)

Tyson, Moses, 'Hand-list of Additions to the Collection of English Manuscripts in the John Rylands Library, 1928–35', *Bulletin of the John Rylands Library*, 19 (1935), 230–54

Warren, C.F.S., untitled note, *Notes and Queries*, 6th ser., 7 (12 May 1883), 366

Willen, Diane, '"Communion of the Saints": Spiritual Reciprocity and the Godly Community in Early Modern England', *Albion*, 27 (1995), 19–41

Wilson, Adrian, 'The Ceremony of Childbirth and Its Interpretation', in Valerie Fildes (ed.), *Women as Mothers in Pre-Industrial England: Essays in Memory of Dorothy McLaren* (London: Routledge, 1990)

Yule, George, 'James VI and I: Furnishing the Churches in His Two Kingdoms', in Anthony Fletcher and Peter Roberts (eds), *Religion,*

Culture and Society in Early Modern Britain: Essays in Honour of Patrick Collinson (Cambridge: Cambridge University Press, 1994)

Dissertations and theses

Cherry, Mary Jane, 'A Classification and Analysis of Selected "Sayings" in Shakespeare's Plays' (unpublished Ph.D. dissertation, The Catholic University of America, 1981)

Heal, Felicity Margaret, 'The Bishops of Ely and Their Diocese during the Reformation Period: ca. 1515-1600' (unpublished Ph.D. dissertation, Cambridge University, 1972)

Knappen, Marshall, 'Richard Greenham and the Practical Puritans under Elizabeth' (unpublished Ph.D. dissertation, Cornell University, 1927)

Mauch, Thomas K., 'The Role of the Proverb in Early Tudor Literature' (unpublished Ph.D. dissertation, University of California, Los Angeles, 1963)

Shipp, Kenneth, 'Lay Patronage of East Anglian Puritan Clerics in Pre-Revolutionary England' (unpublished Ph.D. dissertation, Yale University, 1971)

Primary

Anon., *The Manner of the Cruell Outragious Murther of William Storre Mast. of Art, Minister, and Preacher at Market Raisin in the County of Lincolne Committed By Francis Cartwright. one of his parishioners, the 30. day of August Anno. 1602* (Oxford, 1603)

Ascham, Roger, *The Scholemaster*, ed. R.J. Schoeck (Don Mills, Ontario: J.M. Dent and Sons, 1966)

Bentham, Joseph, *The Saints Societie* (1636)

Bernard, Richard, *The Faithfull Shepheard: Or The Shepheards Faithfulnesse: Wherein is for the matter largely, but for the maner, in few words, set forth the excellencie and necessitie of the Ministerie ...* (1607)

Bolton, Robert, *Some Generall Directions for a Comfortable Walking with God: Delivered in the Lecture at Kettering in Northamptonshire, with enlargement* (2nd edn, 1626)

———, *Instructions For a Right comforting Afflicted Conciences: With speciall Antidotes against some grievous Temptations. Delivered for the most part in the Lecture at Kettering in Northamptonshire* (3rd edn, 1640)

Bucer, Martin, *De regno Christi*, trans. Wilhelm Pauck and Paul Larkin, in *Library of Christian Classics*, vol. 19, *Melanchthon and Bucer* (Philadelphia, PA: The Westminster Press, 1969)

Cardwell, E., *Synodalia* (2 vols, Oxford, 1842)

Carleton, George, *The Life of Bernard Gilpin, a Man Most Holy and renowned among the Northerne English* (1629)

Cartwright, Thomas, *Cartwrightiana*, eds Albert Peel and Leland H. Carlson, Elizabethan Nonconformist Texts, vol. 1 (London: George Allen and Unwin, 1951)

Certain Sermons or Homilies Appointed to be Read in Churches, In the time of Queen Elizabeth of Famous Memory (1683)

Clarke, Samuel, 'Life of Master Richard Greenham', *The Lives of Thirty-Two English Divines*, 3rd edn (London, 1677)

Cooper, Thomas, *The Christians Daily Sacrifice: Containing a daily direction for a settled course of Sanctification* (1608)

Corbett, Richard, *The Poems of Richard Corbett*, ed. J.A.W. Bennett and H.R. Trevor-Roper (Oxford: Clarendon Press, 1955)

Dent, Arthur, *The Plaine Mans Pathway to Heaven* (1625)

Dering, Edward, *A Briefe and necessarie Catechisme or Instruction, very needfull to be known to all Housholders* (1597)

Documents of the English Reformation, ed. Gerald Bray (Minneapolis, MN: Fortress Press, 1994)

Downame, George, *Two sermons, the one commending the ministrie in general: the other defending the office of bishops in particular* (London, 1608)

Elyot, Thomas, *The Banket of Sapience* (1564)

Erasmus, Desiderius, *Adages*, Collected Works of Erasmus, vols 31–4, trans. R.A.B. Mynors and Margaret Mann Phillips (Toronto: University of Toronto Press, 1982–92)

———, *Apophthegmata* (1542)

———, *Christian Humanism and the Reformation: Selected Writings*, ed. John C. Olin (New York: Harper Torchbooks, 1965)

———, *Literary and Educational Writings 2: De Copia / De Ratione Studii*, Collected Works of Erasmus, vol. 24, ed. Craig Thompson (Toronto: University of Toronto Press, 1978)

The First and Second Prayer Books of King Edward the Sixth (London: J.M. Dent and Sons, 1910)

Fraunce, Abraham, *The Arcadian Rhetoric* (London [1588])

Fuller, Thomas, *The Church History of Britain from the Birth of Jesus Christ until the Year M.DC.XLVIII.* (London, 1655)

Gifford, George, *A briefe discourse of certaine points of the religion, which is among the common sort of Christians, which may bee termed the Countrie Divinitie. With a manifest confutation of the same, after the order of a Dialogue* (London, 1582)

Hall, Joseph, *The Works of the Right Reverend Joseph Hall, D.D.*, ed. Philip Wynter (10 vols, Oxford, 1863)

——, *The Collected Poems of Joseph Hall, Bishop of Exeter and Norwich*, ed. A. Davenport (Liverpool: Liverpool University Press, 1949)

——, *Heaven vpon earth, Or Of true Peace, and Tranquillitie of Minde* (London, 1606)

Hoby, Margaret, *Diary of Lady Margaret Hoby 1599-1605*, ed. Dorothy M. Meads (London: George Routledge & Sons, 1930)

Jewel, John, *The Works of John Jewel*, ed. John Ayre, (4 vols, Cambridge: Cambridge University Press, 1847)

Kilby, Richard, *The burthen of a loaden conscience* (1608)

Letters and Papers, Foreign and Domestic of the Reign of Henry VIII, ed. J.S. Brewer et al. (21 vols, London, 1862-1920)

Linaker, Robert, *A Comfortable Treatise for the Relief of such as are Afflicted in Conscience* (1595)

Liturgical Services: Liturgies and Occasional Forms of Prayer set forth in the Reign of Queen Elizabeth, ed. William K. Clay, The Parker Society (Cambridge: Cambridge University Press, 1847)

Lombard, Peter, *Sententiae in IV Libris Distinctae* (Rome: Editiones Collegii S. Bonaventurae Ad Claras Aquas, 1981)

Manningham, John, *The Diary of John Manningham of the Middle Temple 1602-1603*, ed. Robert Parker Sorlien (Hanover, NH: University Press of New England, 1976)

Melanchthon, Philip, *Loci Communes Theologici*, trans. Wilhelm Pauck and Paul Larkin, in *Library of Christian Classics*, vol. 19, *Melanchthon and Bucer* (Philadelphia, PA: The Westminster Press, 1969)

A parte of a register, contayninge sundrie memorable matters written by divers godly and learned in our time, which stande for and desire the reformation of our Church, in discipline and ceremonies, according to the pure worde of God, and the lawe of our lande (Middleburg, 1593)

Pausanias, *Description of Greece*, ed. J.G. Frazer (New York: Biblo and Tannen, 1965)

Perkins, William, *The Work of William Perkins*, ed. Ian Breward (Abingdon, Berks: Sutton Courtney Press, 1970)

——, *Workes* (3 vols, London, 1626-31)

Rainolde, Richard, *The Foundacion of Rhetorike*, intro. Francis R. Johnson (New York: Scholars' Facsimiles and Reprints, 1945)

Religion and Society in Early Modern England: A Sourcebook, eds David Cressy and Lori Anne Ferrell (London: Routledge, 1996)

Richardson, Charles, *A Workeman, That Needeth Not to be Ashamed:*

Or The faithfull Steward of Gods house. A sermon describing the duety of a godly minister, both in his Doctrine and in his Life (London, 1616)

Rogers, Thomas, Miles Christianus (London, 1590)

The Seconde Parte of a Register; being a calendar of manuscripts under that title intended for publication by the Puritans about 1593, and now in Dr William's library, London, ed. A. Peel (2 vols, Cambridge: Cambridge University Press, 1915)

Strype, John, Historical Collections of the Life and Acts of the Right Reverend Father in God, John Aylmer, Lord Bp. of London in the Reign of Queen Elizabeth (new edn, Oxford, 1821)

[Throckmorton, Job], M. Some laid open in his coulers: Wherein the Indifferent Reader may easily see, howe wretchedly and loosely he hath handeled the cause against M. Penri. (La Rochelle, 1589)

The Tudor Constitution, ed. G.R. Elton (Cambridge: Cambridge University Press, 1960)

Tudor Royal Proclamations, ed. Paul L. Hughes and James F. Larkin, (3 vols, New Haven, CT: Yale University Press, 1964-69)

Two Elizabethan Puritan Diaries, ed. M.M. Knappen (Chicago, IL: American Society of Church History, 1933)

The Two Liturgies ... set forth by authority in the Reign of King Edward VI, ed. Joseph Ketley (Cambridge, 1844)

Ursinus, Zacharias, The summe of christian religion (1633)

Visitation Articles and Injunctions of the Period of the Reformation, eds W.H. Frere and W.P. Kennedy, Alcuin Club Collections xiv-xvi (3 vols, London: Alcuin Club, 1910)

Whitgift, John, Works, ed. John Ayre (3 vols, Cambridge: Cambridge University Press, 1851)

Wilson, Thomas, Arte of Rhetorique: 1560, ed. G.H. Mair (Oxford: Clarendon Press, 1909)

——, The Rule of Reason, Conteinyng the Arte of Logike (London, 1563)

Zanchius, Girolomo, H. Zanchius His Confession of Christian Religion (1599)

Index

absolution, 59, 61, 64, 67, 255
abuses
  in church, 17-18, 73, 105, 182,
    202, 226-7
  of superstitious practices, 53, 64,
    178, 196
  see also superstition
adiaphora, 11, 17, 124
adultery, 51, 170, 173, 193, 275,
    302, 303, 304, 329
Adversary, *see* Satan
affections, 115, 119, 136, 141, 143,
    149, 150, 155, 170, 171-2,
    173, 176, 177, 195, 209, 212,
    233, 243, 250, 279, 295, 301,
    302, 314, 316, 322, 327, 339,
    342, 343, 348, 350, 353, 359,
    368
  ordering of, 13, 92-3, 138, 139,
    214, 225, 250
  trial of, 162, 179
  untrustworthiness of, 88, 102-3,
    135-6, 158
afflicted conscience, 5, 6, 8, 31, 33,
    41, 48, 63, 68, 69, 85, 87-98,
    100, 104, 118, 239, 353
  cure of, 91-3, 97-8, 104, 121,
    126, 139, 178, 181, 194
affliction, 48, 71, 87-94, 96-7, 115,
    119, 163, 164, 166, 173, 176,
    189, 197, 200-201, 205, 214,
    230, 241, 243, 244, 246, 250,
    292, 318, 344
Agricola, Rudolphus, 44
Allen, Richard, 27
Ames, William, 112, 118
Anglicans, 8, 100, 124-6
anxiety, 4, 87, 90, 92, 95, 96, 100,
    107, 115, 204
aphorisms, 33
Apochrypha, 108n., 339
apophthegmata, 33
Apostles' Creed, 70, 281
Arianism, 156, 156n.

Ascham, Roger, 44
assurance, 88, 90-91, 96, 113,
    115-16, 119, 136, 148,
    210-11, 236, 281, 288-9, 295,
    331-3; *see also* salvation
atheism, 106, 107, 220, 229
Aylmer, John, 24, 30, 32

Bale, John, 117n.
baptism, 13, 69, 72, 75, 111, 155,
    213, 307, 314-15
  by negligent minister, 151-2
  father's presence at, 69, 154-5
  godparents, 73-4, 152n., 154,
    154n., 156
  interrogatories at, 73, 152, 152n.
  sign of the cross in, 72-73,
    105-6, 124, 186, 226-7
  see also sacraments
Baxter, Richard, 126n.
Becon, Thomas, 9, 27
Bell, Thomas, 64
Bentham, Joseph, 124, 125, 126
Bernard, Richard, 60, 65, 65n., 66,
    122
Beza, Theodore, 46, 50, 108, 108n.,
    117, 249
Bible, *see* scripture
Bilson, Thomas, 123
body, 155, 173, 196, 206, 210, 243,
    249, 259, 336, 337, 346, 347,
    348
  affliction of, 134, 148, 157, 161,
    163, 180, 189, 236
  care of, 94, 148, 151, 173, 184,
    199, 252
Bolgar, Robert, 39n.
Bolton, Robert, 124
Book of Common Prayer, *see* Prayer
  Book
Book of Homilies, 28, 63
Bradford, John, 117n.
Brauer, Jerald C., 121
Breward, Ian, 101n.